Henry Rogers

The Eclipse of Faith

Or a Visit to a Religious Sceptic

Henry Rogers
The Eclipse of Faith
Or a Visit to a Religious Sceptic
ISBN/EAN: 9783743441682

Manufactured in Europe, USA, Canada, Australia, Japa

Cover: Foto ©Lupo / pixelio.de

Manufactured and distributed by brebook publishing software (www.brebook.com)

Henry Rogers

The Eclipse of Faith

THE
ECLIPSE OF FAITH

OR

A VISIT

TO

A RELIGIOUS SCEPTIC

TENTH EDITION

LONDON
LONGMAN, GREEN, LONGMAN, AND ROBERTS
1861

ADVERTISEMENT
TO
THE FIRST EDITION.

HE who reads this book, only superficially, will at once see that it is not all fiction; and he who reads it more than superficially, will as easily see that it is not all fact. In what proportions it is composed of either would probably require a very acute critic accurately to determine. As the Editor makes no pretensions to such acumen — as he can lay claim to only an imperfect knowledge of the principal personage in the volume, and never had any personal acquaintance with the singular youth, some traits of whose character, and some glimpses of whose history are here given, he leaves the above question to the decision of the reader. At the same time, it is of no consequence in the world. The character and purport of the volume are sufficiently disclosed in the parting words of the Journalist. "It aspires," as is justly said, "to none of the appropriate interest either of a novel or a biography." It might have been very properly entitled " Theological Fragments."

March 31. 1852.

CONTENTS.

	Page
Introduction	1
A Genuine Sceptic	24
A Versatile Believer	28
Puritan Infidelity	32
Lord Herbert and Modern Deism	41
Some curious Paradoxes	49
Problems	58
A Dialogue showing that "That may be possible with Man which is impossible with God"	63
A Sceptic's favourite Topics	84
Unstable Equilibrium	86
A Sceptic's First Catechism	89
Some Light on the Mystery	91
Belief and Faith	92
The "Via Media" of Deism	103
A Sceptic's Select Party	145
How it was that Infidelity prevented my becoming an Infidel	168
Skirmishes	193
Christian Ethics	196
The Blank Bible	200
A Dialogue in which it is contended "That Miracles are impossible, but that it is impossible to prove it"	213
The Analogies of an External Revelation with the Laws and Conditions of Human Development	246

	Page
On a prevailing Fallacy	263
Historic Credibility	270
A Knotty Point	280
Medical Analogies	287
Historic Criticism	290
The "Papal Aggression" proved to be impossible	297
The Paradise of Fools	312
A Future Life	328
A Variable Quantity	341
Discussion of Three Points	359
The Last Evening	372

THE

ECLIPSE OF FAITH.

To E. B * * * * *, Missionary in ——, South Pacific.

Wednesday, June 18, 1851.

My Dear Edward,

You have more than once asked me to send you, in your distant solitude, my impressions respecting the religious distractions in which your native country has been of late years involved. I have refused, partly, because it would take a volume to give you any just notions on the subject; and partly, because I am not quite sure that you would not be happier in ignorance. Think, if you can, of your native land as in this respect what it was when you left it, on your exile of Christian love, some fifteen years ago.

I little thought I should ever have so mournful a motive to depart in some degree from my resolution. I intended to leave you to glean what you could of our religious condition from such publications as might reach you. But I am now constrained to write something about it. My dear brother, you will hear it with a sad heart;—your nephew and mine, our only sister's only child, has, in relation to religion at least, become an absolute sceptic!

I well recollect the tenderness you felt for him, doubly endeared by his own amiable dispositions and the remembrance of her whom in so many points he resembled. What must be *mine*, who so long stood to the orphan in the relations which his mother's love and my own affection imposed upon me! It is hardly a figure to say I felt for him as for a son. "Ah!" you will say, as you glance at your own children, "my bachelor brother cannot understand that even *such* an affection is still a faint resemblance of parental love."

It may be so. I know that *that* love is *sui generis;* and, as I have often heard from those who are fathers, its depth and purity were never realised till they became such. But neither, perhaps, can *you* know how nearly such a love as I have felt for Harrington, committed to me in death by one I loved so well — beloved alike for her sake and for his own — the object of so much solicitude during his childhood and youth, — I say you can perhaps hardly conceive how near such an affection may approach that of a parent; how closely such a graft upon a childless stock may resemble the incorporate life of father and son.

You remember what hopes we both formed of his youth, from the promise alike of his heart and of his intellect: how fondly we predicted a career of future usefulness to others, and honour and happiness to himself! You know how often I used to compare him, for the silent ease with which he mastered difficult subjects, and the versatility with which he turned his mind to the most opposite pursuits, to the youthful Theætetus as described in Plato's dialogue; the movements of whose mind Theodorus compares to the "noiseless flow of oil from the flask."

He was just fourteen and a half when you left England; he is now, therefore, nearly twenty-nine. He left me four years ago, when he was just twenty-five — about a year after the termination of his college course, which you know was honourable to him, and gratifying to me. He then went to spend a year, or a year and a half, as he supposed, in Germany. His stay (he was not all the time in Germany, however) was prolonged for more than three years. In the letters which I received from him, and which gradually became more rare and more brief, there was (without one symptom of decay of personal affection) a certain air of gradually increasing constraint, in relation to the subject which I knew and felt to be all-important. Alas! my prophetic soul took it aright; this constraint was the faint penumbra of a disastrous eclipse indeed! He was not, as so many profess to be, convinced by any particular book (as that of Strauss, for example) that the history of Christianity is *false;* nay, he declares that he is not convinced of that even now; he is a genuine sceptic, and is the subject, he says, of invincible *doubts.* Those doubts have extended at length to the whole field of theology, and are due, principally, as he himself has owned, to the spectacle of the interminable controversies which (turn where he would) occupied the mind of Germany. Even when he returned home, he does not appear to have finally abandoned the notion of the possibility of constructing some religious system in the place of Christianity: this, as he affirms, is a later conviction forced upon him by examining the systems of such men as have attempted the solution of the problem. He declares the result wholly unsatisfactory; that, sceptical as he was and is with regard to the truth of Christianity, he is not even *sceptical* with regard to these theories; and he confesses that, since the undoubtedly powerful minds which have framed them have so signally failed in removing his doubts, and affording him a rock to stand upon, he cannot prevail upon himself to struggle further.

And so, instead of stopping at any of those miserable road-side inns between Christianity and Scepticism, through whose ragged windows all the winds of heaven are blowing, and whose gaudy "signs" assure us there is good "entertainment within for man and beast"— whereas it is only for the latter,—Harrington still travelled on in hopes of finding some better shelter, and now, in the dark night, and a night of tempest too, finds himself on the open heath. To employ his own words, " he could not rest contented with one-sided theories or inconsequential reasonings, and has pursued the argument to its *logical* termination." He is ill at ease in mind, I hear, and not in robust health; and I am just going to visit him.

I shall have some melancholy scenes with him; I feel that. Do you remember, when we were in Switzerland together, how, as we wound down the Susten and the Grimsel passes, with the perpendicular cliffs some thousand feet above us, and a torrent as many feet below, we used to shudder at the thought of two men, wrestling upon that dizzy verge, and striving to throw each other over! I almost imagine that I am about to engage in such a strife now, with the additional horror that the contest is (as one may say) between father and son. Nay, it is yet more terrible; for in such a contest *there*, I almost feel as if I could be contented to employ only a passive resistance. But I must here learn to school my heart and mind to an active and desperate conflict. I fear lest I should do more harm than good; and I am sure I shall, if I suffer impatience and irascibility to prevail. I shall, perhaps, also hear from those lips which once addressed me only in the accents of respect and kindness, language indicative of that alienation which is the inevitable result of marked dissimilarity of sentiment and character, and which, according to Aristotle's most just description, will often dissolve the truest friendship; or at least extinguish (just as prolonged absence will) all its vividness. So impossible is it for the full sympathies of the heart to co-exist with absolute antipathy of the intellect! Nay, I shall, perhaps, have to listen to the language which I cannot but consider as "impiety" and "blasphemy," and yet keep my temper.

I half feel, however, that I am doing him injustice in much of this; and I will not "judge before the time." It cannot be that he will ever cease to regard me with affection, though, perhaps, no longer with reverence; and I am confident that not even scepticism can chill the natural kindliness of his disposition. I am persuaded that, even as a sceptic, he is very different from most sceptics. They cherish doubts; he will be impatient of them. Scepticism is, with them, a welcome guest, and has entered their hearts by an open door; I am sure that it must have stormed his, and entered it by a breach.

"No," my heart whispers; "I shall still find you sincere, Harrington; scorning to take any unfair advantage in argument, and impatient of all sophistry, as I have ever found you. You will be fully aware of the moral significance of the conclusion at which you have arrived —even that there is *no* conclusion to be arrived at; and you will be *miserable*, — as all must be who have your power to comprehend it."

Accept this, my dear brother, as a truer delineation of my wanderer than my first thoughts prompted. But then all this will only make it the more sad to see him. Still it is a duty, and it must be done.

I have not the heart at present to give more than the briefest answers to the queries which you so earnestly put to me. No doubt you were startled to find, from the French papers that reached you from Tahiti, and on no less authority than that of the "Apostolic Letter of the Pope," and Cardinal Wiseman's "Pastoral," that this enlightened country was once more, or was on the eve of becoming, a "satellite" of Rome. Subsequent information, touching the course of the almost unprecedented agitation which England has just passed through, will serve to convince you either that Pio Nono's supplications to the Virgin and all the English saints from St. Dunstan downwards, have not been so successful as he flattered himself that they would have been; or that the nation, if it *be* about to embrace Romanism, has the oddest way of showing it. It has acquired most completely the Jesuitical art of disguising its real feelings; or, as the Anglicans would say, of practising the doctrine of "reserve." To all appearance the country is more indomitably Protestant than before.

Nor need you alarm yourself, as in truth you seem too much inclined to do—about the machinations and triumphs of the Tractarian party. Their insidious attempts are no doubt a greater evil than the preposterous pretensions of Rome, to which indeed they gave their only chance of success. The evil has been much abated, however, by those very assumptions; for it is no longer disguised. Tractarianism is seen to be what many had proclaimed it — the strict ally of Rome. The hopes it inspired were the causes of the Pope's presumption and of Wiseman's folly; and by misleading them, it has, to a large extent, undone the projects both of Rome and itself. But even before the recent attempts, its successes were very partial.

The degree to which the infection tainted the clergy was no criterion at all of the sympathy of the people. Too many of the former were easily converted to a system which confirmed all their ecclesiastical prejudices, and favoured their sacerdotal pretensions: which endowed every youngster, upon whom the Bishop laid hands, with "preternatural graces," and with the power of working "spiritual miracles." But the people generally were in little danger of being misled by these absurdities; and *facts*, even before the recent outbreak, ought to have convinced the clergy that if *they* thought proper to go to Rome, their flocks were by no means prepared to follow them. Except among some fashionable folks here and there — young ladies to whom *ennui*, susceptible nerves, and a sentimental imagination, made any sort of excitement acceptable; who turned their arts of embroidery and painting, and their love of music, to "spiritual" uses, thus displaying their piety and their accomplishments at the same time — except among these, I say, and those amongst the more ignorant of our rural population, whom such people influenced, the Anglican movement could not boast of any signal success. In the more densely peopled districts, and amongst the middle classes especially, the failure of the thing was often most ignominious. No sooner were the candles placed upon the "altar" than the congregation began to thin; and by the time the "obsolete" rubrics were all admirably observed, the priest faultlessly arrayed, the service properly *intoned*, and the entire "spiritual" machine set in motion, the people were apt to desert the sacred edifice altogether. It was a pity, doubtless, that when such admirable completeness in the ecclesiastical equipments had been attained, it should be found that the machine would not work; that just when the Church became *perfect*, it should fail for so insignificant an accident as the want of a congregation. Yet so it often was. The ecclesiastical play was an admirable *rehearsal*, and nothing more. Not but what there are many priests who would prefer a "full service" and an ample ceremonial in an empty church, to the simple Gospel in a crowded one; like Handel, who consoled himself with the vacant benches at one of his oratorios by saying that "dey made de music sound de finer." And, in truth, if we adopt to the full the "High Church" theory, perhaps it cannot much matter whether the people be present or not; the *opus operatum* of magic rites and spiritual conjuration may be equally effectual. The Oxford tracts said ten years ago, "*Before* the Reformation, the Church recognised the seven hours of prayer; however these may have been *practically neglected*, or *hidden in an unknown tongue*, there is *no estimating* what influence this may have had on common people's minds *secretly*." Surely you must agree that there *is* no estimating the efficacy of nobody's hearing services which, if heard by anybody, would have been in an unknown tongue.

I repeat that the people of England will never yield to Romanism,—unless, indeed, it shall hereafter be as a reaction from infidelity; just as infidelity is now spreading as a reaction from the attempted restoration of Romanism. That England is not prepared at present is sufficiently shown by the result of the recent agitation. Could it terminate otherwise? Was it possible that England, in the nineteenth century, could be brought to adopt the superstitions of the Middle Age? If she could, she would have deserved to be left to the consequences of her besotted folly. We may say, as Milton said in his day, to the attempted restoration of superstitions which the Reformers had already cast off, "Oh! if we freeze at noon, after their early thaw, let us fear lest the sun for ever hide himself, and turn his orient steps from our ungrateful horizon justly condemned to be eternally benighted."

No, it is not from this quarter that England must look for the *chief* dangers which menace religion, except, indeed, as these dangers are the inevitable, the uniform result of every attempt to revive the obsolete past. The principal peril is from a subtile unbelief, which, in various forms, is sapping the religion of our people, and which, if not checked, will by and by give the Romish bishops a better title to be called bishops *in partibus infidelium* than has always been the case. The attempt to make men believe too much naturally provokes them to believe too little; and such has been and will be the recoil from the movement towards Rome. It is only one, however, of the causes of that widely diffused infidelity which is perhaps the most remarkable phenomenon of our day. Other and more potent causes are to be sought in the philosophic tendencies of the age, and especially a sympathy, in very many minds, with the worst features of Continental speculation. "Infidelity!" you will say. "Do you mean such infidelity as that of Collins and Bolingbroke, Chubb and Tindal?" Why, we have plenty of those sorts too, and — worse; but the most charming infidelity of the day, a bastard deism in fact, often assumes a different form — a form, you will be surprised to hear it, which embodies (as many say) the *essence* of genuine Christianity! Yes; be it known to you, that when you have ceased to believe all that is specially characteristic of the New Testament — its history, its miracles, its peculiar doctrines — you may still be a genuine Christian. Christianity is sublimed into an exquisite thing called modern "spiritualism." The amount and quality of the infidel "faith" are, indeed, pleasingly diversified when you come to examine individual professors thereof; but it is always based upon the principle that man is a sufficient light to himself; that his oracle is within; so clear as either to supersede the necessity — some say even the *possibility* — of all external revelation in any ordinary sense of that term; or, when such revelation is in some sense allowed, to constitute man the absolute arbiter of how much or how little of it is worthy to be received.

This theory we all perceive, of course, cannot fail to recommend itself by the well-known *uniformity* and distinctness of man's religious notions, and the reasonableness of his religious practices! We all know there has never been any want of a revelation!—of which you have doubtless had full proof among the idolatrous barbarians you foolishly went to enlighten and reclaim. I wish, however, you had known it fifteen years ago; I might have had my brother with me still. It is certainly a pity that this internal revelation—the "absolute religion," *hidden*, as Mr. Theodore Parker felicitously phrases it, in *all* religions of all ages and nations, and so strikingly avouched by the entire history of the world,—should render itself suspicious by little discrepancies in its own utterances among those who believe in it. Yet so it is. Compared with the rest of the world, few at the best can be got to believe in the sufficiency of the internal light and the superfluity of all external revelation; and yet hardly two of the "little flock" agree. It is the rarest little oracle! Apollo himself might envy its adroitness in the utterance of ambiguities. One man says that the doctrine of a "future life" is undoubtedly a dictate of the "religious sentiment"—one of the few universal characteristics of *all* religion; another declares *his* "insight" tells him nothing of the matter; one affirms that the supposed chief "intuitions" of the "religious faculty"—belief in the efficacy of prayer, the free will of man, and the immortality of the soul,—are at hopeless variance with intellect and logic; others exclaim, and surely not without reason, that this casts upon our faculties the opprobrium of irretrievable contradictions! As for those "spiritualists"—and they are, perhaps, at present the greater part—who profess, in some sense, to pay homage to the New Testament, they are at infinite variance as to *how much*—whether $7\frac{1}{2}$, 30, or 50 *per cent.* of its records—is to be received. Very few get so far as the last. One man is resolved to be a Christian—none more so—only he will reject all the peculiar doctrines, and all the supernatural narratives of the New Testament; another declares that miracles are impossible and "incredible, *per se;*" a third thinks they are neither the one nor the other, though it is true that probably a comparatively small portion of those narrated in the "book" are established by such evidence as to be worthy of credit. Pray use your pleasure in the selection; and the more freely, as a fourth is of opinion that, however true, they are really of little consequence. While many extol in vague terms of admiration the deep "spiritual insight" of the founders of Christianity, they do not trouble themselves to explain how it is that this exquisite illumination left them to concoct that huge mass of legendary follies and mystical doctrines which constitute, according to the modern "spiritualism," the bulk of the records of the New Testament, and by which its authors have managed to mislead the world; nor how we are to avoid regarding them either as superstitious and fanatical fools, or artful and designing knaves, if nine-tenths, or seven-tenths, of what they record is all to be rejected; nor, if it be affirmed that they never *did* record it, but that somebody else has put these matters into their mouths, how we can be sure that any thing whatever of the small remainder ever came *out* of their mouths. All this, however, is of the less consequence, as these gentlemen condescend to tell us how we are to separate the "spiritual" gold which faintly streaks the huge mass of impure ore of fable, legend, and mysticism. Each man, it seems, has his own particular spade and mattock in his "spiritual faculty;" so off with you to the diggings in these spiritual mines of Ophir. You will say, why not stay at home, and be content at once, with the advocates of the absolute sufficiency of the internal oracle, to listen to its responses exclusively? Ask these men — for I am sure I do not know; I only know that the results are alike different — whether the possessors of "insight" listen to its own rare voice, or put on their spectacles, and read aloud from the New Testament. Generally, as I say, these good folks are resolved that all that is supernatural and specially inspired in the sacred volume is to be rejected; and, as to the rest, which by the way might be conveniently published as the "Spiritualists' Bible' (in two or three sheets 48mo. say), that would still require a careful winnowing; for, while one man tells us that the Apostle Paul, in his intense appreciation of the "spiritual element," made light even of the "resurrection of Christ," and everywhere shews his superiority to the beggarly elements of history, dogma, and ritual, another declares that he was so enslaved by his Jewish prejudices, and the trumpery he had picked up at the feet of Gamaliel, that he knew but little or next to nothing of the real mystery of the very Gospel he preached; that while he proclaims that it is "revealed, after having been hidden from ages and generations," he himself manages to hide it afresh. This you will be told is a perpetual process, going on even now; that as all the earlier "prophets" were unconscious instruments of a purpose beyond their immediate range of thought, so the Apostles themselves similarly illustrated the shallowness of *their* range of thought; that, in fact, the true significance of the Gospel lay beyond them, and doubtless also, for the very same reasons, lies beyond us. In other words, this class of spiritualists tell us that Christianity is a "development," as the Papists also assert, and the New Testament its first imperfect and rudimentary product; only, unhappily, as the development, it seems, may be things so very different as Popery and Infidelity, we are as far as ever from any *criterion* as to which, out of the ten thousand possible developments, is the true; but it is a matter of the less consequence, since it will, on such reasoning, be always something future.

"Unhappy Paul!" you will say. Yes, it is no better with him than it was in our youth some five and twenty years ago. Do you not remember the astute old German Professor in his lecture-room introducing the Apostle as examining with ever increasing wonder the various contradictory systems which the perverseness of exegesis had extracted from his epistles, and at length, as he saw one from which every feature of Christianity had been erased, exclaiming, in a fright, "Was ist das?" But I will not detain you on the vagaries of the new school of spiritualists. I shall hear enough of them, I have no doubt, from Harrington; he will riot in their extravagancies and contradictions as a justification of his own scepticism. In very truth their authors are fit for nothing else than to be recruiting officers for undisguised infidelity; and this has been the consistent termination with very many of their converts. Yet many of them tell us, after putting men on this inclined plane of smooth ice, that it is the only place where they can be secure against tumbling into Infidelity, Atheism, Pantheism, Scepticism. Some of the Oxford Tractarians informed us, a little before crossing the border, that their system was the surest bulwark against Romanism; and in the same way is this exquisite "spiritualism" a safeguard against infidelity.

Between many of our modern "spiritualists" and the Romanists there is a parallelism of movement absolutely ludicrous. You may chance to hear both declaiming, with equal fervour, against "intellect" and "logic" as totally incompetent to decide on "religious" or "spiritual" truth, and in favour of a "faith" which disclaims all alliance with them. You may chance to hear them both insisting on an absolute submission to an "infallible authority" other than the Bible; the one external — that is, the Pope; the other internal — that is, "Spiritual Insight;" both exacting absolute submission, the one to the outward oracle, the Church, the other to the inward oracle, himself; both insisting that the Bible is but the first imperfect product of genuine Christianity, which is perfected by a "development," though as to the direction of that development they certainly do *not* agree. Both, if I may judge by some recent speculations, recoil from the Bible even more than they do from one another; and both would get rid of it — one by locking it up, and the other by tearing it to tatters. Thus receding in opposite directions round the circle, they are found placed side by side at the same extremity of a diameter, at the *other* extremity of which is the — Bible. The resemblances, in some instances, are so striking, that one is reminded of that little animal, the fresh-water *polype,* whose external structure is so absolutely a mere prolongation of the internal, that you may turn him inside out, and all the functions of life go on just as well as before.

It is impossible to convey to you an adequate idea of the *bouleversement* which has taken place in our religious relations — even in each man's little sphere. It is as if the religious world were a masquerade, where you cease to feel surprise at finding some familiar acquaintance disguised in the most fantastical costume. There is our old friend W——, rigorously, as you know, educated in his old father's evangelical notions, ready to be a confessor for the two wax candles, even though unlighted, and to be a martyr for them if but lighted. His cousin in the opposite direction has found even the most meagre naturalism too much for him, and avows himself a Pantheist. L., the son, you remember, of an independent minister, is ready to go nobly to death in defence of the prerogatives of his " apostolical succession ; " and has not the slightest doubts that he can make out his spiritual genealogy, without a link broken, from the first bishop of Rome downwards ! — though, poor fellow, it would puzzle him to say who was his great-grandfather. E——, you are aware, has long since joined the Church of Rome, and has disclosed such a bottomless abyss of " faith," that whole cart-loads of mediæval fables, abandoned even by Romanists (who, by the way, stand fairly aghast at his insatiable appetite), have not been able to fill it. All the saints in the Roman Hagiography cannot work miracles as fast as he can credit them. On the other hand, his brother has signalised himself by an equal facility of stripping himself, fragment by fragment, of his early creed, till at last he walks through this bleak world in such a gossamer gauze of transparent " spiritualism " that it makes you both shiver and blush to look at him. Your old acquaintance P——, true to his youthful qualities (which *now* have most abundant exercise), who has the " charity which believeth all things," though certainly not that which "beareth all things," goes about apologising for all religious systems, and finding truth in every thing; — our beloved Harrington, on the other hand, bewildered by all this confusion, finds truth — in nothing.

Yet you must not imagine that our religious maladies are at present more than *sporadic;* or that the great bulk of our population are at present affected by them: they still believe the Bible to be the revealed Word of God. Should these diseases ever become *epidemic*, they will soon degenerate into a still worse *type*. Many apostles of Atheism and Pantheism amongst our lower classes say (and perhaps truly), that this modern "spiritualism" is but a transition state. In that case, you will have to recall, with a deeper meaning, the song of Byron, which you told me gave you such anguish, as you paced the deck on the evening in which you lost sight of Old England, — "My native land, good night!"

I have sometimes mournfully asked myself, whether the world may not yet want a few *experiments* as to whether it cannot get on better without Christianity and the Bible; but I hope England is not destined to be the laboratory.

I almost envy your happier lot. I picture to myself your unsophisticated folks, just reclaimed from the grossest barbarism and idolatry, receiving the simple Gospel (as it ought to be received) with grateful wonder, as Heaven's own method of making man wise and happy; reverencing the Bible as what it is — an infallible guide through this world to a better; "a light shining in a dark place." They listen with unquestioning simplicity to its disclosures, which find an echo in their own hearts, and with a reverence which is due to a volume which has transformed them from savages into men, and from idolaters into Christians. They are not troubled with doubts of its authenticity or its divinity; with talk of various readings and discordant manuscripts; with subtle theories for proving that its miracles are legends, or its history myths; or with any other of the infinite vagaries of perverted learning. Neither are they perplexed with the assurances of those who tell them that though divine, the Bible is, in fact, a most dangerous book; and who would request them, in their new-born enlightenment, to be pleased to shut their eyes, and to return to a religion of ceremony quite as absurd and almost as cruel as the polytheism they have renounced. I imagine you and your little flock in the sabbath stillness of those mountains and green valleys, of which you give me such pleasant descriptions, exhibiting a specimen of a truly primitive Christianity; I imagine that the peace within is as deep as the tranquillity without.

Yet I know it cannot be; for you and your flock are *men* — and that one word alone suffices to dissolve the charm. You and they have cares, and worse than cares, which make you like all the rest of the world; for guilt and sorrow are of no clime, and the "happy valley" never existed, except in the pages of Rasselas. You are, doubtless, plagued by every now and then finding that some half-reclaimed cannibal confesses that he has not quite got over his gloating recollections of the delicacies of his diabolical *cuisine;* or that *fashionable* converts turn with a yearning·heart, not to theatres and balls, but to the "dear remembrance" of the splendours of tattoo and *amocos;* or that some unlucky wretch who has not mastered the hideous passions of his old paganism has almost battered out the brains of a fellow-disciple in a sudden paroxysm of anger; or that some timid soul is haunted with half-subdued suspicions that some great goggle-eyed idol, with whose worship his whole existence has been associated, is not, what St. Paul declares it *is*, absolutely "nothing in the world." And then you vex your soul about these things, and worry yourself with apprehensions lest "you should have laboured in vain and spent your strength for nought;" and lastly, trouble yourself still more, lest you should lose your temper and your patience into the bargain.

Yes, your scenery is doubtless beautiful, as the sketches you have sent me sufficiently show; especially that scene at the foot of the mountain Moraii or Mauroi, for I cannot quite make out the pencil marks. But, beautiful as they are, they are not more so than those which greet my eye even now from my study window. No — there is no fault to be found with external nature; it is man only who spoils it all. I see nothing in sun, moon, or stars, — in mountain, forest, or stream, that needs to be altered; *we* are the blot on this fair world. "Oh, man," I am sometimes ready to exclaim, "what a —— ;" but I check myself; for as Correggio whispered to himself exultingly, "*I* also am a painter," so must I, though with very different feelings, say, "I also am a man." Johnson said, that every man probably knows worse of himself than he *certainly* knows of most other men; and so I am determined that misanthropy, if it is to be indulged at all, shall, like its opposite, charity, "begin at home."

Yet, now I think better of it, it shall not begin at all; for I recollect that HE also was a "man," who was infinitely more; who has penetrated even this cloudy shrine of clay with the effulgence of His glory; and so let me resolve that our common humanity shall be held sacred for HIS sake, and pitied for its own. Thus ends my little transient fit of spleen, and thus may it ever end!

May we feel, more and more, my dearest brother, the interior presence of that "guest of guests," that Divine Impersonation of Truth, Rectitude, and Love, whose image has had more power to sooth and tranquillise, stimulate and fortify, the human heart than all the philosophies ever devised by man; who has not merely left us rules of conduct, expressed with incomparable force and comprehensiveness, and illustrated by images of unequalled pathos and beauty; who was not merely (and yet, herein alone, how superior to all other masters) the living type of His own glorious doctrine, and affects us as we gaze upon Him with that transforming influence which the studious contemplation of all excellence exerts by a necessary law of our nature; but whose Life and Death include all motives which can enforce His lessons on humanity; — motives, all intensely animated by the conviction that He is a Living Personality, in communion with our own spirits, and attracted towards us by all the sympathies of a friendship truly Divine; "who can be touched with the feeling of our infirmities, though himself without sin." May He become so familiar to our souls, that no suggestions of evil from within, no incursion of evil from without, shall be so swift and sudden that the thought of Him shall not be at least as near to our spirits, intercept the treachery of our infirm nature, and guard that throne which He alone deserves to fill; till, at every turn and every posture of our earthly life, we may realise a mental image of that countenance of divine compassion bent upon us, and that voice of gentle instruction murmuring in our ears its words of heavenly wisdom; till, whenever tempted to deviate from the "narrow path," we may hear Him whispering, "Will ye also go away?" when hated by the world,—"Ye know that it hated *me* before it hated *you*;" when called to perform some difficult duty,—"If ye love me keep my commandments;" when disposed to make an idol of anything on earth,—"He that loveth father or mother more than *me* is not worthy of me;" when in suffering and trial,—"Whom I love I rebuke and chasten;" when our way is dark,—"What I do thou knowest not now, but thou shalt know hereafter;" till, in a word, as we hear His faintest footsteps approaching our hearts, and His gentle signal there according to His own beautiful image, "Behold I stand at the door and knock,"—our souls may hasten to welcome the heavenly guest.

So may it ever be with you and me! And now I find the very thought of these things has cured all my dark and turbulent feelings, as indeed it ever does; and I can say before I go to rest, "Oh man, my brother, I am at peace with thee!"

Ah! what an empire is His! How, even at the antipodes, will these lines touch in your heart a chord responsive to that which vibrates in mine! . . . . . I go to Harrington in a few days, and as our conversation (perhaps, alas! our controversies) will turn upon some of the most momentous religious topics of the day, I shall keep an exact journal — *Boswellize,* in fact — for you as

c

well as I can; and how well some of my earlier days have practised my memory for this humble office, you know. I shall have a pleasure in this, not only because you will be glad to hear all I can communicate respecting one you love so well, but, also, because in this way, I shall, in part at least, fulfil your earnest request to let you know the state of religion amongst us. You will expect, of course, to find only *that* portion of our conversations reported which relates to these subjects; but I anticipate, in discussing others, some compensation for the misery which will, I fear, attend the discussion of these.

Thank your convert Outai for his present of his grim idol. It is certainly " brass for gold," considering what I sent him; but do not tell *him* so. If a man gives us his gods, what more can he do? And yet, it seems, he may be the richer for the loss. Never was a question more senseless than that of the idolatrous fool — " Ye have taken away my gods, and what else have I left?" — His godship was a little injured in his transit; but he was very perfect in deformity before, and his ugliness could not, by any accident, be improved. I have put him into a glass-case with some stuffed birds, at which he ogles, with his great eyes, in a manner not altogether divine. His condition, therefore, is pretty nearly that to which prophecy has doomed all his tribe; if not cast to the "moles and the bats," it is to the owls and parrots. I cannot help looking at him sometimes with a sort of respect as contrasted with his worshippers; for though they have been fools enough to worship him, he has, at least, not been fool enough to worship them. Yet even they are better than the Pantheist who must regard *it* and every thing else, himself included, as a fragment of divinity. I fear that if I could regard either the Pantheist or myself as *divine*, nothing in the world could keep me from blasphemy every day and all day long.

"Again!" you will say, "my brother; is not that old vein of bitterness yet exhausted?" But be it known to you that that last sarcasm was especially intended for my own behoof. She is a sly jade — conscience; like many other folks, she has a trick of expressing her rebukes in general language; as thus — "What a contemptible set of creatures the race of men are!" — hoping that *some* folks will practically take it to heart. Sometimes I do; and sometimes, I suppose, like my fellows, I look very grave, and approvingly say, "It is but too true," with the air of one who philosophically assents to a proposition in which he is totally uninterested; whereupon conscience becomes outrageous and — personal.

I can easily imagine what you tell me, that you hardly know the difference between the missionaries of different denominations, and are very much troubled to remember at times, *which is which*. It is a natural consequence of the relations in which you stand to heathenism. I fancy the sight of men worshipping an idol with four heads and twice as many hands, must considerably abate impressions of the importance of some of the controversies nearer home. Do you remember the passage in "Woodstock," in which our old favourite represents the Episcopalian Rochecliffe and the Presbyterian Holdenough, meeting unexpectedly in prison, after many years of separation, during which one had thought the other dead? How sincerely glad they were, and how pleasantly they talked; when lo! an unhappy reference to the " bishopric of Titus" gradually abated the fervour of their charity, and inflamed that of their zeal, even till they at last separated in mutual dudgeon, and sat glowering at each other in their distant corners with looks in which the "Episcopalian" and "Presbyterian" were much more evident than the "Christian;" and so they persevered till the sudden summons to them and their fellow-prisoners, to prepare for instant execution, dissolved as with a charm the anger they had felt, and " forgive me, oh my brother!" and "I have sinned against thee, my brother!" broke from their lips as they took what they thought would be a last farewell.

I imagine that a feeling a little resembling this, though from a different cause, makes it impossible for you to remember, in the presence of such spiritual horrors as heathenism presents, the immense importance of many of the controversies so hotly waged at home. I can conceive (as some of our zealots would say) that you are *tempted* to a certain degree of insensibility and defection of heart; that you no longer discern the momentous superiority of "sprinkling" over "immersion," or of "immersion" over "sprinkling;" that the "wax candles," "lighted" and "unlighted," appear to you alike insignificant; that even the *jus divinum* of any system of ecclesiastical government is sometimes not discerned with absolute precision; and, in short, that you look with contemptuous wonder on half our "great" controversies. If I mistake not, things are coming to that pass amongst us, that we shall soon think of them almost with contemptuous wonder too.

Vale — et ora pro me, as old Luther used to say at the end of his letters. I will write again soon.

Your affectionate Brother,
F. B.

—— Grange, July 7, 1851.

My Dear Brother,

I HAVE been with Harrington a week: I am glad to say that I was under some erroneous impressions when I wrote my letter. He is *not* a universal sceptic — he is *only* a sceptic in relation to theological and ethical truth. "Alas!" you will say, "it is an exception which embraces more than the general rule; it little matters what else he believes."

True; and yet there is consolation in it; for otherwise it would have been impossible to hold intercourse with him at all. If he had *reasoned*, in order to prove to me that human *reason* cannot be trusted, or I to convince one who affirmed its *universal* falsity, it were hard to say whether he or I had been the greater fool. Your universal sceptic — if he choose to affect that character — no man *is* it — is impregnable; his true emblem is the hedgehog ensphered in his prickles; that is, as long as you are observing him. For if you do not thus irritate his *amour propre*, and put him on the defensive, he will unroll himself. Speaking, reasoning, acting, like the rest of the world, on the implied truthfulness of the faculties whose falsity he affirms, he will save you the trouble of confuting him, by confuting himself.

And I am glad, for another reason, that Harrington does not affect this universal scepticism; for, whereas, by the confession of its greatest masters, it is at best but the play of a subtle intellect, so it does not afford a very flattering picture of an intellect that affects it. I should have been mortified, I confess, had Harrington been chargeable with such a foible.

It is true that, in another aspect, all this makes the case more desperate; for his scepticism, so far as it extends, is deep and genuine; it is no play of an ingenious subtlety, nor the affectation of singularity with him;—and my prognostications of the misery which *such* a mind must feel from driving over the tempestuous ocean of life under bare poles, without chart or compass, are, I can see, verified. One fact, I confess, gives me hopes, and often affords me pleasure in listening to him. He is an *impartial doubter;* he doubts whether Christianity be true; but he also doubts whether it be *false;* and either from his impatience of the theories which infidelity proposes in its place, as inspiring yet stronger doubts, or in revenge for the peace of which he has been robbed, he never seems more at home than in ridiculing the confidence and conceit of that internal oracle, which professes to solve the problems which, it seems, Christianity leaves in darkness; and in pushing the principles on which infidelity rejects the New Testament to their legitimate conclusion.

I told you, in general, the origin and the progress of his scepticism. I suspect there are causes (perhaps *not* distinctly felt by him) which have contributed to the result. These, it may be, I shall never know; but it is hardly possible not to suppose that some bitter experience has contributed to cloud, thus portentously, the brightness of his youth. Something, I am confident, in connection with his long residence abroad, has tended to warp his young intellect from its straight growth. The heart, as usual, has had to do with the logic; and "has been whispering reasons which the reason cannot comprehend." I suspect that passionate hopes have been *buried*—whether in the grave, I know not.—I must add, that an indirect and most potential cause, not indeed of the origination, yet of the continuance of his state of mind, must be sought in what the world would call his good fortune. His maiden aunt by the father's side left her favourite nephew her pleasant, old-fashioned, somewhat gloomy, but picturesque and comfortable house in ——shire, about fifty or sixty acres in land, and three or four hundred a year into the bargain. Poor old lady! I heartily wish she had kept him out of possession by living to a hundred; or dying, had left every farthing to "endow a college or a —— cat." To Harrington she has left a very equivocal heritage. For with this and his little patrimony, he is entirely placed above the necessity of professional life, and fully qualified to live (heaven help him!) as a gentleman;—but, unhappily, as a gentleman whose nature is deeply speculative—whose life has been one of study—and who has no active tastes or habits to correct the morbid portions of his character, and the dangers of his position. With his views already unsettled, he retired a few months ago to this comparative solitude (for such it is, though the place is not many miles from the learned city of ——); and partly from the tendencies of his own mind, partly from want of some powerful stimulus from without, he soon acquired the pernicious habit of almost constant seclusion in his library, where he revolves, as if fascinated, the philosophy of doubt, or some equally distressing themes; all which has now issued as you see. The contemplative and the active life are both *necessary* to man, no doubt; but in how different proportions!

To live as Harrington has lived of late, is to breathe little but azote. I believe that all these ill effects would have been, though not obviated, at least early cured, had he been compelled to mingle in active life—to make his livelihood by a profession. The bracing air of the world would have dissipated these vapours which have gathered over his soul. In very truth, I half wish that he could now be stripped of his all, and compelled to become hedger and ditcher. It would almost be kindness to ruin him by engaging him in some of the worst railway speculations!

I found him all that I had promised to find him; unchanged towards myself; sometimes cheerful, though oftener melancholy, or, at least, to all appearance *ennuyé*; with more causticity and sarcasm in his humour, but without misanthropy; and I must add, with the same logical fairness, the same abhorrence of sophistry, which were his early characteristics.

But the journal of my visit, which I am most diligently keeping, will more fully inform you of his state of mind.

F. B.

JOURNAL OF A VISIT, ETC.

July 1, 1851.

I ARRIVED at —— Grange this day. In the evening, as Harrington and myself were conversing in the library, I availed myself of a pause in the conversation to break the ice in relation to the topic which lay nearest my heart, by saying—

"And so you have become, they tell me, a universal sceptic?"

"Not quite," he replied, throwing one of his feet over the edge of the sofa on which he was reclining, and speaking rather dogmatically (I thought), for a sceptic. "Not quite: but in relation to *religion*, I have certainly become convinced that certainty, like pride, was not made for man, and that it is in vain for man to seek it."

I was amused at the contradiction of a certainty of universal uncertainty, as well as at the discovery that there was nothing to be discovered.

He noticed my smile, and divined its cause.

"Forgive me," he said, "that, like you Christians and believers of all sorts, I sometimes find theory discordant with practice. The generality of people are, you know, a little inconsistent with their creed; suffer me to be so with mine."

"I have no objection, Harrington, in the world; the more inconsistent you are, the better I shall like you; you have my free leave to be, in relation to Scepticism, just what the Antinomian is in relation to Christianity; or as true a sceptic as he was a true Churchman who showed his good principles, according to Dr. Johnson, by never passing a church without taking off his hat, though he never went into it; or even as Falstaff, who had forgotten 'what the inside of a church was made of.'

I shall be contented indeed to see you as little attached to your *no-truth*, as the generality of Christians are to their truth."

"I thank you," said he, a little sarcastically; "I doubt if I shall ever be able to reach so perfect a pitch of inconsistency. But are you wise, my dear uncle, in this taunt? What an argument have you suggested to me, if I thought it worth while to make use of it! how have you surrendered, without once thinking of the consequences, the practical power of Christianity!"

I began to fear that there would be a good deal of sharp-shooting between us.

"I have surrendered nothing," I replied. "If everything is to be abandoned which, though professedly the subject of man's conviction, he fails to reduce to practice, his creed will be short enough. Christianity, however, will be in no worse condition than morals, the theory of which has ever been in lamentable advance of the practice. And least of all can scepticism stand such a test, of which you have just given a passing illustration. Of this system, or rather no-system, there has never been a consistent votary, if we except Pyrrho himself; and whether he were not an insincere sceptic, the world will be always most sincerely sceptical. But forgive me my passing gibe. In wishing you to be as inconsistent as nine-tenths of Christians are, I did not mean to prejudice your arguments, such as they are. I know it is not in your power to be otherwise than inconsistent; and I shall always have that argument against you, so far as it is one."

"And so far as it is one," he replied, "I shall always have the same argument against you."

"Be it so," I replied, "for the present: I am unwilling to engage in polemical strife with you, the very first evening on which I have seen you for so long a time. I would much rather hear a chapter of your past travels and adventures, which you know your few and brief letters — but I will not reproach you — left me in such ignorance of."

He complied with my request; and in the course of

conversation informed me of many circumstances which had formed steps in that slow gradation by which he had reached his present state of mind; a state which he did not affect to conceal. But still I felt sure there were other causes which he did *not* mention.

At length I said, "You must give me the title of an old friend — a father, Harrington, I might almost say" — and the tears came into my eyes — "to talk hereafter fully with you of your *so certain uncertainty* about the only topics which *supremely* affect the happiness of man."

I told him, and I spoke it in no idle compliment, that I was convinced he was far enough from being one of those shallow fools who are inclined to scepticism because they shrink from the trouble of investigating evidence; who find so much to be said for this and so much for that, that they conclude that there is no truth, simply because they are too indolent to seek it. "This," said I, "is the plea of intellectual Sybarites with whom *you* have nothing in common. And as little do you sympathise with those dishonest, though not always shallow thinkers, who take refuge in alleged uncertainty of evidence, because they are afraid of pursuing it to unwelcome conclusions; who are sceptics on the most singular and inconsistent of all grounds, presumption. I know you are none of these."

"I am, I think, none of these," said he, quietly.

"You are not; and your manner and countenance proclaim it yet more strongly than your words. The only genuine effect of a sincere scepticism is and must be, not the complacent and frivolous humour which too often attaches to it, but a mournful confession of the melancholy condition, to which, if true, the theory reduces the sceptic himself and all mankind."

Of all the paradoxes humanity exhibits, surely there are none more wonderful than the complacency with which scepticism often utters its doubts, and the tranquillity which it boasts as the perfection of its system! Such a state of mind is utterly inconsistent with the genuine realisation and true-hearted reception of the theory.

On the most momentous of all subjects, such a creature as man cannot be in universal doubt, and really *feel* his doubts, without being anxious and miserable. When I hear some youth telling me, with a simpering face, that he does not *know*, or pretend to *say*, whether there be a God, or not; or whether, if there be, He takes any interest in human affairs; or whether, if He does, it much imports us to know; or whether, if He has revealed that knowledge, it is possible or impossible for us to ascertain it; when I hear him further saying, that meantime he is disposed to make himself very easy in the midst of these uncertainties, and to await the great revelation of the future with philosophical, that is, being interpreted, with idiotic tranquillity, I see that in point of fact he has never entered into the question at all; that he has failed to realise the terrible moment of the questions (however they may be decided) of which he speaks with such amazing flippancy.

It is too often the result of thoughtlessness; of a wish to get rid of truths unwelcome to the heart; of a vain love of paradox, or perhaps, in many cases (as a friend of mine said), of an amiable wish to frighten "mamas and maiden aunts." But let us be assured that a frivolous *sceptic* — a sceptic indeed — after duly pondering and feeling the doubts he professes to embrace, is an impossibility. What may be expected in the genuine sceptic is a modest *hope* that he may be mistaken; a desire to be confuted; a retention of his convictions as if they were a guilty secret, or the promulgation of them only as the utterance of an agonised heart, unable to suppress the language of its misery; a dread of making proselytes — even as men refrain from exposing their sores or plague-infected garments in the eyes of the world. The least we can expect from him is that mood of mind which Pascal so sublimely says becomes the Atheist. . . . . . "Is this, then, a thing to be said with gaiety? Is it not rather a thing to be said with tears, as the saddest thing in the world?"

The current of conversation after a while, somehow, swept us round again to the point I had resolved to quit for this evening. "But since we are there," said I, "1 wish you would in brief tell me why, when you doubted of Christianity, you did not stop at any of those harbours of refuge which, in our time especially, have been so plentifully provided for those who reject the New Testament? You are not ignorant, I know, of the writings of Mr. Theodore Parker, and other modern Deists. How is it that none of them even transiently satisfied you? An ingenious eclecticism founded on them has satisfied, you see, your old College friend, George Fellowes, of whom I hear rare things. *He* is far enough from being a sceptic."

"Why," said he, laughing, "it is quite true that George is not a sceptic. He has believed more, and disbelieved more, and both one and the other for less reason, than any other man I know. He used to send me the strangest letters when I was abroad, and almost every one presented him under some new phase. No, he is no sceptic. If he has rejected almost everything, he has also embraced almost everything; at each point in his career, his versatile faith has found him some system to replace that he had abandoned; and he is now a dogmatist *par excellence*, for he has adopted a theory of religion which formally abjures intellect and logic, and is as sincerely abjured by them. If the difficulties he has successively encountered had been seen all at once, I fancy he would have been much where I am. Poor George! 'Sufficient unto the day,' with him, is the theology 'thereof.' I picture him to myself going out of a morning, with his new theological dress upon him, and chancing to meet with some friend, who protests that there is something or other not quite 'comme il faut,' he proceeds with infinite complacency to alter that portion of his attire; the new costume is found equally obnoxious to the criticism of somebody else, and off it goes like the rest."

This was a ludicrous, but not untrue, representation of George Fellowes's mind; only the "friend" in the image must be supposed to mean his own wayward fancy; for, though very amiable, he is not particularly amenable to external influences. So dominant, however, is *present* feeling and impulse, or so deficient is he in comprehensiveness, that he often takes up with the most trumpery arguments; that is, for a few days at a time. Yet he does not want acuteness. I have known him shine strongly (as has been said of some one else) upon an *angle* of a subject; but he never sheds over its whole surface an equable illumination. Where evidence is complicated and various, and consists of many opposing or modifying elements, he never troubles himself to compute the sum total, and strike a fair balance. He stands aghast in the presence of an objection which he cannot solve, and loses all presence of mind in its contemplation. He seldom considers whether there are not still greater objections on the *other* side, nor how much farther, if a principle be just, it ought to carry him. The mode in which he looks at a subject often reminds me of the way in which the eye, according to metaphysicians, surveys an extensive landscape. It sees, they say, only a point at a time, — *punctum visibile*, which is perpetually shifting: and the impression of the whole is in fact a rapid combination, by means of memory, of perceptions all but coexistent; if the attention be strongly fixed upon some *one* object, the rest of the landscape comparatively fades from the view. Now George Fellowes seems to me, in a survey of a large subject, to have an incomparable faculty of seeing the *minimum visibile*, and that so ardently, that all the rest of the landscape vanishes at the moment from his perceptions.

"Well," said I smiling, "you must not blame him for his not reaching at once and *per saltum* your position. He has been more deliberate in stripping himself. Yet he has come on pretty well. You ought not to despair of him. I wonder at what point he is now."

"You may ask him to-morrow," said he, "for I am expecting him here to spend a few weeks with me. At whatever point he may be in these days of 'progress,' as they are called, he does not know that I am already arrived at the *ne plus ultra;* for my letters to him were yet briefer and rarer than to you; and I never touched on these topics. Where would have been the use of asking counsel of such an oracle?"

I said I should be glad to see him. "But I shall be still better pleased to hear from you, why you are dissatisfied with any such system as his, and especially why you say he ought in consistency to go much farther."

"I am far from saying that my reasons will be satisfactory, but I will endeavour, if you wish it, to justify my opinion."

"I shall certainly expect no less," replied I: "you are strangely altered, if you are willing to assert without attempting to prove; and if *you* were altered, I am not. When will you let me hear you?"

"Oh, in a day or two, when I have had time to put my thoughts on paper; but, if I mistake not, some of the most important points will be discussed before that; for Fellowes, I hear, is a very knight-errant of 'spiritualism,' and it is a thousand to one but he attempts to convert me. I intend to let him have full opportunity."

"I hardly know," said I, "Harrington, whether I wish him success or not. — But one thing, surely, all must admire in him: I mean his candour. What less than this can prompt him, after abandoning with such extraordinary facility so many creeds and fragments of creeds, after travelling round the whole circle of theology, to confess with such charming simplicity the whole history of his mental revolutions, and expose himself to the charge of unimaginable caprice — of theological coquetry? I protest to you, that *à priori*, I should have thought it impossible that any man could have made so many and such violent turns in so short a time without a dislocation of all the joints of his soul—without incurring the danger of a 'universal anchylosis.'"

"One would imagine," said Harrington, with a laugh, "that in your estimate, his mind resembles that ingenious toy by which the union of the various coloured rays of light is illustrated: the red, the yellow, the blue, the green, and so forth, are distinctly painted on the compartments of a card; but no sooner are they put into a state of rapid revolution than the whole appears white.

Such, it seems, is the appearance of George Fellowes in that rapid gyration to which he has been subjected: the parti-coloured rays of his various creeds are lost sight of, and the pure white of his 'candour' is alone visible!"

"For myself," said I, "I feel in some measure incompetent to pronounce on his present system. When I saw him for a short time a few months ago, he told me that, though his versatility of faith had certainly been great, he must remind me (as Mr. Newman had said) that he had seen *both* sides; that persons, like myself, for example, have had but one experience; whereas he has had *two*."

"If he were to urge *me* with such an argument," replied Harrington, "I should say, 'we are even, then.' But I think even you could reply: 'you certainly do yourself injustice, Mr. Fellowes, in saying you have had *two* experiences. You have had two dozen at least; but whether that can qualify you for speaking with any authority on these subjects I much doubt; to give any weight to the opinions of any man *some* stability at least is necessary.'"

This I could not gainsay. Slow revolutions on momentous subjects, when there has been much sobriety as well as diligence of investigation, are, perhaps, not to be despised as authority. Some superior weight may even be attached to the later and maturer views. But if a man changes them every other day; if they rise and fall with the barometer; if his whole life has been one rapid *pirouette*, it is impossible with gravity to discuss the question, whether at some point he may not have been right. Whoever be in the right, *he* cannot well be who has never long been anything; and to take such a man for a guide, would be almost as absurd as to mistake a weathercock for a sign-post.

"In seeking religious counsel of George Fellowes," said Harrington, "I should feel much as Jeannie Deans, when she went to the 'Interpreter's House,' as Madge Wildfire calls it, in company with that fantastical personage. But he is a kind-hearted, amiable fellow, and, in short, I cannot help liking him."

July 2. Mr. Fellowes arrived this day about noon. He is about a year younger than Harrington. The afternoon was spent very pleasantly in general conversation. In the evening, after tea, we went into the library. I told the two friends that as they had doubtless much to talk of, and as I had plenty of occupation for my pen, I would sit down at an adjoining table with my desk, and they might go on with their chat. They did so, and for some time talked of old College days and on indifferent subjects; but my attention was soon irresistibly attracted by finding them getting into conversation in which, on Harrington's account, I felt a deeper interest. I found my employment impossible, and yet, desiring to hear them discuss their theological differences without constraint, I did not venture to interrupt them. At last the distraction became intolerable; and looking up, I said, "Gentlemen, I believe you might talk on the most private matters without my attending to one syllable you said; but if you get upon these theological subjects, such is my present interest in them," (glancing at Harrington), " that I shall be perpetually making blunders in my manuscript. Let me beg of you to avoid them when I am with you, or let me go into another room." Harrington would not hear of the last; and as to the first he said, and said truly, that it would impede the free current of conversation, " which," said he, " to be pleasurable at all, must wind hither and thither as the fit takes us. It is like a many-stringed lyre, and to break any one of the chords is to mar the music. And so, my good uncle, if you find us getting upon these topics, join us; we shall seldom be long at a time upon them. I will answer for it; or if you will not do that, and yet, though disturbed by our chatter, are too polite to show it, why, amuse yourself (I know your old tachygraphic skill which used so to move my wonder in childhood), I say, amuse yourself, or rather avenge yourself, by jotting down some fragments of our absurdities, and afterwards showing us what a couple of fools we have been." I was secretly delighted with the suggestion; and when the subjects of dispute were very interesting, threw aside my work, whatever it was, and *reported* them pretty copiously. Hence the completeness and accuracy of this admirable journal. I cannot of course always, or even often, vouch for the *ipsissima verba;* and some few explanatory sentences I have been obliged to add. But the substance of the dialogues is faithfully given. I need not say, that they refer only to subjects of a theological and polemical nature.

I hardly know how the conversation took the turn it did on the present occasion; but I think it was from Mr. Fellowes' noticing Harrington's pale looks, and conjecturing all sorts of reasons for his occasional lapses into melancholy.

His friend hoped this and hoped that, as usual.

Harrington at last, seeing his curiosity awakened, and that he would go on conjecturing all sorts of things, said, "To terminate your suspense, be it known to you that I am a bankrupt!"

"A bankrupt!" said the other, with evident alarm; "you surely have not been so unwise as to risk your recently-acquired property, or to speculate in"——

"You have hit it," said Harrington; "I have speculated far more deeply than you suppose."

The countenance of his friend lengthened visibly.

"Be not alarmed," resumed Harrington, with a smile, "I mean that I have speculated a good deal in — philosophy, and when I said I was a bankrupt, I meant only that I was a bankrupt — in faith; having become, in fact, since I saw you last, thoroughly sceptical."

The countenance of Fellowes contracted to its proper dimensions. He looked even cheerful to find that his friend had merely lost his faith, and not his fortune.

"Is that all?" said he; "I am heartily glad to hear it. Sceptic! No, no; you must not be a sceptic either, except for a time," continued he, musing very sagely. "It is no bad thing for awhile: for it at least leaves the house 'empty, swept, and garnished.'"

"Rather an unhappy application of your remnant of Biblical knowledge," said Harrington; "I hope you do not intend to go on with the text."

"No, no, my dear friend; I warrant you we shall find you worthier guests than any such figments of supposed revelation. If you are in 'search of a religion,' how happy should I be to aid you!"

"I shall be infinitely obliged to you," said Harrington, gravely; "for at present I do not know that I possess a farthing's worth of solid gold in the world. Ah! that it were but in your power to lend me some; but I fear" (he added, half sarcastically) "that you have not got more than enough for yourself. I assure you that I am far from happy."

He spoke with so much gravity, that I hardly knew whether to attribute it to some intention of dissembling a little with his friend, or to an involuntary expression of the experience of a mind that felt the sorrows of a genuine scepticism. It might be both.

However, it brought things to a crisis at once. His College friend looked equally surprised and pleased at his appeal.

"I trust," said he, with becoming solemnity, "that all this is merely a temporary reaction from having believed *too much:* the languor and dejection which attend the morrow after a night's debauch. I assure you that I rejoice rather than grieve to hear that you have curtailed your orthodoxy. It has been just my own case, as you know; only I flatter myself, that, perhaps having less subtilty than you, I have not passed the 'golden mean' between superstition and scepticism — between believing too much and believing too little."

I looked up for a moment. I saw a laugh in Harrington's eyes, but not a feature moved. It passed away immediately.

"I tell you," said he, "that I believe absolutely no one religious dogma whatever; while yet I would give worlds, if I had them, to set my foot upon a rock. I should even be grateful to any one, who, if he did not give me Truth, gave me a phantom of it, which I could mistake for reality." He again spoke with an earnestness of tone and manner, which convinced me, that if there were any dissimulation, it cost him little trouble.

"If you merely meant," said Fellowes, "that you do not retain any vestige of your early 'historical' and 'dogmatical' Christianity, why, *I* retain just as little of it. Indeed, I doubt," he continued with, perhaps, superfluous candour, "whether I ever *was* a Christian;" and he seemed rather anxious to show that his creed had been nominal.

"If it will save you the trouble of proving it," said Harrington, "I will liberally grant you both your premises and your conclusion, without asking you to state the one or prove the other."

"Well, then, Christian or no Christian, there was a time, at all events, when I was *orthodox*, — you will grant *that*; when I should have been willing to sign the Thirty-nine Articles; or three hundred and thirty-nine; or the Confession of Faith; or any other compilation, or all others; though, perhaps, if strictly examined, I might have been found in the condition of the infidel Scotch Professor, who being asked, on his appointment to his Chair, whether the 'Confession of Faith' contained all that he believed, replied, 'Yes, Gentlemen, and a great deal more.' I have rejected all 'creeds;' and I have now found what the Scripture calls that 'peace which passeth all understanding.'"

"I am sure it passes mine," said Harrington, "if you really *have* found it, and I should be much obliged to you if you would let me participate in the discovery."

"Yes," said Fellowes, "I have been delivered from the intolerable burden of all discussions as to dogma, and all examinations of evidence. I have escaped from the 'bondage of the letter,' and have been introduced into the 'liberty of the spirit.'"

"Your language, at all events, is richly Scriptural," said Harrington; "it is as though you were determined not to leave the 'letter' of the Scripture, even if you renounce the 'spirit' of it."

"Renounce the spirit of it! say rather that, in fact, I have only now discovered it. Though no Christian in the *ordinary* sense, I am, I hope, something better; and a truer Christian in the spirit than thousands of those in the letter."

"Letter and spirit! my friend," said Harrington, "you puzzle me exceedingly; you tell me one moment that you do not believe in historical Christianity at all, either its miracles or dogmas, — these are fables; but in the next — why no old puritan could garnish his discourse with a more edifying use of the language of Scripture. I suppose you will next tell me that you understand the 'spirit' of Christianity better even than Paul."

"So I do," said our visitor, complacently, "and I think I may say it justly, for after all he was but half delivered from his Jewish prejudices; and when he quitted the nonsense of the Old Testament — though in fact he never *did* thoroughly — he evidently believed the fables of the New just as much as the pure truths which lie at the basis of 'spiritual' Christianity. *We* separate the dross of Christianity from its fine gold. 'The letter killeth, but the spirit giveth life'—'the fruit of the spirit is joy, peace,' not"——

"Upon my word," said Harrington, laughing, "I shall begin to fancy presently that Douce Davie Deans has turned infidel, and shall expect to hear of 'right-hand fallings off and left-hand defections.' But tell me, if you would have me think you rational, is not your meaning this: — that the New Testament contains, amidst an infinity of rubbish, the statement of certain 'spiritual' truths, which, and which alone, you recognise?"

"Certainly."

"But you do not acknowledge that these are *derived* from the New Testament."

"Heaven forbid; they are indigenous to the heart of man, and are anterior to all Testaments, old or new."

"Very well; then speak of them as your heart dictates, and do not, unless you would have the world think you a hypocrite, willing to cajole it with the idea that you are a believer in the New Testament, while you in fact reject it, or one of the most barren and uninventive of all human beings, or fanatically fond of mystical language, — do not, I say, affect this very unctuous way of talking. And, for another reason, do not, I beseech you, adopt the phraseology of men who, according to your view, must surely have been either the most miserable fanatics or the most abominable impostors; for if they believed all that system of miracle and doctrine they professed, and this were not true, they were certainly the first; and if they did not believe it, they were as certainly the second."

"Pardon me; I believe them to have been eminently holy men — full of spiritual wisdom and of a truly sublime faith, though conjoined with much ignorance and credulity, which it is unworthy of us to tolerate."

"Whether it could be ignorance and credulity on *your* theory," retorted Harrington, "is to my mind very doubtful. Whether any men can untruly affirm that they saw and did the things the Apostles *say* they saw and did, and yet be sincere fanatics, I know not; but, even were it so, since it shows (as would also their mystical doctrines which you reject, *if* false) that they could be little less than out of their senses; and, as you further say that the spiritual sentiments you retain in *common* with them, were no gift of theirs, but are yours and all mankind's by original inheritance, uttered by the oracle of the human heart before any Testaments were written — why, speak your thoughts in your own language."

"Ay, but how do we know that these original Christians said that they had seen and done the things you refer to? which of course they never *did* see and do, *because* they were miraculous. How do we know what additions and corruptions as to fact, and what disguises of mystical doctrine, 'the idealising biographers and historians' (as Strauss truly calls them) may have accumulated upon their simple utterances?"

"And how do you know, then, whether they ever uttered these 'simple utterances?' or whether they are not *part* of the corruptions? or how can you separate the one from the other? or how can you ascertain that these men meant what *you* mean, when you thus servilely copy their language?"

"Because I know these truths independently of the Bible, to be sure."

"Then speak of them independently of the Bible. If you profess to have broken the stereotype-plates of the 'old revelation' and delivered mankind from their bondage, do not proceed to express yourself only in fragments from them; if you profess freedom of soul, and the possession of the pure truth, do not appear to be so poverty-stricken as to array your thoughts in the tatters of the cast-off Bible."

"Ay, but the 'saints' of the Bible," replied Fellowes, "are, even by Mr. Frank Newman's own confession, those who have entered, after all, most profoundly into the truths of spiritual religion, and stand almost alone in the history of the world in that respect."

"If it be so, it is certainly very odd, considering the mountain-loads of folly, error, fable, fiction, from which their spiritual religion did not in your esteem defend them, and which you say you are obliged to reject. It is a phenomenon of which I think you are bound to give some account."

"But what is there so wonderful in supposing them in possession of superior 'spiritual' advantages, with mistaken history and fallacious logic, and so forth?"

"Why," answered Harrington, "*one* wonder is that they alone, and amidst such gross errors, should possess these *spiritual* advantages. But, to speak frankly, it also appears to me that your notions of the 'spiritual' are not the *same* as theirs, for you reject the New Testament dogmas as well as its history; if so, it is another reason for not misleading us by using language in deceptive senses. But, at all events, I cannot help pitying your poverty of thought or poverty of expression — one or both; and I beg you, for my sake if not for your own, to express your thoughts as much as possible in your own terms, and avail yourself less liberally of those of David and Paul, whose language ordinary Christians will always associate with another meaning, and can never believe you sincere in supposing that it rightfully expresses the doctrines of your most 'spiritual' infidelity. They will certainly hear your Scriptural and devout language with the same feelings with which they would nauseate that most oppressive of all odours — the faint scent of lavender in the chamber of death. My good uncle here, who cannot be prevailed upon to reject the Bible, will not, I am sure, hear you, without supposing that you resemble those Rationalists, of whom Menzel says, 'These gentlemen smilingly taught their theological pupils that unbelief was the true apostolic, primitive, Christian belief; they put all their insipidities into Christ's mouth, and made him, by means of their exegetical jugglery sometimes a Kantian, sometimes a Hegelian, sometimes one *ian* and sometimes another, 'wie es dem Herrn Professor beliebt:' neither will he be able to imagine that you are not resorting to this artifice for the same purpose. 'The Bible,' says Menzel, 'and their Reason being incompatible, why do they not let them remain separate? Why insist on harmonizing things which do not, and never can, harmonize? It is because they are aware that the Bible has authority with the people; otherwise they would never trouble themselves about so troublesome a book.'—I cannot suspect *you* of such hypocrisy; but I must confess I regard your language as *cant*. As I listen to you, I seem to see a hybrid between Prynne and Voltaire. So far from its being true that you have renounced the 'letter' of the Bible and retained its 'spirit,' I think it would be much more correct to say, comparing your infidel hypothesis with your most spiritual dialect, that you have renounced the 'spirit' of the Bible and retained its 'letter.'"

"But are you in a condition to give an opinion?" said Fellowes, with a serious air. "Mr. Newman says, in a like case, 'the natural man discerneth not the things of the spirit of God, because they are foolishness unto him;' it is the 'spiritual man only who searcheth the deep things of God.' At the same time I freely acknowledge that I never could see my way clear to employ an argument which *looks* so arrogant; and the less, as I believe, with Mr. Parker, that the only true revelation is in all men alike. Yet, on the other hand, I cannot doubt my own *consciousness*."

"Why, no man doubts his *own consciousness*," said Harrington, laughing. "The question is, what is its value? What is the criterion of universal 'spiritual truth,' if there be any?—Those words you have just quoted were well in Paul's mouth, and had a meaning. In yours, I suspect, they would have none, or a very different one. *He* dreamt that he was giving to mankind (vainly, as it seems) a system of doctrines and truths which were, many of them, transcendental to the human intellect and conscience, and which, when revealed, were very distasteful (and not least to *you*); but the assertion of a spiritual monopoly would assuredly sound rather odd in one who professes, if I understand you, that God has given to man (for it is no *discovery* of any individual) an internal and universal revelation! But of your possible *limitations* of your *universal* spiritual revelation, —which all men 'naturally' possess, but which the 'natural man' receiveth not,—we will talk hereafter. Sceptic as I am, I am not a sceptic who is reconciled to scepticism. Meanwhile, you reject the Bible *in toto*, as an external revelation of God, if I understand you."

"*In toto;* and I believe that it has received in this age its death-blow."

"Ay, that is what the infidel has been always promising us; meantime, *they* somehow perish, and *it* laughs at them. You remember, perhaps, the words of old Woolston, so many fragments of whose criticism, as those of many others, have been incorporated by Strauss. He had, as he elegantly expresses it, 'cut out such a piece 'of work for the Boylean lectures as should hold them 'tug as long as the ministry of the letter should last;' for he, too, you see, masked his infidelity by a distinction between the 'letter' and the 'spirit,' though he applied the convenient terms in a totally different sense. Poor soul! The fundamental principles of his infidelity are surrendered by Strauss himself. Similarly, a score of assailants of the Bible have appeared and vanished since his day; each proclaiming, just as he himself went to the bottom, that he had given the Bible its death-blow! Somehow, however, that singular book continues to flourish, to propagate itself, to speak all languages, to intermingle more and more with the literature of all civilised nations; while mankind will not accept, slaves as they are, the intellectual freedom you offer them. It is really very provoking; of what use is it to destroy the Bible so often, when it lives the next minute? I have little doubt *your* new attempts will end just like the labours of the Rationalists of the Paulus school, so graphically described by the German writer whom I have already referred to. 'It is sad, no doubt,' says he, or something to the same effect, ' that after fifty years' exegetical grubbing, weeding, and pruning at the mighty primitive forest of the Bible, the next generation should persist in saying that the Rationalist had destroyed the forest only in his own addled imagination, and that it is just as it was.'"

"Yes; but the new weapons will not be so easily evaded as those of a past age."

"Will they not? we shall see. You must not prophesy; in that, you know, you do not believe."

"No; but nevertheless we shall see so-called sacred dogma and history exploded, for Mr. Newman"——

"Thinks so, of course; and he must be right, because he has never been known to be wrong in any of his judgments, or even to vary in them. But we have had enough, I think, of these subjects this evening, and it is too bad to give you only a controversial welcome. I want to have some conversation with you about very different things, and more pleasant just now. We shall have plenty of opportunity to discuss theological points."

To this Fellowes assented; they resumed general conversation, and I finished my letters.

July 3. We were all sitting, as on the previous day, in the library.

"Book-faith!" I heard Harrington say, laughing; "why, as to that, I must needs acknowledge that the whole school of Deism, 'rational' or 'spiritual,' have the least reason in the world to indulge in sneers at book-faith; for, upon my word, their faith has consisted in little else. Their systems are parchment religions, my friend, all of them;—books, books, for ever, from Lord Herbert's time downwards, are all they have yet given to the world. They have ever been boastful and loud-tongued, but have done nothing; there are no great social efforts, no organisations, no practical projects, whether successful or futile, to which they can point. The old 'book-faiths' which you venture to ridicule have been *something*, at all events; and, in truth, I can find no other 'faith' than what *is* somehow or other attached to a 'book,' which has been any thing influential. The Vedas, the Koran, the Old Testament Scriptures,—those of the New,—over how many millions have *these* all reigned! Whether their supremacy be right or wrong, their doctrine true or false, is another question; but your faith, which has been book-faith and lip-service *par excellence*, has done nothing, that I can discover. One after another of your Infidel Reformers passes away, and leaves no trace behind, except a quantity of crumbling 'book-faith.' You have always been just on the eve of extinguishing supernatural fables, dogmas, and superstitions,—and then regenerating the world! Alas! the meanest superstition that crawls laughs at you, and, false as it may be, is still stronger than you."

"And *your* sect," retorted Fellowes, rather warmly, "if you come to that, is it not the smallest of all? Is *that* likely to find favour in the eyes of mankind?"

"Why, no," said Harrington, with provoking coolness; "but then it makes no *pretensions* to any thing of the kind. It were strange if it did; for, as the sceptic doubts if any truth can be certainly attained by man on those subjects on which the 'rational' or the 'spiritual' deist dogmatises, it of course professes to be incapable of *constructing* any thing."

"And *does* construct nothing," retorted Fellowes.

"Very true," said Harrington, "and therein keeps its word; which is more, I fear, than can be said for your more ambitious spiritualists, who profess to construct, and do not."

"But you must give the school of spiritualism time: it is only just born. You seem to me to be confounding the school of the old, dry, logical deism, with the 'young, fresh, vigorous, earnest school,' which appeals to 'insight' and 'intuition.'"

"No," said Harrington, "I think I do not confound. The first and the best of our English deists derived *his* system as immediately from intuitions as Mr. Parker or you. You know how it sped,—or, if you do not, you may easily discover,—with his successors: they continually disputed about it, curtailed it, added to it, altered it, agreed in nothing but the author's rejection of Christianity, and forgot more and more the decency of his style. So will it be with your Mr. Newman and *his* successors. They will acquiesce in his rejection of Christianity; depend upon it, in nothing more. He may get his admirers to abandon the Bible, but they will have nought to do with the 'loves, and joys, and sorrows,' and raptures, which he describes in the 'Soul;' they would just as soon read the 'Canticles.'"

"I really cannot admit," said Fellowes, "that we modern spiritualists are to be confounded with Lord Herbert."

"Not confounded with him, certainly," replied Harrington, "but *identified* with him you may be; except, to be sure, that he was *convinced* of the immortality of man as one of the few articles of all religion; while many of you deny or doubt it. The doctrines "——

"Call them *sentiments,* rather; I like that term better."

"Oh, certainly, if you prefer it; only be pleased to observe that a sentiment felt is a *fact,* and a *fact* is a *truth,* and a *truth* may surely be expressed in a proposition. That is all I am anxious about at present. If so far, at least, we may not patch up the divorce which Mr. Newman has pronounced between the 'intellect' and the 'soul,' it is of no use for us to talk about the matter. I say that Lord Herbert's articles "——

"There again, 'articles,'" said Fellowes; "I hate the

word; I could almost imagine that you were going to recite the formidable thirty-nine."

"Rather, from your outcry, one would suppose I was about to inflict the forty save one; but do not be alarmed. The articles, neither of Lord Herbert's creed nor of your own, I suspect, are thirty-nine, or any thing like it. The catalogue will soon be exhausted."

"Here again, 'creed;' I detest the word. We have no creed. Your very language chills me. It reminds me of the dry orthodoxy of the 'letter,' 'logical processes,' 'intellectual propositions,' and so forth. Speak of 'spiritual truths' and 'sentiments,' which are the product of immediate 'insight,' of 'an insight into God,' a 'spontaneous impression on the gazing soul,' to adopt Mr. Newman's beautiful expressions, and I shall understand you."

"I am afraid I shall hardly understand myself, then," cried Harrington. "But let us not be scared by mere words, nor go into hysterics at the sound of 'logic' and 'creed,' lest 'sentimental spirituality' be found, like some other 'sentimental' things, a bundle of senseless affectations."

"But you forget that there is all the difference in the world between Herbert and his deistical successors. *They* connected religion with the 'intellectual and sensational,' and *we* with the 'instinctive and emotional' sides of human nature."

"If you think," said the other, "(the *substance* of your religious system being, as I believe, precisely the same as that of Lord Herbert and the better deists), that you can make it more effective than it has been in the past, by conjuring with the words 'sensational and intellectual,' 'instinctive and emotional,' or that the mixture of chalk and water will be more potent with one label than with the other, I fancy you will find yourself deceived. The distinctions you refer to have to do with the theory of the subject, and will make din enough, no doubt, among such as Mr. Newman and yourself; but mankind at large will be unable even to enter into the *meaning* of your refinements. They will say briefly and bluntly, 'What are the *truths*, whether, as Lord Herbert says, they are "innate," or, as *you* say, "spiritual intuitions" (we care nothing for the phraseology of either or both of you), which are to be admitted by universal humanity, and to be influential over the heart and conscience?' Now, I suspect that when you come to the enumeration of these *truths*, your system and that of Lord Herbert will be found the same; only as regards the immortality of the soul *his* tone is firmer than perhaps I shall find yours. But I admit the policy of a change of name; 'Rationalist' and 'Deist' have a bad sound; 'Spiritualist' is a better *nom de guerre* for the present."

"We shall never understand one another," said Fellowes: "the spiritual man"——

"Pshaw!" said Harrington; "you can immediately bring the matter to the test by telling me *what* you maintain, and then I shall know whether your system *is* or *is not* identical with Lord Herbert's; or, rather, tell me what you do *not* believe, and let us come to it that way. Do you believe a single shred of any of the supernatural narratives of the Old or New Testament?"

"No," said Fellowes; "a thousand times no."

"Very well; that gets rid of at least four-sevenths of the Bible. Do you believe in the Trinity, the Atonement, the Resurrection of Christ, in a General Resurrection, in the Day of Judgment?"

"No, not in one of them," said Fellowes: "not in a particle of one of them."

"Pretty well again. You reject, then, the characteristic doctrines of Christianity."

"Not one of them," was the answer.

"We are, indeed, in danger of misunderstanding one another," said Harrington. "But tell me, is it not your boast, as of Mr. Parker, that the truths which are *essential* to religion are not peculiar to *Christianity*, but are involved in all religions?"

"Assuredly."

"If I were to ask you what were the *essential* attributes of a man, would you assign those which he had in common with a *pig?*"

"Certainly not."

"But if I asked you what were those of an *animal*, I presume you would give those which both species possessed, and none that either possessed exclusively?"

"I should."

"Need I add, then, that you are deceiving yourself when you say that you believe all the characteristic doctrines of Christianity, since you say that you believe only those which it has in common with *every* religion? If I were to ask you what doctrines are essential to constitute *any* religion, then you would do well to enumerate those which belong to Christianity and every other. But when we talk of the doctrines peculiar to Christianity, we mean those which discriminate it *from* every other, and not those which are common to it with them."

"But, however," said Fellowes, "none of the doctrines you have enumerated are a part of Christianity, but are mere additions of imposture and fanaticism."

"Then what *are* the doctrines, which, though common to every other religion, are characteristic of *it?* What is left that is essential, or peculiar, to Christianity, when you have denuded it of all that you reject? Is it not, then, assimilated, by your own confession, to every other religion? How shall we discriminate them?"

"By this, perhaps," said Fellowes, "(for I acknowledge some difficulty here), that Christianity contains these truths of absolute religion alone and *pure.* As Mr. Parker says, *This* is the glory of genuine Christianity."

"Do you not see that this is the very question — you yourself being obliged to reject nine-tenths of the statements in the only records in which we know any thing about it? Might not an ancient priest of Jupiter say the same of *his* religion, by first divesting it of all but that which even *you* say it had in common with every other? However, let us now look at the positive side. What is the *residuum* which you condescend to leave to your *genuine* Christianity?"

"Christianity," said Fellowes, rather pompously, "is

not so much a system as a discipline, — not a creed, but a life: in short, a divine philosophy."

"All which I have heard from all sorts of Christians a thousand times," cried Harrington; "and it is delightfully vague; it may mean anything, or nothing. But the *truths*, the *truths*, what are they, my friend? I see I must get them from you by fragments. Your faith includes, I presume, a belief in one Supreme God, who is a Divine Personality; in the duty of reverencing, loving, and obeying him, — whether you know *how* that is to be done or not; that we must *repent* of our sins, — if indeed we duly know what things *are* sins in his sight; that he will certainly forgive to any extent on such repentance, without any mediation; that *perhaps* there is a heaven hereafter; but that it is very doubtful if there are any punishments."

"I do believe," said Fellowes, "these are the cardinal doctrines of the 'Absolute Religion,' as Mr. Parker calls it. Nor can I conceive that any others are necessary."

"Well," said Harrington, "with the exception of the immortality of the soul, on which Lord Herbert has the advantage of speaking a little more firmly, the Deists and such 'spiritualists' as you are assuredly identical. I have simply abridged his articles. The same project as your 'spiritualism,' or 'naturalism,' in all its *essential* features, has been often tried before, and found wanting; that is, of guaranteeing to man a sufficient and infallible internal oracle, independent of all aid from external revelation, and of proving that he has, in effect, possessed and enjoyed it always; only that, by a slight inadvertence (I suppose), he did not know it. The theory, indeed, is rather suspiciously confined to those who have previously had the Bible. No such plenary confidence is found in the ancient heathen philosophers, who, in many not obscure places, acknowledge that the path of mortal man, by his internal light, is a *little* dim. Many, therefore, say that the 'Naturalists' and 'Spiritualists' are but plagiarists from the Bible, and, of course, like other plagiarists, depreciate the sources from which they have stolen their treasures. I think the charge unjust; for whatever their obligations to that mutilated volume, I acknowledge they have transformed Christianity quite sufficiently to entitle themselves to the praise of originality; and if the Battle of the Books were to be fought over again, I doubt whether Moses or Paul would think it worth while to make any other answer than that of Plato in that witty piece, to the Grub Street author, who boasted that *he* had not been in the slightest degree indebted to the classics: Plato declared that, upon his honour, he believed him! Whether the successors of the Herberts and Tindals of a former day are not plagiarists from *them*, is another question, and depends entirely upon whether the writings of their predecessors are sufficiently know to them. Probably the hopeless oblivion which, for the most part, covers them (for the perverse world has been again and again assured of its infallible internal light, and has persisted in denying that it has it) will protect our modern authors from the imputation of plagiarism; but that the systems in question are essentially identical, can hardly admit of doubt. The principal difference is as to the organon by which the revelation affirmed to be internal and universal is apprehended; it affects the metaphysics of the question, and, like all metaphysics, is characteristically dark. But about this you will not get the mass of mankind to *care* any more than you can get yourselves to *agree;* no, nor will you agree even about the system itself. Nay, you modern spiritualists, just as the elder deists, are already quarrelling about it. In short, the universal light in man's soul flickers and wavers most abominably."

"I see," said Fellowes, "you are profoundly prejudiced against the spiritualists."

"I believe not," said Harrington; "the worst I wish them is that they may be honest men, and *appear* what they really *are*."

"I suppose next," exclaimed the other, "you will attribute to the modern spiritualist the scurrility of the elder deists — of Woolston, Tindal, and Collins?"

"No," said Harrington, "I answer no; nor do I

(remember) compare Lord Herbert in these respects with his successors. He was an amiable enthusiast; in many respects resembling Mr. Newman himself. Do you remember, by the way, how that most reasonable rejector of all 'external' revelation, prayed that he might be directed by heaven, whether he should publish or not publish his 'book?' about which, if heaven was very solicitous, this world has since been very indifferent. Having distinctly heard 'a sound as of thunder,' on a very 'calm and serene day,' he immediately received it as a preternatural answer to prayer, and an indubitable sign of heaven's concurrence!"

"No such taint of superstition, however, will be found clinging to Mr. Newman. He has most thoroughly abjured all notion of an external revelation; nay, he denies the possibility of a 'book-revelation of spiritual and moral truth;' and I am confident that his dilemma on that point is unassailable."

"Be it so," answered Harrington; "you will readily suppose I am not inclined to contest that point very vigorously; yet I confess that, as usual, my inveterate scepticism leaves me in some doubts. Will you assist me in resolving them?—but not to-night, let us have a little more talk about old college days — or what say you to a game of chess?"

July 4. I thought this day would have passed off entirely without polemics; but I was mistaken. In the evening, Harrington, after a very cheerful morning, relapsed into one of his pensive moods. Conversation flagged: at last I heard Fellowes say, "I have this advantage of you, my friend, that my sentiments have, at all events, produced that peace of which you are in quest, and which your countenance at times too plainly declares you not to possess. If you had it, you would not take so gloomy a view of things. Like him, from whom I have derived some of my sentiments, I have found that they tend to make me a *happier* man. The Christian, like yourself, looks upon every thing with a jaundiced or distorted eye, and is apt to underrate the claims and pleasures of this present scene of our existence. I can truly say that I now enter into them much more keenly than I could when I was an orthodox Christian. I can say, with Mr. Newman, I now, with deliberate approval, 'love the world and the things of the world.' The New Testament, as Mr. Newman says, bids us watch perpetually, not knowing whether the Lord will return at cock-crowing or midday: 'that the only thing worth spending one's energies on, is the forwarding of men's salvation.' Now I must say with him, that while I believed this, I acted an eccentric and unprofitable part."

"*Only* then?" said Harrington. "You were fortunate."

"He says that to teach the certain speedy destruction of earthly things, as the *New Testament does,* is to cut the sinews of all earthly progress; to declare war against intellect and imagination, against industrial and social advancement."

My gravity was hardly equal to the task of listening to the first part of Mr. Fellowes' speech. To hear that the common and just reproach against all mankind, but especially against all Christians, of taking too keen an interest in the *present,* was in a large measure at least founded upon a mistake; to find, in fact, that there was some danger of an excessive exaggeration of the claims of the future, which required a corrective; that the Christian world, owing to the above pernicious doctrine, might possibly evince too faint a relish for the pleasures or too diminished an estimate of the advantages of the present life; that their "treasure being in heaven," it was not impossible but "their heart" might be too much there also — there perhaps, when it was imperatively demanded in the counting-house, on the hustings, at the mart or the theatre; all this being, as I say, so notoriously contrary to ordinary opinion and experience, seemed to me so exquisitely ludicrous that I could hardly help bursting into laughter, especially as I imagined one of our new "spiritual" doctors ascending the pulpit under the new dispensation, to indulge in exhortations to a keener chase of this world, and "the things of this world." I found afterwards similar thoughts were passing through Harrington's mind, rendered more whimsical by the recollection, that, during college life, his friend (though very far from vicious) had certainly never seemed to take any deficient interest in the affairs of this world, nor to exhibit any predilection for an ascetic life. Indeed, he acknowledged that, after all, he could not sympathise with Mr. Newman's extreme sensitiveness in relation to this matter.*

Harrington answered, with proper gravity, "I am glad to find that any undue austerity of character — of which, however, I assure you, upon my honour, I never suspected you — has received so invaluable a corrective. Still, it is obvious to remark, that if the chief effect of this new style of religion is to abate any excessive antipathy which the New Testament has fostered, or was likely to foster, to the attractions of the present life, it has, I conceive, an easy task. I never remarked in Christians any superfluous contempt of the present world or its pleasures; any indication of an extravagant admiration of any sublimer objects of pursuit. In truth, the tendencies of human nature, as it appears to me, are so much the other way, that the strongest language of a hundred New Testaments would be little heeded. Your corrective is something like that of a moralist who should seriously prove that man was to take care that his appetites and passions are duly indulged, of which ethical writers have, alas! condescended to say but little, supposing that everybody would feel that there was no *need* of solemn counsels on such a subject. It reminds one of the Christmas sermon mentioned in the 'Sketch Book,' preached by the good little antiquarian parson, who elaborately proved, and pathetically enforced on his reluctant auditors, the duty of a proper devotion to the festivities of the season. However, every one must like the complexion of your

* See Phases, p. 205.

theology, though its counsels on this subject do not seem to me of urgent necessity."

"Perhaps," said Fellowes, "I ought rather to have said that Christians inculcate, *theoretically*, a contempt of the present life, while, *practically*, they enter as keenly into its pleasures as the 'worldling'"—uttering the last word with an approach to a sneer.

"You may be sure," said Harrington, "*I* shall leave the Christian to defend himself; but if the case be as you *now* represent it, your new religious system seems to be superfluous as a corrective of any tendencies to Christian asceticism, and can do nothing for us. It appears that your Reformation was begun and ended before your 'spiritual' Luthers appeared."

"Not so," said Fellowes, "for the eagerness with which the Christian pursues the world, while he condemns it, is, as Mr. Greg has recently insisted, 'a gigantic hypocrisy:' it is founded on a lie. Christians say this world is *not* to be the great object for which we are to live, and in which we are to find our happiness; we say it *is*: they say it is *not* our 'country' or our 'home;' we say it *is*: they say that we are to live supremely for the future, and *in* it; we say *for* and *in* the present; that if there be a future world (of which many doubt, and I, for one, have not been able to make up my mind), we are to hope to be happy there, but that the main business is to secure our happiness *here*—to embellish, adorn, and enjoy this our only certain dwelling-place; and, in fact, to live supremely for the *present*. Such is the constitution of human nature."

"I shall not be at the trouble," replied Harrington, "to defend the inconsistencies of the Christian; but your system, I fear, is essentially a brutal theology, and, I am certain, a false philosophy. All the analogies of our nature cry out against it. Why, even with regard to the '*present*,' as you call this life, man is perpetually living *for* and *in* the future. This 'present' (minute as it is) is itself broken up into *many* futures, and it is these which man truly lives for, when he is not a beast; and not for the passing hour. It is not to-day, it is always to-morrow, on which his eye is fixed; and his ever repining nature perpetually confesses its impatient want of something (it knows not what) to come. The child lives for his youth, and the youth is discontented till he is a man; every attainment and every possession palls as soon as it is reached, and we still sigh for something that we have not. It is simply in *analogy* with all this that the Christian and every other religion says (absurdly, if you will, but certainly with a deeper knowledge of human nature than you evince), that as every *little present* has its *little future* for which we live, so the *whole* present of this life has its *great* future, which must, all the way through, be made the *supreme* object of forethought and solicitude: just as we should despise any man who, for a moment's gratification to-day, perilled the happiness of the whole of to-morrow. If Christians are inconsistent in this respect, that is *their* affair; but I am sure their *theory* is more in accordance with the constitution of human nature than yours."—He might have added that there is nothing in the New Testament which forbids to Christians any of the innocent pleasures of this life: the Christian may lawfully appropriate them; his system does not constrain him to hermit-like austerity or puritanic grimace. He may enjoy them, just as a wise man, who will not sacrifice any of the interests of next year for a transient gratification of the passing hour, does not deny himself any legitimate pleasure which is not inconsistent with the more momentous interest. The pilgrim drinks and rests at the fountain, though he does not dream of setting up his tent there.

"Nay," said Fellowes, "but think again of the 'gigantic lie' of making the future world the supreme object, and yet living wholly for this."

"If that be the case," said I, joining in their talk, "there is no doubt a 'gigantic lie' somewhere; but the question is, who tells it? It does not follow that it is Christianity. You may see every day men perilling, nay, losing, some important advantages, by loitering away the very hour which is to secure them,—in reading a novel, enjoying a social hour, lying in bed, and, what not. You do not conclude that the man's estimate of the future—his philosophy of *that*—is any the more questionable for this folly? The ruthless future comes and makes his heart ache; and so may it be with Christianity, for aught any such considerations imply. Your argument only proves that if Christianity be true, man is an inconsistent fool; and, in my judgment, *that* was proved long before Christianity was born or thought of."

"Your theology," cried Harrington, "fairly carried out, would lead most men to the 'Epicurean sty,' which, sceptic as I am, I loathe the thought of; it almost deserves the rebuke which Johnson gave the man who pleaded for a 'natural and savage condition,' as he called it. 'Sir,' said the Doctor, 'it is a brutal doctrine; a bull might as well say, I have this grass and this cow—and what can a creature want more?' No, I am sure that the Christian or any other religionist—inconsistent though he is—appeals in this point to deeper analogies of our nature than you."

"But the fact is," said Fellowes, "that the Christian *depreciates* the innocent pleasures of this life!"

"And my uncle would say, it is his own fault, then."

"Nay, but hear me. I conceive that nothing could be more natural, as several of *our* writers have remarked, than the injunctions of the Apostles to the primitive Christians to despise the world, and so forth, under the influence of that great mistake they had fallen into, that the world was about to tumble to pieces, and"——

"I am not sure," said Harrington, who seemed resolved to evince a scepticism provoking enough, "that they *did* make the mistake, on *your* principles. For I know not, nor you either, whether the expressions on which you found the supposition be not amongst the voluminous additions with which you are pleased to suppose their simple and genuine 'utterances' have been corrupted. But, leaving you to discuss that point, if you like, with my uncle here, I must deny that the *mistake*, supposing it one, makes any thing in relation to our present discussion. You say that the Apostles did *well* and *naturally* to inculcate a light grasp on the world, on the supposition that it was about to pass away; and, therefore, I suppose, you (under a similar impression) would do the same; if so, ought you not *still* to do it? for can it make any conceivable difference to the wisdom or the folly of such exhortations, whether the world passes away from us, or we pass away from the world?—whether it 'tumbles to pieces,' as you express it, or (which is too certain) *we* tumble to pieces? I think, therefore, your same comfortable theology cannot be justified, *if* you justify the conduct of the Apostles under their impression, let it be ever so erroneous. You ought to feel the *same* sentiments; you being, to all practical purposes, under a precisely similar impression."

Fellowes looked as if he were a little vexed at having thus hypothetically justified the conduct of the Apostles. But he was not without his answer, adopted from Mr. Newman. "Yes," said he, "*practically*, no doubt, death is the end of the world to *us;* but to urge this,—what is it, as Mr. Newman says, 'but abominable selfishness preached as religion?' If we are to labour for remote posterity, will not our work remain, though we die? But if the world is to perish in fifty years, or a century, what then?"

"Far be it from me," said Harrington, "to compete with your spiritual philanthropy, which, doubtless, will not be content to work unless under a lease of a million of years or so. I suppose if you thought the world would come to an end in a hundred years (and really I have no proof that the Apostles thought it would end sooner—they spoke of their death as coming first), you would not think it worth while to do any thing; the welfare of your children and grandchildren would appear far too paltry for so ambitious a benevolence as yours! Most people—Christians, sceptics, or otherwise—are contented to aim at the welfare of this generation and the next, and think as little of their great great grandchildren as of their great great grandfathers. That little vista terminates the projects of their philanthropy, just as their own death is to them the end of the world. Meantime, it appears, *you* would be tempted to neglect the *practical* little you could do, because you could not do more than for a century or so! Pray, which is really the more benevolent? Moreover, as not one man in a million can or does think of benefiting any but his immediate generation, you ought, upon *your* principles, still to sit down inactive; for they for whom alone you can work will soon pass away too. But the whole argument is too refined. No mortal—except you or Mr. Newman—would be wrought upon by it."

"Well, but," said Fellowes, "as to the mistake of the Apostles, there can be no doubt of *that;* it really appears to me grossly disingenuous"—looking towards me—"to deny it. What do you say, Mr. B.?" repeating his assertion that the Apostles clearly thought that the end of the world was close at hand—in fact, that it would happen in their generation.

I told him I was afraid I must run the risk of appearing in his eyes "grossly disingenuous;" not that I deemed it necessary to maintain that the Apostles *had* any idea of the period of time which was to intervene between the first promulgation of the Gospel and the consummation of all things; for when I found our Lord himself acknowledging, "of that day and that hour knoweth no man, not even the angels, nor even the Son, but the Father only," I could not wonder that the Apostles were left to mere conjectures on a subject which was *then* veiled even from *his* humanity. I said I even thought it probable that their vivid feeling anticipated the day—that the interval between, so to speak, was "foreshortened" to them; but that I could not see how the question of their inspiration, or the truth of Christianity, was at all involved in their ignorance on that point; unless, indeed, it could be proved that they had positively stated that the predicted event would take place in their own time. This, I acknowledged, I could not find—but much to the contrary; I said that the charge had been so often repeated by the infidel school, that they had persuaded themselves of its truth, and spoke of it as if it were a decided point;

but that as long as the *second* Epistle of St. Paul to the Thessalonians remained, in which the Apostle expressly corrected misapprehensions similar to those which infidelity still professes to found on the *first* Epistle, I should continue to doubt whether Paul did not know his own mind better than his modern commentators. I added that we do not hear that the Thessalonians *persisted* in believing that they had rightly interpreted Paul's words after he had himself disowned the meaning they had put upon them; that this was a degree of assurance possible only to modern critics; and that I was surprised that Mr. Newman should have quietly assumed the alleged "mistake" in his "Phases of Faith," without thinking it worth while even to state the opposing argument from the Second Epistle. I added that the repeated references which both Paul and Peter make to their own death, as certain to take place *before* the dissolution of all things, sufficiently prove that, however their view of the future might be contracted, they did not expect the world to end in *their* day, and ought to have silenced the perverse criticism on the popular expression, "Then *we* which are alive and remain," &c.

Having briefly stated my opinion, Fellowes said he saw that he and I were as little likely to agree as Harrington and he. "However," he continued, turning to his friend, " to go back to the point from which we digressed. My new faith, at all events, makes me happy, which it is plain — too plain — that your want of all faith does not make you."

"Whether it is your new faith," said the other, "makes you happy — whether you were not as happy in your old faith — whether there are not thousands of Christians who are as happy with *their* faith (*they* would say much happier, and I should say so too, if they not only *say* they believe it, but believe it and practise it), I will not inquire; that my want of faith does not make me happy is a sad truth, which I do not think it worth while to deny; though I must confess that there have been many who have shared in my scepticism who have not shared in my misery. It is just because they have not realised what they did *not* believe; even as there are thousands of nominal Christians who do not realise what they say they *do* believe; neither the one nor the other are the happier or the more sorrowful for their pretended tenets. This is simply because they stand in no need of the admirable correctives supplied by your *new* theology. The present engrosses their solicitudes and affections; and the mere *talk* of the belief or the no belief suffices to hush and tranquillise the heart in relation to those most momentous subjects, on which if man has not thought at all, he is a fool indeed. In either case the 'future' and the 'eternal' seem so far removed that they seem to be an 'eternal futurity.' Such parties look at that distant future much as children at the stars; it is a point, an invisible speck, in the firmament. A sixpence held near the eye appears larger; and brought sufficiently close shuts out the universe altogether. But let *us* also forget the future, and have a little talk of the past."

They resumed their conversation on subjects indifferent as far as this journal is concerned, and I bade them good night.

July 5. We were sitting in the library after breakfast. The two college friends soon fell into chat, while I sat writing at my separate table, but ready to resume my capacity of reporter, should any polemical discussion take place. I soon had plenty of employment. After about an hour I heard Harrington say,—

"But I shall be happy, I assure you, to fill the void whenever you will give me something solid wherewith to fill it."

It was impossible that even a believer in the doctrine that no "creed" can be taught, and that an "external revelation" is an impossibility, could be insensible to the charm of making a proselyte.

"What is it," said Fellowes, "that you want?"

"What do I want? I want certainty, or quasi-certainty, on those points on which if a man is content to remain uncertain, he is a fool or a brute; points respecting which it is no more possible for a genuine sceptic — for I speak not of the thoughtless lover of paradox, or the queer dogmatist who *resolves* that nothing is true — to still the soul, than nakedness can render us insensible to cold; or hunger cure its own pangs by saying, 'Go to, now; I have nothing to eat.' The generality of mankind are insensible to these questions only because they imagine, even though it may be falsely, that they possess certainty. They are problems which, whenever there is elevation of mind enough to appreciate their importance, engage the *real* doubter in a life-long conflict; and to attempt to appease the restlessness of such a mind by the old prescriptions — the old quackish Epicurean nostrum of '*Carpe diem*' — 'let us eat, drink, and be merry, for to-morrow we die ' — 'we do not know what the morrow may bring' — is like attempting to call back the soul from a mortal syncope by applying to the nostrils a drop of *eau de Cologne.* 'Enjoy to-day, we do not know what the morrow will bring!' Why that is the very thought which *poisons* to-day. No, a soul of any worth cannot but feel an intense wish for the solution of its doubts, even while it doubts whether they can be solved."

"'*Carpe diem*' certainly would not be my *sole* prescription," said Fellowes; "you have not told me yet what you want."

"No, but I will. The questions on which I want certainty are indeed questions about which philosophers will often argue just to display their vanity, as human vanity will argue about any thing; but they are no sooner felt in their true grandeur, than they absorb the soul."

"Still, what is it you want?"

"I want to know — whence I came? whither I am going? Whether there be, in truth, as so many say there is, a God — a tremendous Personality, to whose infinite faculties the 'great' and the 'little' (as *we* call them) equally vanish — whose universal presence fills all space, in any point of which he exists entire in the amplitude of all his infinite attributes — whose universal government extends even to *me,* and my fellow-atoms, called men; within whose sheltering embrace even I am not too mean for protection;—whether, if there be such a being, he is truly infinite; or whether this vast machine of the universe may not have developed tendencies or involved consequences which eluded his forethought, and are *now* beyond even his control;—whether, for this reason, or for some other necessity, such infinite sorrows have been permitted to invade it;—whether, above all, he be propitious or hostile towards a world in which I feel too surely, in the profound and various misery of man, that his aspects are not *all* benignant — how if he be offended, he is to be reconciled;— whether he is at all accessible, or one to whom the pleasures and the sufferings of the poor child of dust are equally subjects of horrible indifference;— whether, if such Omnipotent Being created the world, he has now abandoned it to be the sport of chance, and I am thus an orphan in the universe;— whether this 'universal frame' be indeed without a mind, and we are, in fact, the only forms of conscious existence;—whether, as the Pantheist declares, the universe itself be God — ever making, never made — the product of an evolution of an infinite series of 'antecedents' and 'consequents;' a God of *which* — for I cannot say of *whom* — you and I are bits; perishable fragments of a Divinity, itself imperishable only because there will always be *bits* of it to perish;— whether, even upon some such supposition, this conscious existence of ours is to be *renewed;* and, if so, under what conditions; or whether, when we have finished our little day, no other dawn is to break upon our night;— whether the *vale, vale in æternum, vale,* is really the proper utterance of a broken heart as it closes the sepulchre on the object of its love."

His voice faltered; and I was confirmed in my suspicions, that some deep secret sorrow had had to do with his morbid state of mind. In a moment he resumed:—

"These are the questions, and others like them, which I have vainly toiled to solve. I, like you, have been rudely driven out of my old beliefs; my early Christian faith has given way to doubt; the little hut on the mountain side, in which I thought to dwell in pastoral simplicity, has been scattered to the tempest, and I am turned out to the blast without a shelter. I have wandered long and far, but have not found that rest which you tell me is to be obtained. As I examine all other theories, they seem, to me, pressed by at least *equal* difficulties with that I have abandoned. I cannot make myself *contented,* as others do, with believing nothing, and yet I have nothing to believe; I have wrestled long and hard with my Titan foes — but not successfully. I have turned to every quarter of the universe in vain; I have interrogated my own soul, but it answers not; I have gazed upon nature, but its many voices speak no articulate language to *me;* and, more especially, when I gaze upon the bright page of the midnight heavens, those orbs gleam upon me with so cold a light and amidst so portentous a silence, that I am, with Pascal, terrified at the spectacle of the infinite solitudes — '*de ces espaces infinis.*' I declare to you that I know nothing in nature so beautiful or so terrible as those mute oracles."

"They are indeed mute," said Fellowes; "but not so that still voice which whispers its oracles *within.* You have but to look inwards, and you may see, by the direct gaze of 'the spiritual faculty,' bright and clear, those great 'intuitions' of spiritual truths which the gauds and splendours of the external universe can no more illustrate than can the illuminated characters of an old missal; — just as little can any *book* teach these truths. You have truly said, the stars will shed no light upon them; they, on the contrary, must illumine the stars; I mean, they must themselves be seen before the outward universe can assume intelligible meaning; must utter their voices before any of the phenomena of the external world can have any real significance!"

"How different," said Harrington, "are the experiences of mankind! You well described those internal oracles, if there are indeed such, as whispering their responses; if they utter them at all, it is to me in a whisper so low that I cannot distinctly catch them. Strange paradoxes! the soul speaks, and the soul listens, and the soul cannot tell what the soul says. That is, the soul speaks to itself, and says, 'what have I said?' I assure you that the ear of my soul (if I may so speak) has often ached with intense effort to listen to what the tongue of the soul mutters, and yet I cannot catch it. You tell me I have only to look down into the depths within. Well, I have. I assure you that I have endeavoured to do so, as far as I know, honestly; and, so far from seeing clear and bright those splendours which you speak of, I can only see as in the depths of a cavern occasional gleams of a tremulous, flickering light, which distinctly shows me nothing, and which, I half suspect, comes from without into these recesses: or I feel as if gazing down an abyss, the bottom of which is filled with water; the light—and that too, for aught I know, reflected from without—only throws a transient glimpse of my own image on the surface of the dark water; that image itself broken and renewed, as the water boils up from its hidden fountain. Or, if I may recur to your own metaphor, instead of hearing in those deep caverns the clear oracles of which you boast, I can distinguish nothing but a scarcely audible murmur; I know not whether it be any thing more than the lingering echoes of what I heard in my childhood: or, rather, my soul speaks to me on all those momentous subjects much as one in sleep often does; the lips move, but no sound issues from them. I retire from these attempts, as those of old from the cave of Trophonius, pale, terrified and dejected. In short," he continued, " I feel much as Descartes says he did when he had denuded himself of all his traditional opinions—a condition so graphically described in the beginning of the second of his Meditations. There is this difference, however, and in his favour: that he imposed upon himself only a self-inflicted doubt which he could terminate at any time. His opinions had been but temporarily laid aside. They were on the shelf, close at hand, ready to be taken down again when wanted. But enough of this.

You will, I know, aid me, if you can. And, now I think of it, do so on one point, by justifying your assertion made the other evening, as to Mr. Newman's dilemma of the ' impossibility of a book-revelation.' "

" I said, I think, that Mr. Newman has satisfactorily proved to me that a book-revelation of moral and spiritual truth is impossible; that God reveals himself to us *within*, and not from *without*."

" As to what is impossible," said the other, " I fancy it would be difficult to get one thoroughly convinced of his ignorance and feebleness to be other than very cautious how he used the word. Perhaps, however, Mr. Newman may be more readily excused than most men for the strength with which he pronounces his opinions; for, as he has passed through an infinity of experiences, it may have given him ' insight' into many absurdities which, to the generality of mankind, do not appear such. I think if *I* had believed half so many things, I should have lost all confidence in myself. What a strong mind, or what buoyant faith he must have!"

" Both — both," said Fellowes.

" Well, be it so. But let us, as you promised yesterday, examine this very point." This led on to a dialogue in which it was distinctly proved, that

THAT MAY BE POSSIBLE WITH MAN WHICH IS IMPOSSIBLE WITH GOD.

" Mr. Newman affirms, you say," said Harrington, " that in his judgment every book-' revelation' is an absurdity and a contradiction; or, in the words quoted by you, ' impossible.' "

" Yes, — of ' moral and spiritual truth.' "

" And of any other truth — as of *historical* truth — you say such revelation is unnecessary ? "

" Yes."

" Moreover, as you and Mr. Newman affirm, the bulk of mankind are not competent to investigate the claims of such an historic revelation ? "

" Certainly."

"And, therefore, it is impossible in *fact*, if not *per se*, unless God is to be supposed doing something both unnecessary and futile."

"I think so, of course," said Fellowes.

"So that *all* book-revelation is impossible."

"I affirm it."

"Very well — I do not dispute it. There still remain one or two difficulties on which I should like to have your judgment towards forming an opinion: and they are on the very threshold of the subject. And, first, I suppose you do not mean to restrict your term of a 'book-revelation' to that only which is literally consigned to a book in our modern sense. You mean an *external* revelation?"

"Certainly."

"If, for example, you could recover a genuine MS. of Isaiah or Paul, you would not think it entitled to any more respect, as *authority*, than a modern translation in a printed book — though it might be free from some errors?"

"I should not."

"You would not allow that parchment, however ancient, has any advantage in this respect over paper, however modern?"

"Certainly not."

"Nor Hebrew or Greek over English or German?"

"No."

"All such matters are in very deed but 'leather and prunella?'"

"Nothing more."

"And for a similar reason, surely, you would reject at once the *oral* teaching of any such man as Paul or Matthew, or any body else, if he professed that what he said was dictated by divine inspiration, concurrently or not with the use of his own faculties? You would repudiate at once his claims, however authenticated, to be your infallible guide; to tell you what you are to believe, and how you are to act? For surely you will not pretend that there is any difference between statements which are merely expressed by the living voice, and those same statements as consigned to a book; except that, if any difference be supposed at all, one would, for some reasons, rather have them in the last shape than in the first."

" Of course there is no difference: to object to a book-revelation and grant a 'lip-revelation' from God, or to deny that lip-revelation (when it is made permanent and diffusible) the authority it had when first given, would be a childish hatred of a *book* indeed," answered Fellowes.

" I perfectly agree with you," replied Harrington. " I understand you, then, to deny that any revelation professedly given to you or to me does, or ever *can*, come to us through any external channel, printed or on parchment, ancient or modern, by the living voice or in a written character; and that this is a proper translation, in a generalised form, of the phrase ' a book revelation?' "

" I admit it. For surely, as already said, it would be truly ridiculous to allow that Paul, if we could but hear his living voice, was to be listened to with implicit reverence as an authorised teacher of divine truth; but that his deliberate utterances, recorded in a permanent form, were to be regarded not merely as less authoritative, but of no authority at all?"

" So that if you saw Peter or Paul to-morrow you would tell him the same story?"

" *Of course* I should," replied Mr. Fellowes.

" And you would *of course* also reject any such revelation, coming from any external source, even though the party proclaiming it confirmed it by miracles? For I cannot see how, if it be true that an external revelation is *impossible,* and that God always reveals himself 'within' us, and never 'out of us' (which is the principle affirmed)—I say, I cannot see how miracles can make any difference in the case."

" No, certainly not. But surely you forget that miracles are impossible on my notion: for, as Mr. Newman says,"——

" Whatever he says, I suppose you will not deny that
F

they are conceivable: and that is all I am thinking of at present. Their impossibility or possibility — I will not dispute with you just now. I am disposed to *agree* with you; only, as usual, I have some doubts, which I wish you would endeavour to solve; but of that another time. Meantime, my good friend, be so obliging as to give me an answer to my question,—whether you would deem it to be your duty to reject any such claims to authoritative teaching, even if backed by the performance of miracles? for, admitting miracles never to have occurred, and even that they never will, you, I think, would hesitate to affirm that you clearly perceive that the very notion involves a contradiction. They are, at least, imaginable, and that is sufficient to supply you with an answer to my question. I once more ask you, therefore, whether, if such a teacher of a book-revelation, in the comprehensive sense of these words already defined, were to authenticate (as he affirmed) his claims to reverence by any number, variety, or splendour of miracles — undoubted miracles — you would any the more feel bound to believe him?"

"What! upon the supposition that there was any thing morally *objectionable* in his doctrine?"

"I will release you on that score, too," said Harrington, in a most accommodating manner. "*Morally*, I will assume there is nothing in his doctrine but what you approve; and as for the rest, — to confirm which I will suppose the revelation given, — I will assume nothing in it which you could *demonstrate* to be false or contradictory; in fact, nothing more difficult to be believed than many undeniable phenomena of the external universe; — matters, for example, which you acknowledge you do not comprehend, but which may possibly be true for aught you can tell to the contrary."

"But if the supposed revelation contain nothing but what, appealing thus to my judgment, I can approve, where is the necessity of a revelation at all?"

"Did I say, my friend, that it was to contain nothing but what is referred to your judgment? nothing but what you would know and approve just as well without it? or even did I concede that you could have known and approved *without* it that which, when it *is* proposed, you do approve? I simply wish an answer to the question, whether, if a teacher of an ethical system such as you entirely approved, with some doctrines attached, incomprehensible it may be, but not demonstratively false or immoral, were to substantiate (as he affirmed) his claims to your belief by the performance of miracles, you would or would not feel constrained any the more to believe him?"

"But I do not see the use of discussing a question under circumstances which it is admitted never did nor ever can occur?"

"You 'fight hard,' as Socrates says to one of his antagonists on a similar occasion; but I really must request an answer to the question. The case is an imaginable one; and you may surely say how, upon the principles you have laid down, you think those principles would compel you to act in the hypothetical case."

"Well, then, if I must give an answer, I should say that upon the principles on which Mr. Newman has argued the question — that all revelation except that which is internal is impossible — I should *not* believe the supposed envoy's claims."

"Whatever the number or the splendour of his miracles?"

"Certainly," said Fellowes, — with some hesitation however, and speaking slowly.

"For that does not affect the principles we are agreed upon?"

"No,"— not seeming, however, perfectly satisfied.

"Very well," resumed Harrington, "that is what I call a plain answer to a plain question. I fancy (waverer that I am!) that I should believe the man's claims. I should be even greatly tempted to think that those things which I could not entirely see *ought* to be contained in the said revelation, were to be believed. But all that is doubtless only because I am much weaker in mind and will than either Mr. Newman or yourself.

You must pardon me; it will in no degree practically affect the question, except on the supposition that the same infirmity is also a characteristic of man in general; that not *I*, from my weakness, am an exception to rule; but you, in your strength. But to dismiss that. You have agreed that a book-revelation is impossible, and not to be believed, even if avouched by miracles. Have men in general been disposed to believe a book-revelation impossible? for if not, I am afraid they would be very liable to run into error, if they share in *my* weaknesses."

"Liable to run into error!" said Fellowes. "Man has been perpetually running into this very error, always and everywhere."

"If it be true, as you say, that man has always and everywhere manifested a remarkable facility of falling into this error, many will be tempted to think that the thing is not so plainly impossible. It seems so strange that men in general should believe things to be possible when they are impossible. However, you admit it as a too certain *fact*."

"I do, for I cannot honestly deny it; but it has been because they have confounded what is historical or intellectual with moral and spiritual truth."

"I am afraid that will not excuse their absurdity, because, as you admit, *all* book-revelation is impossible. —But further, supposing men to have made this strange blunder, it only shows that the 'moral and spiritual' could not be very clearly revealed *within;* and no wonder men began to think that perhaps it might come to them from without! When men begin to mistake blue for red, and square for round, and chaff for wheat, I think it is high time that they repair to a doctor *outside* them to tell them what is the matter with their poor brains. Meantime an external revelation is impossible?"

"Certainly."

"But men, however, have somehow perversely believed it very possible, and that, in some shape or other, it has been given?"

"They have, I must admit."

"Unhappy race! thus led on by some fatality

though not by the constitution of their nature (rather, by some inevitable perversion of it), to believe as possible that which is so plainly impossible. Oh! that it did not involve a contradiction to wish that God would relieve them from such universal and pernicious delusions, by giving them a book-revelation to show them that *all* book-revelations are impossible!"

"That," said Fellowes, laughing, "would indeed be a novelty. Miracles would hardly prove *that.*"

"I think not," said Harrington. "But, as the poet says, 'some god or friendly man' may show the way. Pray, permit me to ask, did *you* always believe that a book-revelation was impossible?"

"How can you ask the question?—you know that I was brought up, like yourself, in the reception of the Bible as the only and infallible revelation of God to mankind."

"To what do you owe your emancipation from this grievous and universal error, which still infects, in this or some other shape, the myriads of the human race?"

"I think principally to the work of Mr. Newman on the 'Soul,' and his 'Phases of Faith.'"

"These have been to you, then, at least a *human* book-revelation that a '*divine* book-revelation is impossible;' a truth which I acknowledge you could not have received by *divine* book-revelation, without a contradiction.—You ought, indeed, to think very highly of Mr. Newman. It is well, when God cannot do a thing, that man can; though, I confess, considering the very wide prevalence of this pernicious error, it would have been better, had it been possible, that man should have had a *divine* book-revelation to tell him that a *divine* book-revelation was impossible. Great as is my admiration of Mr. Newman, I should, myself, have preferred having God's word for it. However, let us lay it down as an axiom that a human book-revelation, showing you that 'a divine book-revelation is impossible,' is not impossible; and really, considering the almost universal error of man on this subject,—now happily exploded,—the book-revelation which convinces man of this great truth ought to be reverenced as of the highest value; it is such that it might not appear unworthy of celestial origin, if it did not imply a contradiction that God should reveal to us in a *book* that a revelation in a *book* was impossible."

Fellowes looked very grave, but said nothing.

"But yet," continued Harrington, very seriously, "I know not whether I ought not, upon your principles, to consider this book-revelation with which you have been favoured, about the impossibility of such a thing, as itself a *divine* revelation; in which case I am afraid we shall be constrained to admit, in *form*, that contradiction which we have been so anxious to avoid, by making 'possible with man what is impossible with God.'"

"I know not what you mean," said Fellowes, rather offended.

"Why," said Harrington, quite unmoved, "I have heard you say you do not deny, in some sense, inspiration, but only that inspiration is preternatural; that every 'holy thought,' every 'lofty and sublime conception,' all 'truth and excellence,' in any man, come from the 'Father of lights,' and are to be ascribed to him; that, as Mr. Parker and Mr. Foxton affirm on this point, the inspiration of Paul or Milton, or even of Christ and of Benjamin Franklin, is of the same nature, and in an intelligible sense from the same source,—differing only in degree. Can you deem less, then, of that great conception by which Mr. Newman has released you, and possibly many more, from that bondage to a 'book-revelation' in which you were brought up, and in which, by your own confession, you might have been still enthralled? Can you think less of this than that it is an 'inspired' voice which has proclaimed 'liberty to the captive,' and made known to you 'spiritual freedom?' If any thing be divine about Mr. Newman's system, surely it must be this. Ought you not to thank God that he has been thus pleased to 'open your eyes, and to turn you from darkness to light'—to raise up in these last days such an apostle of the truth which had lain so long 'hidden from ages and generations?' Can you do less than admire the divine artifice by which, when it was impossible for God *directly* to tell man by external revelation that he could *directly* tell him nothing, He raised up his servant Newman to perform the office?"

"For my part," said Fellowes, "I am not ashamed to say, that I think I ought to thank God for such a boon as Mr. Newman has, in this instance at least, been the instrument of conveying to me: I acknowledge it is a most momentous truth, without which I should still have been in thraldom to the 'letter.'"

"Very well; then the book-revelation of Mr. Newman is, as I say, in *some* sort to *you*, perhaps to *many*, a divine 'book-revelation.'"

"Well, in *some* sense, it is so."

"So that now we have, in *some* sense, a *divine* book-revelation to prove that a *divine* book-revelation is impossible."

"You are pleased to jest on the subject," said Fellowes.

"I never was more serious in my life. However, I will not press this point any further. You shall be permitted to say (what I will not contradict) that though Mr. Newman may be inspired, for aught I know, in that modified sense in which you believe in any such phenomenon—inspired as much (say) as the inventor of Lucifer-matches—yet that his book is not divine—that it is purely human; and even, if you please, that God has had nothing to do with it. But even then I must be allowed to repeat that at least you have derived from a 'book-revelation' what it would not have been unworthy of a *divine* book-revelation to impart, if it could have been imparted without contradiction. Such book-revelation, in this case, must be of inestimable value to man, because, without it, he must have persisted in that ancient and all but inveterate and universal delusion of which we have so often spoken. There is only one little inconvenience, I apprehend, from it in relation to the *argument* of such a book; and that is, that I am afraid that men, so far from being convinced thereby that a divine revelation is impossible, will rather argue the contrary way, and say, 'If Mr. Newman can do so much, what might not God do by the very same method?' If he can thus break the spiritual yoke of his fellow-men by only teaching them *negative* truth, surely it may be possible for God to be as useful in teaching *positive* truth. I almost tremble, I assure you, lest, by his most conspicuous success in imparting to you such important truth, and reclaiming you from such a fundamental error, which lay at the very threshold of your 'spiritual' progress, he may, so far from convincing mankind of the truth of his principle, lead them rather to believe that a 'book-revelation' may have been very possible, and of singular advantage. But, to speak the truth, I am by no means sure that Mr. Newman has not done something more than what we have yet attributed to him, and whether his book-revelation be not also a true *divine* revelation to you."

Fellowes looked rather curious, and I thought a little angry.

"My good friend," said Harrington, "I am sure you will not refuse me every satisfaction you can give, in my present state of doubt and perplexity; that you will render me (as indeed you have promised) all the assistance in your power, by kindly telling me what you know of your own religious development and history. I cannot sufficiently admire your candour and frankness hitherto."

"You may depend upon it," said Fellowes, "I will not hesitate to answer any questions you choose to put. I am not ashamed of the system I have adopted — or rather *selected*, — for I do not agree with any *one* writer, — although I confess I wish I were a better advocate of it."

"O, rest assured that 'spiritualism' can lose nothing by your advocacy. As to your independence of mind, you act, I am sure, upon the maxim *in verba nullius jurare*. Your system seems to me quite a species of eclecticism. There is no fear of my confounding you with the good old lady who, after having heard the sermon of some favourite divine, was asked if she understood him. 'Understand him!' said she; 'do you think I would presume — blessed man?' Nor with the Scotch woman, who required, as a condition of her admiration, that a sermon should contain some things at least which transcended her comprehension. 'Eh! it is a' vara weel,' said she, on hearing one which did not fulfil this reasonable condition; 'but do ye call that fine preaching? — there was na ae word that I could na explain mysel.'"

Fellowes smiled good-naturedly, and then said, "I was going to observe, in relation to the present subject, that it is 'moral and spiritual' truth which Mr. Newman says it is impossible should be the subject of a book-revelation."

Harrington, apparently without listening to him, suddenly said, "By the bye, you agree with Mr. Newman, I am sure, that God is to be approached by the individual soul without any of the nonsense of mediation, which has found so general — all but universal — sanction in the religious systems of the world?"

"Certainly," said Fellowes, "nor is there probably any 'spiritualist' (in whatever we may be divided) who would deny that."

"Supposing it true, does it not seem to you the most delightful and stupendous of all spiritual truths?"

"It does indeed," said Fellowes.

"Could you always realise it, my friend?" said Harrington.

"Nay, I was once a firm believer in the current orthodoxy, as you well know."

"*Now* you see with very different eyes. You can say, with the man in the Gospel, 'This I know, that whereas I was blind, now I see.'"

"I can."

"And you attribute this happy change of sentiment to the perusal of those writings of Mr. Newman, from which you think that I also might derive similar benefits?"

"I do."

"It appears then that to *you*, at least, my friend, it is possible that there may be a book-revelation of 'moral and spiritual truth' of the highest possible significance and value, although you do not consider the book to be *divine;* now, if so, I fancy many will be again inclined to say, that what Mr. Newman has done in your case, God might easily do, if He pleased, for mankind in general; and with this advantage, that He would *not* include in the same book which revealed truth to the mind, and rectified its errors, an assurance that *any* such book-revelation was impossible."

"But, my ingenious friend," cried Fellowes, with some warmth, "you are inferring a little too fast for the premises. I do not admit that Mr. Newman or any other spiritualist has revealed to me any truth, but only that he has been the instrument of giving shape and distinct consciousness to what was, in fact, uttered in the secret oracles of my own bosom before; and, as I believe, is uttered also in the hearts of all other men."

"I fear your distinction is practically without a difference. It will certainly not avail us. You say you were once in no distinct conscious possession of that system of spiritual truth which you now hold; on the contrary, that you believed a very different system; that the change by which you were brought into your present condition of mind — out of darkness into light — out of error into truth — has been produced chiefly by Mr. Newman's deeply instructive volumes. If so, one will be apt to argue that a book-revelation may be of the very utmost use and benefit to mankind in general — if only by making that which would else be the inarticulate mutter of the internal oracle distinct and clear; and that if God would but give such a book, the same value at least might attach to it as to a book of Mr. Newman's. It little matters to this argument — to the question of the possibility, value, or utility of an external revelation — whether the truths it is to communicate be absolutely unknown till it reveals them, or only *not known*, which you confess was your own case. If your natural taper of illumination is stuck into a dark lantern, and its light can only flash upon the soul when some Mr. Newman kindly lifts up the slide for you; or if your internal oracle, like a ghost, will not speak till it is spoken to; or, like a dumb demon, awaits to find a voice, and confess itself to be what it is, at the summons of an exorcist;—the same argument precisely will apply for the possibility and utility of a book-revelation from God to men in general. What has been done for you by man, even though no more were done, might, one would imagine, be done for the rest of mankind, and in a much better manner, by God. If that internal and native revelation which both you and Mr. Newman say has its seat in the human soul, be clear without his aid, why did he write a syllable about it? If, as you say, its utterances were not recognised, and that his statements have first made them familiar to you, the same argument (the Christian will say) will do for the Bible. It is of little use that nature teaches you, if Mr. Newman is to teach nature."

Fellowes was silent; and, after a pause, Harrington resumed; he could not resist the temptation of saying, with playful malice,—

"Perhaps you are in doubt whether to say that the internal revelation which you possess does teach you clearly or darkly. It is a pity that nature so teaches as to leave you in doubt till some one else teaches you what she *does* teach you. She must be like some ladies who keep school indeed, but have accomplished masters to teach everything. Pray, which of your 'spiritual' writers shall we call the Professor of 'Spiritual Insight?' Would it not be advisable, if you are in any uncertainty, to write to Mr. Newman to ask whether the internal truths which *no* external revelation can impart be articulate or not; or whether, though a book from God could not make them plainer, you are at liberty to say that a book of Mr. Newman's will? It is undoubtedly a subtle question for him to decide for you;

namely, what is the condition of your own consciousness? But I really see no help for it, after what you have granted; nor, without his aid, do I see whether you can truly affirm that you have an internal revelation, independently of *him* or not. And whichever way he decides, I am afraid lest he should prove both himself and you very much in the wrong. If he decides for you that your internal revelation must and did anticipate any thing he might write, and that it was perfectly articulate, as well as inarticulately present to your 'insight' *before*, it will be difficult to determine why he should have written at all; he would also prove, not only how superfluous is your gratitude, but that *he* understands your own consciousness better than you do. If he decides it the other way, and says you had a 'revelation' before he revealed it, yet that he made it utter articulate language, and interpreted its hieroglyphics — then it once more seems very strange that either you or he should contend that a 'book-revelation' is impossible, since Mr. Newman has produced it. If, however, he decides in the first of these two ways, I fear, my good friend, that we shall fall into another paradox worse than all, for it will prove that the 'internal revelation' which *you* possess is better known to Mr. Newman than to *yourself*, which will be a perfectly worthy conclusion of all this *embarras*. It would be surely droll for you to affirm that you possess an internal revelation which renders all 'external revelation' impossible, but yet that its distinctness is unperceived by yourself, and awaits the assurance of an external authority, which at the same time declares all 'external revelation' impossible!"

"There is still another word," said Fellowes, "which you forget that Mr. Newman employs — he says that an *authoritative* book-revelation of moral and spiritual truth is impossible."

"Why," said Harrington, laughing, "while you were without the truth, as you say you *were*, it was not likely to be authoritative: if, when you have it, it is recognised as authoritative, which you say is the case with the truth you have got from Mr. Newman — if you acknowledge that it *ought* to have authority as soon as known —that is all (so far as I know) that is contended for in the case of the Bible. If you mean by 'authoritative,' a revelation which not only *ought* to be, but which *is* so, I think mankind make it pretty plain that neither the 'external' nor the 'internal' revelation is particularly authoritative. In short," he concluded, "I do not see how we can doubt, on the principles on which Mr. Newman *acts* and yet denies, that a book-revelation of moral and spiritual truth is very possible ; and, if given, would be signally useful to mankind in general. If Mr. Newman, as you *admit*, has written a book which has put you in possession of moral and spiritual truth, surely it may be modestly contended that God might dictate a better. Either you were in possession of the truths in question before he announced them, or you were not; if not, Mr. Newman is your unspeakable benefactor, and God may be at least as great a one; if you were, then Mr. Newman, like Job's comforters, ' has plentifully declared the thing as it is.' If you say, that you were in possession of them, but only by implication ; that you did not see them clearly or vividly till they were propounded —that is, that you saw them, only practically you were blind, and knew them, only you were virtually ignorant; still, whatever Mr. Newman does (and it amounts, in *fact*, to revelation), that *may* the Bible also do. If even that be not possible, and man naturally possesses these truths explicitly as well as implicitly, then indeed the Bible is an impertinence — and so is Mr. Newman."

After a pause, Harrington suddenly asked—

"Do you not think there is some difference between yourself and a Hottentot?"

"I should hope so," said Fellowes, with a laugh.

"But still the Hottentot has all the 'spiritual faculties' of which you speak so much?"

"Certainly."

"What makes this prodigious difference? — for of that, as a fact, we cannot dispute."

"Different culture and education, I suppose."

"This culture and education is a thing external?"

"It is."

"This culture and education, however, must be of immense importance indeed, since it makes all the difference between the having or the not having, practically, any just religious notions, or sentiments, or practices (even in your estimation), whatever our internal revelation."

"But still I hold, with Mr. Parker, that the 'absolute religion' is the same in all men. The difference is in circumstantials only, as Mr. Parker says."

"When it serves his turn," said Harrington; "and he says the contrary, when *it* serves his turn; then the depraved forms of religion are hideous enough. When he wishes to commend his 'absolute religion,' they merely differ in circumstantials. Circumstantials! I have hardly patience to hear these degrading apologies for all that is most degrading in humanity. If the 'absolute religion,' as he vaguely calls it, be present in these systems of gross ignorance and unspeakable pollution, it is so incrusted and buried, that it is indiscernible and worthless. Rightly, therefore, have you expressed a hope that there is a 'prodigious difference' between you and a Hottentot. You adhere to that, I presume."

"Of *course* I shall," said Fellowes.

"Well, let us see. Would you think, if you were turned into a Hottentot to-morrow, you had a religion worthy of the name, or not?"

"I am afraid I should not."

"You *hope* it, you mean. Well, then, it appears that culture and education do somehow make all the difference between a man's having a religion worthy of the name, and the contrary?"

"I must admit it, for I cannot deny it in point of fact."

"And you also admit that, in nine hundred and ninety-nine cases out of a thousand, or in a much larger proportion, taking all the nations of the world since time began, the said culture and education have been wanting, or ineffably bad?"

"Yes."

"So that there have been very few, in point of fact, who have attained that 'spiritual' religion for which you and our spiritualists contend; and those few *chiefly*, as Mr. Newman admits, amongst Jews and Christians, though they too have had their most grievous errors, which have deplorably obscured it?"

"Yes."

"It appears then, I think, that if we allow that the internal revelation, without a most happy external culture and development, will not form any religion at all worthy of the name, and that that happy culture and development (from whatsoever cause) are not the condition of our race; it appears, I say, rather odd to affirm that any divine aid in this absolutely necessary *external* education of humanity, is not only superfluous, but *impossible*."

Another pause ensued, when Harrington again said, "You will think me very pertinacious, perhaps, but I must say that, in my judgment, Mr. Newman's theory of *progressive* religion (for he also admits a doctrine of *progress*) favours the same sceptical doubts as to the impossibility of a book-revelation. You do not deny, I suppose, that he does think the world needs enlightening?"

"Had he not believed that, he would not have written."

"_ suppose not. However, how the world should need it, if your principles be true, and every man brings into the world his own particular lantern — 'enter moonshine' — I do not quite understand; or, if it is in need of such illumination notwithstanding, why it should not be possible for an *external* revelation to supply it still better than your illuminati, I am equally unable to understand. But let that pass. Mr. Newman concludes that the world does stand in need of this illumination, and that it has had it at various times. It is his opinion, is it not, that men began by being polytheists and idolaters?"

"It is so; and surely all history bears out the theory."

"Many doubt it. I will not venture to give any opinion, except that there are inexplicable difficulties, *as usual*, on both sides. Just now I am quite willing to take his statement for granted, and suppose that man in the infancy of his race was, in spite of the aid of his very peculiar illumination — which seems to have 'rayed our darkness' — as very a Troglodyte in civilisation and religion as you (for the special glory of his Creator, I suppose, and the honour of your species) can wish him to have been. Well, man began by being a polytheist, and *very gradually* emerged out of that pleasant condition — or rather an infinitesimal portion of the race has emerged out of it into the *better* forms of idolatry — (poor wretch!), and from thence to monotheism; that, in short, his polytheism is not the corruption of his monotheism, but his monotheism an elevation of his polytheism. Yet it is, after all, a cheerless 'progress,' which often 'advances backward.' Mr. Newman says that 'the law of God's moral universe, as known to us, is that of *progress;* that we trace it from old barbarism to the *methodized* Egyptian idolatry, to the more flexible polytheism of Syria and Greece,' and so forth; and so in Palestine, from the 'image worship in Jacob's family to the rise of spiritual sentiment under David, and Hezekiah's prophets.'* Yet he also tells us, 'ceremonialism more and more incrusted the restored nation, and Jesus was *needed* to spur and stab the consciences of his contemporaries, and recall them to more spiritual perceptions.' Well, thus came Christ to 'stab and spur;' and faith, I think, 'stab and spur' were again needed by the end of the third century. Successive reformers are needed to 'stab and spur' the thick hide of humanity, without which it will not, it seems, go forward, but perversely go backward; and even with this perpetual application of the goad of some spiritual *mohout*, man crawls on at an intolerably slow pace. However, 'stab' and 'spur' are *needed*, which is all I am now intent upon."

* Phases, p. 223

"Yes; but each of those great souls, who have stimulated the dull mind of ordinary humanity, derived from its *own* internal illumination that spiritual light which they have communicated to the rest of mankind!"

"For *themselves*, perhaps, my friend," said Harrington, "and if they had kept it to *themselves* in many instances, probably the world would have been no loser. That they had it from within, is true—if your theory is true. But to others, to the bulk of mankind, they have imparted this light; it has been to *mankind* an external revelation; it is from without, not from within, that this light has been received, and that the boasted 'progress' of the race has been secured. It remains, therefore, only for your Christian opponent to ask, how it should be *impossible* that mankind should be indebted to an external revelation by God, when it is plain that they are indebted to the like from man? and whether it is not conceivable, that if Moses, and Socrates, and Paul, could do so much for them, God could do a trifle more? You will say, perhaps, on the old plea, that these profounder spirits only made articulate that which already existed inarticulately in the hearts of those whom they addressed; that they only chafed into life the marble statue of Pygmalion—the dormant principles and sentiments which had a home in the human heart before, only they were unluckily treated as strangers. Well; the same thing may the apologist for the Bible say—merely adding, perhaps, that it does more effectually the business of thus awakening 'dormant' powers, and giving a substantive form to the shadowy conceptions of mankind. But it is still, in either case, to the bulk of the world, an external revelation, an outward aid which gives them the actual conscious possession of spiritual light, and secures the vaunted progress of humanity. Such are some of my difficulties respecting your theory of the impossibility and inutility of any and all external revelations. I must, in candour, say that our discussion has left them where they were."

"There is one thing," he added, "about your system which I acknowledge would be consolatory to me if it were but true. If man be really in possession of an internal and universal revelation of moral and spiritual truth, you neither can nor need take any trouble to enlighten and convert him. It relieves one of all superfluous anxiety on that score."

"Pardon me," said Fellowes, "it is Mr. Newman's spiritual theory alone which *does* allow the prospect of success to any such efforts. As he truly says, when the spiritual champion has thrown off the burden of an historical Christianity, he advances, as lightly equipped as Priestley himself. I should say much more lightly. 'What,' says he, 'may we now expect from the true theologian when he attacks sin, and vice, and gross unspirituality?' 'The weapon he uses (to employ Mr. Newman's own language) is as lightning from God, kindled from the spirit within him, and piercing through the unbeliever's soul, convincing his conscience of sin, and striking him to the ground before God; until those who believe receive it not as the word of man, but as what it is, in truth, the word of God. Its action is directly upon the conscience and upon the soul; and hence its wonderful results; not on the critical faculties, upon which the Spirit is powerless.'* Again, he says that such a preacher 'will have *plenty to say alike to the vulgar and to the philosophers*, appreciable by the soul!' Hear him again: 'Then he may speak with confidence of what he knows and feels; and call on his hearers of themselves to try and prove his words. Then the conversion of men to the love of God may take place by *hundreds and thousands*, as in some former instances. Then, at length, some hope may dawn that Mohammedans and Hindoos may be joined in one fold with us, under one Shepherd, who will only have regained his older name of the Lord God.'"†

"By all the gods and goddesses of all the nations," said Harrington, "I *cannot* understand it. How man-

---

* Soul, p. 244. † Soul, p. 258.

kind should need such teaching, if *your* theory be true; how, if they need it, it is possible that you should give it, if all external revelation of moral and spiritual truth be impossible; how, if it *is* possible, it should be impossible for a God, by a Bible, to give the like; how you can get *at* the souls of people at all except through the intervention of the senses and the intellect — the latter of which you say has nothing to do with the 'soul,' and surely the former can have as little; — or how, if you *can* get at them by this intervention, it is impossible that a Bible should, is all to me a mystery. But let that pass. If your last account be true, one thing is clear: that a splendid career is open to you and your friends. You can immediately employ this irresistible 'weapon' for the verification of your views and the conversion of the human race. You can renew, or rather realise, the triumphs of early Christianity; — I say, realise, for you and Mr. Newman believe them to be, for the most part, *fabulous*, and that it was the army of Constantine that conquered the empire for Christianity; but *you* can turn such fables into truths. Surely the least you can do is to be off as a missionary to China or India. Go to Constantinople, my dear fellow, and take the great Turk by the beard. Nor can Mr. Newman do less than repair to Bagdad upon a second and more hopeful mission. You will let me know when you have demolished Mohammedanism, and got fairly into Thibet. Alexander's career will be nothing to it. But, alas! I fear it will be only *another* variety of that *impossible* thing — a book-revelation!"

"Nay," said Fellowes, "we must first finish our mission at home, and try our weapons upon you and such as you. We must subdue such as you first."

"Then you will never go," said Harrington.

"Never mind," I said, "Mr. Fellowes; Harrington is very mischievous to-day. But, as he said he would not contest the ground of your *dictum*, that a book-revelation of moral and spiritual truth is impossible, so he has not entered into it. Will you let me, on some future day, read to you a brief paper upon it? I have no skill

— or but little — in that erotetic method of which Harrington is so fond." He assented; and here this long conversation ended.

July 7. Harrington and I spent a portion of this morning alone (Fellowes was gone out for a day or two), conversing on various subjects. I hardly know how it was, but I felt a strong reluctance to enter, with formality, on that one which yet lay nearest my heart — whether from the fear lest I should do more harm than good; lest controversy should, as so often happens, indurate rather than soften the heart; or perhaps I had some secret distrust of my own temper or of his. Yet, if I felt anything of the last, I am sure I did him injustice; and (I hope) myself. Be it as it may, I thought it better just to exchange a shot now and then — sometimes it was a red-hot shot, too, on both sides — as we passed and repassed, in the current of conversation, than come to a regular set-to, yard-arm to yard-arm. From whatever cause, he gave me abundant opportunity of recurring to the subject, for he was perpetually, and, I believe, unconsciously, leading the conversation towards it; not, I think, from confidence in his logical prowess, but from the restlessness in which (he did not pretend to disguise it) his state of scepticism had plunged him. It was curious, indeed, to see how every thing, sooner or later, fell into one channel. For example, I happened to remark, that a cottage in the valley, which we saw from his library window, would make a pretty object in a picture, — it was the only sign of life in the little valley. "I should like the view itself all the better without it," said he. I observed that a painter would feel very differently; and if there were no such object, he would be sure to put one in. "Oh, certainly," he replied, " a *painter* would, and justly; there is no doubt that the *shadow* of animated existence is very admirable; a picture, I admit, is wonderfully more picturesque with such a *picture* of life; especially as the painter can and does remove every thing offensive to his fastidious art.

He is very apt to regard the objects in his landscapes much as a poet does a cottage, according to Cowper's confession. 'By a cottage,' says he to Lady Hesketh, 'you must always understand, my dear, that a poet 'means a house with six sashes in front, two comfortable 'parlours, a smart staircase, and three bed-rooms of con-'venient dimensions.'—As I have looked sometimes down a mountain glen, and seen the most picturesque huts upon its sides, I have thought how little the painter could dispense with them. But, then, how easily the philosopher can: for, alas! I have taken wing from my station, and looked in through the miserable casement, and seen not only what is disgusting to the senses — which is a small matter — but ignorance, and disease, and fear, and guilt, and racking pain, and doubt, and death; and I have not been able to help saying, in pity, 'Oh, for absolute solitude! — how much nature would be 'improved if the human race were annihilated!'"

"The human race," said I, laughing, "is very much obliged to the pity which would thus exterminate them; but as one of them, I should decidedly object to so sweeping a mode of improving the picturesque. Besides, I suppose you make an exception in favour of yourself, otherwise the picturesque would vanish just when it was brought to perfection. — I am often inclined to say, with Paley, though I remember well having sometimes felt as you do, — 'It is a happy world after all.' I admit, however, that a buoyant, cheerful, habitual conviction of this will depend on the constitution of the mind, and even vary with the same mind in its different moods. But I am sure it may be a *really* happy world, whatever its sorrows, to any one who will view it as he ought."

"I wish you could teach me the art."

"It is," said I, "to exercise the faith and the hope of a Christian; humbly to regard this life — as what it is — a scene of discipline and schooling; — a pilgrimage to a better. It is an old remedy, but it has been often tried; and to millions of our race has made this world more than tolerable, and death tranquil, nay, triumphant.

—Do you remember Schiller's 'Walk among the Linden Trees?'"

"Perfectly well."

"Do you not remember how the two youths differ in their estimate of the beautiful in nature? 'Is it possible,' says Edwin, 'you can thus turn from the cup of joy sparkling and overflowing as it is?'—'Yes,' said Wollmar, 'when one finds a spider in it; and why not? In your eyes, to be sure, Nature decks herself out like a rosy-cheeked maiden on her bridal-day. To me she appears an old withered beldame, with sunken eyes, furrowed cheeks, and artificial ornaments in her hair. How she seems to admire herself in this her Sunday finery! But it is the same worn and ancient garment, put off and on some hundreds of thousands of times.' But how natural is the explanation of all given at the beautiful close of the dialogue! 'Here,' said the jocund Edwin, 'I first met my Juliet.' —'And it was under these linden trees,' says Wollmar, 'that I lost my Laura.' It was their mood of mind, and not the outward world, that made all the difference. All nature, innocent thing! must consent to take her hue from it. You have, I fear, lost your Laura"—simply alluding to his early faith; "or shall I suppose, from your present mood, that you have just met with your Juliet?" I spoke, of course, of his philosophy.

He was looking out of the window; but on my turning my gaze towards him, I saw such a look of peculiar anguish, that I felt I had inadvertently touched a terrible chord indeed. I turned the conversation hastily, by remarking (almost without thinking of what I said) on the beautiful contrast between the light blue of the sky and the green of the lawn and trees; and proceeded to remark on the degree in which the mere organic or sensational pleasures of vision formed an ingredient in the pleasurable associations of the complex "beautiful."

He gradually resumed conversation; and we discussed the subject of the "beautiful" for some time. Yet I know not how it was, nor can I trace the steps by which we deviated,—only that Rousseau's summerday dreams on the Lake of Bienne was a link in the chain,—we somehow soon found ourselves on the brink of the great controversy respecting the "Origin of Evil." "I have read many books on that subject," said I; "but I intend to read no more; and I should think *you* have had enough of them."

"Why, yes," said he, laughing; "whatever philosophers may have thought of the *origin* of evil, it is a great aggravation of it to read their speculations. The best thing I know on the subject — and it exhausts it — is half-a-dozen lines in 'Robinson Crusoe.'"

"Robinson Crusoe!" said I.

"Certainly," he replied: "do you not remember that when he caught his man Friday, the 'intuitional consciousness'—the 'insight'—the 'inward revelation' of that worthy savage not being found quite so perfect as Mr. Parker would fancy, Robinson proceeds to indoctrinate him in the mysteries of theology? Friday is much puzzled, as many more learned savages have been before him, to find that the infinite power, wisdom, and goodness of God had made every thing very good, and that good it would have continued had it not been for the opposition of the devil. 'Why God not kill debbil?' asks poor Friday. On which, says Robinson, 'though I was a very old man, I found that I was but a young doctor in divinity.' Ah! if all doctors in divinity had been equally candid, the treatises on that dread subject would not have been quite so voluminous; for we close them all alike, with the unavailing question, 'Why God not kill debbil?'"

Observing his tendency to gravitate towards the abyss, I at last said to him, "I think, if I were you, having decided that there is no religious truth to be found, I should dismiss the subject from my thoughts altogether. Do as the Indian did, who struggled as long as he could to right his canoe when he found he was in the stream of Niagara; but finding his efforts unavailing, sat himself down with his arms folded, and went down the falls without stirring a muscle. *Let us talk no more on the subject.* Why should you perplex yourself, as you apparently do, about a thing so hopeless to be found out as *truth?* 'What is truth?' said Pilate; and, as Bacon says, 'he would not wait for an answer.' It was a question to which, most probably, he, like you, thought no answer could be given. If I were *you*, I should do the same. Why perplex yourself to no purpose?"

"I should answer," said he, "as Solon did when asked why he grieved for his son, seeing all grief was unavailing? 'It is for that very reason that I grieve,' was the reply. And in like manner I dwell on the impossibility of discovering truth because it *is* impossible."

I acknowledged that it was a sufficient reason, and that it went to account in some degree for a fact I had remarked in the few sceptics I had come across—genuine or otherwise,—that they seemed less capable of reposing in their *professed* convictions than any one else: it is of no avail, they say, to reason on such subjects: and yet they are perpetually reasoning! They will neither rest themselves nor let any one else rest. He confessed it, and said, "The state of mind is very much as you have described it; and you have described it so exactly, that I almost think you, my dear uncle, must know the heart of a sceptic, and have been one yourself some time or other!"

We wound up the morning, which was beautiful, by taking a ride, in the course of which I was amused with an instance of the sensitiveness with which Harrington's cultivated mind recoiled from the grossness of vulgar and ignorant infidelity. We called at the cottage of a little farmer, a tenant of his, somewhat notorious both for profanity and sensuality. Presuming, I suppose, on his young landlord's suspected heterodoxy, and thinking perhaps to curry favour with him, he ventured (I know not what led to it) to indulge in some stupid joke about the legion and the herd of swine. "Sir," said he, scratching his head, "the devil, I reckon, must have been a more clever fellow than I thought, to make two thousand hogs go down a steep place into the sea—it is hard enough even to make them go where they *will*, and almost impossible to make them go where they won't."

"The devil, my good friend," said Harrington, very gravely, "*is* a very clever fellow; and I hope you do not for a moment intend to compare yourself with him. As to the supposed miracle, it would, no doubt, be hard to say which were most to be pitied, the devils in the swine, or the swine with the devils in them; but has it never struck you that the whole may be an allegorical representation of the miserable and destructive effects of the *union* of the two vices of sensuality and profanity? *They* also (if all tales be true) lead to a steep place, but I have never heard that it ends in the water. Now," he continued, "I dare say you would laugh at that story which the Roman Catholics tell of St. Antony; namely, that 'he preached to the pigs!'—yet it has had a very sound allegorical interpretation; we are told that it *meant* merely that he preached to country farmers; which, you see, is no more than I have been doing."

It was one of the many things which made me a sceptic as to whether *he* was one. "Harrington," said I, "at times I find it impossible to believe that you doubt the truth of Christianity."

"Suppose I were to answer, that at times I *doubt* whether I *doubt* it or not, would not that be a *thorough* sceptic's answer?" I admitted that it would be indeed.

July 8. I was already in the library, writing, when Harrington came in to breakfast. "You seem busy, early," said he. I told him I was merely endeavouring to manifest my love for his future children.

"You know," said I, "what Isocrates says, that it is right that children, as they inherit the other possessions, should also inherit the friendships of their fathers."

"My children!" said he, very gravely; "I shall never have any."

"Oh, yes, you will, and then these sullen vapours of

doubt will roll off before the sunlight of domestic happiness. It will allure you to love *Him* who has given you so much to love. Yes," said I, gaily, "I shall visit you one day in happier moods; when you will wonder how you could have indulged all your present thoughts of God and the universe. As you gaze into the face of innocent childhood, which shows you what faith in God is by trust in you, you will say, 'Heaven shield the boy from being what his father has been!'—you will feel that such thoughts as yours will not *do*, as the world says; and we shall all go together, you with your wife on your arm, to church there in the valley, in the bright sun and deep quiet of a Sabbath morning, and amidst the music of the Sabbath bells; and as the tranquil scene steals into your very soul, you will say, "No; scepticism was not made for man.'"

"It is a pleasant romance," he replied, gloomily, "and nothing more. I shall *never* love, and shall therefore never wed; though, I suppose, *that* does not *logically* follow. However, it does with *me;* and, consequently, I presume the children are also only *in posse*. However, what is this instance of your kindness to my possible children?" he added, more cheerfully.

"I was endeavouring," said I, " on the bare possibility of your retaining as a father all the feelings you *seem* to entertain at present, to compile for your children (as they must be taught something, and you would wish them, as you say, to know the *truth*) a short catechism. I think the questions in Watts' First Catechism might do for the poor little souls. The answers (as usual) might not be wholly intelligible till they got older; but still might awaken some notion which in time might ripen into confirmed scepticism."

"Well," said he, laughing, "let me hear what sort of 'religious' instruction you have provided."

"I had only finished one question," I replied, "when you came in: but I almost think it may be considered a 'Summa Theologiæ' of itself. It is this —

"'*Can you tell me, child, who made you?*'

"'I cannot, certainly, tell who made me; neither can

my father; but, from the continual misery, confusion, and doubt, which I feel in myself and see around me' — here the little pupil is to be cautioned not to laugh; the mirth in the *eye*, perhaps, cannot be extinguished — 'I am led to doubt whether I was made by one who cares for me or takes any interest in me.' (*Good child.*)"

As I looked up, after reading this *first truth* of sceptical theology, I observed in Harrington's face something of the same look of sorrow which I had noted the day before. Suddenly he said, as if to prevent any chance recurrence to painful topics:

"I very gradually became a doubter. I was perhaps *becoming* so when, two years ago I became an *idolater*, and my idol crumbled to pieces at my feet. That transient vision of the *beautiful* half reclaimed me from my doubts; the darkness of the succeeding night taught me juster views of the miseries of man and the incomprehensible riddle of his existence; and I half blushed at my glimpse of *selfish* happiness."

So saying, he suddenly left the room. Some part of the mystery I felt was unravelled. Alas! the logic of the head!—how fatally fortified by the logic of the heart! And so, thought I to myself, even Harrington too is in part the dupe of that cunning spirit of delusion which, in various forms, is resolved to cast God, and a Redeemer, and Immortality, out of the universe, in compliment to man's wonderful elevation, purity, unselfishness, and philanthropy! One man tells me, with Shaftesbury, that he does not want any "immortal hopes," or any such "bribes" of prudence, to make *him* virtuous or religious — delicate, noble-minded creature! — that he can serve and love God equally well, though he were sure of being annihilated to-morrow morning! Another declares that he would not accept heaven itself if purchased by a single pang, voluntary or involuntary, endured by any other being in God's universe! Another swears that such is his sympathetic benevolence that he "would not accept that same heaven if he thought any other being was to be shut out of it;" I wonder whether he condescends to accept any blessing *now*, while a single fellow-creature remains destitute of it! A fourth (a lady too) declares "there is no theory of a God, of an author of nature, of an origin of the universe, which is not utterly repugnant to her faculties, which is not (to her feelings) so irreverent as to make her blush, so misleading as to make her mourn;" and now Harrington, instead of being thankful for his glimpse of happiness, and yielding to the better instincts and convictions it partly awakened, and learning patience, submission, and faith under his shattered hopes, is taken captive on the same weak side; and (all unconscious that he shares in the prophet's feeling, "I do well to be angry") fancies that his present gloom is more truly in unison with the condition of the universe, and that he is bound to be most philanthropically misanthropical. Oh! well does the BOOK say of this heart of ours, "DECEITFUL ABOVE ALL THINGS!" Such are our mingled follies and wickedness, so ludicrous, so sorrowful, are the features presented in this great tragi-comedy — THE LIFE OF MAN — that it is impossible to play consistently either Democritus or Heraclitus.

July 9. Mr. Fellowes returned this morning. We had a very pleasant day — theology being excluded. In the evening my companions were again pleased to disturb my occupations; but it was only a short skirmish. Fellowes was endeavouring to enlighten his friend respecting the mysteries of "belief" and "faith," as expounded by some of his favourite writers; he contended (making that sheer separation between "the intellectual" and "spiritual," which so many of the spiritual school affect) not only that there may be correct belief without true faith, which, in an intelligible sense, few will deny; but that there may be a true faith with a false belief, or even with none, in the strict sense of the word. Referring to a recent acute writer in one of our religious periodicals, he argued that belief is properly an intellectual process, founded on a presumed preponderance of *reasons* or *supposed* reasons, for it; and that whether those reasons amount to demonstration, or whether the scale be turned by a grain, matters not; the product is purely *logical*, and has no more to do with "faith" than a "belief" in any proposition of Euclid.

"But at all events," he proceeded, "whether you choose to call some of these acts of *reason* by the name of belief or not, faith is something quite independent of it. As Mr. Newman says, in his 'Phases,' 'Belief is one thing and faith another?' 'belief is purely intellectual; faith is properly spiritual.' 'Nowhere from any body of priests, clergy, or ministers, as an order, is religious progress to be anticipated till *intellectual creeds are destroyed.*' See, too, how tenderly he speaks even of atheism. 'I do not know,' he says, 'how to avoid calling this a *moral* error; *but I must carefully guard against seeming to overlook that it may still be a merely speculative error*, which ought not to separate our hearts from any man.' Similarly, he charitably restricts 'idolatry' in any 'bad sense' to a voluntary worshipping of what the worshipper feels not to deserve his adoration; and as I, for one, doubt whether this is ever the case, this delightful charity is comprehensive indeed. Mr. Parker's discourse is full of the same beautiful and tolerant maxims. 'Each religious doctrine,' he says, 'has some time stood for a truth. . . . Each of these forms of religion (polytheism and fetichism, to wit) did the world service in its day.' No one form of religion is absolutely true; faith may be compatible with them all."

"Let me understand you, if possible," said Harrington; "for at present I fear I do not. That there may be belief without faith in a very intelligible sense, I can understand. You say there can be faith without belief, and a true faith that is connected with *any* belief, *however erroneous*, do you not?"

"Provided it contains the absolute religion."

"Well, and even the lowest fetichism does that, according to Mr. Parker, whom you defend. Now this Protean *faith* is what I do *not* understand."

"That," said Fellowes, "I can easily conceive; and, let me add, no sceptic *can* understand it."

"I see no reason why he should *not*," said Harrington, laughing, "if, as you and Mr. Newman suppose, the 'spiritual' can be so perfectly divorced from the 'intellectual.' According to your reasoning, the atheist and the idolater cannot be incapable of exercising this mysterious 'faith' — when their errors are supposed purely speculative, — since faith has *nothing* to do with the intellect; neither, therefore, ought the sceptic to be quite beyond the pale of your charity. Nay, his intellect being a *rasa tabula* in these matters, I should think he is in more favourable circumstances than *they* can be. But seriously, let me try, if possible, to fathom this curious dogma — I beg your pardon — *sentiment*, I mean. Belief without faith in an intelligible sense (if by this last we mean a condition of the emotions or affections), I can understand; though, if the truth believed be of a *nature* to excite to emotion and dictate action, and fail to do so, I doubt whether men in general would not call that belief spurious. For example, if a man, on being told that his house was on fire, sat still in his neighbour's chimney-corner, and took no notice of the matter, most persons would say that his assent was no true *belief*, for it did not produce its *effects*, did not produce *faith*. But whether faith can ever exist independently of *belief*, — whether it is not always involved with it, — and whether there can be a faith worth a farthing that is not based on a *true* belief, — that is the point on which I want light. If I understand you, you think an acceptable faith may or may not coexist with a true belief; and men who believe in Jupiter or Jehovah, in one God or a thousand, who worship the sun or an idol, or a cat, or a monkey, may all have an equally acceptable faith."

"I affirm it."

"That as there may be belief in a truth without faith, so there may be faith, though the intellect believes in a falsehood; — that faith, in fact, is independent of *knowledge*, or of any particular condition of the intellect?"

"I do not like the terms in which you express the sentiment; but I, for one, believe it substantially correct."

"Never mind the form; I am quite willing to employ other terms, if you will supply them."

"Well, then," said Fellowes, "I should say with Mr. Parker that the principle of true faith may be found to coexist with the grossest and most hideous misconceptions of God, while the absence of it may coexist with the truest and most elevated belief."

"That, I think, comes to much the same as I said. — Now about the latter position we have no dispute; it is the former that I want light upon. The latter only shows that a belief, which *ought* to be practical, and if not practical is nothing, is but a species of hypocrisy; and, of course, *I* have nothing to say for it. My uncle here, who is still one of the orthodox, who believes that an 'acceptable faith' and a belief in the divinity of a monkey or a cat are somehow quite incompatible, would be among the first to acknowledge the latter position. He would say, 'No doubt there has often been such a thing as "dead orthodoxy," — a creed of the "letter," — a religion exclusively dependent on logic, and having nothing to do with the feelings; — belief that is not sublimated into faith; — a system of arteries and veins infiltrated with some coloured substance, like the specimens in an anatomical museum, but in which none of the life-blood of religion circulates. But surely,' he would say, 'it does not follow, that because there has been belief without faith, there is or can be any faith independent of *some* belief, or an acceptable faith without a *true* belief.'"

"I affirm," said Fellowes, "that 'faith' has nothing to do with the intellect, but is a state of the affections exclusively. I affirm, with a recent acute writer, that there is, properly speaking, no belief at all that is distinguishable from *reason*. For what is meant by belief of a proposition but the receiving that proposition as *true* upon evidence, from a supposed preponderance of reasons in its favour? Now, whether that preponderance be a ton weight or a single grain, down goes the balance, and reason as strictly decides that it is to be received as if it were a mathematical demonstration.

If the arguments, whether abstract or otherwise, absolutely demonstrative or only probable, are supposed to be exactly balanced, there is no reason for deciding in favour of one side more than the other; and there is therefore no belief, for the very reason that reason cannot be exercised."

"Very well indeed," said Harrington, "so far as it goes; but I forthwith see, that, so far from deriving any benefit from this ingenious reasoning, there is no such thing as either *faith* or *belief:* belief and faith have both vanished at the same time; the first is resolved into reason, and the second, we shall soon see, becomes impossible."

"Belief may," said Fellowes, "but faith never. Its divine beauty is all the brighter, when happily divorced from logic and syllogisms, its misalliance with which can only be compared to that cruel punishment by which the living was chained to the dead. Say what you will, it still reigns and triumphs in the soul, in spite of all."

"I am perfectly convinced," said Harrington, "that the modern spiritualist will not bring his 'faith' into any ignominious slavery to intellect or syllogisms. But clear up my doubts if you can. I know that the writers you are fond of quoting, very generally give an illustration of the nature of *faith* by pointing to the ingenuous trust of a child in the wisdom and kindness of a parent."

"They do; and is it not a beautiful illustration? *That* is genuine faith indeed!"

"I am willing to take the illustration. The child has faith, we see, in his father's superior wisdom and experienced kindness."

"Yes."

"He believes them, therefore."

"Certainly."

"But *belief* is *reason.*"

"Certainly; but faith is more than that."

"No doubt; but he *does* believe these things."

"Yes, certainly."

"And if he did *not* believe them he would cease to have *faith*. If, for instance, he be convinced that his father is mad, or cruel, or unjust, the state of affection which you call *faith* will diminish, and at last cease."

"Perhaps so," said Fellowes.

"Perhaps so, my friend! I really cannot receive your answer, because I am convinced that it does not express your sentiments."

"Well, I believe that the state of affection which we call 'faith' would be impossible under such circumstances."

"But *belief* is *reason*."

"Yes."

"Must we not say, then, that the child's faith *depends* on the condition of his *belief*, that is, on his *reason*, so that the 'faith' is possible *when* he believes, and *so long* as he believes, that his father is wise and kind, but is impossible *when* he believes, and *as soon* as he believes, the contrary?"

"Yes, I admit *that*."

"It appears, then, that faith in this case — perhaps the best illustration that could be selected — so far from being a state of the affections *exclusive* of the intellect, is *not* exclusive of it, but absolutely dependent on it, inasmuch as it is absolutely dependent on belief, and that is dependent on reason. It exists in connection with it, and is never independent of it. If the contrary be affirmed, I doubt whether there can be any such thing as 'faith' in the world. *Belief* becomes *reason*, and *faith*, having nothing, you say, to do with the intellect, becomes impossible. — But now, let it be supposed (as, indeed, I cannot *but* suppose), that *some* belief, that is reason, enlightened or not (generally the last), is involved in every act of faith; you yet affirm most distinctly that it is a state of the affections quite independent of the *truth* or *falsehood* of any such intellectual propositions as may be involved with it."

"I do."

"It *ought* to follow, then, that it matters not what is the object of belief, provided there is 'faith;' and this, if you observe, is very much what the language of Mr. Newman would imply, while it is the very essence of Mr. Parker's teaching."

"You mean Father Newman, perhaps?"

"Why no, I did not; but, to tell you the truth, either would illustrate my meaning; there not appearing to me much difference between them in this respect. Whether you worship an image of a 'winking virgin,' or, according to the other Dromio, the 'ideal' of an idolater, — whether (provided always it be with *sincerity* and *trust!*) you adore the Jehovah of the Hebrews, or, 'the image which fell down from Jupiter,' ought to make, upon your theory, no great difference."

"Well, in whatever difficulty the controversy may involve us, can we deny this conclusion?"

"Truly," replied Harrington, "I think it does not involve *me* in any difficulty; it shows me that if *this* be the 'faith,' to which you attach so much importance, it really is not worth the powder and shot that must be expended in the controversy. For my own part, I do not hesitate to say that I would rather be absolutely destitute of 'faith' altogether, than exercise the most plenary faith ever bestowed upon a tawdry image of the Virgin, or some misshapen beast of an idol of Hindoo or Hottentot workmanship."

"Ah! my friend," cried Fellowes, "do not thus blaspheme the most holy feelings of humanity, however misapplied!"

"I do not conceive that I do, in declaring abhorrence and contempt of such perversions of 'sentiment,' however 'holy' you may call them. Hideous as they are, however, they are less hideous than the half-length apologies for them on the part of cultivated and civilised human beings, like our 'spiritual' infidels. Your tenderness is ludicrously misplaced. I wonder whether the *same* apology would extend to those exercises of simple-minded 'faith' in which it is said that the Spanish and Portuguese pirates sometimes indulged, when they implored the benediction of the saints on their predatory expeditions! And yet I see not how it could be avoided; for the exorbitancies of these pirates were not more hateful to humanity than are the rites practised, and the duties enjoined, by many forms of religion. What delightful ingenuous 'faith' and genuine 'simplicity' of mind did these pirates manifest!"

"How can you talk so, when we make it a mark of a false revelation, that it contradicts any intuition of our moral nature?"

"Then cease to talk of your 'absolute religion,' as capable in any way of consecrating the hateful forms of false and cruel superstition, for which you and Mr. Parker condescend to be the apologists. The fanaticism of such pious and devout beasts as those saint-loving pirates, is not a more flagrant violation of the principles of morality than the acts which flow directly as the immediate and natural expression of the infinitely varied, but all-polluting forms of idolatry, with which you are pleased to identify your 'absolute religion,' and in *all* of which you suppose an acceptable 'faith,' to be very possible. You see how Mr. Parker extends the apology to the foulest acts of his Tartar and Calmuck scoundrels; acts called murders in the codes of Christendom and civilisation, but varnished over by the beautiful 'faith' which somehow still lurks under the most frightful practices of a simple-minded barbarian. If this faith will shelter the abominations of a gross idolatry, I see not what else it may *not* sanctify.—But, in fact, neither in the case of idolaters, or any other religionists, is it true that 'faith' is independent of 'belief;' in the case of your Calmuck, for example, the 'belief' is vile, and, therefore, the 'faith' vile too; a faith practical enough, certainly, but one that as certainly does *not* 'work by love;' and which I think would be well exchanged for a dead orthodoxy, or anything else."

It is not difficult to see the source of the fallacy into which Mr. Fellowes had fallen. It lies in the attempt to make a distinction in *fact*, as well as in *theory*, between the "intellectual" and "emotional" parts of our nature. It is very well for the spiritual and mental analyst to consider separately the several principles which constitute humanity, and which act, and react, and interact, in endless involution. That there may be acts of belief that terminate chiefly in the intellect, and may be wholly worthless, who denies? The drunkard, for example, may admit that sobriety is a duty; but yet if he gets drunk every night of his life, we shall, of course, think little of that act of belief,—of his daily repetition of *moral* orthodoxy. In the same manner, a man may admit that it is his duty to exercise implicit love, gratitude, and obedience towards the great object of worship; but if his habitual conduct shows that he has no thought of *acting* in accordance with this maxim, he must be regarded, in spite of the orthodoxy of his speculative creed, as no better than a heathen; or worse.

But though it is very possible that a true belief may not involve true faith, does the converse follow,—that, therefore, true faith is essentially different from it, and independent of it? All history shows, that when religion is practical at all,—that is, issues in faith,—such faith is as the truth or falsehood *believed;* the emotional and active conditions of the soul are coloured, as usual, by *knowledge* and *intellect.* These, again, are not independent of the will and the affections, as we all familiarly know. And hence the fallacy of supposing that no man is to be thought better or worse for his "intellectual creed." His "creed" may be his "crime;" and surely none ought to see this more clearly than the writers who deny it; for why their eternal invectives against "dogmas,"—and especially the tolerably universal dogma that men are responsible for the formation of their opinions,—except upon the supposition that men *are* responsible for framing and maintaining them? If they are not, men should be left alone; if they are, they are to be thought of as "worse and better" for their "intellectual creeds."

Before the conclusion of the conversation, Mr. Fellowes asked me for my opinion.

"If," said I, "faith be defined independently of an act of intellect, then, I think, with our sceptical friend here, there can be no such thing at all. For I neither know, nor can conceive, of any such unreasonable exercise of the emotions or affections. If it be meant, on the other hand, that though *some* act of the intellect be indeed uniformly involved, yet that it matters not *what* it is, and that faith does not take its complexion, as of moral value, from it, then I also think, with Harrington, that it is impossible to deny that such a doctrine will sanctify any sort of worship, and any sort of deity, provided men be sincere; are you prepared to contend for so much?"

Mr. Fellowes put an adroit objection here. "Why," said he, "you will not deny, surely, that even Scripture often commends as good a faith which is founded on a very imperfect conception of the spiritual realities to which it is directed!"

"It is ingeniously put, I admit. I grant that there are here, as in so many other cases, limits which, though it may not be very easy to assign them, as plainly exist. But that does not answer my question. I want to know whether the principle is to be applied *without limits at all*, as your speculative theory demands? In other words, will it or not sanctify acts of the most degrading and pernicious idolatry, ·of the most debasing superstition, because allied to that state of the affections in which you make the *essence* of faith consist? If it will not, then your objection to me is nothing; it merely asks me to assign limits, within which the exercise of the affection in question may be acceptable, or almost equally acceptable, in cases of a partially enlightened understanding. If it will, then it leaves you open, as I conceive, and fairly open, to all the objections which have been so brusquely urged against you by your friend, in whose indignant protest against the detestable apologies for the lowest forms of religious degradation, in which so many 'spiritual' writers indulge, I for one heartily sympathise."

I ventured to add, that the account of "faith" as a state of the emotions exclusively, given by some of his favourite writers, is perfectly arbitrary. "Belief," say they, "is wholly intellectual: Faith is wholly moral."

Now it would be of very little consequence, provided the terms were generally understood, whether they be so used or not; men would in that case suppose, that faith, thus restricted, uniformly *implies* a previous process of mind which is to be called exclusively *belief.* I added, however, that I did not believe that the word "faith" was ever thus understood in popular use; but that, on the contrary, it was employed to imply belief founded on knowledge or supposed knowledge, and also where the belief was, in its very nature, practical, or claimed emotion, a *conduct* and *a state of the affections* corresponding thereto. "But this," said I, "merely respects the popular use of the words, and it is hardly worth while to prolong discussion on it. As to the reasoning which would show that *belief* does not properly exist at all, because it may be all resolved into *reason,* founded on the preponderance of evidence, where it does not matter whether that preponderance be a ton or a scruple;—surely it is over-refined. Men will always *feel* that there is a marked difference between the states of mind in which they assent to a proposition of which they have no more doubt than they have of their own existence, or to a proposition in the mathematics,—and to one in which they feel that only a few grains turn the scale. To this conscious difference in the condition of mind, they have given (and I suppose will continue to give) very different names; and though they will not say that they *believe* that two and two make four, but that they *know* it, they will say that they believe that they will die before the end of the century, though they will not say that they *know that.* The distinction between the certain and the probable is *felt* to be far too important not to be marked by corresponding varieties of speech; and speech has made them accordingly."

July 10. This morning Harrington fulfilled his promise of acquainting me with a few of the principal reasons which prevented his taking refuge in the "halfway houses" between the Bible and Religious Scepticism:

Mr. Fellowes was an attentive listener. Harrington had entitled his paper —

REASONS FOR DECLINING THE VIA MEDIA BETWEEN REVEALED RELIGION AND ATHEISM, — OR SCEPTICISM; WITH SPECIAL REFERENCE TO THE THEORIES OF MR. THEODORE PARKER AND MR. FRANCIS NEWMAN.

I shall be brief; not being solicitous to suggest doubts to others, but merely to justify my own.

Both Mr. Parker and Mr. Newman make themselves very merry with a "book-revelation" as they call it; and if they had given me anything better — more rational or more certain than the Bible — how gladly could I have joined in the ridicule! As it is, I doubt the solidity of the theories they support, and *hardly* doubt that if the *principles* on which they reject the Bible be sound, they ought to go much farther. Both affirm the absurdity of a special *external* revelation to man; both, that the fountain of spiritual illumination is exclusively from *within*, and not from *without*. A few brief citations will set this point in a clear light. "Religion itself," says Mr. Parker, "must be the same thing in each man; not a *similar* thing, but just the *same;* differing only in degree."* "The *Idea of God*, as a fact given in man's nature, is *permanent and alike in all;* while the sentiment of God, though vague and mysterious, is always the same in itself."† "Of course, then, there is no difference but of words between *revealed* Religion, and *natural* Religion; for all natural religion is revealed in us or it could not be felt."‡ The Absolute Religion which he affirms to be universally known, he defines as "Voluntary obedience to the Law of God — inward and outward Obedience to that law he has *written on our nature*, revealed in various ways through Instinct, Reason, Conscience, and the Religious Sentiment."§ Similarly, Mr. Newman says, "*What* God reveals to us he reveals *within*, through the medium of our moral and

---

* Discourses of Matters pertaining to Religion, p. 36.
† Ibid. p. 21.   ‡ Ibid. p. 33.   § Ibid. p. 34.

spiritual senses."* "Christianity itself has practic[ally] confessed, what is theoretically clear"—you must t[ake] his word for both, what he calls his *arguments*, assertions only—"that an authoritative *external* rev[ela]tion of moral and spiritual truth is essentially impossi[ble] to man."† "No book-revelation can (without sapp[ing] its own pedestal) authoritatively dictate laws of hum[an] virtue, or alter our *à priori* view of the div[ine] character."‡

Happy race of men, one is ready to exclaim, with [the] Idea of God, *one* and *the same* in all; this "Absol[ute] Religion," which is *also* "universal;" this internal re[ve]lation, which supersedes, by anticipating, all poss[ible] disclosures of an external revelation, and renders it [an] "impertinence." Men in all ages and nations m[ust] exhibit a delightful unanimity in their religious noti[ons], sentiments, and practices!

They *would* do so, cries Mr. Parker; but unhapp[ily], though the "idea" of God is "one and the same, [and] perfect" in all "when the proper conditions" are comp[lied] with, yet *practically*, in the majority of cases, th[e] proper "conditions are not observed;"§ "the concept[ion] which men universally form of God, is always imperf[ect,] sometimes self-contradictory and impossible;" "[the] primitive simplicity and beauty" of the "idea" are l[ost.] And thus it is, he tells us, that, owing to this awkw[ard] "conception," the vast majority of the human race h[as] been, and are, and for ages *will* be, sunk in the gros[s] Fetichism—Polytheism—and every form of abs[urd] and misshapen Monotheism;—the horrors of all w[hich] he proceeds faithfully, but not *too* faithfully, to descr[ibe] and sometimes, when he is in the mood, to soften [and] extenuate; in order that he may find that the "[poor] Calmuck," and even the savage, "whose hands [are] smeared over with the blood of human sacrifices"— yet in possession of the "absolute Idea," and the "a[bso]lute Religion."

---

* Soul, p. 59.   Ibid. p. 59.   ‡ Ibid. p. 58.
§ Discourses, p. 19.

And what must we infer from Mr. Newman? The unanimity anticipated would, doubtless, be obtained, only that, unfortunately, there are various principles of man's nature which traverse the legitimate action and impede the due development of the "spiritual faculty;" and so man is apt to wander into a variety of those "degraded types" of religious development, which the dark panorama of this world's religions has ever presented to us, and presents still. "Awe," "wonder," "admiration," "sense of order," "sense of design," may all mislead the unhappy "spiritual faculty" into quagmires; and, in point of fact, have wheedled and corrupted *it* ten thousand times more frequently than it has hallowed *them*. This all history, past and present, shows.

It is certainly unfortunate, and as mysterious, that those unlucky "conceptions" of God should have the best of it — or rather, that the *"idea"* of God should have the worst of it; nor less so that Awe, Reverence, and so forth, should thus put the "spiritual faculty" so hopelessly *hors de combat*.

Nevertheless, two questions naturally suggest themselves. Since the destructive "conceptions" have almost everywhere impaired the "Idea," and the "degraded types" seduced the "spiritual faculty,"— 1st, What *proof* have we that man has an original and universal fountain of spiritual illumination in himself? and 2ndly, If he have, but under *such* circumstances, is its utility so unquestionable that no space is left for the offices of an external revelation?

First. What is the evidence of the uniform existence in man of any such definite faculty?

When we say that any principle or faculty is common to the whole species, do we not make the proof of this depend upon the uniformity of the phenomena which exhibit it? When we say, for example, that hunger and thirst are universal appetites, is it not because we find them universal; or if we say that the senses of sight and hearing are characteristic of the race, do we not contend that these are so, because we find them uniform in such an immense variety of instances, that the exceptions are not worth reckoning? If men sometimes saw black where others saw white, some objects rectilinear which others saw curved, some objects small which others saw large,—nay, the very same men at different times seeing the same objects differently coloured, and of varying forms and magnitudes, and every second man *almost* stone blind into the bargain,—I rather think, that, instead of saying that all men were endowed with one and the same power of vision, we should say that our nature exhibited only an imperfect and rudimentary *tendency* towards so desirable a faculty; but that a clear, uniform, well-defined faculty of vision there certainly was not. As I gaze upon the spectacle of the infinite diversities of religion, which variegate, but alas! do not beautify the world, what is there to remind me of that uniformity of result, of which I *do* see the indelible traces in every faculty really characteristic of our nature; as, for example, in our senses and our appetites? Powerfully does Hume urge this argument in his "Natural History of Religions."*

I have my *doubts*—admire the modesty of a sceptic—whether the entire phenomena of religion do not favour the conclusion, that man, in this respect, exhibits only the traces of an imperfect, truncated creature; that he is in the predicament of the *half-created* lion so graphically described by Milton:—

> "Now half appeared
> The tawny lion, pawing to get free
> His hinder parts;"

only, unfortunately, *man's* "hinder parts"—his lower nature—have come up first, and appear, unhappily, prominent; while his nobler "moral and spiritual faculties" still seem stuck in the dust!

There is, indeed, *another* hypothesis, which squares, perhaps, equally well with the phenomena,—I mean that of the BIBLE;—that man is *not* in his original

---

* Introduction.

state; that the religious constitution of his nature, in some way or other, has received a shock. But *either* this, *or* the supposition that man has been insufficiently equipped for the uniform elimination of religious truth, is, I think, alone in harmony with the facts; and to those facts, patent on the page of the whole world's history, I appeal for proof that man has not, on these highest subjects, the certitude of any internal revelation, marked by the remotest analogy to those other undoubted principles and faculties which exhibit themselves with undeniable uniformity.

It will perhaps be said, that the spiritual phenomena are not *so* uniform as those of sense — as Mr. Parker and Mr. Newman both abundantly admit, — but that there is an *approximate* uniformity. And you must seek it, says Mr. Parker, in the "Absolute Religion," which animates *every* form of religion, and is equally found in all. I know he chatters about this incessantly; but when I attempt thus to "hunt the one in the many," as Plato would call it — to seek the elusive unity in the infinite multiform — to discover what it is which *equally* embalms all forms, from the Christianity of Paul to the religion of the "grim Calmuck," I acknowledge myself as much at a loss as Martinus in endeavouring to catch the abstraction of a Lord Mayor: Mr. Parker, on the other hand, is like Crambe, "who, to show his acuteness, swore that he could form an abstraction of a Lord Mayor not only without his horse, gown, and gold chain, but even without stature, feature, colour, hands, head, feet, or any body, which he supposed was the abstract of a Lord Mayor." Or if it be vain to attempt to abstract this Absolute Religion from all religions, as Mr. Parker indeed admits, — though it is truly *in* them, — and I take his definition from his "direct consciousness," — which direct consciousness we can see has been *directly* affected by his abjured Bible, — namely, "that it is voluntary obedience to the will of God — outward and inward," — why, what on earth does this vague generality do for us? What *sort* of God? Is *he* or *it* one or many? Of infinite attributes or finite? of goodness and mercy equal to his power, or not? What *is* his will? *How* is he to be worshipped? Have we offended him? Is he placable or not? Is he to be approached only through a mediator of some kind, as nearly all mankind have believed, but which Mr. Parker denies — a queer proof, by the way, of the clearness of the internal oracle, if he be right; — or is he to be approached, as Mr. Parker believes, and Mr. Newman with him, without any mediator at all? Is it true that man is immortal, and knows it by immediate "insight," as Mr. Parker contends, or does the said "insight," as Mr. Newman believes, tell us nothing about the matter? Surely the "Absolute Religion," after having removed from it *all* in which different religions differ, is in danger of vanishing into that imperfect susceptibility of *some* religion, which I have already conceded, and which is certainly *not* such a thing as to render an external revelation very obviously superfluous. It may be summed up in one imperfect article. All men and each may say, "I believe there is *some* being, superior in *some* respects to man, whom it is my duty or my interest to" — *cætera desunt.*

To affirm that every man has this "Absolute Religion" without external revelation, is much as if a man were to say that we have an "Absolute Philosophy" on the same terms, in virtue of man's having faculties which prompt him to philosophise in *some* way. All religions contain the Absolute Religion, says Mr. Parker: Just, I reply, as all philosophies contain the absolute philosophy. The philosophy of Plato, of Aristotle, of Bacon, of Locke, of Leibnitz, of Reid, are all *philosophies*, no doubt; but that is all that is to be said. Even *contraries* must resemble one another in *one* point, or they could not be contrasted. In truth, there is, I think, a striking analogy between man's spiritual and intellectual condition; only his intellect is a *little* less variable than his "spiritual faculty;" far more so, however, than his senses. His animal nature is more defined than his intellectual, his intellectual than his spiritual and moral. All the phenomena point *either* to an imperfect organisation of his nobler faculties, or to the doctrine of the "Fall."

But further; surely if this internal oracle exists in man, every sincere and earnest soul, on interrogating his consciousness, would hear the indubitable response, — would enjoy the beatific vision of "spiritual insight." If this be asserted, I for one have to say to this representation, that, so far as my own consciousness informs me, I have honestly, sincerely, and with utmost diligence, interrogated my spirit; and I solemnly protest, that, apart from those external influences, and that external instruction which the revelation from *within* is supposed to anticipate and supersede, I am not conscious that I should have any of the sentiments which either of the above writers makes the sum of religion. Even as to that fundamental position, — the existence of a Being of unlimited power and wisdom (his unlimited *goodness*, I believe that nothing *but* an external revelation can absolutely certify to us), I feel that I am much more indebted to those inferences from *design*, which these writers make so light of, than to any *clearness* in the imperfect intuition; for if I found — and surely this is the true test — the traces of design less conspicuous in the physical world, confusion there as in the moral, and in both greater than is now found in either, I extremely doubt whether the faintest surmise of such a Being would have suggested itself to me. But be that as it may; as to the other cardinal sentiments of these authors, — the nature of our relations to this Being — his placability if offended, — the terms of forgiveness, if any, — whether, as these gentlemen affirm, he is accessible to all, without any atonement or mediator: — as to all this, I solemnly declare, that, apart from external instruction, I cannot, by interrogating my racked spirit, catch even a murmur. That the response must be faint, indeed in *other* men; so faint as to render the pretensions of the certitude of the internal revelation, and its independence of all external revelation, perfectly preposterous, I infer from this, — that men have, for the most part, arrived at diametrically opposite conclusions from those of these interpreters of the spiritual revelation. As to the articles, indeed, of man's immortality and a future state, it would be truly difficult for *my* "spiritual insight" to verify *theirs;* for, according to Mr. Parker, his "insight" affirms that man *is* immortal, and Mr. Newman's "insight" declares nothing about the matter!

Nor is my consciousness, so far as I can trace it, mine only. This painful uncertainty has been the confession of multitudes of far greater minds; they have been so far from contending that we have naturally a clear utterance on these great questions, that they have acknowledged the necessity of an external revelation; and mankind *in general*, so far from thinking or feeling such light superfluous, have been constantly *gaping* after it, and adopted almost anything that but *bore the name.*

What, then, am I to think of this all-sufficient revelation from *within?*

There is, indeed, an amusing answer of Mr. Newman's to the difficulty; but, then, it formally surrenders the whole argument. He says to those who affirm they are unconscious of those facts of spiritual pathology which he describes in his work on the "Soul," that the consciousness of the spiritual man is not the less true, that the *unspiritual* man is not privy to it; and somewhere quotes with much unction the words, "For the spiritual man judgeth all things, but himself is judged of no man."

"I shall be curious to know," said I, interrupting him, "what you will reply to that argument."

"Reply to it," said he eagerly; "does it require any reply? However, I will read what I have written. — Is it not plain, that while Mr. Newman is professedly anatomising the spiritual nature of man, as *man* — the functions and revelations of that inward oracle which supersedes and anticipates all external revelation, — he is, in fact, anatomising his *own?* What title has he, when avowedly explaining the phenomena of the religious faculty, which he asserts to be inherent in *humanity* — though how they should need explaining, if his theory be true, I know not, — what title has he, when men deny that they are conscious of the facts he describes, to take refuge in his own private revelations, and that of the few whose privilege it is to be 'born again,' by a mysterious law which he says it is impossible for us to investigate?—'We cannot pretend,' he says, 'to sound the mystery *whence comes* the new birth in certain souls. To reply, 'The Spirit bloweth where He listeth,' confesses the mystery, and declines to explain it. But it is evident that *individuals* in Greece, in the third century before the Christian era, were *already* moving *towards* an intelligent *heart-worship*, or had even *begun* to practise it!"*

High time, I think, that after some thousands of years some few *individuals* should begin to manifest the phenomena of the universal revelation from *within*, if such a thing be!

This is not to delineate the religious nature of humanity, but to reveal—yes, and to reveal *externally*—the religious nature of the elect few,—and few they are indeed,—who, by a mysterious infidel Calvinism, are permitted to attain by direct intuition, and independent of all external revelation, the true sentiments and experiences of "spiritual insight." If this be Mr. Newman's solution of our difficulties, it is utterly nugatory. It is not to dissect the soul, "its sorrows and aspirations;" it is merely to give us the pathology—perhaps the morbid pathology—of Mr. Newman's soul, *its* sorrows and *its* aspirations. If the answer merely respected the *practical* value of a theory of spiritual sentiments, which all acknowledged, then Mr. Newman's answer might have some force; for, certainly, only he who reduced that theory to practice, or attempted to do so, would have a right to conclude against the experience of him who did. But it is obvious, that the question affects the *theory itself*, and especially the consciousness of those terms of possible communion with God, those relations of the soul to him, on the reception of which all the said spiritual experience must depend.

* Soul, p. 64.

How, then, stands the argument? I ask how I shall know the intimations of the spiritual faculty, which renders all "external revelation" an impertinence? I am told, with delicious vagueness, that I must *gaze* on the phenomena of spiritual consciousness; I say I exercise earnest and sincere self-scrutiny, and that I can discern nothing but shadowy forms, most of which do *not* answer to those which these new spiritualists describe; and then Mr. Newman turns round and says, that the unspiritual nature cannot discern them! What is this but to give up the only question of any importance to humanity,—which is, not what are Mr. Newman's spiritual phenomena; if they are known to himself, it is well; he has been very long in discovering them, in spite of the clearness of the internal revelation;— but what are those of *man?* If the former be alone in question, Mr. Newman is safe indeed; he is intrenched in his own peculiar consciousness, of which I am quite willing to admit that all other men, (as well as I,) are inadequate judges. But the monograph of a solitary enthusiast is of the least possible consequence to humanity. For reasons similar to those which render us incompetent to pronounce on *his* experience, he is incapable of judging of ours.—There is only one other answer that I know of, and that is the answer which Fellowes made to me the other day when you were not by:—"Oh! but you *have* the same spiritual consciousness as I have, only you are not *aware* of it." I contented myself with saying, that I was just as able to comprehend a perception which is not perceived, as a consciousness which when sought was not to be found. The question is one of consciousness; you say you have it, I do not deny it; *I* have it not. Now if we are not disputing as to whether it be a characteristic of *humanity*, it little matters; if we are, I plainly have the best of it, because the want of uniformity in the phenomena is destructive of the hypothesis.

But I proceed to ask my *second* question. Is the "absolute religion" of Mr. Parker, or the "spiritual faculty" of Mr. Newman, of such singular use as to supersede all external revelation, since by the unfortunate "conceptions" of the one, and the "degraded types" of the other, it has for ages left man, and does, *in fact*, now leave him, to wallow in the lowest depths of the most debasing idolatry and superstition; since by the confession of these very writers, the great bulk of mankind have been and are hideously mal-formed, in fact, spiritual cripples, and have been left to wander in infinitely varied paths of error, but *always* paths of error? — for Judaism and Christianity, though *better* forms, are, as well as other forms, — according to these writers, — full of favours and fancies, of lying legends and fantastical doctrines. Think for a moment of a "spiritual faculty," so bright as to anticipate all essential spiritual verities, — the universal possession of humanity, — which yet terminates in leaving the said humanity to grovel in every form of error, between the extremes of Fetichism, which consecrates a bit of stone, and Pantheism, which consecrates all the bits of stone in the universe, — in fact, a sort of comprehensive Fetichism; which leaves a man to erect every thing into a God, provided it is none, — sun, moon, stars, a cat, a monkey, an onion, uncouth idols, sculptured marble; nay a shapeless trunk — which the devout impatience of the idolater does not stay to fashion into the likeness of a *man*, but gives it its apotheosis at once! Think of the venerable wide-spread empire of the different forms of polytheism, the ancient Egyptian, Greek, Roman, Chinese, and Hindoo mythologies; and then acknowledge, that if man has this *faculty*, it is either the most idle prerogative ever bestowed on a rational creature, or that, somehow or other, as the Bible affirms, it has been denaturalised and disabled. If, on the other hand, man has this faculty, and yet has never *fallen*, it can only be because he never *stood;* and then, no doubt, as old John Bunyan hath it, — "He that is *down* need fear no *fall!*"

There *is* an answer, indeed, but it is one which, in my judgment, covers those who resort to it with the deepest shame. It is that which apologises for all these abominations, — so humiliating and odious, — by representing them as less humiliating and odious than they are. It is true that Mr. Parker, when it is his cue, is most eloquent in his denunciations of the infinite miseries and degradation which have followed the exorbitancies of the religious principle. Thus he says of superstition (and there are other innumerable passages to a similar effect), "To dismember the soul, the very image of God, — to lop off the most sacred affections, — to call Reason a liar, Conscience a devil's oracle, and cast Love clean out from the heart, — this is the last triumph of superstition, but one often witnessed in *all* the three forms of Religion — Fetichism, Polytheism, Monotheism; in all ages before Christ, in all ages after Christ." Far be it from me to deny it, or the similar horrors which he liberally shows flow from fanaticism. But, then, at other times, that quintessence of all abstractions, which all religions alike contain, — the "absolute religion," — imparts such perfume and appetising relish to the whole composition, that, like Dominie Sampson in Meg Merrilies' *cuisine*, Mr. Parker finds the devil's cookery-book not despicable. The things he so fearfully describes are but *perversions* of what is essentially good! The "forms," the "accidentals," of different religions become of little consequence; whether it be Jehovah or Jupiter, the infinite Creator or a divine cat, a holy and gracious God that is loved, or an impure demon that is feared, — all this is secondary, provided the principles of *faith, simplicity,* and *earnestness,* — that is, blind credulity and idiotic stupidity, — inspire the wretched votary: as if the *perversions* this author deplores and condemns were not the necessary consequences of such religions themselves, or, rather, as if they were aught but the religions! In virtue of the "absolute religion," many a savage smeared with "human sacrifice," and the Christian martyr perishing with a prayer for his persecutors, are hastening together to the celestial banquet. I hope the "savage" will not go with "unwashen hands," I trust he may be Pharisee enough for that: I also hope the two will not sit next one another; otherwise the savage may be tempted to offer up a *second* sacrifice.

and the Christian martyr be a martyr a second time. Hear our author:—" He that worships *truly*, by whatever form,"—that is, who is *sincere* in his fetichism, his idolatry, his sacrifices, *though* they may be human,—" worships the only God; He hears the prayer, whether called Brahma, Pan, or Lord, or called by no name at all. Each people has its prophets and its saints; and many a swarthy Indian, who bowed down to wood and stone, — many a grim-faced Calmuck, who worshipped the great God of storms, — many a Grecian peasant, who did homage to Phœbus Apollo, when the sun rose or went down,—yes many a savage, his hands smeared all over with human sacrifice, — shall come from the East and the West, and sit down in the Kingdom of God, with Moses and Zoroaster, with Socrates and Jesus."* The charity which hopes that men my be forgiven the *crime* of "religions," which, if there be a God at all, must be "abominations," one can understand; but these maudlin apologies for the religions themselves,—as if they were not themselves crimes, and involved crimes in their very *practice*, — I do not understand. According to this, all that man has to do is to be *sincere* in any thing, however diabolical, and it is at once transmuted into a virtue which nothing less than heaven can reward!

Mr. Newman sometimes follows closely in Mr. Parker's steps in the exercise of this bastard toleration, this spurious charity; though, in justice, I must say, he does not go *his* length. Yet who can read without laughter that definition of idolatry, made apparently for the same preposterous purpose— to sanctify the hideous absurdities of the "religious sentiment," and to save the credit of the "internal oracle?" He says,—"to worship *as perfect and infinite* one whom *we know* to be imperfect and finite, this is idolatry, and (in any bad sense) this alone. . . . . . . A man can but adore his own highest ideal; to forbid this is to forbid all religion to him. If, therefore, idolatry is to mean any thing wrong and bad, the word must be reserved for the cases in which a man

---

* Discourses, p. 83.

degrades his ideal by worshipping something that falls short of it."*

So that the most degraded idolater, if he but come up to his own *ideal* of the Divinity, is none at all, but a respectable worshipper! It may be; but the idolater's ideal of God is, generally, the reality of what others call the devil!—Only think of the divine *ideal* of a man who worships an image of his own making with ten heads and twenty hands! The definition reminds me of that passage in which Pascal's Jesuit Father defines the mortal sin of "idleness:"—"It is," says he, "a grief that spiritual things should be spiritual, as if it should be regretted that the sacraments are the source of grace; and it is a mortal sin." "O! Father," said I, "I cannot imagine that any one can be *idle* in such a sense." "So Escobar says, 'I confess it is very seldom that any person falls into the sin of idleness.' Now, surely, you must see the necessity of a good *definition!*"

No, no; few but Mr. Parker will affirm that the various religions which have overshadowed the world are essentially more *one* in virtue of the "absolute religion," than they are different in virtue of their principles, tendencies, practices, and forms: while in none —*if* we except Judaism and Christianity —is there enough of the "absolute religion" to keep them *sweet*.

These apologies, odious as they are, are necessary if the credit of the "spiritual faculty" and the "absolute religion" is to be at all preserved. But, unhappily, it is not a tone which can be consistently maintained. Sometimes the religions of mankind are all tolerable enough, from the presence of the all-consecrating element; and sometimes, in spite of this great antiseptic, they are represented as the rotten putrid things they are! And then another answer, equally empty with the former, is hinted to save the credit of the darling oracle. Its due influence has been perverted, its just expansion prevented, by the influence of national religions, by the intervention of the "historical" and "traditional," by false

---

* Soul, p. 55, 56.

and pernicious education;—these things, it seems, have poisoned the waters of spiritual life in their source, else they had gushed out of the hidden fountains of the heart pure as crystal!

Yes, it is too plain; "Bibliolatry" and "Historical Religion," in some shape,—Vedas, Koran, or Bible,— have been the world's bane. Had it not been for these, I suppose, we should every where have heard the invariable utterance of "spiritual religion" in the one dialect of the heart.

It is too certain that the world has found its spiritual "Babel:" the one dialect of the heart is yet to be heard.

But I am not sure that the apologetic vein would not be wiser. For what is this plea but to acknowledge, that man is so *constituted* that the boasted "religious sentiment," the "spiritual faculty,"—if it exist at all, and is any thing more than an ill-defined tendency,— instead of being a glorious light which anticipates all external revelation, and renders it superfluous, is, in fact, about the feeblest in our nature; which every where and always is seduced and debauched by the most trumpery pretensions of the "historical" and "traditional!" It is not so with people's eyes; it is not so with people's appetites; no parental influence or early instruction can make men think that green is blue, or stones and chalk good for food. Yet *this* glorious faculty uniformly yields,—goes into shivers in the encounter! I, at least, will grant to Mr. Parker all he says of the pernicious and detestable character of the infinite variety of "false conceptions of God," and to Mr. Newman all *he* says of the "degraded types" of religion; but then it was *Man* himself that framed all those false "conceptions," and all those "degraded types." How came he thus universally to triumph over that divinely implanted faculty of spiritual discernment, which, if it exist, must be the most admirable feature of humanity; which these writers tell us anticipates all external *truth*, but which, it seems, greedily swallows all external *error?* It almost universally submits to the most contemptible pretensions of a revelation, and acknowledges that it dares not to pronounce on that, even when false, of which, even when true, it is to be the sole source! There never was an "historical" religion, however contemptible, that did not make its thousands of proselytes. Man has been easily led to embrace the most absurd systems of mythology and superstition, and is willing even to go to death for them.

So far from venturing to set up the claims of the internal oracle in competition, man all but uniformly takes his religion from his fathers (no matter what), just as he takes his property; only the former, however worthless, he holds as infinitely the more precious. Even when he surrenders it, he still surrenders it to some other "historical" religion; it is to *that* he turns. Such men as Mr. Newman and Mr. Parker,—though every one can see that *their* system too has been derived from *without*, that it is, in fact, nothing but a distorted Christianity,— may be numbered by units. The vast bulk of mankind are unresisting victims of the "traditional" and "historical;" nay, rather eagerly ask for it, and willingly submit to it. What, then, can I infer, but either, 1st, that this vaunted internal faculty which supersedes all necessity of an external revelation is a delusion, and exists only as a vague and imperfect tendency; or, 2ndly, that, as Christians say, it lies in ruins, and needs that external revelation, the possibility of which is denied; or, 3rdly, that God has somehow made a great mistake in mingling the various elements of man's composition, and miscalculated the overmastering power of the "historical" and "traditional;" or, 4thly, that man, having the original faculty still bright and strong, and that brightness and strength *sufficient* for his guidance and support, is more hopelessly, deliberately, and diabolically wicked, in thus every where and always substituting error for truth, and superstition for religion, in thus giving the historical and traditional the uniform ascendancy over the moral and spiritual,—than even the most desperate Calvinist ever ventured to represent him! Surely, according to this theory, he is the most detestable beast that ever crawled on the face of the earth, and, in a new and more portentous sense, "loves darkness rather than light." The fact is, that,—so far from having even a *suspicion* that an external revelation is useless or impossible,—man, as already said, greedily seeks for it and devours it.

Nay, so far from its being authenticated by the history, or vouched by the consciousness of the race, this very proposition—that man stands in no need of an external revelation,—first comes to him, and rather late too, by an external revelation; even the revelation of such writers as Mr. Parker and Mr. Newman. The last has been a student of theology for twenty years, and has only just arrived at this conviction, that he needed no light, inasmuch as he had plenty of light "within." Brilliant, surely, it must have been! I can only say for myself, that I do not, even with such aid, find myself in any superfluous illumination, and would gladly accept, with Plato, some divine communication, of which, heathen as he was, he acknowledged the necessity.

The mode of accounting for man's universal aberrations, from the tyranny of "bibliolatry" and superstitious and pernicious "education,"—seeing that it is a tyranny of man's *own* imposing,—is exactly like that by which some theologians seek to elude the argument of man's depravity; it is owing, they say, to the influence of a *universally depraved education!* But whence that universally depraved education they forget to tell us. Meantime, the inquirer is apt to put that universal proclivity in the matter of *education* to that very depravity for which it is to account.

Similarly, one is apt to infer, from man's tendency to deviate into any path of religious superstition and folly, that the spiritual lantern he carries within casts but a feeble light upon his path. This plea, therefore, is utterly worthless; for if it were true, that the influence of tradition and historic association, when once set up, could thus darken and debauch the natural faculty, whose specific office it was to convey, like the eye, specific intelligence, it would not account for the *first* tendencies of man to disown its authority in favour of an absurd and uniform submission to the usurpations of tradition and priestcraft. The faculty is universally feeble against this influence; it *staggers;* whether from weakness or drunkenness little matters, except that the last is the viler infirmity of the two. — If we find a river turbid, it is of no consequence whether it was so as it issued from its fountain, or from pollutions which have been infused into its current lower down, — it is a turbid river still.

On the whole, so far from admitting the principle of Mr. Newman, that a "book-revelation" of moral and spiritual truth is unnecessary, I should rather be disposed to infer the very contrary, from the uncertainty, vacillation, and feebleness of man's spiritual nature. I should be disposed to infer it, whether I look at the lessons which experience and history teach, or those taught by my own anxious and sincere scrutiny of my own consciousness. If it *be*, on the other hand, as he says, "impossible," mankind are in a very hopeless predicament, since it only proves that the "spiritual insight" of man having unhappily failed the great majority of our race, it cannot be supplied by any external aid; that the malady, which is but too apparent, is also as apparently without a remedy.

For myself, I must say that I find myself hopelessly at issue with him in virtue of the above axiom, whether I receive or reject his theory of religious truth; for, if that axiom be true, I must reject his *theory* of religion, — since it is nothing but a *book-revelation* to me, — issued by Mr. Newman, instead of the Bible or the Koran. On the other hand, if that theory be true, and I accept it, his *maxim* must be false, for the very same reason; since he himself will have given me a *double* book-revelation, — a revelation at once of the *theory* and of the *genesis* of religion, both of which are in many respects absolute novelties to my consciousness.

But further; if we take the genesis of religion as described by either of these writers, and consider the infinite corruptions to which they both acknowledge a perverted, imperfect "development" of the "religious sentiment" and the "spiritual faculty" has led, one would imagine that an external communication from heaven might be both very possible and very useful; useful if only by cautioning men against those "false conceptions" which have so uniformly swamped the "idea," and those "degraded types," into which all the various principles of our nature have wheedled the "spiritual faculty." Only listen to a brief specimen of the "byepath meadows" which entice the poor soul from the direct course of its development, and judge whether a communication from heaven, if it were only to the extent of a sign-post by the way side, might not be of use! First comes "awe."—"But even in this early stage," says Mr. Newman, "*numberless* deviations take place, and mark especially the rudest Paganism. We may embrace them under the general name of Fetichism, which here claims attention. . . . But even in the midst of enlightened science, and highly literate ages, errors *fundamentally identical* with those of Fetichism may and do exist, and with the very same results."* Then comes "wonder:" "But of this likewise we find numerous degraded types in which the rising religion is marred. . . . Of this we have eminent instances in the Gods of Greece, and in the fairies of the German and Persian tribes. . . . Under the same head will be included the grotesque devil-stories and other legends of the Middle Ages. . . . Yet the *dreadful alternative* of gross superstition is this, that the graver view tends to cruel and horrible rites, while the fanciful and sportive sucks out the life-blood of devout feeling."† Then comes the "sense of beauty:" "This was strikingly illustrated in Greek sculpture. A statue of exquisite beauty, representing some hero, or an Apollo, *because* of its beauty, seemed to the Greeks a fit object of worship. . . . An *opposite* danger is often remarked to accompany the use of *all* the fine arts as handmaids to religion; namely, that the would-be worshipper is so absorbed in mere beauty as never to rise into devotion."‡ Then comes the

---

* Soul, p. 7. 10.   † Ib. p. 14–16.   ‡ Ib. p. 21. 23.

"sense of order;" but, alas! Atheism and Pantheism, and other "degrading types," may be begotten of it!

As I look at men thus tumbling into error, along this wretched causeway to heaven, I seem to be viewing Addison's bridge of human life, with its broken arches, at each of which thousands are falling through. This way to the "celestial city" ought to be called the "North-West Passage;" it has *one,* and only one trait of your Christian path: there will be "*few* that find it."

If, then, by the confession of these writers, the "false conceptions" and the "degraded types,"—the result of what are as truly "principles" of man's nature as the supposed "spiritual faculty,"—only that this last always has the *worst* in the conflict,—have universally, and for unknown ages, involved man in the darkest abysses of superstition, crime, and misery, surely external revelation is any thing but superfluous; and if impossible, so much the worse.

The same truth is even formally evinced by the self-destructive course which both writers employ; for as the *conditions* of the development of our "spiritual nature," when not complied with, lead to all the deplorable consequences which they acknowledge, how do they propose to rectify them? Why, by "external" culture, proper discipline and training, judicious instruction; by *enlightening* mankind,—as we may suppose they are doing by these hopeful books of theirs! If man can do so much by *his* books, is it *impossible* that a book from God might do something more? But on this I will say nothing, since you tell me that you have heard attentively the conversation I had with my friend Fellowes the other day. I will therefore omit what I had written on this point. . . .

But I proceed to another position, maintained by these writers, on which I confess I am equally sceptical. If they concede (as how can they help it?) that the "religious sentiment" and the "spiritual faculty" have somehow left humanity involved in the most deplorable perplexities and the most humiliating errors, they yet assure us that there is "a good time coming;"—an auspicious "progress" in virtue and religion, *very* gradual indeed, but sure and illimitable for the race collectively! Yes, "progress," that is the word; and a "progress" for the world at large, of which they speak as certainly as if they had received, at least on *that* point, that external revelation, the possibility of which they deny. A matter of spiritual "insight" I presume none will declare it to be, and the data are certainly far too meagre and unsatisfactory to make it *calculation*. Is Saul among the prophets? Yes; but, as usual, the truth (if it *be* a truth) for which they contend, is, as with other parts of their system, a plagiarism from the abjured Bible. Now, if I must believe prophecy, I prefer the magnificent strains of Isaiah to the sentimental prose either of Mr. Parker or of Mr. Newman.

I must modestly doubt whether, apart from the representations of the "books" they abjure as special "revelations," there is any thing in the history of the world which will justify a sober-minded man in coming to any positive conclusion as to this promised "progress," this infidel millenium, either the one way or the other. The chief facts, apart from such special information, would certainly point the other way. Look at the condition of the immense majority of the race in *every* age, so far as we can gather any thing from history,—compare it with that of the immense majority *at the present moment;*—what does it tell us? Why, surely, that if there *be* a destiny of indefinite "progress" in religion and virtue for the race collectively, the hand of the great clock moves so immeasurably slow that it is impossible to note it. The experience of the individual, nay, of recorded history,—if we can say there is any such thing,—fails to trace the movement of the index on the huge dial. If there be this progress for the race *collectively*, it must be accomplished in a cycle vast as those of the geological eras;—a deposit of a millionth of an inch of knowledge and virtue over the whole race in fifty million years or so! Mr. Newman is pleased to say, "Some nations sink, while others rise; but the lower and higher levels are both generally ascending." Has this level *for the whole race* been raised perceptibly within the memory of so-called history?

Observe; I am not denying that the notion *may be* true: I am literally the sceptic I profess to be; I know not — apart from *special* information from a superhuman source — whether it be true or false. I am only venturing to laugh at men, who, denying any such information, affect to speak with any confidence on the solution of this prodigious problem, the data for solving which I contend we have not; while those we *have*, apart from the direct assurance of supposed inspiration, more *plausibly* point to an opposite conclusion. The conclusion which would more *naturally* suggest itself from the history of the past would be that of perpetual advance and perpetual retrogression, *contemporaneously* going on in different portions of the race, — perpetual flux and reflux of the waves of knowledge and science on different shores; though, alas! as to "*religion and virtue*," I fear that these, like the Mediterranean, are almost without their tides. For an intellectual "progress" in the race collectively, far more plausible arguments can be adduced than for a similar religious progress; yet how much might be said that appears to militate even against *that!* Think of the frequent and signal checks to civilisation; its transference from seat to seat; the decay of races once celebrated for knowledge and art; the inundations of barbarism from time to time; — these things alone might make a sober man pause before he predicted for the *entire* race a certain progress even in art and science. Experience would at most justify a philosopher in saying, "Perhaps, yes; perhaps, no." But the argument becomes incomparably more doubtful when we come to "religion," and especially that particular form of it which such writers as Messrs. Parker and Newman believe will be preeminent and universal, towards which consummation it does not appear at present that the smallest conceivable advance has been made; since, with the exception of that infinitesimal party, of which they are among the chief, the immense majority of mankind persist in rejecting the sufficiency of the "internal" oracle, and are still found as strongly convinced as ever both of the possibility and necessity of an "external" revelation, and that, in some shape or other, it has been given! Nay, the facts, so far as we have any, seem all to point the other way; for no sooner had men been put approximately in possession of the pure "spiritual truth," which both Mr. Newman and Mr. Parker suppose to be characteristic in larger measure of Judaism and Christianity than of any other religion, than they busily began the work, not of *improvement*, but of *corruption*. The Jews corrupted their pure monotheistic truths into what these writers believe the fables, legends, miracles, and absurd dogmas of the Old Testament; and, as if *that* were not enough, proceeded to bury them in the huge absurdities of the Rabbinical traditions; the Christians, in like manner, corrupted the yet purer truths, which these writers affirm Christianity teaches, with what they also affirm to be the load of myth, fiction, false history, and monstrous doctrine, which make up nine-tenths of the New Testament; and, as if *that* were not enough, proceeded, just as did the Jews, to "expand" the New Testament itself into the worse than Rabbinical traditions of the Papacy! From approximate "spiritual truth" to the supposed legends and false dogmas of the Pentateuch, from the supposed legends and dogmas of the Pentateuch to the absurdities of the Talmud;—again, from the approximate "spiritual truth" of Christianity to the supposed legends and fanciful doctrines of the New Testament, and from the legends and doctrines of the New Testament to the corruptions of the Papacy;—surely these are queer proofs of a tendency to progress! A tendency to retrogradation is rather indicated. No sooner, it appears, does man proceed to obtain "spiritual truth" *tolerably* pure, as tested by such writers, than he proceeds incontinently to adulterate it! This unhappy and uniform tendency is also a curious comment on the impotence of the internal spiritual oracle, as against the ascendancy of the "historical" and "traditional."

Similar arguments of doubt may be derived from other facts.

Over how many countries did primitive Christianity soon degenerate into such odious idolatry, that even the delusions of the "false prophet" have been considered (like the doom to "labour") as a sort of beneficent curse in comparison! What, again, for ages, was the history of those "Shemitic races," in which, of all "races," was found, according to Mr. Parker, the happiest "religious organisation," by which they *discovered*, earlier than other "races," the great truths of Monotheism? One incessant *bulimia* for idolatry was their master-passion for ages; while for many ages past, as has been remarked by a countryman of Mr. Parker, their "happy religious organisation" has been in deplorable ruins.

I humbly venture, then, once again, to doubt whether any sober-minded man, apart from "special inspiration," can affirm that he has any grounds to utter a word about a "progress" in religion or virtue for the race collectively. But it is easy to see where these writers obtained the notion; they have stolen it from that Bible, which as a special revelation they have abjured.

I cannot help remarking here, that it is a most suspicious circumstance, if there be indeed any universal and sufficient "internal revelation," that these writers find every memorable advance of what *they* deem religious truth in unaccountable connection either with the happy "religious organisation of one race," according to Mr. Parker, or in equally strange connection with the records of "two books" originating among that race, according to Mr. Newman. "The Bible," says the latter, "is pervaded by a sentiment, which is implied every where, viz. *the intimate sympathy of the Pure and Perfect God with the heart of each faithful worshipper.* This is that which is wanting in Greek philosophers, English Deists, German Pantheists, and all formalists. This is that which so often edifies me in Christian writers and speakers when I ever so much disbelieve the letter of their sentences."*

* Phases, p. 188.

It is unaccountably odd that the universal spiritual faculty should act thus capriciously, and equally odd that Mr. Newman does not perceive, that if it were not for the "Bible," his religion would no more have assumed the peculiar cast it has than that of Aristotle or Cicero. Sentiments due to the still active influences of his Christian education he imputes to the direct intuitions of spiritual vision, just as we are apt to confound the original and acquired perceptions of our eyesight. — He is in the condition of one who mistakes a reflected image for the object itself, or a forgotten suggestion of another for an original idea. In the *camera obscura* of his mind, he flatters himself that the coloured forms there traced are the original inscriptions on the walls, forgetful of the little aperture which has let in the light; and not even disturbed by the untoward phenomenon — that the ideas thus contemplated are all upside down.

But, surely, it is natural to ask, — how is it that Greek philosophers, Hindoo sages, Egyptian priests, English Deists, — and men of all other religions, — having always had access to the fountain of natural illumination *within*, have not also had their "Baxters, Leightons, Watts, Doddridges?" that the whole style of thought on this subject is so totally different in them all, by Mr. Newman's own confession? If man possess the "spiritual faculty" attributed to him, — if it be a characteristic of humanity, — it will be surely generally manifested; and even if those disturbing causes — which he and Mr. Parker so plentifully provide, — by which the *genesis* of religion is so unhappily marred, but which, alas! no revelation from without can ever counteract, — prevent its *uniform*, or nearly uniform, display, still its principal indications (partial though they may be every where) ought, at least, to be every where indifferently diffused throughout the race. Its manifestation may be *sporadic*, but it will be in one race as in another; it will not be suspiciously confined to a single race with a peculiarly felicitous "religious organisation," or to "two books" exclusively originating with that favoured race.

For his "spiritual" illumination, it is easy to see Mr.

Newman's exclusive dependence on that Bible which he abjures as a *special* revelation. If it has not been so to mankind, it has at least been so to Mr. Newman. To it he perpetually runs for argument and illustration. Among those who will accept his infidelity, I apprehend there will be few who will not recoil from his representations of spiritual experience, so obviously nothing more than a disguised and mutilated Christianity. They will say that they do not wish the "new cloth sewed on to the old garment;" scarcely a soul amongst them will sympathise with *his* soul's "sorrows," or share *his* soul's "aspirations!"

But however these things may be, I now proceed to what I acknowledge is the most weighty topic of my argument; which is to prove that, if I acquiesce, on Mr. Newman's grounds, in the rejection of the Bible as a special revelation of God, I am compelled on the very *same* principles to go a few steps further, and to express doubts of the exclusively divine original of the *World*, and the administration thereof, just as he does of the divine original of the Bible. If I concede to Mr. Newman, however we may differ as to the moral and spiritual faculties of man, that these are yet the sole and ultimate court of appeal to us; that from our "intuitions" of right and wrong, of "moral and spiritual truth," be they more perfect according to him, or more rudimentary and imperfect according to me, we must form a judgment of the moral bearings of every presumed *external* revelation of God, I cannot do otherwise than reject much of the revelation of God in his presumed *Works* as unworthy of him, just as Mr. Newman does very much in his supposed *Word* as equally unworthy of him. Mr. Newman says, "Only by discerning that God has Virtues, similar in kind to human Virtues, do we know of his truthfulness and his goodness. . . . . The nature of the case implies, that the human mind is competent to sit in moral and spiritual judgment on a professed revelation, and to decide (if the case seems to require it) in the following tone: — 'This doctrine attributes to God that which *we* should all call harsh, cruel, or unjust in man:

it is therefore intrinsically inadmissible; for if God may be (what we should call) *cruel*, he may equally well be (what we should call) a *liar;* and, if so, of what use is his word to us?'"* Similarly Mr. Newman continually affirms, that God reveals himself, when he reveals himself at all, *within*, and not *without;* as he says in his "Phases,"—"Of our moral and spiritual God we know nothing *without*,—every thing *within.* It is *in the spirit* that we meet him, not in the *communications of sense.*" †
If I acquiesce in this judgment, I must apply the reasoning of the above passage to the "external revelation" of God in his *Works*, as well as to that in his *Word;* and the above reasoning will be equally valid, merely substituting one word for the other. We are to *decide*, if the case seem to require it, in the following tone, — " These phenomena — this conduct — implies what *we* should call in man harsh, or cruel, or unjust; it is therefore intrinsically inadmissible as *God's* work or *God's* conduct."

Acting on his principles, Mr. Newman refuses to "depress" his conscience (as he says) to the Bible standard. He affirms, that in many cases the Bible sanctions, and even enjoins, things which shock his moral sense as flagrantly immoral, and he *must* therefore reject them as supposed to be sanctioned by God. He in different places gives instances;— as the supposed approbation of the assassination of Sisera by the wife of Heber, the command to Abraham to sacrifice his son, and the extermination of the Canaanites. Now, whether the Bible represents God, or not, in all these cases as sanctioning the things in question, I shall not be at the pains to inquire, because I am willing to take it for granted that Mr. Newman's representation is perfectly correct. I only think that he ought, in consistency, to have gone a little further. Let him defend, as in perfect harmony with his "intuitions" of right and wrong, the undeniably similar instances which occur in the administration of the universe ; or, if it be found impossible to solve those

---

* Soul, p. 58. † P. 52.

difficulties, let him acknowledge, either that our supposed essential "intuitions" of moral rectitude are not to be trusted, as applicable to the Supreme Being, and that therefore the argument *from* them against the Bible is inconclusive; or, that no such Being exists; or, lastly, that He has conferred upon man an intuitive conception of moral equity and rectitude, — of the just and the unjust, — in most edifying contradiction to his own character and proceedings!

Here Fellowes broke in: —

"If indeed there *be* any such instances; but I think Mr. Newman would reply, that they will be sought for in vain in the 'world,' however plentiful, as I admit they are, in the Bible."

"I know not whether he would deny them or not," said Harrington; "but they are found in great abundance in the world notwithstanding, and this is my difficulty. If Mr. Newman were the creator of the universe, no question none of these contradictions between 'intuitions' within, and stubborn 'facts' without, would be found. He has created a God after his own mind; if he could but have created a universe also after his own mind, we should doubtless have been relieved from all our perplexities. But unhappily we find in it, as I imagine, the very things which so startle Mr. Newman in the scriptural representations of the divine character and proceedings. Is he not, like all other infidels, peculiarly scandalized, that God should have *enjoined* the extermination of the Canaanites? and yet does not God *do* still more startling things every day of our lives, and which appear *less* startling only because we are familiar with them? at least, if we believe that the elements, pestilence, famine, in a word, destruction in all its forms, really fulfil *his* bidding? Is there any difference in the world between the cases, except that the terrible phenomena which we find it impossible to account for, are on an infinitely larger scale, and in duration as ancient as the world? that they have, in fact, been going on for thousands of weary years, and for aught you or I can tell, and as Mr. Newman seems to think probable, for millions of years? Does not a pestilence or a famine send thousands of the guilty and the innocent alike — nay, thousands of those who know not their right hand from their left, to one common destruction? Does not God (if you suppose it his doing) swallow up whole cities by earthquake, or overwhelm them with volcanic fires? I say, is there any difference between the cases, except that the victims are very rarely so wicked as the Canaanites are said to have been, and that God in the one case *himself* does the very things which he commissions men to do in the other? Now, if the *thing* be wrong, I, for one, shall never think it less wrong to do it oneself than to do it by proxy."

"But," said Fellowes, rather warmly, for he felt rather restive at this part of Harrington's discourse, "it is absurd to compare such *sovereign* acts of inexplicable will on the part of God, with his *command* to a being so constituted as man to perform them."

"Absurd be it," said Harrington, "only be so kind as to *show* it to be so, instead of saying so. I maintain that the one class of facts are just as 'inexplicable,' as you call it, as the other, and only appear otherwise because, in the one case, we daily see them, have become accustomed to them, and, what is more than all, cannot deny them, — which last we can so promptly do in the other case; for Moses is not here to contradict us. But I rather think, that a being constituted morally and intellectually like us, who had never known any but a world of happiness, would just as promptly deny that God could ever perform such feats as are daily performed in *this* world! I repeat, that if for some reasons ('inexplicable,' I grant you) God does not mind *doing* such things, he is not likely to hesitate to *enjoin* them; for reasons perhaps equally inexplicable. I say *perhaps*; for, as I compare such an event as the earthquake in Lisbon, or the plague in London, with the extermination of the Canaanites, I solemnly assure you that I find a greater difficulty, as far as my 'intuitions' go, in supposing the former event to have been effected by a *divine* agency than the latter. If we take the Scripture history, we must at least allow, that the race thus doomed had long tried the patience of heaven by their flagrant impiety and unnatural vices; that they had become a centre and a source (as we sometimes see collections of men to be) of moral pestilence, in the vicinage of which it was unsafe for man to dwell; that, as the Scriptures say (whether truly or falsely I do not inquire), they had 'filled up the measure of their iniquities.' Let this be supposed as fictitious as you please, still the whole proceeding is *represented* as a solemn judicial one; and supposing the events to have occurred just as they are narrated, it positively seems to me much less difficult to suppose them to harmonise with the character of a just and even beneficent being than those wholesale butcheries which have desolated the world, in every hour of its long history, without any discrimination whatever of innocence or guilt; which, if they have inflicted unspeakable miseries on the immediate victims, have produced probably as much or more in the agony of the myriad myriads of hearts which have bled or broken in unavailing sorrow over the sufferings they could not relieve. Such things (I speak now only of what man has not in any sense inflicted) are, in your view, as undeniably the work of God as is the extermination of the Canaanites according to the Bible. Why, if God does not mind *doing* such things, are we to suppose that he minds on some occasions ordering them to be *done;* unless we suppose that man — delicate creature! — has more refined intuitions of right and wrong, and knows better what they are than God himself. Now, Mr. Newman and you affirm, that to suppose God should have *enjoined* the destruction of the Canaanites is a contradiction of our moral intuitions; and that for this and similar reasons you cannot believe the Bible to be the *word* of God; I answer, that the things I have mentioned are in still more glaring contradiction to such 'intuitions;' than which none appears to me more clear than this, — that the morally innocent ought not to suffer; and I therefore doubt, whether the above phenomena are the work of God. I must refuse, on the very same principle on which Mr. Newman disallows the Bible to be a true revelation of such a Being, to allow the entire universe to be so. — In equally glaring inconsistency with what appears to me a first principle of moral rectitude, is the entire administration of this lower world, — namely, that he who suffers a wrong to be inflicted on another when *he can prevent* it, is responsible for the wrong itself. The whole world is full of such instances."

"Ay," said Fellowes, eagerly, "we ought to prevent a wrong, provided we have the *right* as well as the *power* to interfere."

"I am supposing that we have the right as well as the power; as, for example, to prevent a man from murdering his neighbour, or a thief from entering his dwelling. There are, no doubt, many acts which, from our very limited right, we should have no business to prevent; as, for example, to prevent a man from getting tipsy at his own table with his own wine. But no such limitation can apply to Him who is supposed to be the Absolute Monarch of the universe; and yet He (according to *your* view) notoriously does not interpose to prevent the daily commission of the most heinous wrongs and cruelties under which the earth has groaned, and hearts have been breaking, for thousands of years. You will say perhaps, that in all such instances we must *believe* that there are some reasons for His conduct, though we cannot guess what they are. Ah! my friend, if you come to *believing*, you may believe also that the difficulties involved in the scriptural representations of the divine character and proceedings are susceptible of a similar solution. If you come to *believing*, I think the Christian can believe as well as you, and rather more consistently. But let me proceed."

He then read on.

It is plain, that, in accordance with our primitive 'moral intuitions' (if we have any), we should hold him who had the power to prevent a wrong and did not use it, as a participator and accomplice in the crime he did not prevent. Applying, therefore, the principles of Mr. Newman, I must refuse to acknowledge such conduct on the part of the Divine Being, and to say, that such things are not done by him. If I may trust my *whisper* of him, derived from *analogous* moral qualities in myself, I must believe that an administration which so ruthlessly permits these things, is not *his* work; but that his power, wisdom, and goodness have been thwarted, baffled, and over-mastered by some 'omnipotent devil,' to use Mr. Newman's expression; if it be his work, then that whisper of him cannot be trusted: the heathen was right, '*Sunt superis sua jura*.' In other words, I feel that I must become an Atheist, a Pantheist, a Manichæan, or—what I am—a *sceptic*.

All these perplexities are increased when I trace them up to that profound mystery in which they all originate,—I mean the permission of physical and moral evil. Either evil could have been prevented or not; if it could, its immense and horrible prevalence is at war with the intuition already referred to; if it could not, who shall prove it? I am no more able to contradict the intuitions of the intellect than those of the conscience; and if anything can be called a contradiction of the former it is to be told that a Being of infinite power, wisdom, and beneficence *could* not construct a world without an immensity of evil in it; no reason being assignable, or even imaginable, for such a proposition, except the fact that such a world has not been created! I am therefore compelled to doubt, whether this entire universe be the fabrication of such a Being. It is impossible to express my astonishment at the ease with which Mr. Newman disposes of the difficulties connected with the origin and perpetuation of physical and moral evil. His arguments are just two of the most hackneyed common-places with which metaphysicians have attempted to evade these stupendous difficulties; and it is not too much to say, that there never was a man who was not resolved that his theory must stand, who pretended to attach any importance to them. They are most gratuitously assumed, and even then are most trivial alleviations; a mere plaister of brown-paper for a deep-seated cancer.

I certainly know of no other man who has stood so unabashed in front of these awful forms. One almost envies him the truly child-like faith with which he waves his hand to these Alps, and says, 'Be ye removed and cast into the sea;' but the feeling is exchanged for another, when he seems to rub his eyes and exclaim, 'Presto, they are gone sure enough!' while you still feel that you stand far within the circumference of their awful shadows.

As to physical evil, Mr. Newman tells us, ' Here it may be *sufficient* to remark, that the difficulty turns on the Epicurean assumption, that physical ease and comfort is the most valuable thing in the universe: but that is not true even with brutes. There is a certain *perfection* in the nature of each, consisting in the full development of all their powers, to which the existing order manifestly tends. . . . As for susceptibility to pain, it is obviously essential to every part of corporeal life, and to discuss the question of *degree* is absurd. On the other hand, human capacity for sorrow is equally necessary to our whole moral nature, and sorrow itself is a most essential process for the perfecting of the soul.'*

This, then, is the fine balm for all the anguish under which the world has been groaning for these thousands of years! But, first, how does suffering tend to the perfection of the whole *lower* creation? It enfeebles, and at last destroys them, I know; but I am yet to learn that it is *essential* to the perfection of animal life. Again, how does it minister to that of man, except he be more than the insect of a day, of which Mr. Newman's theology leaves him in utter doubt? And if he *be* immortal, how does it operate beneficially except as an instrument of moral improvement? And how rarely (comparatively) do we see that it has that effect! How often is it *most* prolonged and torturing in those who seem least to need it, and in those who are absolutely as yet incapable of learning from it; or alas! are too evidently *past* learning from it! How often do we see, slowly sinking under

* Soul, p. 43, 44.

the protracted agonies of consumption, cancer, or stone, all these various classes of mortals, without our being able to assign or even conjecture the slightest reason for such experiments! I acknowledge freely that we can give *no* reasons for them; but it is to mock miserable humanity to give *such* reasons as these; *doubly* to mock it, if men be the ephemeral creatures which Mr. Newman's theology leaves in such doubt; since in that case, we see not only (what we see at *any* rate) that physical evil does not always, nor even in *many* instances, produce a salutary moral effect, but that it hardly matters whether it does or not; for just as the poor patient may be beginning to be benefited by his discipline, and generally in *consequence* of it, he is unluckily annihilated; he dies of his medicine! Surely if physical evil be this grand elixir, never was such a precious balm so improvidently expended. We may well say, only with much more reason, what the Jews said of Mary's box of ointment—'Why was all this waste?'—To be sure it is 'given' in abundance 'to the poor.'

And, at the best, this exquisite reasoning gives no account whatever of that suffering which falls upon innocent infancy and childhood. It *destroys* them, however, and effectually prevents their attaining the 'perfection' which it is so admirable an instrument of developing, and that too before they can be morally benefited by the 'salutary' sorrow it brings!

"Susceptibility to pain," says Mr. Newman, "is essential to corporeal being."

Yes, *susceptibility* to pain; just as a created being must be *liable* to annihilation. *Must* he be annihilated? Just as a hungry stomach must be *liable* to starvation. *Must* it be starved? The primary office of *susceptibilities* to pain would seem to be to forewarn us to provide against it. They certainly *have* that effect. Does it necessarily follow that they must involve anguish and death? Unless it be supposed, indeed, that nature having provided such an admirable apparatus of 'susceptibilities' of pain, thought it a thousand pities that they should not be employed.

But when it comes to 'moral evil,' which Mr. Newman acknowledges cannot be so lightly disposed of, what then?

Why then he says, 'let the Gordian knot be cut.'

Well, what then? Why, then, Mr. Newman frankly 'assumes' that it is 'transitory and finite,'* and will one day vanish from the universe,—a supposition for which he condescends to give no reason whatever.

Stat pro ratione voluntas.

That this 'moral evil' should have existed at all, much more to so immense an extent, under the administration of *supposed* infinite power, wisdom, and benevolence, is the great difficulty; that it will ever cease to be, is a pure assumption for the nonce; but if it will one day entirely vanish, it is gratuitous to suppose it might not have been prevented.

I, of course, acknowledge that we can give no answer to the questions involved in this transcendent mystery—that our ignorance is absolute; but I do say, that if I am to trust to those 'intuitions' of the Divine Goodness, on whose warranty Mr. Newman and Mr. Parker reject the Bible, as containing what is unworthy of their conceptions of God, I am compelled to proceed further in the same direction; and repudiate, as unworthy of him, not merely some of the phenomena of the Book which men profess to be his *word*, but also some of the phenomena of that universe which men profess to be his *work*. If I can only judge, as these gentlemen urge, of such a Being by the analogies of my own nature, no 'intuition' of theirs can possibly *seem* stronger than do mine—that beings absolutely innocent ought not to suffer; that to inflict suffering upon them is injustice; and that to permit any evils which we can prevent is in like manner to be accomplices in the crime. On those very principles of all moral judgment which Mr. Newman says are innate and our only rule, I say I am compelled to these conclusions; for if God does those things which are *ordinarily* attributed to Him, he acts as much in contra-

---

* Soul, p. 45.

vention of these intuitions as in any acts attributed to him in the Bible. If it be said that there *may be reasons* for such apparent violations of rectitude which we cannot fathom, I deny it not; but *that* is to acknowledge that the supposed maxims derived from the analogies of our own being are most deceptive as applied to the Supreme; it is to remit us to an act of absolute faith, by which, with no greater effort, nor so great, we may be reconciled to similar mysteries of the Bible. But, above all, is it to remit us to such an act of faith, to say that the origin and permission of physical and moral evil are inexplicable; while it is to *double* this demand on faith, to declare that it was all *necessary*, and could not be evaded in the construction of the universe even by infinite power, directed by infinite wisdom, and both animated by an infinite benevolence! As far as I can trust my reason at all, nothing seems more improbable; and if I receive it by a transcendent exercise of faith, I may, as before, give the Bible the benefit of a like act. I am compelled, therefore, on such principles, either to adopt a Manichæan hypothesis of the universe, or do — what I have done — adopt none at all.

I was talking to a friend on these subjects the other day: 'Ah! but,' said he, 'many of these difficulties you mention oppress every hypothesis — Christianity just as much as the rest.'

This, I replied, is no answer to *me*, nor to *you*, if you have a particle of candour; still less is it one to the Christian, who consistently applies the *same* principle of absolute faith to things apparently *à priori* incredible, whether found in the works or in the word of God. But if you think the argument of any force, apply it to the next Christian you meet, and see what answer he will make to you; it will not trouble him. But it is far more ridiculous addressed to me. I ask for something in the place of that Bible, of which the faithful application of your own principles deprives me; and when I affirm that the difficulties of the universe are no less than those of the Bible I have surrendered, you tell me that the perplexities of my new position are no greater than those of the old! That clearly will not do —I must go further. If I am to yield to pretensions of any kind, I would infinitely prefer the yoke of the Bible to that of Messrs. Parker and Newman; for it is to nothing else than their dogmatism I must yield, if I admit that the difficulties which compel me to *doubt* in the one case are less than those which compel me to *doubt* in the other.

But it is not even true that the difficulties in question are left where they were by the adoption of any such theory as that of either Mr. Parker or Mr. Newman. I contend that they are all indefinitely increased. The Bible does at least give me a *plausible* account of some of the mysteries which baffle me: it tells me that man was created holy and happy; that he has fallen from his 'excellent estate;' and hence the misery, ignorance, and guilt, in which he is involved, and which have rendered revelation necessary.

But—and it brings me to the last step of my argument—if I accept the theory of the universe propounded by these writers, not only am I left without any such approximate solutions, or, if that be thought too strong a term, without any such alleviations, but all the difficulties, as regards the character, attributes, and administration of God, are increased a thousandfold. The Scripture account of the 'Fall'—however inexplicable it may be that God should have *permitted* such a catastrophe—yet does expressly assert that, somehow or other, it is man's fault, not God's; that man is not in his normal condition, nor in the condition for which he was created. Dark as are the clouds which envelope the Divine Ruler, 'their skirts are tinged with gold,'—pervaded and penetrated throughout their dusky depths by that Mercy which assures us that, in some intelligible sense, this condition of man is contrary to the Divine Will, which, from the first, resolved to remedy it; and that a day is coming when what is mysterious shall be explained—so far, at least, that what has been 'wrong' shall be 'righted.' But what is the theory of the universe propounded by these writers? So hideous (I solemnly declare it) that I feel ten times more compelled to reject the universe as a work of an infinitely gracious, wise, and powerful Creator, than if the difficulties had been simply left where the Bible leaves them. According to their theory, man is now just what he was at first — as he came from his Creator's hand; or rather in some parts of the world (thanks to himself though) a little *better* than he was originally; I must believe that God cast man forth, so constituted by the unhappy mal-admixture of the elements of his nature — with such an inevitable subjection of the 'idea' to the 'conception,' of the 'spiritual faculty' to the 'degraded types' — that for unnumbered ages — for aught we know, myriads of ages — man has been gradually crawling up, a very sloth in 'progress' (poor beast!), from the lowest Fetichism to Polytheism — from Polytheism, in all its infinitude of degrading forms, to imperfect forms of Monotheism; and how small a portion of the race have even imperfectly reached this last term, let the spectacle of the world's religions at the present moment proclaim! From the more imperfect forms of Monotheism, the race is gradually to make 'progress' to something else — heaven knows what! but certainly something still far below the horizon — still concealed in the illimitable future. For this gradual transformation from the veriest religious grub into the spiritual Psyche, man was expressly equipped by the constitution of his nature — he was created this grub! For all this truly geological spiritualism, and for all the infinitude of hideous superstitions and cruel wrongs involved in the course of this precious development, Mr. Parker tells us there was a *necessity* — nothing less! It was *necessary*, no doubt, for his logic, that he should say so; but apart from his own argumentative exigencies, it is impossible even to imagine any necessity whatever. It was an 'ordeal,' it seems, through which man was obliged to pass. What is all this, but to acknowledge the unaccountable nature of the problem?

With this "religious" theory admirably coincides the hypothesis of man's having been originally created a *savage*, from which he was gradually *exalted* to the lowest stages of civilisation — a theory which I thought had (in mere shame) been abandoned to some few Deists of the last century, or the commencement of this. It is true that these writers do not expressly endorse it; but it is easy to see that they favour it; and it is most certain that it alone is consistent with their parallel theory of man's 'religious development' from the vilest Fetichism to (shall we say?) a mythical Christianity; though even to that very few have yet arrived. I say the originally 'savage state of man' is the necessary complement of this theory, according to which the Great Father — supposed a Being of infinite power, wisdom, and goodness — threw his miserable offspring on the face of the earth, with an admirable 'absolute religion' no doubt, and an admirable 'spiritual-faculty,' but the 'idea' so inevitably subject to thwarting 'conceptions,' and the 'spiritual-faculty' so perpetually debauched by 'awe and reverence,' and the whole rabble of emotions and affections with which it was to keep company — in fact, with the elements of his nature originally so ill-poised and compounded—that every where and for unnumbered ages man has been doomed and necessitated, and for unnumbered ages *will* be doomed and necessitated, to wallow in the most hideous, degrading, cruel forms of superstition,—inflicting and suffering reciprocally all the dreadful evils and wrongs which are entailed by them. For this, then, man was *created;* such a thing he was — through this 'ordeal' he passes — by original destination. If *this* be the picture of the Father of All, he is less kind to *his* offspring than the most intimate 'intuitions' teach them to be to theirs. The voice of nature teaches them not to expose their children; the universal Father, according to this theory, remorselessly exposed his! Such a God, projected by the 'spiritual faculties' of Mr. Newman and Mr. Parker, may be imagined to be a more worthy object of worship than the 'God of the Bible:' he shall never receive mine. If I am to abjure the Bible because it gives me unworthy conceptions of the Deity, I must, with more reason, abjure, on similar grounds, such a detestable theory of man's creation, destination, and history.

As to that 'progress' which is promised for the *future*, it is like the necessity for the *past*, purely an invention of Mr. Parker; if I receive it, I must receive it simply as matter of prophecy. If the *necessity* has continued so long, then, for aught I know, it may continue for ever; the evil is all too certain — the bright futurity is still a futurity. But if it ever became a reality, it would not neutralise one of the dark imputations which such a theory of the original destination and creation of man casts on the Divine character; not to say, that if Mr. Newman's doubts of man's immortality be well founded, that better future will be of no more avail to the myriads of our race who have suffered under the long iron *régime* of *necessity*, than a reprieve to the wretch who was executed yesterday!

I told Harrington I must have a copy of the paper he had just read. I should like, with his leave, to publish it!

"O, and welcome," said he. "Only remember that its *tendency* is to show that there is no tenable resting-place between a revealed religion and none at all; between the Bible and scepticism. If you make men sceptics, — mind, it is not my fault."

"I will take the risk," said I. "I *wish* the controversy to be brought to the issue you have mentioned. I *know* there will never be many sceptics, any more than there will be many atheists; and if men are convinced that the *Via Media* is as hard to find as you suppose — or as that between Romanism and Protestantism — they will take refuge in the BIBLE. And if it be the BOOK OF GOD indeed, this is the issue to which the great controversy *will* and ought to come. But how is it you were not tempted to become an atheist rather than a sceptic?"

"Why," said he, with a smile, "the great master of the *Modern Academy* had fortified me against *that*.

·Hume, you know, confesses that if men be discovered without any impressions of a Deity — genuine atheists — we may assume that they will be found the most degraded of the species, and only one remove above the brutes. Now I have no wish to be set down in that category."

"Very different," said I, "is the account our modern atheists give of themselves: they are contending that the banishment of God from the universe, by one or other of the various theories of Atheism or Pantheism (which I take to be the same thing, with different names), is the tendency of all modern science, and, that when that science is perfect, God will be no more."

"My dear uncle," replied Harrington, "you are insufficiently informed in the mysteries of modern theology. There *are* no atheists, properly speaking; they who are so called *merely* deny any personal, conscious, intelligent sovereign of the universe. Even those who *call themselves* so, and will have it that they *are* so, are told that they are none. I myself have perused statements of some of our modern 'spiritualists,' who knew every thing, even other people's consciousness, quite as well as their own (and perhaps better), that the said atheists are mistaken in thinking themselves such; that such genuine love of the spirit of universal nature is something truly divine, and that they are animated by 'a deeply religious spirit,' though they never suspected it!"

"Well," said I, "if you had too much *reason*, as you flattered yourself (adopting Hume's criterion), to become an atheist, could you not have adopted such views as those of Mr. G. Atkinson and Miss Martineau, who both possess surely (as they claim to possess) that 'religious reverence' of nature of which you have just spoken?"

"Why," he replied, "I am afraid that if I had too much *reason* for the one, I have not *faith* enough for the other. That the miracles and prophecies of the Bible may possibly have been true — only the effect of *mesmerism;* — that things quite as wonderful, or more so, happen every day by this wonderful agent; — that every phenomenon that takes place does so in virtue of a perfectly wise LAW — without any wise LAWGIVER; — that this *wise law* has, it seems, *prearranged* that man should generally exhibit an inveterate tendency to religious systems of some kind, though all religions are absurd, and persist in believing in his free will, though free will is a downright impossibility; — that these contradictions and absurdities of man are the result of an *irreversible necessity*, and yet that Mr. Atkinson may hope to *correct* them; — that by the same necessity, man is in no degree culpable or responsible, and yet that Mr. Atkinson may perpetually blame him; — that no man *can* do any thing 'wrong,' and yet that till he believes *that*, man will never *cease* to do it; — that people may read without their eyes, and distinguish colours as *colours* though they are born blind; — that Bacon was an atheist, and that this may be proved by *induction* from his own writings; — these and other paradoxes, which I must believe, if I believe Mr. Atkinson, require a faith which it would really be unreasonable to expect from such a sceptic as I am."

July 18*th*. Till three days ago, nothing since my last date has occurred having any special relation to the sole object of this journal. I was glad to escape on the 13th to a quiet church some miles off, and, after a plain and simple, but earnest, sermon from a venerable clergyman (of whom I should like to know a little more), I further refreshed my spirit by a long and solitary ramble of some hours through the beautiful scenery in the midst of which Harrington's dwelling is situated. In the course of it I reviewed my own early conflicts, and augured from them happier days for my beloved nephew. I went carefully over all the main points of the argument for and against the truth of Christianity which in youth had so often occupied me, and resolved that on some fair opportunity I would recount my story to him and Mr. Fellowes. I little thought then that I should have a larger and very miscellaneous audience to listen to me. But this will account for my not being to *seek* (as they say) when the occasion presented itself.

Three days ago (the 15th) a queer company assembled in Harrington's quiet house. The conversations and incidents connected with that day have led me to take refuge for the last two mornings in the solitude of my own chamber, that I might, undisturbed, recall and record them with as much accuracy and fulness as possible. Very much, indeed, that I wished to remember has vanished; but the substance of what too many said, as well as what I said myself, made too deep an impression to be easily obliterated.

Be it known to you, my dear brother, that I have been not a little amused, I may even say instructed, by a trick played by your madcap nephew, for the honour and glory, I suppose, of his scepticism, or from some other motive not easily divined. He promised me significantly an entertainment, in which I should enjoy the "feast of *reason* and the flow of *soul*," by which I little thought that he was going to collect a rare party of "Rationalists" and "Spiritualists," — in fact, representatives of all the more prominent forms, whether of belief or unbelief. I may as well call it the

Sceptic's Select Party.

You remember, I doubt not, the humorous paper in the Spectator, in which Addison introduces the whimsical nobleman who used to invite to his table parties of men (strangers to one another), all characterised by some similar personal defect or infirmity. On one occasion, twelve wooden-legged men found themselves stumping into his dining-room, one after another, and making, of course, a terrible clatter; on another, twelve guests, who all had the misfortune to squint, amused their host with their ludicrous cross lights; and on a third, the same number of stutterers entertained him still more, not only by their uncouth impediment, but by the anger with which they began to sputter at one another, on the supposition that each was mocking his neighbour. A shorthand writer, behind the scenes, was employed to take down the conversation, which says the witty essayist, was easily done, inasmuch as one of the gentlemen was a quarter of an hour in saying "that the ducks and green peas were very good," and another almost an equal time in assenting to it. At the conclusion, however, the derided guests became aware of the trick their entertainer had played upon them; and from their hands, quicker than their tongues, he was obliged to make a precipitate retreat. Our dinner party of yesterday did not break up in any such *fracas,* nor was the conversation so unhappily restricted. Yet the company was hardly better assorted. To bring it together, Harrington ransacked his immediate circle, and Fellowes unconsciously *recruited* for him in the university town. Our host had provided for our mutual edification an Italian gentleman with whom he had had some pleasant intercourse on the Continent (by the way, he spoke English uncommonly well), and now staying with a Roman Catholic in the neighbourhood; this latter gentleman himself, with whom Harrington, by means of his former friend, has knocked up an acquaintance (he is a liberal Catholic of the true British species); our acquaintance, Fellowes, with his love of "insight" and "spiritualism;" a young surgeon from ———, a rare, perhaps unique, specimen of conversion to certain crude atheistical speculations of Mr. Atkinson and Miss Martineau; a young Englishman (an acquaintance of Harrington's), just fresh from Germany, after sundry semesters at Bonn and Tübingen, five hundred fathoms deep in German philosophy, and who hardly came once to the surface during the whole entertainment; three Rationalists (acquaintances of Fellowes), standing at somewhat different points in the spiritual thermometer, one a devoted advocate of Strauss: add to these a Deist, no unworthy representative of the old English school; one or two others further gone still; a Roman Catholic priest, an admirer of Father Newman, who therefore believes every thing; our sceptical friend Harrington, who believes nothing; and myself, still fool enough to believe the Bible to be "divine," and you will acknowledge that a more curious party never sat down to edify one another with their absurdities and contradictions.

Questionable as was the entertainment for the mind, that for the body was unexceptionable. The dinner was excellent; our host performed his duties with admirable tact and grace; and somehow speedily put everybody at his ease. Relieved, according to the judicious modern mode, of the care of supplying the plates of his guests, he had eye, ear, and tongue for every one, and leisure to direct the conversation into what channel he pleased. He took care to turn it for some time on indifferent topics; and each man lost his reserve and his frigidity almost before he was aware; so that by the time dinner was fairly over every one was ready for animated conversation. If any one began to have queer suspicions of his neighbours, he felt, as on board ship, that he was *in* for it, and bound, by common politeness, to make the best of it.

The Deist, addressing himself to the Italian gentleman, asked him if he had heard lately from Italy. He replied in the negative.

"I can tell you some news then," said he. "They say that the head of the illustrious Guicciardini family has been just imprisoned at Florence, having been detected reading in Diodati's Bible a chapter in the Gospel of St. John. Supposing the fact true, for a moment, may I ask if it would be the wish of the Roman Catholic Church, were she to regain her power in England, to imprison every one who was found reading a chapter in John? If so, England would have to enlarge her prisons."

"Not much," said one of the Rationalist gentlemen, laughing; "for if things go on as they have done, there will not, in a few years, be many who will be found reading a chapter in John."

"Perhaps so," said Harrington, smiling, "but, if for the reason *you* would assign, few will be found in church either; and the ecclesiastical authorities might perhaps put you in prison for that instead."

"Oh! I will answer for *him*," said the Deist, who

knew something of his plasticity; "our friend is ver[y] accommodating, and though he would not *like* to go t[o] church, he would still less like to go to prison. And t[o] church he would go; and look very devout into th[e] bargain. But, however, I should like to hear what you[r] Italian guest has to say to my question."

The impatience of the English Catholic could not b[e] repressed.

"If," said he, "the Roman Catholic religion were t[o] regain its ascendancy to-morrow, it would leave our entire code of laws, our liberties and privileges, just as it found them; it is one of the many calumnies with which our Church is continually treated, to say that she would act otherwise; and were it not so I would immediately desert her."

The Catholic priest did not look well pleased with this frank avowal.

"I quite believe you," said our host. "I believe you are too much of an Englishman to say or to act otherwise."

"So do I," said the Deist; "I moreover agree with you that if the Roman Catholic religion were to regain her ascendancy to-morrow, she would leave all our privileges intact; but would she the next day, and the day after that? In other words, is it an essential principle with her to persecute, — as in this instance, to imprison for peeping between the leaves of the Bible, — or is it not? Do you think, Signor, that in such acts the principles of your *church* are complied with or violated?"

The Italian gentleman looked perplexed; he presumed that the Catholic Church complied with the actual laws of every country; and if such country chose to deny religious liberty, the church did not deem it requisite to declare opposition.

"I fear that is no answer to my question," cried the other, a little cavalierly. "It cannot serve you, Signor. It would not, indeed, serve you any where; for we know the anxiety with which Rome has expressly secured, in her recent concordat with Spain, the recognition of the most intolerant maxims. But least can it serve you in the papal states, where, unluckily for your observation, the Pope is *monarch*. Your remark would imply that your Church favoured the principles of religious liberty rather than otherwise, but did not deem it right to *oppose* the will of civil governments. Are we to understand by that, that the chief of the papal states abhors as a pope what he does as a sovereign? That in the one capacity he protests against what he allows in the other? No, no," continued this somewhat brusque assailant, "it is too late to talk in that way. If the Church of Rome really approve of religious liberty — of such principles as those which govern England — where are her protests and her efforts against intolerance and persecution where she still retains power? It is the least that humanity can expect of her. If not, let her plainly say that when she regains power in England she will *reform* us to the condition of Spain and Italy in this matter. For my part, I frankly acknowledge that I have more respect for a Roman Catholic who proclaims that it *is* inconsistent for his church to *tolerate* where it has the power to *repress;* because I see that that is her uniform practice, and therefore ought to be her avowed maxim."

The Roman Catholic Priest, who is a devoted admirer of Father Newman, said that he thought so too; and quoted some candid recent admissions to that effect from certain English Roman Catholic periodicals. "To employ," said he, " the very words of a recent convert to us from the Anglican Church, 'The Church of Rome may say, I *cannot* tolerate you; it is inconsistent with my principles; but you can tolerate me, for it is not inconsistent with yours.'"

The Deist remarked that it was straightforward; that he admired it; "though as an *argument*," said he, "it is much as if a robber should say to an honest man on the king's highway, 'How advantageously I am situated! You *cannot* rob me, for it is inconsistent with your principles; but I *can* rob you, for I have none.'"

Another of the company observed that he feared it was in vain for the Church of Rome to contend that she was favourable to freedom of opinion, in any degree or form, so long as the "Index Expurgatorius" was in existence, or such stringent means adopted to repress the circulation and perusal of the Scriptures.

The liberal English Catholic again chafed at this last indictment. "It was," he said, "another of the calumnies with which his church was treated."

"Hardly a calumny, my good Sir," replied the other, "in the face of such facts as that which gave rise to the present conversation, of the encyclical letters of Pius VII., Leo XII., of Gregory XVI., and many other Popes, and the well-known fact that it is impossible to obtain in Rome itself a copy of the Scriptures, except at an enormous price, and even then it must be read by special license. Pardon me," he continued, still addressing the English Catholic, "I mean nothing offensive to you; but neither I nor any other English Protestant can consent to admit you sincerely liberal English Roman Catholics to be in a condition to give us the requisite information touching the maxims and principles of your church. You have been too long accustomed to enjoy and revere religious liberty not to imagine your church sympathises with it; you do not realise what she is abroad; and if you be sincere in condemning such acts as that which led to this conversation, as inconsistent with her genuine principles, *why* the ominous silence of you and your co-religionists in all such cases? Where are your protests and efforts? How is it you do not denounce maxims and practices so rife throughout Papal Christendom, since you say you would denounce them, if it were attempted to realise them here? When you protest with one voice against these things as inconsistent (so you say) with the principles of your *Church*, and as therefore deeply dishonouring her — whether your views on this point be right or wrong — we shall at least admit you to have a title to give us an opinion on the subject."

"Even then, though," said the Deist, "we may still think it *safer* to consult the opinions and, what is more, the practices, of the vast majority of the Roman Catholic

Church, and her conduct in the countries in which she holds undisputed sway, and therefore I am anxious to hear whether the Signor would justify imprisonment for reading the Bible."

Our host seemed to think that the conversation had proceeded in this direction quite far enough; and, lest his foreign guest should be made uncomfortable by these close inquiries, observed, sarcastically, that he was glad to find that the querists were so anxious to secure the inestimable privilege of freely reading the Scriptures. "It is the more admirable," said he to the last speaker, "as I am aware it is most disinterested; you having too little value for the Scriptures to read them yourself. *Sic vos non vobis:* you labour for others. You remind me of the colloquy in the 'Citizen of the World' between the debtor in gaol and the soldier outside his prison window. They were discussing, you recollect, the chances of a French invasion. 'For my part,' cries the prisoner, 'the greatest of my apprehensions is for our freedom; if the French should conquer, what would become of English liberty?' 'It is not so much our liberties,' says the soldier, with a profane oath, 'as our religion, that would suffer by such a change; ay, our religion, my lads!'"

The company laughed, and the assailants forgot the former topics. Our host went on further to encourage his foreign guest, though in a left-handed way, with a gravity which, if I had not known him, would not only have staggered but even imposed upon me.

"For my part," said he, "my good Sir, if I were you, I should not hesitate to acknowledge at once that it is not only the true *policy*, but the solemn *duty*, of the Church of Rome to seclude as much as possible the Scriptures from the people." The gentleman looked gratified, and the guests were all attention. "In my judgment much more can be said on behalf of the practice than at first appears; and if I sincerely believed all *you* do, I should certainly advocate the most stringent measures of repression."

The foreigner began to look quite at his ease. "For

example," continued Harrington, in a very quiet tone, "supposing I believed as *you* do, that the Holy Virgin is entitled to all the honours which you pay her, so that, as is well known, in Italy and other countries, she even eclipses her son, and is more eagerly and fondly worshipped, — it would be impossible for me to peruse the meagre accounts given in the New Testament of this so prominent an object of Catholic reverence and worship — to read the brief, frigid, not to say *harsh* speeches of Christ — to contemplate the stolidity of the Apostles with regard to her throughout their Epistles — never even mentioning her name, — I say it would be impossible for me to read all this without having the idea suggested that it was never intended that I should pay her such homage as you demand for her, or without feeling suspicious that the New Testament disowned it and knew nothing of it."

"Very true," said the Italian; "I must say I have often felt that there is such a danger myself."

"Similarly, what a shock would it perpetually be to my deep reverence for the spiritual head of the church, and my conviction of his undoubted inheritance, from the Prince of the Apostles, of his august prerogatives, to find no trace of such a personage as the Pope in the sacred page, — the title of 'Bishop of Rome,' never whispered — no hint given that Peter was ever even there! — I really think it would be impossible to read the book without feeling my flesh creep and my heart full of doubt. Similarly, take that stupendous mystery of 'transubstantiation;' though it *seems* sufficiently asserted in one text, which therefore it were well (as is, indeed, the practice with every pious Catholic) continually to quote *alone*, yet when I look into other portions of the New Testament, I see how perpetually Christ is employing metaphors equally strong, without any such mystery being attached to them. I cannot but feel that I and every other vulgar reader would be sure to be exposed to the peril of suspecting that in that single case a metaphorical meaning was much more probable than so great a mystery."

" You reason fairly, my dear Sir," said the Italian.

" Again," continued Harrington, blandly bowing to the compliment, " believing, as I should, in the efficacy of the intercessions of the saints, in the worship of images, in seven sacraments, in indulgences, and the necessity of observing a ritual incomparably more elaborate than an undeveloped Christianity admitted, how very, *very* apt I should be to misinterpret many passages, both in the Old Testament and the New! How is it possible that the vulgar reader should be able to limit the command not to bow down ' to *any* graven image' to its true meaning — that is, ' to any image' except those of the Virgin and all the saints; to interpret aright the passages which speak so absolutely about the *one* Mediator and Intercessor, when there are thousands; how will he be necessarily startled to find 'seven' sacraments grown out of ' two;' how will he be shocked at the apparent — of course *only* apparent — contempt with which St. Paul speaks of ritual and ceremonial matters; of the futility of ' fasts' and distinctions of ' meats and drinks,' of observing ' days and months and years,' and so on. His whole language, I' contend, would necessarily mislead the simple into heresies innumerable. Of numberless texts, again, even if the meaning were not mistaken, the *true* meaning would never be discovered unless the Church had declared it. Who, for example, would have supposed that the doctrine of the Pope's supremacy and universal jurisdiction lay hid under expressions such as, ' I say unto thee that thou art Peter,' and ' Feed my sheep;' or that the two swords of the Prince of the Apostles meant the temporal and spiritual authority with which he was invested? Under such circumstances, I must say, that if I were a devout Catholic, I should plead for the absolute suppression of a book so infinitely likely — nay, so necessarily certain — to mislead."

" It is precisely on that ground," said the Italian, " and on that ground only, the welfare of the Church, that our Holy Mother does not approve of the Bible being read generally. The true theory of the Roman Catholic Church would never be elicited from it."

"Precisely so," said our host gravely; "I am sure it could not."

"But then," remarked our friend, the Deist, "since the Church of Rome holds this book to be the inspired revelation of God to mankind, is it not singular to say that this 'revelation' requires to be carefully *concealed* from mankind; that the Bible is invaluable, indeed, but only while it is unread; and that, in fact, the Church knows herself better than Jesus Christ himself did? for in that book we are supposed to have the words of Him and her founders, and yet it seems they *could* only mislead! 'Never man spake like this man,' may well be said of Christ, if this were true."

"Never mind him, Signor," said our host. "He secretly cannot but approve of your *end*, though he disapproves the *means*." The Deist looked surprised.

"Why, have you not sometimes said that you believe the Bible to be, in many respects, a most pernicious book? that many of the most obstinate and dangerous prejudices of mankind are principally due to it? and that you wish it were in your power to *destroy* it?"

"Well, I certainly have thought so, if not said so."

"Then you approve of the *end*, though you disapprove of the *means*. You ought to *thank* our friend here, and regret that his work is not done more effectually. But enough of this. I must not have my respected Roman Catholic guests alone put on the defensive. The Signor fairly tells us what his system is in relation to the Bible, and why he would place it under lock and key; he tells you also what better thing he substitutes when he removes the Bible. I really think it is but fair and candid in you to do as much. I know you all believe not only that you are in quest of religious truth, but that you have found it to some extent or other:—for my own part I am exempted from speaking; for I have given over the search in despair."

This frank acknowledgment was followed by some

highly curious conversation, of which I regret my inability to recall all the particulars. Suffice it to say, that there were not two who were agreed either as to the *grounds* on which Christianity was deemed a thing of nought, or on what was to be substituted in its place; one even had his doubts whether any thing *need* be substituted, and another thought that any thing *might* be. One of the Rationalists was a little offended at being supposed willing to 'abandon' the Bible at all; he declared on the contrary, his unfeigned reverence for the New Testament at least, as containing, in larger mass and purer ore than any other book in the world, the principles of *ethical* truth; he was willing even to admit — with exquisite *naïveté* — that it was inspired in the same sense in which Plato's dialogues and the Koran were inspired; he merely dispensed with all that was supernatural and miraculous and mystical! The Deist laughed, and told him that he believed just as much, if *that* constituted a Christian. "I believe," said he, "that the New Testament is quite as much inspired as the Koran of Mahomet; and that it contains more of ethical truth (however it came there) than is to be found in any other book of equal bulk. But," he proceeded, "if you dispense with all that is miraculous in the facts, and all that is peculiar and characteristic in the doctrines — that is, all which discriminates Christianity from any *other* religion, I am afraid that your Christianity is own born brother to my Infidelity. As for your reverence for this inspired book, since you must reject ninety per cent. of the whole, it seems to me very gratuitous; equally so, whether you suppose the compilers *believed* or *disbelieved* the facts and doctrines you reject; if the former, and they were deceived, they must have been inspired idiots; if the latter, and were deceiving others, they were surely inspired knaves. For my part," he continued, "while I hold that the book somehow does unaccountably contain more of the morally true and beautiful than any book of equal extent, I also hold that Christianity itself is a pure imposture from beginning to end."

This coarse avowal of adherence to the elder, and,

after all, more intelligible deism, brought down upon him at once two of the company. One was the disciple of Strauss (I mean as regards his theory of the origin of Christianity, not as regards his Pantheism); the other a Rationalist, with about the same small tatters of Christianity fluttering about him; but who was a little disposed, like so many German theologians, to consider Strauss as somewhat *passé*. Unhappily, they got athwart each other's bows shortly after they came into action. They both enlarged — really in a very edifying manner, I could have listened to them for an hour — on the absurdity of the Deist's argument. "What!" cried one; "the purest system of ethics from the most shameless impostors!" "And what do you make of the infinitely varied and inimitable marks of simplicity and honesty in the writers?" cried the other. "And who does not see the impossibility of getting up the miracles so as to impose upon a world of bitter and prejudiced enemies in open day?" exclaimed the Rationalist. "They were obviously mere myths," cried the Straussian. "*That* I must beg to doubt," said the other. — And now, as they proceeded to give each his own solution of the difficulty, the scene became comic in the extreme. The Rationalist ridiculed the notion that nations and races, all of whom, in the nature of things, must have been prejudiced against such myths as those of Christianity, *could* originate or *would* believe them; and still more the notion, that in so short a space of time these wildest of wild legends (if legends at all) could induce the world to acquiesce in them as historic realities! In his zeal, he even said that, though not altogether satisfied with it, he would sooner believe all the frigid glosses by which the school of Paulus had endeavoured to resolve the miracles into misunderstood 'natural phenomena.' As the dispute became more animated between these three champions, they exhibited a delicate trait of human nature, which I saw our sceptical host most maliciously enjoyed. Each became more anxious to prove that his *mode* of proving Christianity false was the *true* mode, than to prove the falsehood of Christianity itself. "I tell you what," said the Straussian, with some warmth, "sooner than believe all the absurdities of such an hypothesis as that of Paulus, I could believe Christianity to be what it professes to be." "I may say the same of that of Strauss," said the other, with equal asperity; "if I had no better escape than his, I could say to him, as Agrippa to Paul, 'Almost thou persuadest me to be a Christian.'" "For my part," exclaimed the Deist, who was perfectly contented with his brief solution — the difficulties of the problem he had never had the patience to master — "I should rather say, as *Festus* to Paul, 'Much learning has made you *both* mad:' and sooner than believe the impossibilities of the theory of either, — sooner than suppose men *honestly* and *guilelessly* to have misled the world by a book which you and I admit to be a tissue of fables, legends, and mystical nonsense, — I could almost find it in my heart to go over to the Pope himself."

"Good," whispered our host to me, who sat at his left hand; "we shall have them all becoming Christians, by and by, just to spite one another." — The admirer of Mr. Atkinson and Miss Martineau here reminded the company that the miracles of the New Testament *might* be true, — only the result of mesmerism. "Christ," said he, "to employ the words of Mr. Atkinson, was constitutionally a *clairvoyant*. . . . . . . Prophecy, and miracle, and inspiration, are the effects of *abnormal* conditions of man. . . . . Prophecy, clairvoyance, healing by touch, visions, dreams, revelations, . . . are *now known* to be simple matters in nature, which may be induced at will, and experimented upon at our firesides, here in England (climate and other circumstances permitting), as well as in the Holy Land."* But no one seemed prepared to receive this hypothesis. At last our host, addressing the Deist, said, "But you forget, Mr. M., that though you find it insurmountably difficult to conceive a book full of lies (as you express it) to have been, consciously or un-

---

* He cited the substance of these sentiments. I have since referred to, and here quote, the *ipsissima verba.*—See 'Letters, &c.,' pp. 175, 212.

consciously the product of honest and guileless minds, you ought also to find it a little difficult to conceive a book (as you admit the New Testament to be) of profound moral worth, produced by shameless impostors. But let that pass. Let us assume that Christianity, as a supernaturally revealed and miraculously authenticated system, is false, though you are dolefully at variance as to how it is to be proved so; let us assume, I say, that this system *is* false, and dismiss it. I am much more anxious to hear what is the positive system of religious truth, which you are of course each persuaded is the true one. I have left off to 'seek,' but if any one will find the truth for me without my 'seeking' it, how rejoiced shall I be!"

Painful as were the "revelations" which ensued, I would not have missed them on any account. "In vino veritas," says the proverb, which on this occasion lied most vilely; yet it was true in the only sense in which "*veritas*" is there used; for there was unbounded candour and frankness, under the inspiring hospitality of our host, aided by his skilful management of the conversation. Nor was there, I am bound to say, much of coarse ribaldry, even from the free-spoken representative of the Tindals and Woolstons of other days. But the varieties of judgment and opinion in that small company were almost numberless. Fellowes, and two of the Rationalists, were firm believers in the theory of "insight;" that the human spirit derives, by immediate intuition from the "depths" of its consciousness, a "revelation of religious and spiritual truth." They differed, however, as to several articles; but especially as to the little point, whether the fact of man's future existence was amongst the intimations of man's religious nature; one contending that it was, another that it was not, and Fellowes, as usual, with several more of the company, declaring that *their* consciousness told them nothing about the matter either way. But when some one further declared, amidst these very disputes, that this internal revelation was so clear and plain as not only to anticipate and supersede any "external" revelation, but to render it "impossible" to be given, our host suddenly broke out into a fit of laughter. The disputants were silent, and every one looked to him for an explanation. He seemed to feel that it was due, and after apologising for his rudeness, said that while some of them were asserting man's clear internal revelation, he could not help thinking of the whimsical contrast presented by the diversified speculations and opinions of even this little party, and the infinitely more whimsical contrast presented by the gross delusions of polytheism and superstition, which in such endless variations of form and unchanging identity of folly have misled the nations of the earth for so many thousands of years. "And just then," said he, "it occurred to me, what a curious commentary it would be on the asserted unity and sufficiency of 'internal revelation,' if the 'Great Exhibition of the *Industry* of all Nations' were followed up by a 'Great Exhibition of the *Idolatry* of all Nations' under the same roof. Thither might be brought specimens of the ingenious handicraft of men in the manufacture of deities: we might have the whole process, in all its varieties, complete; the raw material of a God in a block of stone or wood, and the most finished specimen in the shape of a Phidian Jupiter; the countless bits of trumpery which Fetichism has ever consecrated; the divine monsters of ancient Egypt, and the equally divine monsters of modern India; the infinite array of grim deformities hallowed by American, Asiatic, and African superstition. I imagined, notwithstanding the vastness of that Crystal Pantheon, there would still be crowds of their godships who would be obliged to wait outside, having come too late to exhibit their perfections to advantage. However, as I went in fancy up the long aisles, and saw, to the right and the left, the admiring crowds of worshippers, grimacing, and mowing, and prostrating themselves, with a folly which might lead one reasonably to suppose, that miserable as were the gods, they were gods indeed compared with such worshippers, I imagined my worthy friend Fellowes in the corner where the Bible, in its 120 languages, is now kept, employed in delivering a lecture on the admirable clearness of those intuitions of spiritual truth which constitute each man's particular oracle, and the superfluity of all 'external' revelation. This was, I confess, a little too much for my gravity, and I was involuntarily guilty of the rudeness for which I now apologise." It was certainly a ridiculous vision enough; and we made ourselves very merry by pursuing it for a little while.

Presently the company resumed their solutions of the great problem. The Deist remarked, "that *one* and only *one* thing was plain, and indubitable,"—for he was a dogmatist in his way;—it was, "that intellect and power to an indefinite extent had been at work in the universe, but whether the Being to whom these attributes belonged took any cognizance of man, or his actions, he had never been able to make up his mind." "Yet surely it *does* make a slight difference," said Harrington, "since if God takes no cognizance of man, then, as Cicero long ago remarked of the idle dogs of Epicurus,—I mean gods of Epicurus, I beg their pardon,—but really it does not matter *which* consonant comes first,—atheism and deism are much the same thing." "Why," said the Deist, "there is as much difference as in the theories of our 'intuitional' friends here, one of whom admits, and another denies, the future existence of man; for if we be the ephemeral insects the latter supposes, it little matters *what* system of religion we espouse or abjure. However, I am clear that *if* God require any duty of us, it is that we should *reverence* him as the Creator of all things,—prayer to him is an absurdity,—and perform those offices of honest men which are so clearly the dictates of conscience,—the reward and punishment being exclusively the result of present *laws*."

"Which laws," said his next neighbour, "often secure no reward or punishment at all,—or rather, often give the reward to the vice of man, and the punishment to his virtue." "Very true," rejoined the Deist, "and I must say,"—sagely shaking his head,—"that such things make me often suspect the whole of that slippery, uncertain thing called 'natural religion,' whether as taught by the elder deists or modified by our modern spiritualists. Surely they may be abundantly charged with the same faults with which they tax the Christian; for they are full of interminable disputes about the 'truths' or 'sentiments' of their theology."

One of those who had gone further than our Deist, felt disposed to question all '*immutable* morality' and original 'dictates of conscience.' "I doubt," said he, "whether those dictates are any clearer than those dogmas of 'natural religion' which have been so justly oppugned; and I judge so for the same reason; the endless disputes of men with regard to the source, — the rule, — the obligation of what they call duty; and which are exactly similar to the disputes which we charge upon the Natural Religionist and the Christian." And here he ran through half a dozen of the two score theories which the history of Ethics presents, making rare work with Plato and Aristotle, Hobbes, Cudworth, Mandeville, and Bentham. "Meantime," he concluded, "we do see, in point of fact, that the moral rule is most *flexible*, and to an *indeterminate* degree the creature of association, custom, and education; so that I am inclined to think that that alone is obligatory which the positive laws and institutions of any society render binding." "So that," cried Harrington, "a man both may and ought to thieve in ancient Sparta, may expose his parents in Hindostan, and commit infanticide in China!" "It is a pity," archly whispered the Italian guest, "that this gentleman was not born in China."

"It is a respectable, but very old, speculation," said Harrington, "of which many ancient moralists avowed themselves the advocates, but of which it is only fair to admit that Plato and many other heathens were heartily ashamed."

It seemed as if the bathos of theological and ethical absurdity could not lie deeper; but I was mistaken. The admirer of Mr. Atkinson declared with great modesty that he thought, as did his favourite author, that the whole world had been *mad* on the subject of theology and morality;—that the prime error consisted in the superficial notion of a Personal Deity, and the foolish attribution of the notion of "sin" and "crime" to human motives and conduct, instead of regarding the former as a name of an absolutely unknown cause of the entire phenomena of the universe, and the latter as part of a series of rigidly necessary antecedents and consequents, for which man is no more to be either blamed or praised than the sun for shining or the avalanche for falling; he added that only in this way could man attain peace. "As Mr. Atkinson beautifully says, 'What a hopeful and calming influence has such a contemplation of nature! At this moment it is not I, but the nature within me, that dictates my speech and guides my pen. I am what I am. I cannot alter my will, or be other than what I am, and cannot deserve either reward or punishment.' But I feel with him, 'We may preach these things, and men may think us mad, or something worse.'" *

"And perhaps justly," said Harrington, with a laugh, "for Nature has surely, after so many thousands of years, let you know what her *law* is, and you say that that law is necessary and irreversible, and yet you strive to alter it! You had better leave men to their *necessary* absurdities."

"Nay," said the other, "as Mr. Atkinson says, from the recognition of a universal law we shall develope a universal love; the disposition and ability to love without offence or ill-feeling towards any; or, as Miss Martineau represents it,—When the mind has completely surmounted every idea of a personal God, of a supreme will, 'what repose begins to pervade the mind! What clearness of *moral purpose* naturally ensues! and what healthful activity of the *moral faculties!* † . . . What a new perception we obtain of the "beauty of holiness" —the loveliness of a healthful moral condition—accordant with the laws of nature, and not with the requisitions of theology!'" ‡

* P. 190, 191.   † P. 219.   ‡ P. 219.

I got him afterwards to show me these passages, for I could hardly believe that he had quoted them right.

"And as for morality," continued he, "the knowledge which mesmerism gives of the influence of body on body, and consequently of mind on mind, will bring about a morality we have not yet dreamed of. And who shall disguise his nature and his acts when we cannot be sure at any moment that we are free from the *clairvoyant* eye of some one who is observing our actions and most secret thoughts; and our whole character and history may be read off at any moment?" *

What an admirable substitute, thought I, for the idea of an omnipresent and omniscient Deity! Who will not abstain from lying and stealing when he thinks there is possibly some *clairvoyant* at the antipodes in mesmeric *rapport* with his own spirit, and perhaps, by the way, in very sympathising *rapport*, if the *clairvoyant* happen to be in Australia?

It was at this point that our young friend from Germany broke in. "I hold that you are right, Sir," he said to the last speaker, "in saying that God is not a *Person*; but then it is because, as Hegel says, he is *Personality itself*—the universal personality which realises itself in each human consciousness, as a separate thought of the one eternal mind. Our *idea* of the absolute is the absolute itself; apart from and out of the universe, therefore, there is no God."

"I think we may grant you that," said Harrington, laughing.

"Nor," continued the other, "is there any God apart from the universal consciousness of man. He——"

"Ought you not to say *it?*" said Harrington.

"*It*, then," said our student, "is the entire process of thought combining in itself the objective movement in nature with the logical subjective, and realising itself in the spiritual totality of humanity. He (or it, if you will) is the eternal movement of the universal ever raising itself to a subject, which first of all in the subject

---

* H. G. A. to H. M., p. 280.

comes to objectivity and a real consistence, and accordingly absorbs the subject in its abstract individuality. God is, therefore, not a person, but personality itself."

Nobody answered, for nobody understood.

"Q. E. D.," said Harrington, with the utmost gravity.

Thus encouraged, our student was going on to show how much more *clear* Hegel's views are than those of Schelling. "The only real existence," he said, "is the relation; subject and object which seem contradictory are really one—not one in the sense of Schelling, as opposite poles of the same absolute existence, but one as the *relation* itself forms the very *idea*. Not but what in the threefold rhythm of universal existence there are affinities with the three potencies of Schelling; but——"

"Take a glass of wine," said Harrington to his young acquaintance, "take a glass of wine, as the Antiquary said to Sir Arthur Wardour, when he was trying to cough up the barbarous names of his Pictish ancestors, 'and wash down that bead-roll of unbaptized jargon which would choke a dog.'"

We laughed, for we could not help it.

Our young student looked offended, and muttered something about the inaptitude of the English for a deep theosophy and philosophy.

"It is all very well," said he, "Mr. Harrington; but it is not in this way that the profound questions which, under some aspects, have divided such minds as Fichte, Schelling, and Hegel; and under others, Göschel, Hinrichs, Erdmann, Marheineke, Schallar, Gabler——"

Harrington burst out laughing. "They divide a good many philosophers of that last name in England also," said he.

"Why, what have I said?" replied the other, looking surprised and vexed.

"Nothing at all," said Harrington, still laughing. "Nothing that I know of; I am sure I may with truth affirm it. But I beg your pardon for laughing; only I could not help it at finding you, like so many other young philosophers born of German theology and philosophy, attempting to frighten me by a mere roll-call of formidable names. Why, my friend, it is because these things have, as you say, divided these great minds so hopelessly that I am in difficulty; if the philosophers had *agreed* about them, it would have been another story. One would think, to hear them invoked by many a youth here, that these powerful minds had *convinced* one another; instead of that they have simply *confounded* one another. It was the very spectacle of their interminable disputes and distractions in philosophy and theology—ever darker and darker, deeper and deeper, as system after system chased each other away, like the clouds they resemble through a winter sky;—I say it was the very spectacle of their distractions which first made me a sceptic; and I think I am hardly likely to be reconvinced by the mere sound of their names, ushered in by vague professions of profound admiration of their profundity! The praise is often oddly justified by citing something or other, which, obscure enough in the original, is absolute darkness when translated into English; and must, like some versions I have seen of the Classics, be examined in the original in order to gain a glimpse of its meaning."

The student acknowledged that there was certainly much vague admiration and pretension amongst young Englishmen in this matter; but thought that profounder views were to be gathered from these sources than was generally acknowledged.

"Very well," replied Harrington; "I do not deny it—perhaps it is so; and whenever you choose to justify that opinion by expressing in intelligible English the special views of the special author you think thus worthy of attention, whether he be from Germany or Timbuctoo, I humbly venture to say that I will (so far from laughing) examine them with as much patience as yourself. But if you wish to cure me of laughing, I beseech you to refrain from all vague appeals to wholesale authority.

"The most ludicrous circumstance, however," he continued, " connected with this German mania is, that in many cases our admiring countrymen are too late in changing their metaphysical fashions; so that they sometimes take up with rapture a man whom the Germans are just beginning to cast aside. Our servile imitators live on the crumbs that fall from the German table, or run off with a well-picked bone to their kennel as if it were a treasure, and growl and show their teeth to any one that approaches them, in very superfluous terror of being deprived of it. It would be well if they were to imitate the importers of Parisian fashions, and let us know what is the philosophy or theology *à la mode*, that we may not run a chance of appearing perfect frights in the estimate even of the Germans themselves."

Coffee was here brought in; and Harrington said, "Thank you, gentlemen, for your candour, though your unanimity does not seem very admirable. In one sentiment, indeed, you are pretty well agreed—that the Bible is to be discarded, though you are infinitely at variance as to the *grounds* on which you think so; our Catholic friends deeming it too precious to be intrusted to every body's hands, and the rest of you, as a gift not worth receiving. But as to the systems you would substitute in its place, they are so portentously various that they are hardly likely to cure *me* of my scepticism; nor even my worthy relative here"—pointing to me—"of his old-fashioned orthodoxy. He will say, 'Much as we theologians differ as to the interpretation of Scripture, our differences are neither so great nor so formidable as those of these gentlemen. I had better remain where I am.'"

Several of the guests stared at me as they would at the remains of a *megatherium*.

"Is it possible," said one at last, "that you, Sir, can retain a belief in the divine inspiration of the Bible—excluding incidental errors of transcription, and so on?"

"It is not only possible," said I, "but certain."

"Do you mean," said the other, "that you can give satisfactory answers to the objections which can be brought against various parts of it?"

"By no means," said I; "while I think that many may be *wholly* solved, and more, partially, I admit there are some which are altogether insoluble."

"Then why in the name of wonder do you retain your belief?"

"Because I think that the evidence for retaining it is, on the whole, stronger than the evidence for relinquishing it: that is, that the objections to admitting the objections are stronger than the objections themselves."

"But how do you manage in a controversy with an opponent as to those insoluble objections?"

"I admit them."

"Then you allow his position to be more tenable and reasonable than yours?"

"No," said I; "I take care of *that*."

"How so?"

"I transfer the war, my good Sir; a practice which I would recommend to most Christians in these days. When I meet with an opponent of the stamp you refer to — who thinks insoluble objections *alone* are sufficient reasons for rejecting any thing, I say to him, 'My friend, this Christianity, if so clearly false, is not worth talking about: let us quit it. But as you admit with me, that religious truth is of great moment, and as you think you have it, pray oblige me by your system.' To tell you the truth, I never found any difficulty in propounding plenty of insoluble objections; but if you think differently, you or any gentleman present can make experiment of the matter now."

"Nay, my dear uncle," said Harrington, "you are invading my province. It is I only who can consistently challege all comers; like the ancient Scythians, I have every thing to gain and nothing to lose."

Whether it was out of respect for the host, or that each felt, after the recent disclosures, that he would not only have Harrington and myself, but every body else, *down* upon him, nobody accepted his challenge.

At last one of them said, he could not even yet comprehend how it was that I could remain an old-fashioned believer in these days of 'progress?' "It was infidelity itself," I replied, "that early robbed me of the advantages of being an infidel."

Several expressed their surprise, and I told them that after we had taken tea in the drawing-room (to which we were then summoned) I would, if they felt any curiosity upon the matter, and would allow a little scope to the garrulity of an old man, tell them

How it was that Infidelity prevented my becoming an Infidel.

After tea I gave my story, as nearly as I can recollect, in the following way. Of course, I cannot recall the precise words; but the order of the *thoughts*, — how often have they been pondered! — I cannot be mistaken about.

It is now thirty years ago or more since I was passing through many of the mental conflicts in which I see so many of the young in the present day involved. I have no doubt that the majority of them will come out, probably after an *eclipse* more or less partial, very orthodox Christians — so great are the revolutions of opinion which an experience of human life and the necessities of the human heart work upon us! As I look around me I see few of my youthful contemporaries who have not survived their infidelity.

Far be it from me — (I spoke in a tone which, I imagine, they hardly knew whether to take as compliment or irony) — to affirm that the infidels of this day are like those I knew in my youth. I have no hesitation in saying of *us* that a perfectly natural recoil — partly intellectual and partly moral — from the *supernatural* history, the *peculiar* doctrines, but, above all, the severe *morality* of the New Testament, was at the bottom of our unbelief. I have long felt that the reception of that book on the part of any human being is not the least of its proofs that it is divine; for I am persuaded there never was a book naturally more repulsive either to the human head or heart. *All the prejudices* of man are necessarily arrayed against it. *I* felt these prejudices, I am now distinctly conscious; nor was I insensible to the palpable *advantages* of infidelity;—its accommodating morality; its large margin for the passions and appetites; its *doubts* of any future world, or its *certainty* that, if there were one, it would prove a universal paradise (for *doubts* and *certainties* are equally within the compass of human *wishes*); the absolute abolition of hell, and every thing like it. I say I saw clearly enough the *advantages* which infidelity promised, and I acknowledge I was not insensible to them. I think no young men are likely to be.

I do not insinuate that similar advantages have any thing to do with those many peculiar *revelations* of religion which different oracles have in our day substituted for the New Testament. The arguments *against* Christianity, indeed, I do not find much altered; the substitutions for it, though, as before, distractingly various, are, I confess, in some respects different. Nay, we see that many of our 'spiritualists' complain chiefly of the' moral and spiritual *deficiencies* of Christianity; they are afraid, with Mr. Newman, of the conscience of man being DEPRESSED to the Bible standard! So that we must suppose that the aims of some, at least, of our infidel reformers are prompted by a loftier ideal of 'spiritual' purity than Christianity presents!

It certainly was not so *then;* I felicitate some of you, gentlemen, on being so much holier and wiser, not only than we were, but even than Christ and his Apostles.

I have said I was not insensible to the *advantages* of infidelity; but nature had endowed me with prudence as well as passions: and I wanted evidence for what appeared to me its most gratuitous philosophy of the future—for its too uncertain doubts of *all* futurity, or its too doubtful certainty of none but a happy one! I also wanted evidence of the falsehood of Christianity itself. As to the former, I shall not trouble you with my difficulties; there were indeed then, as now, an admirable variety of theories; but if I could have been convinced of the futility of the claims of Christianity, I believe I should have been easily satisfied as to a substitute; or rather, unable to decide between Chubb and

Bolingbroke, Voltaire and Rousseau, I should most likely have *tossed up* for my religion.

It was the distractions with regard to the evidences of Christianity that ruined me; and at last *condemned* me to be a Christian.

I was first troubled, like so many in our day, about the *miracles*. I could hardly bring my mind to believe them. One day, talking with a jovial fellow whom I casually met (not of very strong mind indeed, but who made up for it by very strong passions) over the improbability of such occurrences, he exclaimed, as he mixed his third glass of brandy and water, 'I only wonder how any one can be such a fool as to believe in any stuff of that sort! Do you think that if the miracles had been really wrought, there *could* have been any doubters of Christianity?' He tossed off the brandy and water with a triumphant air; and I quite forgot his argument in compassion for his bestiality. I expostulated with him. 'You may spare your breath, Mr. Solomon,' said he, 'May this be my poison (as it *will* be my poison),' mixing a fourth glass, 'if I need any sermons on the subject. Hark ye—I am *perfectly* convinced that the habit I am chained to will be the destruction of health—of reputation—of my slender means—will reduce to beggary and starvation my wife and children—and yet,' drinking again, 'I know I shall never leave it off.'

'Good heavens!' said I. 'Why you seem as plainly convinced of the infatuation of your conduct as if a miracle had been wrought to convince you of it.'

'I am,' he said, unthinkingly; 'ten thousand miracles could not make it plainer; so you may "spare your breath to cool your porridge," and preach to one who is not already in the condemned cell.'

I was exceedingly shocked; but I thought within myself,—It appears then that man may act against convictions, as strong as any that a miracle could produce. It is clear there are no LIMITS to the perversity with which a depraved will and passions can overrule evidence, even where it is *admitted* by the reason to be *invincible*. It does not follow, then, that a miracle (which cannot present conclusions more clear) *must* triumph over them. If the passions can defy the understanding where it coolly acknowledges they cannot pervert the evidence, how much more easily may they *cajole* it to suggest doubts of the evidence itself! And what more easy than in relation to miracles? Such a phenomenon might from novelty produce a transient impression; but that would pass away, just as the vivid feelings sometimes excited by a sudden escape from death pass away; the half-roused debauchee resumes his old career, just as if he had never looked over the brink of eternity and shuddered with horror as he gazed. He who had *seen* a miracle, might, very soon, and probably would, if he did not *like* the doctrine it was to confirm, persuade himself that it was an illusion of his senses, for they *have* deceived him; unless indeed he saw a new miracle every day, and then he would be certain to get *used* to it. How much more easily could the Jews do this, who both hated the doctrine of Him who taught, and, not thinking miracles impossible, could conveniently refer them to Beelzebub!

I felt therefore that the brandy and water logic had perfectly convinced me that this was far too precarious ground on which to conclude that the miracles of the New Testament had never been wrought.

I was further confirmed in my convictions of the illogical nature of all *à priori* views on the subject, by the whimsical differences of opinion among my infidel friends.

One told me that it was plain that miracles were " incredible" and " impossible," *per se:* but he was immediately contradicted by a second, who said that he really could not see any thing incredible or impossible about them; that all that was wanting to make them credible was *sufficient* evidence, which perhaps had in no case been given.

A third said, that it was of little consequence; that no miracle could prove a moral truth; and, taking a view diametrically opposite to that of my first acquaintance, swore that if he saw a score of miracles, he should not be a bit the more inclined to believe in the *authority* of a religion authenticated by them.

Here was a fine beginning for an ingenuous neophyte, who was eager to be fully initiated in infidel theology!

It set me to examine the miracles themselves, and the evidence for them.

"They were the simple result of fraud practising upon simplicity," said one of the genuine descendants of Bolingbroke and Tindal.

I pondered over it a great deal. At last I said one day to another infidel acquaintance, "You ask me to believe that the miraculous events of the New Testament were contrivances of fraud; which, though ventured upon in the very eyes of those who were interested in detecting them, who *must* have been prejudiced against them, nay the majority of whom (as the events show) were determined, whether they detected them or not, not to believe those who wrought them, were yet successfully practised, not only on the deluded disciples of the impostors, but on their unbelieving persecutors, who admitted them to be miracles, only of Beelzebub's performing. I really know not how to believe it. As I look at the general history of religion, I see that this open-day appeal to miracles—especially such as raising the dead—among prejudiced spectators interested in unmasking them, is, if unsupported by truth, just the thing under which a religious enterprise inevitably fails."

I reminded him that the French prophets in England got on pretty well till their unlucky attempt to raise the dead, when the bubble burst instantly; that for this reason the more astute impostors have refrained from any pretensions of the kind, from Mahomet downwards;* that the miracles they professed to have wrought were conveniently wrought in *secret*, on the safe theatre of their mental consciousness; or that they were reserved for times when their disciples were pre-determined to believe them, because they were cordial believers already

---

* How discreetly cautious again have the Mormonites been on this point!

in the religion which appealed to them! I said nothing of the unlikelihood of the instruments — Galilean Jews — whom the theory invests with such superhuman powers of deception; or of the prodigious intellect and lofty ambition with which it also so liberally endows these obscure vagabonds, who not only conceived, in spite of their narrow-hearted Jewish bigotry, such a system as Christianity, but proclaimed their audacious resolve of establishing it on the ruins of every other religion — Jewish or Heathen; I said nothing of the still stranger moral attributes with which it invests them (in spite of their being such odious tricksters, in spite of all their grovelling notions and exclusive prejudices) as the teachers of a singularly elevated and catholic morality; what is still stranger, as suffering for it — strangest of all, as apparently practising it; I said nothing of what is still more wonderful, their acting this inconsistent part from motives we cannot assign, or even imagine; their encountering obloquy, persecution, death in the prosecution of their object, whatever it was; I said nothing of the innumerable, and one would think inimitable, traits of nature and sincerity in the narrative of those who record these miracles, and which, if simulated by such liars, would be almost a miracle itself; a narrative in which majestic indifference to human criticism is every where exhibited; in which are no apologies for the extraordinary stories told; no attempt to conciliate prejudice; no embellishment; no invectives (as Pascal says) against the persecutors of Christ himself; — they are simple witnesses, and nothing more, and are seemingly indifferent whether men despise them or not. I repeat, I said nothing of all these paradoxes; I insisted that the mere *fact* of the successful machination of false miracles, of *such* a nature, at so many points, in open day, in defiance of every motive and prejudice which must have prompted the world to unmask the cheat; of a conspiracy successfully prosecuted, not by *one*, but by *many* conspirators, whose fortitude, obstinacy, and circumspection, both when acting together and acting alone, never allowed them to betray themselves, was, *per se*, incredible; 'and yet,' said I to my friend, 'you ask me to believe it?'

"*I* ask you to believe it?" cried he, in surprise which equalled my own. "I am not fool enough to ask you to believe any thing of the kind; and they are fools who do. The miracles fraudulent machinations! no, no; it was, as you say, evidently impossible. And where shall we look for marks of simplicity and truthfulness, if not in the records which contain them? The fact is," said he (I should mention that it was just about the time that the system of "naturalism" was culminating under the auspices of Paulus of Heidelberg, from whom, at second hand, my infidel friend borrowed as much as he wanted); "The fact is, that the compilers of the New Testament were pious, simple-minded, excellent enthusiasts, who sincerely, but not the less falsely, mistook *natural* phenomena for *supernatural* miracles. What more easy than to suppose people dead when they were not, and who were merely recovered from a swoon or trance? than to imagine the blind, deaf, or dumb, to be miraculously healed, when in fact they were cured by medical skill? than to fancy the blaze of a flambeau to be a star, and to shape thunder into articulate speech, and so on? Christ was no miracle-worker, but he was a capital doctor."

I pondered over this "*natural*" explanation for a long time. At last I ventured to express to a third infidel friend my dissatisfaction with it. "Not only," said I, "is such a perpetual and felicitous genius for gross blundering, such absolute craziness of credulity, in strange contrast with the intellectual and moral elevation which the New Testament writers every where evince, and especially in the conception of that Ideal of Excellence which even those who reject all that is supernatural in Christianity acknowledge to be so sublime a masterpiece;—in whose discourses, the most admirable ethics are illustrated, and in whose life they are still more divinely dramatised;—not only is such ludicrous madness of fanaticism at variance with the tone of sobriety and simplicity every where traceable; but,—what is more—

when I reflect on the *number* and *grossness* of these supposed illusions, I find it hard to imagine how even *one* individual could have been honestly stupid enough to be beguiled by them; and utterly impossible to suppose that a *number* of men should on many occasions have been *simultaneously* thus befooled! But, what is much more, how can those who must often have *managed* the phenomena which were thus misinterpreted into miracles — how, especially, can the great Physician himself, who knew that he was only playing the Doctor, be supposed *honestly* to have allowed the simple-minded followers to persist in so strange an error? Either he, or they, or both, *must*, one would think, have been guilty of the grossest frauds. But the mere number and simultaneity of such strange illusions, under such a variety of circumstances, render it impossible to receive this hypothesis. I cannot see, I said, that it is so *very* easy for a *number* of men to have been continually mistaking 'flambeaux' for 'stars,' 'thunder' for 'human speech,' and 'Roman soldiers' for 'angels?'"

My friend laughed outright. "I should think it is *not* easy, indeed!" he exclaimed, "especially that last. For my part, *I* see clearly on this theory that either the Apostles *or* their commentators were the most crazy, addle-headed wretches in the world. Either Paulus of Tarsus or Paulus of Heidelberg was certainly *cracked: I* believe the last. No, my friend; depend upon it that the Gospels consist of a number of *fictions* — many of them very beautiful — invented, I am inclined to believe, for a very pious purpose, by highly imaginative minds."

This set me thinking again. And, in time, my doubts, as usual, assumed a determinate shape, and I hastened to another oracle of infidelity in hopes of a solution.

If the New Testament be supposed a series of fictions, I argued, — the work of highly imaginative minds for a pious purpose, — there is, perhaps, a slight *moral* anomaly in the case (but I do not insist upon it): I mean that of supposing pious men writing fictions which they evidently *wish* to impose on the world as simple history, and which they must have known would, if received at all, be actually regarded as such; as, *in fact*, they have been. I do not *quite* understand how pious men should thus endeavour to cheat men into virtue, nor inculcate sanctity and truth through the medium of deliberate fraud and falsehood. But let that pass; perhaps one could forgive it. Other anomalies, far more inexplicable, strike me. That Galilean Jews (such as the history of the time represents them), with all their national and inveterate prejudices,—wedded not more to the law of Moses than to their own corruptions of it, bigoted and exclusive beyond all the nations that ever existed, eaten up with the most beggarly superstitions,—should rise to the moral grandeur, the nobility of sentiment, the catholicity of spirit which characterise the Gospel, and, above all, to such an ideal as Jesus Christ,—this is a moral anomaly, which is to me incomprehensible; the improbability of Christianity having its *natural* origin in such a source is properly measured by the hatred of the Jews against it, both then, and through all time. I said I could as little understand the *intellectual* anomalies of such a theory. Could men, among the most ignorant of a nation sunk in that gross and puerile superstition of which the New Testament itself presents a true picture, and which is reflected in the Jewish literature of that age, and ever since; a nation, whose master minds then, and ever since (think of that!) have given us only such stuff as fills the Talmud;—could such men, I said, have created *such* fictions as those of the New Testament— reached such elevated sentiments, or conveyed them in such perfectly original forms; embodied truth so sublime in a style so simple? Throughout those writings there is a peculiar tone which belongs to no other compositions of man. While the individuality of the writers is not lost, there are still peculiarities which pervade the whole, and have, as I think, justly been called a Scripture *style*. One of their most striking characteristics, by the way, is a severely simple *taste;* a uniform freedom from the vulgarities of conception, the exaggerated sentiment, the mawkish nonsense and twaddle which disfigure such an infinitude of volumes of religious biography and fiction which have been written since. Could *such* men attain this uniform elevation? Could *such* men have *invented* those extraordinary fictions—the miracles and the parables? Could they, in spite of their gross ignorance, have so interwoven the fictitious and the historical as to make the fiction *let into* the history seem a natural part of it? Could they, above all, have conceived the daring, but glorious, project of embodying and dramatising the ideal of the system they inculcated in the person of Christ? And yet they have succeeded, though choosing to attempt the wonderful task in a life full of unearthly incidents, which they have somehow wrought into an exquisite harmony! But even if one such man in such an age and nation could have been found equal to all this, could we, I argued, believe that several (with undeniable individual varieties of manner) were capable of working into the picture similarly unique, but different materials, with similar success, and of reproducing the same portrait, in varying posture and attitude, of the great Moral Ideal? Could we believe that in achieving this task, not one, but several, were intellectual magicians enough to solve that great problem of producing compositions in a form independent of language — of laying on colours which do not fade by time; in so much that while Homer, Shakspeare, Milton, suffer grievous wrong the moment their thoughts are transfused into another tongue, these men have written in such a way that their wonderful narrative naturally adapts itself to every dialect under heaven?

These intellectual anomalies, I confessed — if these had been all — staggered me. As Lord Bacon said that he would sooner believe 'all the fables of the Talmud than that this universal frame was without a mind,' so I affirmed I could sooner believe all those fables, than that minds that can *only* produce Talmuds should have conceived such *fictions* as the Gospels. I said I could as soon believe that some dull chronicler of the middle ages composed Shakspeare's Plays, or that a ploughman had written Paradise Lost; only that, to parallel the present case, we ought to believe that *four* ploughmen wrote *four* Paradise Losts! Nay, I said, I would as soon believe that most laughable theory of learned folly, that the monks of the middle ages compiled all the classics. Nor could it help me to say that it was *Christians*, not *Jews*, who compiled the New Testament; for they must have been Jews before they were Christians; and the twofold moral and intellectual problem comes back upon our hands, — to imagine how the *Jewish* mind could have given birth to the *ideas* of Christianity, or have embodied them in such a surpassing form. And as to the intellectual part of the difficulty, — unhappily abundant proof exists in *Christian* literature that the early Christians could as little have manufactured such fictions as the Jews themselves! The New Testament is not more different from the writings of Jews, or superior to them, than it is different from the writings of the Fathers and superior to *them*. It stands alone like the peak of Teneriffe. The Alps amidst the flats of Holland would not present a greater contrast than the New Testament and the Fathers. And the further we come down, the less capable morally, and nearly as incapable intellectually, do the rapidly degenerating Christians appear of producing such a *fiction* as the New Testament; so that if it be asked whether it was not possible that some Christians of after times might have *forged* these books, one must say with Paley, that they *could* not.

And, by the by, gentlemen, said I (interrupting my narrative, and addressing the present company), I may remind some of you who are great admirers of Professor Newman, that he admits (as indeed all must, who have had an opportunity of comparing them) the infinite inferiority of the Fathers, though he does not attempt to account, as surely he *ought*, for so singular a circumstance. He says in his Phases, "on the whole, this reading [of the Apostolical Fathers] greatly exalted my sense of the unapproachable greatness of the New Testament. The moral chasm between it and the very earliest Christian writers seemed to me so vast, as only to be accounted for by the doctrine . . . . . . that the New

Testament was dictated by the immediate action of the Holy Spirit."*

But to resume the statement of my early difficulties. I said I felt that the anomalies involved in the theory of the *fictitious* origin of the New Testament were almost endless; that, however hard to believe that any men, much less such men as Jews of that age, were capable of such achievements as I had already specified, I must, if I received this theory, believe much more still; for the men, with all their wisdom, were fools enough to make their enterprise infinitely more hazardous—by entrusting the execution of it to a league of many minds, thus multiplying indefinitely their chances of contradiction; by adopting every kind and style of composition, full of reciprocal allusions; and, above all, by dove-tailing their fabrications into *true history*, thus encountering a perpetual danger of collision between the two; all as if to accumulate upon their task every difficulty which ingenuity could devise! *Could* I believe that such men as those to whom history restricts the problem, had been able, while thus giving every advantage to the detection of imposture, to invent a narrative so infinitely varied in form and style, composed by so many different hands, traversing in such diversified ways, contemporary characters and events, involving names of places, dates, and numberless specialities of circumstance, and yet maintain a general harmony of so peculiar a kind—such a *callida junctura* of these most heterogeneous materials, as to have imposed on the bulk of readers in all ages an impression of their heartless truth and innocence, and that they were writing *facts*, and not fictions? Above all, could they be capable of fabricating those deeply-latent coincidences, which, if fraud employed them, overreached fraud itself; lying so deep as to be undiscovered for nearly eighteen centuries, and only recently attracting the attention of the world in consequence of the objections of infidels themselves? We know familiarly enough, that to sustain any verisimi-

* Phases. p. 25.

litude in a fictitious history (even though only *one* man has the manufacture of it), is almost impossible, because the relations of *fact* that must be anticipated and provided against are so infinitely various, that the writer is certain to betray himself. The constant detection of very limited fabrications of a similar nature, when evidence is sifted in a court of justice, shows us the impossibility of weaving a plausible texture of this kind. Many things are sure to have been forgotten which *ought* to have been remembered. If this be the case, even where *one* mind has the fabrication of the whole, how much more would it be the case if many minds were engaged in the conspiracy? Should we not expect, at the very least, the hesitating, suspicious, self-betraying tone usual in all such cases? Could we expect that general air of truth which so undeniably prevails throughout the New Testament—the inimitable tone of nature, earnestness, and frank sincerity, which, in the case of such extravagant forgeries, would alone be marvellous traits? But, at all events, could we expect those minute coincidences, which lay too deep for the eye of all ordinary readers, and would never have been discovered had not infidelity provoked Paley and others to excavate those subterranean galleries in which they are found?

And here again I interrupted my narrative to remark, that Professor Newman acknowledges the force of these coincidences, and, as usual, gives *no account* of them; does not *attempt* to account for them. He says of the Horæ-Paulinæ, in his " Phases," ' This book greatly enlarged my mind as to the resources of historical criticism. Previously my sole idea of criticism was that of the direct discernment of style; but I now began to understand what powerful argument rose out of combinations; and the very complete establishment which this work gives to the narrative concerning Paul in the latter half of the Acts, appeared to me to reflect critical honour on the whole New Testament.' *

But once more to resume my statement. Upon men-

---

* Phases, p. 23.

tioning these and such like considerations to my infidel friend, who pleaded that the New Testament was *fiction*, he replied, "As to the *harmony* in these fictions—if they be such—you must acknowledge that it is not absolute: there are discrepancies."

Yes, I said, there are discrepancies, I admit; and I was about to mention that as another difficulty in the way of my reception of this theory: I refer to the nature and the limits of those discrepancies. If there had been an *absolute* harmony, even to the minutest point, I am persuaded that on the principles of evidence in all such cases, many would have charged collusion on the writers, and have felt that it was a corroboration of the theory of the *fictitious* origin of these compositions. But as the case stands, the discrepancies, if the compositions be fictitious indeed, are only a proof that these men attained a still more wonderful skill in aping verisimilitude than if there had been no discrepancies at all. They have left in the historic portions of their narrative an air of general harmony, with an exquisite congruity in points which lie deep below the surface,—a congruity which they must be supposed to have known would astonish the world when once discovered; and have at the same time left certain discrepancies on the surface (which criticism would be sure to point out), as if for the very purpose of affording guarantees and vouchers against the suspicion of collusion! The discords increase the harmony. Once more,—I asked could I believe *Jews*, Jews in the reign of Tiberius or Nero, equal to all these wonders?

But all this, even all this, I said, was as *nothing* compared with another difficulty involved in this theory. How came these fictions, containing such monstrous romance, if romance at all, and equally monstrous doctrines, to be *believed;* to be believed by multitudes of Jews and Gentiles, both opposed and equally opposed to them by previous inveterate superstition and prejudice? How came so many men of such different races and nations of mankind to hasten to unclothe themselves of all their previous beliefs in order to adopt these fantastical fables? How came they to persist in regarding them as authoritative truth? How came so many in so many different countries to do this *at once?* Nay, I added with a laugh, I think there are distinct traces, as far as we have any evidence, that these very peculiar fictions must have been believed by many *before* they were even compiled and published.

My infidel friend mused, and at last said, " I agree with you that these compositions could not have been fictions in the *ordinary* sense—that is, deliberately composed by a conspiracy of highly imaginative minds. That last argument alone, of their *success,* is conclusive against *that;* but may they not have been legends which gradually assumed this form out of floating traditions and previous popular and national prepossessions?" In short, he faintly sketched a notion somewhat similar to that mythic theory, since so elaborately wrought out by Strauss.

I answered somewhat as follows: In the first place, on this hypothesis, all the intellectual and moral anomalies of the last theory reappear. That such legends should have been the product of the Jewish mind (whether designedly or undesignedly, consciously or unconsciously, makes no difference) is one of the principal difficulties. If it had been objected to Père Hardouin, that 'Virgil's Æneid' could not have been composed by one of the monks of the middle ages, I suppose that it would have been no relief from the difficulties of his hypothesis, to say that it was a gradual, unconsciously formed *deposit of the monkish mind!*—But besides all this, I said the theory was loaded with other absurdities especially its own; for we must then believe all the indications of historic *plausibility,* to which I had adverted in speaking of the previous theory, to be the work of *accident;* a supposition, if possible, still more inconceivable than that some super-human genius for fiction had been employed on their elaboration. Things moulder into *rubbish,* but they do not moulder into *fabrics.* And then (I continued) the greatest difficulty, as before, reappears—how came these queer legends, the product whether of design or accident, to be *believed?* Jews and Gentiles were and must have been thoroughly opposed to them.

To this he replied, " I suppose the belief, as *you* also do, anterior to the *books,* which express that belief, but did not cause it. I suppose the Christian system already existing as a floating vapour, and merely condensed into the written form. It was a gradual formation like the Greek and Indian mythologies." I thought on this for some time, and then said something like this: —

Worse and worse; for I fear that the age of Augustus was no age in which the world was likely to frame a mythology at all: — if it had been such an age the problem does not allow sufficient time for it: — if there had been sufficient time it would not have been *such* a mythology; — and if there had been any formed, it would not have been rapidly embraced, any more than other mythologies, by men of different races, but would have been confined to that which gave it birth.

As to the *first* point, you ask me to believe that something like the mythology of the Hindoos or Egyptians could spring up and *diffuse itself* in such an age of civilisation and philosophy, books and history; whereas all experience shows us that only a time of barbarism before authentic history has commenced, is proper to the birth of such monstrosities; that this congelation of tradition and legend takes place only during the long frosts and the deep night of ages, and is impossible in the bright sun of history; in whose very beams, nevertheless, these prodigious icicles are supposed to have been formed!

As to the *second* point, you ask me to believe that the thing should be done almost instantly; for in A. D. 1, we find, by all remains of antiquity, that both Jews and Gentiles were reposing in the shadow of their ancient superstitions; and in A. D. 60, multitudes among *different* races had become the bigoted adherents of this novel *mythology!*

As to the *third* point, you ask me to believe that *such* a mythology as Christianity could have sprung up when those amongst whom it was supposed to have originated, and those amongst whom it is supposed to have been propagated, must have equally loathed it.—National prepossessions of the Jews! Why, the kind of Messiah on which the national heart was set, the inveteracy with which they persecuted to the death the one that offered himself, and the hatred with which, for 1800 years, they have recoiled from him, sufficiently show how preposterous *this* notion is! As a nation, they were, ever have been, and are now, *more* opposed to Christianity than any other nation on earth.—Prepossessions of the Gentiles! There was not a Messiah that a *Jew* could frame a notion of, but would have been an object of intense loathing and detestation to them all! Yet you ask me to believe that a mythology originated in the prejudices of a nation, the vast bulk of whom from its commencement have most resolutely *rejected* it, and was rapidly propagated among other nations and races, who must have been prejudiced against it; who even abjured in its favour those venerable superstitions which were consecrated by the most powerful associations of antiquity!

As to the *fourth* point, you ask me to believe that at a juncture when all the world was divided between deep-rooted superstition and incredulous scepticism;—divided, as regards the Jews, into Pharisees and Sadducees, and, as regards the Gentiles, into *their* Pharisees and Sadducees, that is, into the vulgar who believed, or, at least, practised all popular religions, and the philosophers who laughed at them all, and whose combined hostility was directed against the supposed new mythology,—it nevertheless found favour with multitudes in almost all lands! You ask me to believe that a *mythology* was rapidly received by thousands of different races and nations, when all history proclaims, that it is with the utmost difficulty that any such system ever passes the limits of the race which has originated it; and that you can hardly get another race even to look at it as a matter of philosophic curiosity! You ask me to believe that this system was received by multitudes among many different races, both of Asia and Europe, without *force*, when a similar phenomenon has never been witnessed in relation to any mythology whatever! Thus, after asking me to burden myself with a thousand perplexities to account for the *origin* of these fables, you afterwards burden me with a thousand more, to account for their *success!* Lastly, you ask me to believe, not only that men of different races and countries became bigotedly attached to legends which none were *likely* to originate, which all were likely to *hate,* and, most of all, those who are supposed to have originated them; but that they received them as historic *facts,* when the known recency of their origin must have shown the world that the supposed facts were the legendary birth of yesterday; and that they acted thus, though those who propagated these legends had no military power, no civil authority, no philosophy, no science, no one instrument of success to aid them, while the opposing prejudices which every where encountered them, had! I really know not how to believe all this.

"There are certainly many difficulties in the matter," candidly replied my infidel friend. But, as if wishing to effect a diversion,—" Have you ever read Gibbon's celebrated Chapter?"

Why yes, I told him, two or three years before; but he does not say a syllable in solution of my chief difficulties: he does not tell me any thing as to the *origin* of the *ideas* of Christianity, nor who could have written the wonderful books in which they are embodied; besides, said I, in my simplicity, he yields the point, by allowing miracles to be *the* most potent cause of the success of Christianity.

"Ah," he replied, "but every one can see that he is there speaking ironically."

Why, then, said I, laughing, I fear he is telling us how the success of Christianity *cannot* be accounted for, rather than how it *can.*

"Oh! but he gives you the *secondary* causes; which it is easy to see he considers the principal; and also sufficient."

I will read him again, I said, and with deep attention. Some time after, in meeting with the same friend, I began upon Gibbon's *secondary* causes.

"They have given you satisfaction, I hope?"

Any thing but that, I replied; they do not, as I said before, touch my principal difficulties; and even as to the *success* of the system when once elaborated,—his reasons are either a mere re-statement of the difficulty to be solved, or aggravate it *indefinitely*.

"You are hard to be pleased," he replied.

I said I was, except by solid arguments. But does Gibbon offer them? I asked.

He tells us, for example, that the virtues, energy, and zeal of the early Church was a main instrument of the success of Christianity; whereas it is the very origination of the early Church, with all these efficacious endowments, that we want to account for: it is as though he had told me that we might account for the *success* of Christianity, from the fact that it had *succeeded* to such an extent as to render its further success very probable! As for the rest of his secondary causes, they are difficulties in its way rather than auxiliaries. He asks me to believe that the *intolerance* of Christianity, — by which it refused all alliance with other religions, and insisted in reigning alone or not at all; by which it spat contempt on the whole rabble of the Pantheon, — was likely to facilitate its reception among nations, whose pride and whose pleasure alike it was to encourage civilities and compliments between their Gods, each of whom was on gracious visiting terms with its neighbours! He asks me, in effect, to believe that the austerity of the Christians tended to give them favour in the eyes of an accommodating and jovial Heathenism; that the severity of manners by which they reproved it, and which to their contemporaries must have appeared (as we know from the Apologists it *did*) much as Puritan grimace to the Court of Charles II., was somehow attractive! That the scruples with which they recoiled from all usages and customs which could be associated with the elegant pomp of Pagan worship, and the suspicion with which, as having been linked with idolatry, they looked on every emanation of that spirit of beauty which reigned over the exterior life of Paganism, would operate as a charm in their favour! That their studied absence from all scenes of social hilarity, their grave looks on festal days, their ungarlanded heads, their simple attire, their utter estrangement from the Graces, which in truth were the only legitimate Gods in Greece, and the true mothers of the whole family of Olympus, would be likely to conciliate towards the Gospel the favourable dispositions of classic antiquity! I have not so read history, nor so learnt human nature.—Again, he asks me to believe, that the immortality which Christianity promised the heathen — *such* an immortality — was another of the things which tended to give it success; — on the one hand, a menace of retribution, not for flagrant *crimes* only, which heathenism itself punished, nor for those lax manners which the easy spirit of paganism had made venial, but for *spiritual* vices, of which it took no account, some of which it had even consecrated as virtues; and, on the other hand, an offer of a paradise which promised nothing but delights of a spiritual order; a paradise which, whatever material or imaginative adjuncts it might have, certainly disclosed none; which presented no one thing to gratify the prurient curiosity of man's fancy, or the eager passions of his sensual nature; which must, in fact, have been about as inviting to the soul of a heathen as the promise of an eternal Lent to an epicure! Surely these were resistless seductions. Yet it is to such things as auxiliaries that Gibbon refers me for the success of Christianity. Verily it is not without reason that he is called a master of irony!

My friend fairly acknowledged the difficulties of the subject, but said he *could* not believe in the truth of Christianity.

I repaired to another infidel acquaintance. "It is a perplexing, a very perplexing, controversy, no doubt," was his reply; "but every thing tends to show that Christianity resembles in its principal features all those other religions which you admit to be false. All have their prodigies and miracles — their revelations and inspirations — their fragments of truth, and their masses of nonsense. They are all to be rejected together."

I again puzzled for a long time over this aspect of

the case. At last I said to him,—This seems a curious way of disposing of the *evidence* for Christianity; for if there be any true religion, it is likely, as in all other cases, that the counterfeits will have some features in common with it. It would follow also, that there can be no true *philosophy;* since, while there are scores of philosophies, only one can be true.—But I have another difficulty; on comparing Christianity with other systems, I find vital differences, both as regards *theory* and *fact.*—As regards theory I find an insuperable difficulty, not merely in imagining how Jews, Greeks, or Romans, any or all of them, should have been the originators of Christianity, but how *human nature* should have been fool enough to originate it at all! For I am asked to believe that man, such as I know him through all history, such as he appears in so many forms of religion which have been his undoubted and most *worthy* fabrication, did, whether fraudulently or not, whether designedly or unconsciously, frame a religion which is in striking contrast with all his ordinary handiwork of this sort! This religion enjoins the austerest morality; human religions generally enjoin a very lax one;—this demands the most refined purity, even of the thoughts and desires; other religions usually attach to external and ceremonial observances greater weight than to morality itself:—this is singularly simple in its rites; *they* for the most part consist of little else:—this exhibits a singular silence and abstinence in relation to the future and invisible; *they* amply indulge the imagination and fancy, and are full of delineations calculated to gratify man's most natural curiosity:—this takes under its special patronage those virtues which man is least likely to love or cultivate, and which men in general regard as pusillanimous infirmities, if not vices; *they* patronise the most energetic passions—the passions which made the demigods and heroes of antiquity. I am not saying which is the *better* in these respects; I am only saying that human nature appears more true to itself in the last. And so notorious is all this, that the corruptions of Christianity, as years rolled on, ever tended to assimilate it to the other religions of the earth; to abate its spirituality; to relax its austere code of morals; to commute its proper claims for external observances; to encumber its ritual with an infinity of ceremonies; and, above all, to uncover the future and invisible on which it left a veil, and add a *purgatory* into the bargain! Thus, whether contrasted with other religions, or with its corrupted self, Christianity does not seem a religion which *human nature* would be pleased to invent.*

Again, is it like the *other* religious products of human nature, in daring to aspire to universal dominion, and that, too, founded on *moral* power alone? Never, till Christianity appeared, had such an imagination ever entered the mind of man! Other religions were national affairs; their gods never dreamed of such an enterprise as that of subduing all nations. They were naturally contented with the country that gave them birth, and the homage of the race that worshipped them. They were, when not themselves assailed, very tolerant, and did the civil thing by all other gods of all other nations, and were even content to expire with great propriety (they usually did so) with the political extinction of the race of their votaries! Christianity alone adopts a different tone; "Go ye, and preach the Gospel to *all* nations," and declares not only that it *will* reign, but that none other *shall*. It will not endure a rival; it will not consent to have a statue with the mob of the Pantheon. Whether this ambition — call it pride and folly, if you will, as you well may if the thing be merely human — was *likely* to suggest itself to man, considering the local and national character of other religions, and the apparent hopelessness of any such enterprise, I have my

---

* A few only of the characteristics, by which the theory of Christianity is distinguished from that of other religions, are here given. The Editor cannot refrain from recommending the reader to peruse Archbishop Whately's admirable volume on the "*Peculiarities* of the Christian Religion," as also his eminently philosophical "Essay on Christian Self-denial." The more this whole subject is impartially considered, the more it will be felt, not how much Christianity resembles other religions, but how much it differs from them.

doubts. Arrogance it may be; but it is not such arrogance as is very natural to man.

These, I said, were amongst a few of the things in which I must say I thought the theory of Christianity very unlike that of any religion human nature was likely to invent.

If, I continued, I examine the past history and present position of Christianity, with an impartial eye, I see that it presents in several most important respects a contrast with other religions in point of *fact*. I shall content myself with enumerating a few. Look, then, at the perpetual spirit of aggression which characterises this religion; its undeniable power (in whatever it consists, and from whatever it springs) to prompt those who hold it to render it *victorious* — a spirit, which has more or less characterised its whole history; which still lives, even in its most corrupt forms, and which has not been least active in our own time. I do not see any thing like it in other religions. Till I see Mollahs from Ispahan, Brahmins from Benares, Bonzes from China, preaching *their* systems of religion in London, Paris, and Berlin; supported year after year by an enormous expenditure on the part of their zealous compatriots, and the nations who support them taking the liveliest interest in their success or failure; till I see this (call it fanatical if you will, the money thus expended wasted, the men who give it fools), I shall not be able to pronounce Christianity simply on a par with other religions.

Till the sacred books of *other* religions can boast of at least a hundredth part of the same efforts to translate and diffuse them as have been concentred on the Bible; till we find them in at least half as many languages; till they can render those who possess them at least a tenth part as willing to make costly efforts to insure to them a circulation co-extensive with the family of man; till they occupy an equal space in the literature of the world, and are equally bound up with the philosophy, history, poetry of the community of civilised nations; till they have given an equal number of human communities a *written* language, and may thus boast of having imparted to large sections of the human family the germ of *all* art, science, and civilisation ; till they can cite an equal amount of testimonies to their beauty and sublimity *from those who reject their divine original;* I shall scarcely think Christianity can be put simply on a par with other religions.

Till it can be said that the sacred books of other religions are equally unique in relation to all the literature in which they are embedded; similar neither to what precedes nor what comes after them,—their enemies themselves being judges; till they can be shown to be as superior to all that is found in contemporaneous authors as the New Testament is to the writings of Christian Fathers or the Jewish Rabbis, I cannot say that Christianity is just like any other religion.

Till we can find a religion that has stood as many different assaults from infidelity in the midst of it,— educated infidelity, infidelity aided by learning, genius, philosophy, freely employing all the power of argument and all the power of ridicule to disabuse its votaries; till we can find a religion which can point to an equal array of educated men, philosophic in spirit, rich alike in learning and genius, deeply skilled in the investigation of evidence, deliberately declaring that its claims are well sustained,—we cannot say that Christianity is just like any other religion.

Till it can be shown that another religion, to an equal extent, has propagated itself without force amongst totally different races, and in the most distant countries; and has survived equal revolutions of thought and opinion, manners and laws, amongst those who have embraced it, it cannot be said that Christianity is simply like any other religion.

Till it can be shown that the sacred books of other religions have contained predictions as definite and as unlikely to be fulfilled as the success of early Christianity against all the opposition of prejudice and persecution— its voluntary reception amongst different races, contrary to all the analogies of religious history—and the continued preservation of the Jews among all nations without forming a part of any, I cannot think that Christianity is precisely in the condition of any other religion.

Such, gentlemen, were some few of the differences in *fact* which seemed to me, not less than its theory, to discriminate Christianity from other religions. Had I, in those days of my youth, been favoured with the views of modern " spiritualism," I should then have said one thing more;—that till it is shown that some other religion has possessed an equal power of moulding those characters whom Mr. Newman acknowledges to be the best examples of " spiritual " religion, and can point to oracles equally pervaded by that "sentiment" which he declares is wanting in Greek philosophers, English Deists, and German Pantheists, but which, he admits, pervades the Bible; till I see the devout men whom *he* extols produced by other religions; or rather, I ought to say, produced without or in spite of them (in regions where Christianity however is unknown), by the unaided " spiritual faculty," I cannot but think that the position of Christianity is somewhat discriminated from that both of *other* religions and of " Naturalism."

Such, I said (in conclusion), was an imperfect outline of some of my early conflicts, and such the cruel mode in which my unbelieving friends laughed at each other's hypotheses, and left me destitute of any. Finding that they conclusively confuted one another, and perceiving at last that the idea of the superhuman origin of Christianity did, and, as Bishop Butler says, alone can, resolve all the difficulties of the subject, I was compelled to forego all the advantages of infidelity, and condescended to " depress " my conscience to the " Biblical standard!" Would to heaven that it had never been depressed *below* it!

I am bound to say my auditors listened with courtesy.

The conversation was now carried on in little knots: I, who was glad of a rest, was occupied in listening to a conversation between Harrington and his Italian friend, who was urging him to take refuge from such a Babel of discords as his company had offered, in the only secure asylum. Harrington told him, with the utmost gravity, that one great objection to the Church of Rome was the unseemly liberty she allowed to the *right of private judgment;* that he found in her communion distractions the most perplexing, especially as between English and Foreign Romanists!

After the party had broken up, and we were left alone, Mr. Fellowes, turning to me, said, " You lay great stress on the origination of such a character as Christ. But can we make its reality a *literary* problem? May it not have been imaginary? As Mr. Newman says, ' Human nature is often portrayed in superhuman dignity; why not in superhuman goodness?'"

"That the origination," said I, "of *such* a Moral Ideal, in so peculiar a form, by *such* men as Galilean Jews, is unaccountable enough, I fancy all will admit; but it is, you observe, only *one* of the *numberless* points which are unaccountable; neither do I make this one feature, or any of the other singular characteristics of the New Testament, merely a *literary* problem. The whole, you see, is a vast *literary, moral, intellectual, spiritual,* and *historical* problem. But it is too much the way with you objectors to say, ' this may, perhaps, be got over,' and ' that may be got over;' the question is, as Bishop Butler says, whether *all* can be got over; for if all the arguments for it be not false, Christianity is true."

"You charge us with the very conduct," retorted Fellowes, "which Mr. Newman objects to Christians. They, says he, affirm that this objection is of little weight, and that is of little weight; whereas *altogether* they amount to considerable weight."

"I admit it," said I; "and those are very unfair who deny it. But still, since there are these things of weight on both sides, the argument returns, on which side does the balance on the sum-total of evidence lie?"

"But," said Fellowes, "how *few* are competent to compute *that!*"

"You are really pleasant, Mr. Fellowes," I replied; "I thought the question we were arguing was as to the *truth* or the *falsehood* of Christianity, not whether the bulk of mankind are fully competent to form an independent and profound judgment on its evidences: very few are competent to do so either on this or any other complex subject: certainly not (as our differences show) on the subject of your 'spiritualism.' But the incompetency of the great bulk of mankind to deal with complicated evidence, makes a thing neither true nor false; perhaps on this, as on so many other subjects, the few must thoroughly sift the matter for the many. If your present objection were of force, what would become of truth in politics, law, medicine, in all which the great majority must trust much to the conclusions of their wiser fellow-creatures? Your observation is no confutation of the evidences for Christianity: it is simply a satire upon God and the condition of the human creatures he has made!"

"Well, let that pass," said Fellowes: "I was going to say further that it is not so clear to every one that Christ is so very wonderful an ideal of humanity. Do you remember that Mr. Newman says in his 'Phases' that, when he was a boy, he read Benson's Life of Fletcher of Madely, and thought Fletcher an *absolutely* perfect man? and he also says that he imagines, if he were to read that book again, he would think Fletcher a *more* perfect character than Jesus Christ. Have you nothing to say to that?"

"NOTHING," said I, "except to point you to the infinitely different estimates of Christ formed by other men who yet think of historical Christianity much as you do. How differently do such writers as Mr. Greg and Mr. Parker speak! How do they almost exhaust the resources of language to express their sentiments of this wonderful character! As to Mr. Newman's *impression*, I do not think it worth an answer. When a man so far forgets himself as to say what he can hardly help knowing will be unspeakably painful to multitudes of his fellow-creatures, on the strength of *boyish* impressions,— not even thinking it worth while to verify those impressions, and see whether, after thirty or forty years, he is not something more than a boy,—I think it is scarcely worth while to reply. Christianity is willing to consider the arguments of *men*, but not the impressions of *boys*."

"But we must not be too hard," said Harrington, "upon Mr. Newman; it is evident, from his Hebrew Monarchy, that as he takes a benevolent pleasure in defending those whom nobody else will defend—in petting Ahab, whom he pronounces rather weak than wicked, and palliating the conduct of Jezebel, whose character was, it seems, grievously deteriorated by contact with the 'prophets of Jehovah,' so he has a chivalrous habit of depressing those who have been particularly the objects of veneration. Elisha, Samuel, and David, are all brought down a great many degrees in the moral scale. He has simply done the same with Christ."

"Well," said Fellowes, "I cannot help agreeing with Mr. Newman in thinking that when one hears men made the objects of extravagant eulogy, it almost 'tempts one, even though a stranger to their very name, to 'pick holes,' as the saying is.'"

"It may be so," said I; "but it is a tendency against which we should guard. It would lead us, like him of Athens, to *ostracise* Aristides: we should be weary of hearing him continually called 'The Just.'"

"However," rejoined Fellowes, "I *am* weary of hearing Christ so perpetually called our example.—As Mr. Newman says, he cannot, except in a very modified sense, be such. 'His garments will not fit us.'"

"Did you ever hear," said I, "that fathers and mothers ought to set an example to their children?"

"Certainly."

'Yet surely not in all things can they be such. *Their* garments surely will not fit their children."

"No," said Harrington; "those of the father at all events will not, if they are girls, nor of the mother, if they are boys. Fellowes, I think you had better say nothing on this subject. If *men* of fifty can, in all essential points, be beautiful *examples* to *girls* of ten,—in gentleness, in patience, in humility, in kindness, in integrity, in candour, and so forth,—and all the more impressively for the wide interval between them, why I suppose Jesus Christ may be as much to his disciples."

"But again," urged Fellowes to me, "you, like so many men, seem to lay such stress on the superiority of the *morality* of the New Testament. I cannot see it. I confess, with Mr. Foxton, and many more, that it seems to me that it has not such a very great advantage over that of many heathen moralists who have said the same things — Plato, for example."

I replied that, of course, it would be of no avail to affirm in general (what I was yet convinced was true), that the New Testament inculcated a system of ethics much more just and comprehensive than any other volume in the world. I told him, however, that I thought he would not deny that its *manner* of conveying ethical truth was *unique;* that it not only contained more admirable and varied summaries of duty than any other book whatever, but that we should seek in vain in any other for such a profusion of just maxims and weighty sentiments, expressed with such comprehensive brevity, or illustrated with so much beauty and pathos. I remarked that, if he would be pleased to do as I had once done — compile a selection of the principal precepts and maxims from the most admirable ethical works of antiquity (those of Aristotle, for example), and compare them with two or three of the summaries of similar precepts in the New Testament, he would at once feel how much more vivid, touching, animated, and even comprehensive, was the Scriptural expression of the same truths. But I further observed, that even to obtain the *means* of such comparison, he must reject from Plato or the Stagyrite twenty times the bulk of questionable speculations and dreary subtleties, which in these authors too uniformly separate by long intervals those gems of moral truth, which every where sparkle on the pages of the New Testament.

I told him that I could not help laying great stress on the degree and manner in which this element enters into the composition of the New Testament; that ethical truths are there expressed in every variety of form which can fix them upon the imagination and the heart, with an entire absence of those prolix discussions and metaphysical refinements which form so large a portion of Aristotle and Plato. If we find in these writers a moral truth expressed with something approaching the comprehensive beauty and simplicity of the Gospels, we are filled with surprise and rapture, and dig out with joy the glittering fragment from the mass of earthy matter — oppressive disquisitions about "ideas" and "essences," "energies" and "entelechies," and so forth, — in which it is sure to be embedded. I promised, if health and life were given, to exhibit some day these gems, with a sufficient portion of the surrounding earth still attached to them, and to contrast them with those of the New Testament. "In this strange volume," I continued, "the most beautiful ethical maxims exist in unexampled profusion. After reading Aristotle's ethics, I feel, when I turn to the New Testament, as Linnæus is said to have felt when he first saw, growing wild, the masses of blooming gorse, which he had never seen in his cold north, except as a sheltered exotic. Whether it was *likely* that contemporaries of the *Pharisees*, who were sunk in formalism, and who had *glossed* away every moral and spiritual precept of the Law, could reach and maintain such elevation of tone, — I leave you to judge." But though I felt all this, I acknowledged that it was difficult to express it; and said that, perhaps, the best way to compare the morality of the New Testament with the ethical system of any philosopher, or the code of any legislator, would be to imagine them all in succession *universally* adopted, and then see how much would have to be objected to — how much "brick" was mingled with the "porphyry." "If, for example," said I, "Plato, who, I admit, so often flashes upon us the sublimest and most comprehensive *principles* of morals, and whose ethical system you say is identical with that of Christianity, had the forming of a republic, you would have community of women and property — women trained to war — infanticide under certain circumstances — young children led to battle (though at a safe distance), that 'the young whelps might early scent carnage, and be inured to slaughter!'

Both with him and Aristotle slavery would be a regularly sanctioned and perfectly natural institution. Not only did they entertain very lax notions of the relations of the sexes, but the tone in which they speak of the most abominable corruptions — I do *not* except cannibalism — to which humanity has ever degraded itself, implies that they regarded such things as comparatively *venial*. I know no greater single names than these, and I presume that these points you would find some difficulty in digesting." He admitted it.

I told him I supposed he would take equal objections to the Gentoo, or the Roman, or the Spartan code, as also to the Koran. He admitted all this too.

"But now, if we take the Christian code, and suppose the New Testament made the literal guide of life in every man, tell me, Mr. Fellowes, what would be the consequence? What would you wish otherwise?"

"Why," said Harrington, smiling, "he would, perhaps, object that there would be no more war, and that retaliation would be impossible."

"The former," said I, "we could all endure, I suppose; nor be unwilling to give up the latter, seeing that there would, in that case, be no wrongs to avenge. It would not matter that you would be compelled to turn your right check to him who smote you on the left (let the interpretation be as literal as you will), since no one would strike you on the left; nor that you must surrender your cloak to him who took away your coat, since no one would take your coat. But tell me, is there any thing more serious that would follow from the literal and universal adoption of the ethics of the New Testament?" Fellowes acknowledged that he knew of nothing, unless it was a *sanction* of slavery.

"I do not admit that the New Testament *sanctions* it," I replied; "and I will, if you like, give my reasons in full another time. But is there any thing else?" He said he did not recollect any thing.

"But you would recoil from the literal realisation of the systems and codes we have mentioned?" He confessed this also

"The superiority of the Christian code, then," said I, "is practically acknowledged.—And it is further often confessed, in a most significant way, by the mode in which the enemies of Christianity taunt its disciples. When they speak of the vices and corruptions of the heathen, they blame, and justly blame, the *principles* of their vicious systems; and ask how it could be otherwise? When they blame the Christian, the first and the last thing they usually do, is to point in triumph to the *contrast* between his principles and practice." "How much better," say they, "is his code than his conduct!" It is as a hypocrite that they censure *him*. It is sad for him that it should be so; but it is a glorious compliment to the morality of the New Testament. Its enemies know not how to attack its disciples, except by endeavouring to show that they do *not* act as *it* bids them. "Surely," said I, in conclusion, " this *uniform* excellence of the Christian ethics, as compared with other systems, is a peculiarity worth noting, and utterly incomprehensible upon the hypothesis that it was the unaided work of man. That there are points on which the moral systems of men and nations *osculate*, is most true; that there should have been certain approximations on many most important subjects was to be expected from the essential identity of human nature, in all ages and countries; but their deviations in some point or other—usually in several—from what we acknowledge to be both right and expedient, is equally undeniable. That when such men as Plato and Aristotle tried their hands upon the problem, they should err, while the writers of the New Testament should have succeeded—that these last should do what all mankind besides had in some points or other failed to do, is sufficiently wonderful;—that *Galilean Jews* should have solved the problem, is, whether we consider their age, their ignorance, or their prepossessions, to me utterly incredible."

It was now very late, and we rose to retire. Mr. Fellowes said, "I should be glad to know what answer you would make to Mr. Newman's observations on three points — one of them just alluded to — on which he affirms that undue credit has been given to Christianity;—I mean its supposed elevating influence in relation to women—its supposed mitigation of slavery—and its supposed triumphs before Constantine."

I said I would scribble a few remarks on the subject, and would give them to him in a day or two. I remarked that Mr. Newman had treated these great subjects very briefly, but that I could not be quite so concise as he had been.

The discussions of the preceding day had made so deep an impression upon me, that when I went to bed I found it very difficult to sleep; and when I did get off at last, my thoughts shaped themselves into a singular dream, which, though only a dream, is not, I think, without instruction. I shall entitle it

The Blank Bible.

Ἔτλην γεγωνεῖν νυκτίφοιτ' ὀνείρατα.
                                  Æschyl. Prom. Vinct. 657.

I thought I was at home, and that on taking up my Greek Testament one morning to read (as is my wont) a chapter, I found, to my surprise, that what seemed to be the old familiar book, was a total blank; not a character was inscribed in it or upon it. I supposed that some book like it had, by some accident, got into its place; and without stopping to hunt for it, took down a large quarto volume which contained both the Old and New Testaments. To my surprise, however, this also was a blank from beginning to end. With that facility of accommodation to any absurdities which is proper to dreams, I did not think very much of the coincidence of two blank volumes having been substituted for two copies of the Scriptures in two different places, and therefore quietly reached down a copy of the Hebrew Bible, in which I could just manage to make out a chapter. To my increased surprise, and even something like terror, I found that this also was a perfect blank. While I was musing on this unaccountable phenomenon, my servant entered the room, and said that thieves had been in the house during the night, for that her large Bible, which she had left on the kitchen table, had been removed, and another volume left by mistake in its place, of just the same size, but made of nothing but white paper. She added, with a laugh, that it must have been a very queer kind of thief to steal a Bible at all; and that he should have left another book instead, made it the more odd. I asked her if any thing else had been missed, and if there were any signs of people having entered the house. She answered in the negative to both these questions; and I began to be strangely perplexed.

On going out into the street, I met a friend, who, almost before we had exchanged greetings, told me that a most unaccountable robbery had been committed at his house during the night, for that every copy of the Bible had been removed, and a volume of exactly the same size, but of pure white paper, left in its stead. Upon telling him that the same accident had happened to myself, we began to think that there was more in it than we had at first surmised.

On proceeding further we found every one complaining, in similar perplexity, of the same loss; and before night it became evident that a great and terrible "miracle" had been wrought in the world; that in one night silently, but effectually, that hand which had written its terrible menace on the walls of Belshazzar's palace, had reversed the miracle; had spunged out of our Bibles every syllable they contained, and thus reclaimed the most precious gift which heaven had bestowed, and ungrateful man had abused.

I was curious to watch the effects of this calamity on the varied characters of mankind. There was universally, however, an interest in the Bible now it was *lost*, such as had never attached to it while it was *possessed;* and he who had been but happy enough to possess fifty copies might have made his fortune. One keen speculator, as soon as the first whispers of the miracle began to spread, hastened to the depositories of the Bible Society and the great book-stocks in Paternoster Row, and offered to buy up at a high premium any copies of the Bible that might be on hand; but the worthy merchant was informed that there was not a single copy remaining. Some, to whom their Bible had been a "blank" book for twenty years, and who would never have known whether it was full or empty, had not the lamentations of their neighbours impelled them to look into it, were not the least loud in their expressions of sorrow at this calamity. One old gentleman, who had never troubled the book in his life, said it was "confounded hard to be deprived of his *religion* in his old age;" and another, who seemed to have lived as though he had always been of Mandeville's opinion, that "private vices were public benefits," was all at once alarmed for the *morals* of mankind. He feared he said, that the loss of the Bible would have "a *cursed* bad effect on the public virtue of the country."

As the fact was universal and palpable, it was impossible that, like other miracles, it should leave the usual loopholes for scepticism. Miracles in general, in order to be miracles at all, have been singular or very rare violations of a general law, witnessed, by a few, on whose testimony they are received, and in the reception of whose testimony consists the exercise of that faith to which they appeal. It was evident that, whatever the reason of *this* miracle, it was not an exercise of docile and humble faith founded on evidence no more than just sufficient to operate as a moral test. This was a miracle which, it could not be denied, looked marvellously like a "judgment." However, there were, in some cases, indications enough to show how difficult it is to give such evidence as will satisfy the obstinacy of mankind. One old sceptical fellow, who had been for years bed-ridden, was long in being convinced (if, indeed, he ever was) that any thing extraordinary had occurred in the world; he at first attributed the reports of what he heard to the "impudence" of his servants and dependents, and wondered that they should dare to venture upon such a joke. On finding these assertions backed by those of his acquaintance, he pished and pshawed, and looked very wise, and ironically congratulated them on this creditable conspiracy with the insolent rascals, his servants. On being shown the old Bible, of which he recognised the binding, though he had never seen the inside, and finding it a very fair book of blank paper, he quietly observed that it was very easy to substitute the one book for the other, though he did not pretend to divine the motives which induced people to attempt such a clumsy piece of imposition; and on their persisting that they were not deceiving him, swore at them as a set of knaves, who would fain persuade him out of his senses. On their bringing him a pile of blank Bibles, backed by the asseverations of other neighbours, he was ready to burst with indignation. "As to the volumes," he said, "it was not difficult to procure a score or two 'of commonplace books,' and they had doubtless done so to carry on the cheat; for himself, he would sooner believe that the whole world was leagued against him, than credit any such nonsense." They were angry, in their turn, at his incredulity, and told him that he was very much mistaken if he thought himself of so much importance that they would all perjure themselves to delude him, since they saw plainly enough that he could do that very easily for himself, without any help of theirs. They really did not care one farthing whether he believed them or not: if he did not choose to believe the story, he might leave it alone. "Well, well," said he, "it is all very fine; but unless you show me, not one of these blank books, which could not impose upon an owl, but one of the *very blank Bibles themselves*, I will not believe." At this curious demand, one of his nephews who stood by (a lively young fellow) was so excessively tickled, that though he had some expectations from the sceptic, he could not help bursting out into laughter; but he became grave enough when his angry uncle told him that he would leave him in his will nothing but the family Bible, which he might make a ledger of if he pleased. Whether this resolute old sceptic ever vanquished his incredulity, I do not remember.

Very different from the case of this sceptic was that of a most excellent female relative, who had been equally long a prisoner to her chamber, and to whom the Bible had been, as to so many thousands more, her faithful companion in solitude, and the all-sufficient solace of her sorrows. I found her gazing intently on the blank Bible, which had been so recently bright to her with the lustre of immortal hopes. She burst into tears as she saw me. "And has your faith left *you* too, my gentle friend?" said L. "No," she answered, "and I trust it never will. He who has taken away the Bible has not taken away my memory, and I now recall all that is most precious in that book which has so long been my meditation. It is a heavy judgment upon the land; and surely," added this true Christian, never thinking of the faults of others, "I, at least, cannot complain, for I have not prized as I ought that book which yet, of late years, I think I can say, I loved more than any other possession on earth. But I know," she continued, smiling through her tears, "that the sun shines, though clouds may veil him for a moment; and I am unshaken in my faith in those truths which have been transcribed on my memory, though they are blotted from my book. In these hopes I have lived, and in these hopes I will *die*." "I have no consolation to offer to you," said I, "for you need none." She quoted many of the passages which have been, through all ages, the chief stay of sorrowing humanity; and I thought the words of Scripture had never sounded so solemn or so sweet before. "I shall often come to see you," I said, "to hear a chapter in the Bible, for you know it far better than I."

No sooner had I taken my leave than I was informed that an old lady of my acquaintance had summoned me in haste. She said she was much impressed by this extraordinary calamity. As, to my certain knowledge, she had never troubled the contents of the book, I was surprised that she had so taken to heart the loss of that which had, practically, been lost to her all her days.

"Sir," said she, the moment I entered, "the Bible, the Bible." "Yes, madam," said I, "this is a very grievous and terrible visitation. I hope we may learn the lessons which it is calculated to teach us." "I am sure," answered she, "I am not likely to forget it for a while, for it has been a grievous loss to me." I told her I was very glad. "Glad!" she rejoined. "Yes," I said, "I am glad to find that you think it so *great* a loss, for that loss may then be a gain indeed. There is, thanks be to God, enough left in our memories to carry us to heaven." "Ah! but," said she, "the hundred pounds, and the villany of my maid-servant. Have you not heard?" This gave me some glimpse as to the secret of her sorrow. She told me that she had deposited several banknotes in the leaves of her family Bible, thinking that, to be sure, nobody was likely to look *there* for them. "No sooner," said she, "were the Bibles made useless by this strange event, than my servant peeped into every copy in the house, and she now denies that she found any thing in my old family Bible, except two or three blank leaves of thin paper, which she *says*, she destroyed; that if any characters were ever on them they must have been erased, when those of the Bible were obliterated. But I am sure she lies; for who would believe that heaven took the trouble to blot out my precious bank-notes? They were not God's word, I trow." It was clear that she considered the "promise to pay" better by far than any "promises" which the book contained. "I should not have cared so much about the Bible," she whined, hypocritically, "because, as you truly observe, our memories may retain enough to carry us to heaven" — a little in that case would certainly go a great way, I thought to myself — "and if not, there are those who can supply the loss. But who is to get my banknotes back again? Other people have *only* lost their Bibles." It was, indeed, a case beyond my power of consolation.

The calamity not only strongly stirred the feelings of men, and upon the whole, I think, beneficially, but it immediately stimulated their ingenuity. It was wonderful to see the energy with which men discussed the subject, and the zeal, too, with which they ultimately exerted themselves to repair the loss. I could even hardly regret it, when I considered what a spectacle of intense activity, intellectual and moral, the visitation had occasioned. It was very early suggested that the whole Bible had again and again been quoted piecemeal in one book or other; that it had impressed its own image on the surface of human literature, and had been reflected on its course as the stars on a stream. But, alas! on investigation, it was found as vain to expect that the gleam of star-light would still remain mirrored in the water, when the clouds had veiled the stars themselves, as that the bright characters of the Bible would remain reflected in the books of men when they had been erased from the book of God. On inspection, it was found that every text, every phrase which had been quoted, not only in books of devotion and theology, but in those of poetry and fiction, had been remorselessly expunged. Never before had I had any adequate idea of the extent to which the Bible had moulded the intellectual and moral life of the last eighteen centuries, nor how intimately it had interfused itself with habits of thought and modes of expression; nor how naturally and extensively its comprehensive imagery and language had been introduced into human writings, and most of all, where there had been most of genius. A vast portion of literature became instantly worthless, and was transformed into so much waste paper. It was almost impossible to look into any book of merit, and read ten pages together, without coming to some provoking erasures and mutilations, some "hiatus valde deflendi," which made whole passages perfectly unintelligible. Many of the sweetest passages of Shakespere were converted into unmeaning nonsense, from the absence of those words which his own all but divine genius had appropriated from a still diviner source. As to Milton, he was nearly ruined, as might naturally be supposed. Walter Scott's novels were filled with perpetual *lacunæ*. I hoped it might be otherwise with the philosophers, and so it was; but even here it was curious to see what strange ravages the visitation had wrought. Some of the most beautiful and comprehensive of Bacon's Aphorisms were reduced to enigmatical nonsense.

Those who held large stocks of books knew not what to do. Ruin stared them in the face; their value fell seventy or eighty per cent. All branches of theology, in particular, were a drug. One fellow said, that he should not so much have minded if the miracle had spunged out what was *human* as well as what was divine, for in that case he would at least have had so many thousand volumes of fair blank paper, which was as much as many of them were worth before. A wag answered, that it was not usual, in despoiling a house, to carry away any thing except the *valuables*. Meantime, millions of blank Bibles filled the shelves of stationers, to be sold for day-books and ledgers, so that there seemed to be no more employment for the paper makers in that direction for many years to come. A friend, who used to mourn over the thought of palimpsest manuscripts—of portions of Livy and Cicero erased to make way for the nonsense of some old monkish chronicler,—exclaimed, as he saw a tradesman trudging off with a handsome morocco-bound quarto for a day-book, "Only think of the pages once filled with the poetry of Isaiah, and the parables of Christ, spunged clean to make way for orders for silks and satins, muslins, cheese, and bacon!" The old authors, of course, were left to their mutilations; there was no way in which the confusion could be remedied. But the living began to prepare new editions of their works, in which they endeavoured to give a new turn to the thoughts which had been mutilated by erasure, and I was not a little amused to see that many, having stolen from writers whose compositions were as much mutilated as their own, could not tell the meaning of their own pages.

It seemed at first to be a not unnatural impression that even those who could recall the erased texts as they perused the injured books,—who could *mentally* fill up the imperfect clauses,—were not at liberty to inscribe them; they seemed to fear that if they did so the characters would be as if written in invisible ink, or would surely fade away. It was with trembling that some at length made the attempt, and to their unspeakable joy found the impression durable. Day after day passed; still the characters remained; and the people at length came to the conclusion that God left them at liberty, if they could, to reconstruct the Bible for themselves out of their collective remembrances of its divine contents. This led again to some curious results, all of them singularly indicative of the good and ill that is in human nature. It was with incredible joy that men came to the conclusion that the book might be thus recovered nearly entire, and nearly in the very words of the original, by the combined effort of human memories. Some of the obscurest of the species, who had studied nothing else but the Bible, but who had well studied *that*, came to be objects of reverence among Christians and booksellers; and the various texts they quoted were taken down with the utmost care. He who could fill up a chasm by the restoration of words which were only partially remembered, or could contribute the least text that had been forgotten, was regarded as a sort of public benefactor. At length, a great public movement amongst the divines of all denominations was projected to collate the results of these partial recoveries of the sacred text. It was curious, again, to see in how various ways human passions and prejudices came into play. It was found that the several parties who had furnished from memory the same portions of the sacred text, had fallen into a great variety of different readings; and though most of them were of as little importance in themselves as the bulk of those which are paraded in the critical recensions of Mill, Griesbach, or Tischendorf, they became, from the obstinacy and folly of the men who contended about them, *important* differences, merely because they were *differences*. Two reverend men of the synod, I remember, had a rather tough dispute as to whether it was *twelve* baskets full of fragments of the *five* loaves which the *five* thousand left, and *seven* baskets full of the *seven* loaves which the *four* thousand had left, or *vice versâ:* as also whether the words in John, vi. 19, were " *about* twenty or five and twenty," or " *about* thirty or five and thirty furlongs."

To do the assembly justice, however, there was found an intense *general* earnestness and sincerity befitting the occasion, and an equally intense desire to obtain, as nearly as possible, the very words of the lost volume; only (as was also, alas! natural) vanity in some; in others, confidence in their strong impressions and in the accuracy of their memory; obstinacy, and pertinacity in many more (all aggravated as usual by controversy, caused many odd embarrassments before the final adjustment was effected.

I was particularly struck with the varieties of reading which mere prejudices in favour of certain systems of theology occasioned in the several partisans of each. No doubt the worthy men were generally unconscious of the influence of these prejudices; yet, somehow, the memory was seldom so clear in relation to those texts which told *against* them as in relation to those which told *for* them. A certain Quaker had an impression that the words instituting the Eucharist were preceded by a qualifying expression, " and Jesus said *to the twelve,* Do this in remembrance of me;" while he could not exactly recollect whether or not the formula of " baptism" was expressed in the general terms some maintained it was. Several Unitarians had a clear recollection that in several places the authority of manuscripts, as estimated in Griesbach's recension, was decidedly against the common reading; while the Trinitarians maintained that Griesbach's recension in those instances had left that reading undisturbed. An Episcopalian began to have his doubts whether the usage in favour of the interchange of the words "bishop" and " presbyter" was so uniform as the Presbyterian and Independent maintained, and whether there was not a passage in which Timothy and Titus were expressly called " bishops." The Presbyterian and Independent had similar biases; and one gentleman, who was a strenuous advocate of the system of the latter, enforced one equivocal remembrance by saying, he could,

P

as it were, distinctly see the very spot on the page before his mind's eye. Such tricks will imagination play with the memory, when preconception plays tricks with the imagination! In like manner, it was seen that while the Calvinist was very distinct in his recollection of the ninth chapter of Romans, his memory was very faint as respects the exact wording of some of the verses in the Epistle of James; and though the Arminian had a most vivacious impression of all those passages which spoke of the claims of the law, he was in some doubt whether the apostle Paul's sentiments respecting human depravity, and justification by faith alone, had not been a little exaggerated. In short, it very clearly appeared that tradition was no safe guide; that if, even when she was hardly a month old, she could play such freaks with the memories of honest people, there was but a sorry prospect of the secure transmission of truth for eighteen hundred years. From each man's memory seemed to glide something or other which he was not inclined to retain there, and each seemed to substitute in its stead something that he liked better.

Though the assembly was in the main most anxious to come to a *right* decision, and really advanced an immense way towards completing a true and faithful copy of the lost original, the disputes which arose, on almost every point of theology, promised the world an abundant crop of new sects and schisms. Already there had sprung up several whose names had never been heard of in the world, but for this calamity. Amongst them were two who were called the "*Long Memories*" and the "*Short Memories.*" Their general tendencies coincided pretty much with those of the orthodox and the Rationalists.

It was curious to see by what odd associations, sometimes of contrast, sometimes of resemblance, obscure texts were recovered, though they were verified, when once mentioned, by the consciousness of hundreds. One old gentleman, a miser, contributed (and it was all he did contribute) a maxim of prudence, which he recollected, principally from having systematically *abused* it. All the ethical maxims, indeed, were soon collected; for though, as usual, no one recollected his own peculiar duties or infirmities, every one, as usual, kindly remembered those of his neighbours. Husbands remembered what was due from their wives, and wives what was due from their husbands. The unpleasant sayings about " better to dwell on the housetop," and " the perpetual dropping on a very rainy day," were called to mind by thousands. Almost the whole of Proverbs and Ecclesiastes were contributed, in the merest fragments, in this way. As for Solomon's " times for every thing," few could remember them all, but every body remembered some. Undertakers said there was a " time to mourn;" and comedians that there was a " time to laugh;" young ladies innumerable remembered there was a " time to love;" and people of all kinds that there was a " time to hate;" every body knew there was a "time to speak;" but a worthy Quaker reminded them that there was also a " time to keep silence."

Some dry parts of the laws of Moses were recovered by the memory of jurists, who seemed to have no knowledge whatever of any other parts of the sacred volume; while in like manner one or two antiquarians supplied some very difficult genealogical and chronological matters, in equal ignorance of the moral and spiritual contents of the Scriptures.

As people became accustomed to the phenomenon, the perverse humours of mankind displayed themselves in a variety of ways. The efforts of the pious assembly were abundantly laughed at; but I must, in justice, add, without driving them from their purpose. Some profane wags suggested there was now a good opportunity of realising the scheme of taking " *not* " out of the Commandments, and inserting it in the Creed. But they were sarcastically told that the old objection to the plan would still apply; that they would not sin with equal relish if they were expressly commanded to do so, nor take such pleasure in infidelity, if infidelity became a duty. Others said that if the world must wait till the synod had concluded its labours, the prophecies of the New Testament would not be written till some time after their fulfilment; and that if all the conjectures of the learned divines were inserted in the new edition of the Bible, the declaration in John would be literally verified, and that " the world itself would not contain all the books which would be written."

But the most amusing thing of all, was to see, as time made man more familiar with this strange event, the variety of speculations which were entertained respecting its *object* and *design*. Many began gravely to question whether it was the duty of the synod to attempt the reconstruction of a book of which God himself had so manifestly deprived the world, and whether it was not a profane, nay, an atheistical, attempt to frustrate his will. Some, who were secretly glad to be released from so troublesome a book, were particularly pious on this head, and exclaimed bitterly against this rash attempt to counteract and cancel the decrees of heaven. The Papists, on their part, were confident that the design was to correct the exorbitancies of a rabid Protestantism, and show the world, by direct miracle, the necessity of submitting to the decision of their church and the infallibility of the supreme Pontiff; who, as they truly alleged, could decide all knotty points quite as well without the Word of God as with it. On being reminded that the writings of the Fathers, on which they laid so much stress as the vouchers of their traditions, were mutilated by the same stroke which had demolished the Bible (all their quotations from the sacred volume being erased), some of the Jesuits affirmed that many of the Fathers were rather improved than otherwise by the omission, and that they found these writings quite as intelligible and not less edifying than before. In this, many Protestants very cordially agreed. On the other hand, many of our modern infidels gave an entirely new turn to the whole affair, by saying that the visitation was evidently not in judgment, but in mercy; that God in compassion, and not in indignation, had taken away a book which men had regarded with an extravagant admiration and idolatry, and which they had exalted to the place of that clear internal oracle which he had planted in the human breast; in a word, that if it was a rebuke at all, it was a rebuke to a rampant "Bibliolatry." As I heard all these different versions of so simple a matter, and found that not a few were inclined to each, I could not help exclaiming, "In truth the devil is a very clever fellow, and man even a greater blockhead than I had taken him for." But in spite of the surprise with which I had listened to these various explanations of an event which seemed to me clear as if written with a sunbeam, this *last* reason, which assigned as the cause of God's resumption of his own gift, an extravagant admiration and veneration of it on the part of mankind — it being so notorious that those who professed belief in its divine origin and authority had (even the best of them) so grievously neglected both the study and the practice of it — struck me as so exquisitely ludicrous that I broke into a fit of laughter, which awoke me. I found that it was broad daylight, and the morning sun was streaming in at the window, and shining in quiet radiance upon the open Bible which lay on my table. So strongly had my dream impressed me, that I almost felt as though, on inspection, I should find the sacred leaves a blank, and it was therefore with joy that my eyes rested on those words, which I read through grateful tears: "The gifts of God are *without repentance.*"

July 19. This morning my friends treated me to a long dialogue, in which it was contended

THAT MIRACLES ARE IMPOSSIBLE, BUT THAT IT IS IMPOSSIBLE TO PROVE IT.

"I think, Fellowes," Harrington began, "if there be any point in which you and I are likely to agree, it is in that dogma that miracles are impossible. And yet here, as usual, my sceptical doubts pursue and baffle me. I wish you would try with me whether there be not an escape from them." Fellowes assented.

"As I have to propose and explain my doubts," said Harrington, "perhaps you will excuse my taking the 'lion's share' of the conversation. But now, by way of beginning in some way, — what, my dear friend, *is* a miracle?"

"What is a miracle? Ay — that is the question; but though it may be difficult to find an exact definition of it, it is easily understood by everybody."

"Very likely; then you can with more ease give me *your* notion of it."

"If, for example," said Fellowes, "the sun which has risen so long every morning, were to rise no more: or if a man, whom we knew to be dead and buried, were to come to life again; or, if what we know to be water were at once to become wine, none would hesitate to call *that* a miracle."

"You remember, perhaps," said Harrington, "an amusing little play of Socratic humour in the dialogue of Theætetus, somewhere in the introduction, when the ironical querist has asked that intelligent youth what science is?"

"I cannot say that I do; for though I have read that dialogue, it is some years ago."

"Let me read you the passage, then. Here it is," said Harrington, reaching down the dialogue and turning to the place. 'Tell me frankly,' says Socrates, 'what do you think *science* is?' 'It appears to me,' says Theætetus, 'that such things as one may learn from Theodorus here — namely, geometry, as well as other things which you have just enumerated; and again, that the *shoemaker's* art, and those of *other* artizans, — all and each of them are nothing else but science.' 'You are munificent indeed,' said Socrates; 'for when asked for *one* thing, you have given *many*.' — I almost think," continued Harrington, "that if Socrates were here, he would do what I should not presume to do, — banter you in a somewhat similar way. He would say, that having asked what a miracle was, Mr. Fellowes told him, that half-a-dozen things were miracles, but did not tell him what every miracle was; that is, never told him what made all miracles such. Suffer me again to ask you what a miracle is?"

"I recollect now enough of the charming dialogue from which you have taken occasion to twit me, to answer you in the same vein. As it turns out, Socrates appears to be at least equally ignorant with Theætetus as to the definition of which he is in search. I think it may be as well for me to do at once, what certainly Theætetus would have done, had he known that his reprover was as much in the dark as himself."

"What is that?" said Harrington.

"He would have cut short a good deal of banter by at once turning the tables upon his ironical tormentor; acknowledging his impotence and making *him* give the required definition. Come, let me take that course."

"I have no objection, my friend, if you will first, as you say, *acknowledge* your impotence; only I would not advise you, for in that case you would be obliged to confess that you have resolved *with me* that a miracle is impossible, and yet that you are not quite sure that you can tell, or rather own that you cannot, what a miracle is? Let me entreat you to essay some definition; and if you break down, I have no objection to take my chance of the honour of success or the ignominy of failure."

"The fact is," answered Fellowes, "that, like many other things, it is better understood——"

"Than described, as the novelists say, when they feel that their powers of description fail them. But this will hardly do for us; we are philosophers, you know (save the mark!) in search of *truth*.—A thing that is well known by *everybody*, and is capable of being described by *nobody*, would be almost a miracle of itself; and I think it imports us to give some better account of the matter. I can see that my orthodox uncle there is already secretly amusing himself at the anticipation of our perplexities."

I took no notice of the remark, but went on writing.

"Well, then, if I *must* give you some definition," said Fellowes, "I know not if I can do better than avail myself of the usual one, that it is a suspension or violation of a law of nature. Is not that the account which Hume gives of the matter?"

"I think it is. I am afraid, however, that at the very outset we should have some difficulty in determining one of the phrases used in this very definition,—namely, how are we to understand a *law* of nature? I do not ask whether *law* implies a lawgiver; you will assert it, and I shall not gainsay it: it is at present immaterial.— But do you not mean by a *law* of nature (I am asking the question merely to ascertain whether or not we are thinking of the same thing) just this;—the *fact* that similar phenomena uniformly reappear in an observed series of antecedents and consequents, which series is invariable so far as *we* know, and so far as *others* know, whose experience we can *test*. Is not that what you mean? You do not, I presume, suppose you know any thing of the connection which binds together causes and effects, or the manner in which the secret bond (if there be any) which unites antecedents and consequents, in any natural phenomena, is maintained?"

"I certainly make no such pretensions; all that I mean by a law of nature is just what you have mentioned. I shall be well content to adhere to your explanation," answered Fellowes.

"So that when we observe similar phenomena reproduced in the aforesaid series of antecedents and consequents, we call that a law of nature, and affirm that a violation of that law would be a miracle—and impossible?"

"Certainly."

"And further, do you not agree with me that such invariable series is sufficiently certified to us by our own uniform experience,—that of all our neighbours and friends,—and, in a word, that of all whose experience we can *test*?"

"I agree with you."

"I am content," replied Harrington; "but at the outset it seems to me that the expression I have used requires a little expansion to meet the sophistry of our opponents. I will either explain myself now, and then leave you to judge; or I will say no more of the matter here, but pursue our discussion, and let the difficulty (if there be one) disclose itself in the course of it, and be provided for as may be in our power."

"What is it?"

"It is this;—that it cannot with truth be said, in relation to many phenomena, that (so far as our experience informs us) they *do* follow each other in an absolutely invariable order; which phenomena, nevertheless, we believe to be as much under the dominion of *law* as the rest; and any violation of this law, I presume, you would think as much a miracle as any other. For example, we do not find the same remedies or the same regimen will produce the same effects upon different individuals at different times; again, the varieties of the weather, in every climate, are dependent upon so many causes, that it transcends all human skill to calculate them. Yet I dare say you can easily imagine certain *degrees and continuity* of change in these variable phenomena which you would not hesitate to call as much *miracles* as if the dead were raised, or the sun stayed in mid-heaven."

"Yes, unquestionably," replied Fellowes: "if I found, for instance, that a dozen men could take an ounce of arsenic or half a pound of opium with impunity, I should not hesitate to regard it as a miracle, although the precise amount sufficient to kill in any particular case might not be capable of being ascertained. In the same manner, if I found that though the amount of heat and cold in summer and winter in our climate is subject to marked variations, yet that suddenly for several consecutive years we had more frost in July than in December; that gooseberries and currants were getting ripe on Christmas day, and men were skating on the Serpentine on the 10th of August, I should certainly argue that a change tantamount to a miracle had been wrought in nature."

"You have just expressed my own feelings on that point," said Harrington; "and it was this very consideration which made me say that, in order to render my expression perfectly clear, and to obviate misconception and misrepresentation, we must endeavour to include this very frequent case of a certain limited variation from the order of nature as consistent with the *absence* of miracle; and a certain degree of that variation as inconsistent with it."

"Will you just state our criterion once more, with the limitation attached; and then I shall know better whether we are certainly agreed in the criterion we ought to employ."

"I say, then," resumed Harrington, "that our uniform experience, that of our friends and neighbours, and of all whose experience we have the opportunity of *testing*, as to the order of nature—meaning by that either an order absolutely invariable or varying only within *limits* which are themselves absolutely invariable—justifies us in pronouncing an event contradicting such experience to be an *impossibility*. If the principle is worth any thing, let us embrace it, and inflexibly apply it."

"And I, for one," replied Fellowes, "am quite satisfied with the principle and the limitations you have laid down; and am so confident of its correctness, that I do not hesitate to say that all the miraculous histories on record are to be summarily rejected."

"For example," said Harrington, "we have seen the sun rise every morning and set every evening all our lives; and every one whose experience we can test has seen the same. Every man who has come into the world has come into it but one way, and has as certainly gone out of it, and has not returned; and every one whose experience we can test affirms the same. We therefore conclude, on this uniform and invariable experience, that the same sequences took place yesterday and the day before, and will take place to-morrow and the day after; and we may fearlessly apply this principle both to the past and the future. I know of no other reason for rejecting a miracle; and if I am to apply the principle at all to phenomena which have not fallen under my own observation, I must apply it without restriction."

"I am quite of your mind."

"You think, with me, that *our* experience — the experience of those about us — the experience of all whose experience we have the means of testing — is sufficient to settle the question as to the experience of those whose experience we have *not* the means of testing; who lived, for example, a thousand years before we were born; or in a distant part of the world, where we have never been?"

"Certainly; why should we hesitate so to apply it?"

"I am sure I know not; and you see I am *not* unwilling so to apply it. Only I asked the question, because we must not forget that many say it is begging the point in dispute; for, as a 'miracle' has not been exerted on *us* to give us a vision of the *past* experience of man, or his *present* experience in any part of the world we never visited, our opponents affirm that to say that the experience we trust to has been and is the *universal* experience of man, is a clear *petitio principii*."

"Surely," said Fellowes, "it may be said that the *general* experience of mankind has been of such a character?"

"Exactly so, as a postulate from our experience, as a *generalised assumption* that *our* experience may be taken as a specimen and criterion of *all* experience. We assume *that* — we do not *prove* it. It is just as in any other case of induction; we say, 'Because this is true in twenty or thirty or a hundred instances (as the case may be), which we can *test* — *therefore* it is generally or universally true;' we do not say because this is true in these instances, and because it is *also* generally or universally true, therefore it is so! No; our true premise is restricted to what alone we *know* from our experience and the experience of all whose experience we can *test* if we please. This is our *real* ground on which we are to justify our rejection of all miracles; and let us adhere to it. As to your *general* experience, you see, the advocate of miracles easily gets over that. He says, 'Why, no one pretends that miracles are as "plenty as blackberries;" otherwise they would no longer be miracles; these are comparatively rare events, of course; and *being* rare, are necessarily at variance with *general* experience;' and for my part, I should not know how to answer the objection."

"Well, then," said Fellowes, "let us adhere to that which is our real ground of objection, and let us consistently apply it."

"With all my heart," said Harrington: "we agree, then, that our own uniform experience, — that of all our neighbours and friends, — in fact, of all whose experience we can test, is a sufficient criterion of a law of nature, and justifies us in at once rejecting as impossible any alleged fact which violates it."

"Certainly."

"For example, if it were asserted that last year the sun never rose on a certain day, or, rather, for twenty-four hours the rotation of the earth ceased, we should instantly reject the story, without examination of witnesses, or any such thing."

"No doubt of *that*."

"And just so in other cases. — This, then, is our ground. You would not (if I may advise) lay much stress on the fact that there have been so many stories of a supernatural kind *false ?* "

"Why, I do not know whether it would not be wise to insist upon *that* argument. It seems to be not without weight," urged Fellowes.

"Perhaps so," replied Harrington; "but it has, you see, this inconvenience, of proving more than you want. The greater part by far of all religions have been false. But you affirm that there is *one little* system absolutely true. The greater part of the theories of science and philosophy, which men, from time to time, have framed, have also been *false;* and yet *you* believe that there is such a thing as true philosophy and true science. Similarly, the generality of political governments have been founded on vicious principles, yet *you* hope for a political millennium at last. In short, the argument would go to prove, that, as there can never have been any true miracles because there have been so many false ones, so, for similar reasons, it is mere 'vanity and vexation of spirit' to search after truth in religion, or science, or politics; and though a sceptic, like myself, might not much mind it, perhaps it would trammel such a *positive* philosopher as you. Nay, a pertinacious opponent might even say, that, as you believe that in all these last cases there is a substance, else there would not have been the shadows, so, with reference to miracles, the very general belief of them rather argues that there *have* been miracles, than that there have been none. My advice is, that we adhere to those reasons we have assigned, for they are our real reasons."

"Be it so; I hate miracles so much, that I care not by what means the doltish delusion is dissipated."

"Only that the weapons should be fair?"

"Oh! of course."

"To resume, then. I say, that if we were told that last year an event of such a miraculous nature occurred as that the earth did not revolve for twenty-four hours together, we should at once reject it, without any examination of witnesses, or troubling ourselves with any thing of the kind."

"Unquestionably."

"And if it were said to have occurred twenty years ago, we should take the same course."

"Certainly."

"And so, if any such event were said to have occurred eighteen hundred years ago."

"Agreed."

"And if such events were said at *that* day to have occurred eighteen hundred years previously, we believe, of course, the men of that time would have been equally entitled to reason in the same way about them as ourselves; and, in short, that *we* may fearlessly apply the same principle to the same epoch."

"Of course."

"And so for two thousand years before that; and, in fact, we must believe that every thing has always been going on in the same manner,—the sun always rising and setting, men dying and never rising again, and so forth."

"Exactly so, even from the beginning of the Creation," said Fellowes.

"The beginning of the Creation! My good fellow, I do not understand you. As we have been going back we have seen that there is no period at which the same principle of judgment will not apply, and, following it fearlessly, I say that we are in all fairness bound to believe that there *never* has been a period when the present order has been different from what it is; in other words, that the progression has been an eternal one."

"I cannot admit that argument," said Fellowes.

"Then be pleased to provide me with a good answer to it, which will still leave us at liberty to say, that a miracle (that is, a variation from the order of nature as determined by our uniform experience, and by that of the whole circle of our contemporaries), is impossible, and that we may reject at once any pretension of the kind."

"But I do not admit that the *creation* of any thing or of all things is of the nature of a *miracle*."

Harrington smiled. "I am afraid," said he, "that to common sense, to fair reasoning, to any philosopher worthy of the name, there would be no difference, except in *magnitude*, between such an event as the sudden appearance of an animal (say man) for the *first* time in our world, or the *first* appearance of a tree (such a thing never having been before), and the restoration to life of a dead man. Each is, to all intents and purposes, a violation of the present established series of antecedents and consequents, and comes strictly within the limits of our definition of a miracle; and a miracle, you know, is impossible. The only difference will be, that the *miracle* in the one case will be greater and more astonishing than that in the other."

"But it is impossible, in the face of geologists, to contend that there have not been many such revolutions in the history of the world as these. Man himself is of comparatively recent introduction into our system."

"I cannot help what the geologists affirm. If we are to abide by our *principle*, we have no warrant to believe that there have been any such violations, or infractions, or revolutions of nature's laws in the world's history. If they contend for the interpolation of events in the history of the universe, which, by our criterion, are of the nature of miracles, and we are convinced that miracles are impossible,—we must reject the conclusions of geologists."

"But may we not say, that the great epochs in the history of the universe are themselves but the manifestation of *law?*"

"In no other sense, I think, than the advocate of miracles is entitled to say that the intercalation of miracles in the world's history is also according to law,—parts, though minute parts, of a universal plan, and permitted for reasons worthy of the Creator. To both, or neither, is the same answer open. Your objection is, I think, a mere sophistical evasion of the difficulty. There is no difference whatever in the *nature* of the events, except that the variations from the 'established series of sequences' is infinitely greater in those portentous revolutions of the universe to which the geologist points your attention. The application of our principle (as you affirm with me) will justify us in at once pronouncing any variation from the 'established series,' whether occurring yesterday, a year ago, a thousand years ago, or a million of years ago, incredible; it will, in the same manner, justify the men of any age in saying the same of all previous ages; and I, therefore, while contending for your principle with you, carry it consistently out, and affirm that the established series of antecedents and consequents (as we now find it) must be regarded as *eternal*, because creation would do what a miracle is supposed to do, and a miracle, you know, is impossible. You are silent."

"I am not able to retract acquiescence in the principle,

and I am as little inclined to concede the conclusions you would draw from it."

"As you please; only, in the latter case, provide me with an *answer*. If you saw now introduced on the earth for the first time a being as unlike man as man is unlike the other animals, — say with seven senses, wings on his shoulders, a pair of eyes behind his head as well as in front of it, and the tail of a peacock, by way of finishing him off handsomely, — would you not call such a phenomenon a miracle?"

"I think I should," said Fellowes, laughing.

"And if the creature died, leaving no issue, would you continue to call it so?"

"Yes."

"But if you found that he was the head of a *race* as man was, and a whole nation of such monsters springing from him, then would you say that this wonderful intrusion into the sphere of our experience was *no* miracle, but that it was merely according to *law*?"

"I should."

"Verily, my dear friend, I am afraid the world will laugh at us for making such fantastical distinctions. This infraction of 'established sequences' ceases to be miraculous, if the wonder is perpetuated and sufficiently multiplied! Meantime, what becomes of the prodigy during the time in which it is *uncertain* whether any thing will come of it or not? You will say, I suppose, (the interpolation in the 'series' of phenomena being just what I have supposed) that it is *uncertain* whether it is to be regarded as miraculous or not, *till we know whether it is to be repeated or not*.

"I think I must, if I adhere to the principle I am now defending."

"Very well; only in the meantime you are in the ludicrous position of facing a phenomenon of which you do *not know* whether you will call it a miracle or not, — the contingency, meantime, on which it is to be decided, not at all, as I contend, affecting the matter; since you allow that it is the infraction of the previously established order of sequences, as known to uniform experience, which constitutes a miracle! If so I must maintain that the creation of man was, for the same reasons, of the essence of a miracle. You seem to think there is no objection to the admission of miracles, provided they are astounding and numerous enough; or provided they are a long time about, instead of being instantaneously wrought. I must remind you, that to the *principle* of our argument these things are quite immaterial. Whether the revolution by which the established order of sequences is absolutely infringed—the face of the universe or of our globe transformed, or an entirely new race (as, for example, man) originated— I say, whether such change be produced slowly or quickly, is of no consequence in the world to our argument. It is whether or not a series of phenomena be produced as absolutely transcending the sphere of all experience, as those events we admit to be *impossible*, called 'miracles.' That the introduction of man upon the earth for the first time (for you will not allow his race eternal), or the origination of a sun, is not at all to be reckoned as transcending that experience, I cannot understand. Nor can I understand it a bit better by your saying that it is in conformity with the vague something you are pleased to call a *law*. It is a very safe phrase, however; for, as neither you nor any one else can interpret it, no one can refute you. This *law* is a most convenient thing! It repeals, it appears to me, all other laws—even those of logic. Perhaps it would be better to say that miracles are no miracles when they are '*lawful*' miracles. No: let us keep our principle intact from all such dangerous admissions as these. In that way only are we safe."

"Safe, do you call it? I see not how, if we carry out this principle in the way and to the extent you propose, we can reply to the atheist or to the pantheist, who tells us that the universe is but an eternal evolution of phenomena in one infinite series, or in an eternal recurrence of finite cycles."

"And what is that to *you* or *me*? How can we help our principle (if we are to hold it at all) leading to some such conclusion? We are, I presume, anxious to know the *truth.* You see that Strauss, who is the most strenuous asserter of the *impossibility* of miracles, is also a pantheist. I know not whether you may not become one yourself."

"Never," said Fellowes, vehemently; "never, I trust, shall I yield to that 'desolating pantheism' (as worthy Mr. Newman calls it), which is now so rife."

"I think Mr. Newman's principles *ought* to guide you thither. You seem to hold fast by his skirts at present; but I very much doubt whether you have yet reached the termination of your career. You have, you must admit, made advances quite as extraordinary before."

"We shall see.—But I suppose you have reached the end of the objections which your wayward scepticism suggests against a conclusion which we both admit; or have you any more?"

"Oh, plenty; and amongst the rest, I am afraid we must admit—whether we admit or not your expedient of *law*—a miracle, or something indistinguishable from it, as involved in the creation and preservation of the *first* man,—since you *will* have a first man."

"What do you mean?"

"I mean, that, supposing the creation of man to be no miracle, because he entered by *law;* or that that *first* fact (which would *otherwise* be miraculous) is not such simply because it is the *first* of a series of such facts,—I should like to see whether we have not even then to deal with a miracle, or a fact as absolutely *unique;* and which was not connected with *any series* of similar facts."

"I think you would find it very hard to prove it."

"*Nous verrons.*—I am sure we shall not disagree as to the fact that man, however he came into the world, sooner or later, by ordinary or extraordinary methods, by some *lawful* wedlock of nature, or by some miracle which is *not* 'lawful,' is endowed by nature with various faculties and susceptibilities."

"Certainly," said Fellowes, laughing; "if you demand my assent to nothing more than that, I shall easily admit your premises and deny your conclusion."

"You will also admit, I think, that the process by which man comes to the use of these faculties, and powers, and so forth, is very gradual?"

"Assuredly."

"And will you not also admit that the development and command of these is something very different from the 'potentialities' themselves, as my uncle here would call them;—that, for example, we have the faculty of vision; but that the *art* of seeing involves a slow and laborious process, acquired not without the concurrent exercise of other senses; and that the *apparatus* for walking is perfect even in an infant; but that the *art* of walking is, in fact, a wonderful acquisition; further, that the command given us by these faculties, as actually exercised, is immensely greater than would be conferred by each alone? In one word, you will allow that man, when he comes to the use of his faculties, is, as has been well said, a *bundle of habits*, or, as Burke puts it, is a creature who, to a great extent, has the making of himself."

"I am much at my ease," said Fellowes; "I shall not dispute any of these premises either."

"And will you not also admit that as man comes into the world *now*, a long time is required for his development; and that during that time he is absolutely dependent on the care of those who have already in their turn required *similar* care?"

"Seeing that we have had fathers and mothers—as I suppose our grandfathers and grandmothers also had— there can be as little doubt of this as of the preceding points," said Fellowes, rather condescendingly.

"And that many of the functions which thus task their care, are necessary for our existence, and for any chance of our being able to *develope into men?*"

"I think so, of course."

"So that, if an infant were exposed on a mountain side or forest, you would have no doubt he would perish (unless it pleased some kind-hearted wolf to suckle him) before he could come to the use of his faculties, and develope them by exercise."

"I think," said the other, "your premises perfectly innocent; I shall not contest them."

"A little further," said Harrington, "we may go together; and then, if I mistake not, you will pause before you go one step further. This, then, is the *normal* condition of humanity?"

"Yes."

"Do you think the first man was like us in these respects?"

"I cannot tell."

"I dare engage you cannot—it is a very natural answer. But he either *was*, I suppose, or was *not*. That, I think, you will grant me." He assented, though rather reluctantly.

"Pray please yourself," said Harrington; "for it is quite immaterial to me which alternative you take. If man *was* in our condition, then, though the 'lawful miracle' by which he was brought into the world might have made him a baby of six feet high, he would have been no more than a baby still. All that was to constitute him a *man*—all those *habits* by which alone his existence was capable of being preserved, and without which he must have perished immediately after his creation, in which case you and I should have been spared the necessity of all this discussion on the subject —would have to be learned; and his existence during that time—and a long time it must have been, having no teachers and aids as we have—must have been preserved by a—miracle. If he were taught by the Creator himself, then we have the miracle in *that* direction. If he were not brought into the world under the same conditions of development as we are, but with *habits ready made*—if, indeed, that be not a contradiction—then we have a miracle in *that* direction; if he had his faculties preternaturally quickened and expanded, so as to acquire instantaneously, or possess by instinct, what we acquire by a long and slow process, and not for many years— then we have a miracle in *that* direction. If you do not like these suppositions, I see but one other; and that is, that being a baby—though, as I said, a baby six feet high—he had an angel nurse sent down expressly to attend him, and to push or wheel him about the walks of paradise in a celestial go-cart. But then, I think that in this last particular we shall hardly say that we have got rid of a miracle, though it would doubtless be a miracle of a very ludicrous kind. If you can imagine any other supposition, I shall be glad to hear it."

"I acknowledge I can form no supposition on the subject."

"Only remember that if you could, the theory would still suppose man's actual preservation and development effected under totally different conditions from those which have formed the *uniform experience* of all his posterity; and so far from any subterfuge of a *law* stepping in, it is a single expedient provided for our first parent alone."

"I do not think we are at all in a condition to consider any such case, about which we cannot know any thing," replied Fellowes.

"Neither do *I;* but pardon me—the question *I* asked does not depend upon any such knowledge; it is a question which is wholly independent whether of our ignorance or our knowledge. Granting, as you do, that man was *created*, but that it was no miracle, nor any thing analogous to one (as *you* say), still *either* he was created subject to *our* conditions of development and preservation, or he was *not;* if he was not, then I fear we have in form the miracle we wish to evade; if he was, then I fear also that there are but the three imaginable modes of obviating the difficulty, which I have so liberally provided; and supposing there were a thousand, I fear still that they all involve a departure from the 'uniform course of nature.'"

"But I do not see," replied Fellowes, "that it is absolutely necessary, supposing that the first man was thrown upon the green of paradise——"

"Or in a forest, or on a moor," said Harrington, "for you know nothing of paradise."

"Well then in a forest, or on a moor;—I say if man were cast out there, the same helpless being, which all his posterity are,—unfortified, as the lower animals are, by feathers or hair, or by instincts equal to theirs,—who can affirm that it was beyond the *possibilities* of his nature, that he might survive this cruel experiment? crawl, perhaps, for an indefinite period on all-fours— live on berries, and at last, by very slow degrees doubtless, but still at last, emerge into——"

"The dignity of a savage," cried Harrington, "as the *first* step towards something better,—his Creator having beneficently created him something infinitely worse! Surely you must be returning to a savage yourself, even to hint at such a pedigree. But, I have done: till those cases of which certain philosophers have said so much, have been authenticated; till you can produce an instance of a new-born babe, exposed on a mountain side, in all the helplessness of his natal hour, and self-preserved— nay, two of them—for you must at least have a pair of these 'babes in the wood;' and till, moreover, it can be shown that they would have survived this experiment so as to preserve the characteristics of humanity a little better than the 'wild boy of Germany,' and were fit to be the heads of the human family, I shall at times be strangely tempted to embrace *any* theory as infinitely more probable. I cannot think it was in *this* way that our first parents made their *entrée* into the world. I hope not, for the credit of the Creator, as well as for the happiness of his offspring. Of the *moral* bearings of such a brutal theory, I say nothing; but if it be true, all I can say is, that I am glad that you and I, my dear Fellowes, are not the immediate *children*, but so fortunate as to be only the great-great-great-great grandchildren of God! You have well called it a 'cruel experiment:' according to this the first Father of all thrust forth his children into the world to be for an indefinite time worse than the beasts, who were carefully provided against miserable man's inconveniences! Certainly, I think you may alter the account of man's creation, given in Genesis, to great advantage. Instead of God's saying, 'Let us create man in *our* image,' he must be supposed to have said, 'Let us create man in the image of a BEAST;' and in the image of a BEAST created he him, male and female created he them; and very imperfect beasts they must have been, after all. This is that old savage theory which I had supposed was pretty well abandoned. If the necessity of denying miracles imposes any necessity of believing *that*, I fear I shall sooner be got to believe a thousand."

"Well," said Fellowes, who seemed ashamed of this theory, but knew not how to abandon it; "I cannot believe there have been any *miracles*, and, what is more, I will not."

"That is perhaps the best reason you have given yet," said Harrington. "The Will is indeed your only irresistible logician. You are one degree, at all events, better off than I, for I can hardly say either that I believe, or that I do *not* believe in miracles."

"And yet," continued Harrington, after a pause, "two or three other strange consequences seem to follow from that seemingly undeniable principle on which we base the conclusion that there neither has been nor can be any such thing as a miracle; in other words, a departure from the established series of sequences which, as tested by our own experience, and by that of other men, we are convinced is stable. Will you see with me whether there is any fair mode of escaping from them? I should be very glad if I could do so."

"What are they?"

"Why first, I am afraid it must be said, that we must entirely justify a man in the condition of the Eastern prince mentioned by Hume, who could not be induced to believe that there was such a thing as ice. I am afraid that he was quite in the right; and yet we know that in fact he was wrong."

"You are not, then, satisfied with Hume's own solution?"

"So far from it, that I cannot see, upon the principles on which *we* refuse to believe miracles, that it is even intelligible. We agree, do we not, that from the experience we have, (and so far as we can ascertain, from every body else's,) of the uniform course of events, of the established order of sequences, we are to reject any assertion of a violation of those sequences; as, for example, of a man's coming into the world in any preternatural manner, or when he has once gone out of it, coming into it again; and that we are entitled to do this without any examination of the witnesses to any such fact, merely on the strength of the principles aforesaid?"

"I admit that we have agreed to this."

"Now was not the assertion that in a certain quarter of the world water became solid as stone, could be cut into pieces, and be put into one's pockets, contrary, in a similar manner, to all the phenomena which the said prince had witnessed, and also to the uniform experience of all about him from his earliest years?"

"It certainly was."

"He was *right*, then, in rejecting the fact; that is, he was right in rejecting the possibility of such an occurrence," said Harrington.

"But did we not ourselves say, with Hume, that as we see that there is not an absolute uniformity in the phenomena of nature, but that they are varied within certain limits in different climates and countries, so it does not become us to say that a phenomenon, though *somewhat* variable, *is* a violation of the usual order of sequences?"

"We did: but we also agreed, I think, that those variations were to be within invariable limits, as tested by the whole of our experience; we did not include within those variations what is diametrically *contrary* (as in the present case) to all our own experience and that of every body about us. If it is to extend to *such* variations, what do we say but this, that the order of nature is uniform and invariable, except where—it is the reverse; and, as it seems it sometimes is so, see what comes of the admission. A man asserts the reality of a miracle which you reject at once as simply impossible; as contrary to your experience and that of every one whose experience you can test. It will be easy for him to say, and upon Hume's evasion he *will* say, that it was performed, for aught you know, under conditions so totally different from those which *ordinarily* obtain in relation to the same order of events, that you are no adequate judge as to whether it was possible or not. He acknowledges that a miracle is a very *rare* occurrence; that it is performed for special ends; is strictly limited to time and place, like those phenomena the Indian prince was asked to believe; and that your experience cannot embrace it, nor is warranted in pronouncing upon it. I really fear that if our incredulous prince is to be condemned, our principle will be ruined. I am anxious for his safe deliverance, I assure you."

"Still I cannot see that we can deny that phenomena *may* be manifested in virtue of the laws of nature, totally different from those which we have ever seen or heard of."

"What! So different that the phenomena in question shall be a *total departure* from that order of nature of which alone we and all about us are cognisant; in fact, all but the *one* man, who tells us the strange thing, we being at the same time totally incapable of testing his experience?"

"Yes," said Fellowes; "I *must* grant it."

"I see," said Harrington, "you are bent on the destruction of our criterion. Do you not perceive that if our experience and that of the immense majority, or of all about us, be not a sufficient criterion of the laws of nature, our argument falls to the ground? 'Your principle,' our adversaries will say, 'is a fallacious one; nature has her laws, no doubt, which apply to miracles as to every other phenomenon; but in assuming your experience to be a sufficient criterion of these laws, you have not been interpreting *her* laws, but imposing upon her your own.' If unknown powers of nature may thus reverse our experience and the experience of all those whose experience, under the given conditions, we have opportunities of testing, we ought to abstain from saying that some unknown powers may not also have wrought miracles. Let us then affirm consistently the sufficiency of our criterion; and the prince aforesaid must do the same; and it warranted him, I say, in believing that there neither was nor could be such a thing as ice."

"But this seems ridiculous," said Fellowes; "for according to this, different and opposite experiences may, in different places, give different and opposite measures of the laws of nature; which nevertheless are supposed to be invariably the same, or invariably within the limits certified by that experience."

"I cannot help it: upon that same experience *we* must believe it true that there are no miracles, and our unbelieving prince, that there could be no such thing as ice; for to *him* it was a miracle. If we do not reason thus, may we not be compelled to admit that our uniform experience, with its limited variations, is no rule at all, and that there are cases for which it makes no provision? and may not the advocate for miracles say that miracles are amongst them? No, let us adhere to our *principle*, and adhering to it, I wish to know whether the prince in question was not quite right in saying that there neither was nor could be such a thing as ice; for the assertion that there was, was contrary to all his experience, and to that of every soul about him."

"I must say, that if we look only to the principle of this uniform experience, he was *right.*"

"But he rejected the *truth?*"

"He certainly did."

"And he was *right* in rejecting the truth?"

"Certainly, upon *your* principle."

"Upon *my* principle! Do not say upon my principle, unless you mean to deny that you too embrace it; if you give up that principle, you lay yourself open at once to the retort that your position is insecure; that you have taken your experience as a sufficient criterion of the possibilities of events, when it is in fact merely a measure of such as have fallen under your own observation."

"Perhaps," said Fellowes, "I should say that the prince in question was justified at *first* in rejecting the fact, but that when he found other men, whose veracity he could not suspect, coming from the same regions of the world, and affirming the same phenomenon, it was his business to correct his experience, and to admit that the fact was so."

"I am surprised to hear you say so; you are again ruining our principle. Do you admit that the assertion that there was a place on earth at which water in large quantities became solid, was apparently as great a violation of all the experience of this man as what is ordinarily called a miracle is of ours?"

"I cannot deny that it was so."

"But yet you think, that though justified in disbelieving it at *first*, he would not be so when others, whose veracity and motives he had no reason to suspect, told him the same tale?"

"Yes."

"Why, then is not this plainly to make a belief of such events depend upon *testimony*, and do we not give up altogether our sufficient principle of rejection of *all* such testimony? You are yielding, without doubt, the principle of our opponents, who affirm that there is no event so improbable that a certain combination of testimony would not be sufficient to warrant your reception of it; because, as they say, that testimony might be given under such circumstances, so variously certified, and so above suspicion,—that it would be more improbable that the statement to which it applied (however strange), should be false, than that the testimony should not be true; in other words, that the falsehood of the testimony would be the greater *miracle* of the two. And they say this, because (as they assert) the uniform experience on which we found our objection to any miraculous narrative is no less applicable to the world of mind than to the world of matter; that there is not, indeed, an absolute uniformity of experience in the *former*, as neither is there in the *latter;* but that neither in one nor in the other is there any absolute *bouleversement* of the principles and constitution of nature; which they say would be implied, if under *all* conceivable circumstances testimony might prove false. And yet now you seem to admit the very thing for which they contend; and in contending for it, you give up your case. Doing so, you certainly get rid of one of the paradoxical conclusions which my wretched scepticism sometimes suggests to me, as throwing a doubt on the integrity of our principle; I say your admission gets rid of it. But then it is with the ruin of the principle itself."

"What was that paradox?"

"It is this; that if we adhere to our principle, we must deny that *any* amount of testimony is sufficient to warrant the belief of a miracle."

"That is what we do maintain."

"I thought so; but you seem to me to have hastily given it up. Let us then again maintain that our prince, in denying what was a miracle to him, was not only consistent in saying that it could not be, when *first* asserted to him, but also when *last* asserted; and died an orthodox infidel in the possibility of ice, or an orthodox believer in the eternal fluidity of water, whichever you prefer to consider it."

"Well, and what then?"

"Why then, let *us* act upon our principle with equal consistency in other cases; for you say that there is no amount or complexity of evidence which would induce you to believe in a miracle."

"I do."

"Let us suppose it was asserted that a man known to have been dead and buried, had risen again, and after having been seen by many, had at last, in the presence of a multitude, on a clear day, ascended to heaven through the calm sky, without artificial wings or balloon, or any such thing; that he was seen to pass out of sight of the gazing crowd who watched and watched in vain for his return; and that he had never more been seen. Let us suppose that the witnesses who saw this, constantly affirmed it; that amongst them were many known to you, whose veracity you had no reason to suspect, and who had no imaginable motive to deceive you; let us suppose further that they persisted in affirming this in spite of all contumely and contempt, insult and wrong; amidst threats of persecution, and persecution itself; lastly, let there be amongst them many, who *before* this event had been as strenuous assertors of the impossibility of a miracle as yourself: I want to know whether you would believe this story thus authenticated, or not?"

"But it is, I think, unfair to put any such case; for there never *was* such an event so authenticated."

"It is quite sufficient to test our *principle*, that you can imagine such testimony. If that principle is sound, it is plain that it will apply to all *imaginable* degrees of testimony as well as to all *actual*. *No testimony*, you say, can establish a miracle. This is true or not. If you admit that there are any degrees in this matter, you come at last to the old argument, which you abjure; namely, that whether a miraculous event has taken place or not depends on the *degree* of evidence with which it is substantiated, and that must be the result of a certain investigation of it in the particular *alleged* case. You remember the story of the ring of Gyges, which made the wearer invisible. Plato tells us how a man *ought* to act, and how a good man would act, if he had such a ring. Cicero tells us how absurd it would be to reply to his reasoning (as one did), by saying that there never was such a ring. It was not necessary to the force of the illustration that there should be such a ring. So neither is it necessary to my argument that there should be such testimony as I have supposed, to enable us to see whether we are prepared to admit the truth of your principle, that *no* evidence can establish a miracle. Once more, then, I ask you whether, on the supposition of such testimony, you would reject the supposed fact, or not?"

"Well, then, I should say, that since *no* testimony can establish a miracle, I *should* reject it."

"Bravo, Fellowes! I do of all things like to see an unflinching regard to a principle, when once laid down."

"But, would not *you* also reject it, upon the same principle?"

"Of course I should, if the principle be true; but ah! my friend, pardon me for acknowledging my infirmities; my miserable scepticism tosses me to and fro. I have not your strength of Will; and I fear that the rejection in such a case would cost me many qualms and doubts. Such is the infirmity of our nature, and so much may be said on all sides! And I fear that I should be more likely to have these uneasy thoughts, inasmuch as I fancy I see a difficult dilemma (I but now referred to it), which would be proposed to us by some keen-sighted opponent — I say not with justice — who would endeavour to show that we had abandoned our principle in the very attempt to maintain it; that the bow from which we were about to launch so fatal an arrow at the enemy, had broken in our hands, and left us defenceless."

"What dilemma do you refer to?" said Fellowes.

"I think such an adversary might perhaps say: 'That same uniform experience on which you justify the rejection of all miracles, — does it extend only to *one* part of nature, to the physical and material only, or to the mental and spiritual also?' In other words, if there were such things as miracles at all, might there be miracles in connection with mind as well as in connection with matter? What would you say?"

"What *can* I say but what Hume himself says, so truly and so beautifully, in his Essay on 'Necessary Connection,' and 'On Liberty and Necessity,' namely, 'that there is a uniformity in both the moral and physical world; and that nature does not transgress certain limits in either the one or the other?' You must remember that he says so?"

"I do," said Harrington. "Now, I am afraid our astute adversary would say that such a complication of false testimony, as we have supposed, would itself be a flagrant violation of the established series of sequences, on which, as applied to the physical world, we justify the rejection of *all* miracles; that we have got rid of a miracle by admitting a miracle; that our uniform experience has broken down with us."

"But, again I say, there never was such a case of testimony," urged Fellowes.

"I wish this could help us; but it plainly will not; because we have concluded that if there *were* such testimony we *must* believe it false, and therefore should admit that the *miracle* of its falsehood was, in that case, necessary to be believed; not to say that there *has been*, in the opinion of millions, testimony often given to miracles, which, *if* false, does imply that the laws of human nature must have been turned *topsy-turvy* — and I, for my part, know not how to disprove it. If, in such cases, the testimony, the falsity of which would be a miracle, is not to be rejected, then we must admit that the miracle which it supports is true. — I must leave it there," said Harrington, with an air of comic resignation; "I cannot answer for any thing, except that you may reject both miracles *alternately*, if that will be any comfort to you, without being able to disbelieve both *simultaneously*. If you believe the testimony false, you must believe the alleged miracle false; but you will have then the moral miracle to believe. If you believe the testimony true, you will then believe the physical miracle true. Perhaps the best way will be to disbelieve both *alternately* in rapid succession, and you will then hardly perceive the difficulty at all!"

There was here a brief pause. Harrington suddenly resumed. "These are very perplexing considerations. One thing, I confess, has often puzzled me much; and that is, — what should we do, in what state of mind should we be, if we *did* see a miracle?"

"Of what use is the discussion of such a particular case, when you know it is impossible that we should ever see it realised?" replied Fellowes.

"Of course it is; just as it is *impossible* that we should ever see levers perfectly inflexible, or cords perfectly flexible. Nevertheless it is perfectly possible to entertain such a hypothetical case, and to reason with great conclusiveness on the consequences of such a supposition; and in the same way we can imagine that we have seen a miracle; and what then?"

"Why, if we were to *see* one, of course seeing is believing. We must give up our principle," said Fellowes, laughing.

"Do you think so? I think we should be very foolish, then. How can we be *sure* that we have seen it? Can it appeal to any thing stronger than our *senses*, and have not our senses often beguiled us? Must we not rather abide by that general induction from the evidence to which our ordinary experience points us? In other words, ought we not to adhere to the great principle we have already laid down, that a miracle is impossible?"

"But, according to this, if we err in that principle, and God were to work a miracle for the very purpose of convincing us, it would be impossible for him to attain his purpose."

"I think it would, my friend, I confess; just for the reason that since we believe a miracle to be impossible, we must believe it impossible for even God to work one; and therefore if we are mistaken, and it *is* possible for him to work one, it is still *impossible* that he should convince us of it."

"I really know not how to go that length."

"Why not? You acknowledge that your senses have deceived you; you know that they have deceived others; and it is on that very ground that you dispose of very many cases of supposed miracles which you are not willing, or are not able, to resolve otherwise. If I believe, then, that a miracle is impossible, I must admit that, if I err in that, it is still impossible for God himself to convince me of it."

Fellowes looked grave, but said nothing.

"And do you know," said Harrington, "I have sometimes thought that Hume, so far from representing his argument from 'Transubstantiation' fairly (there is an obvious fallacy on the very face of it, to which I do not now allude), is himself precisely in the condition in which he represents the believer in miracles?"

Fellowes smiled incredulously. "First, however,"

said he, "what is the more *notorious* fallacy to which you allude?"

"It is so barefaced an assumption that I am surprised that his acuteness did not see it; or that if he saw it, he could have descended to make a point by appearing *not* to see it. It has been often pointed out, and you will recollect it the moment I name it. You know he commences with the well-known argument of Tillotson against Transubstantiation, and flatters himself that he sees a *similar* argument in relation to miracles. Now it certainly requires but a moderate degree of sagacity to see that the very point in which Tillotson's argument *tells*, is that very one in which Hume's is totally unlike it. Tillotson says, that when it is pretended that the bread and wine which are submitted to *his own* senses have been 'transubstantiated into flesh and blood,' the alleged phenomena contradict *his* senses; and that as the information of his senses as much comes from God as the doctrines of Scripture (and even the miracles of Scripture appeal to nothing stronger), he must believe his senses in this case in preference to the assertions of the priest. Hume then goes on quietly to take it for granted that the miracles to which consent is asked, in like manner contradict the testimony of the senses of *him* to *whom the appeal is made;* whereas, in fact, the assertor of the miracle does not pretend that he who denies them has ever seen them, or had the opportunity of seeing them. To make the argument analogous, it ought to be shown that the objector, having been a spectator of the pretended miracles, when and where they were affirmed to have been wrought, had then and there the testimony of his *senses* that no such events had taken place. It is mere juggling with words to say that never to have seen a *like* event is the same argument of an event's never having occurred, as never to have seen that event when it was alleged to have taken place under our very eyes!"

"I give up the reasoning on this point," said Fellowes; "but how, I should like to know, do you retort the argument upon him?"

"Thus; you see that *we* maintain that a miracle is incredible *per se*, because impossible; not to be believed, therefore, on *any* evidence."

"Certainly."

"If, then, we saw what *seemed* a miracle, we should distrust our senses; we should say that it was most likely that they *deceived* us. Hear what Voltaire says in one of his letters to D'Alembert; 'Je persiste à penser que cent mille hommes qui ont vu ressusciter un mort, pourraient bien être cent mille hommes qui auraient la berlue.' And what he says of *their* bad eyes, there is no doubt he would say of his own, if he had been one of the hundred thousand."

"I think so, certainly."

"And Strauss, and Hume, and Voltaire, and you and I, and all who hold a miracle impossible, would distrust our senses, and fall back upon that *testimony* from the general experience of others, which alone could correct our own halting and ambiguous experience?"

"Certainly."

"It appears, then, my good fellow, that the position of those who deny and those who assert miracles is exactly the reverse of Hume's statement. The man who believes 'Transubstantiation' distrusts his senses, and rather believes testimony: and even so would he who has fully made up his mind, on our sublime principle, as to the impossibility of miracles, when any thing which has that appearance crosses his path; he is prepared to deny his senses, and to trust to testimony—to that general experience of others which comes to him and can come to him only in that shape. It is *we*, therefore, and not our adversaries, who are liable to be reached by this unlucky illustration."

Fellowes himself seemed much amused by finding the tables thus turned. For my part, I had difficulty in repressing a chuckle over this display of sceptical candour and subtlety.

"There is perhaps another paradox which may be as well mentioned," resumed Harrington. "It is a little trying to my scepticism, but perhaps will not be to your faith. I mean this. We are constrained to believe from our '*uniform experience*' criterion that no miracle has ever occurred or ever will; in short, it is, as we say, *impossible*. Now the principle which undoubtedly leads us to the conclusion we may regard as a principle of our *nature*, if ever there were one; that is, we are so constituted as to infer the perpetual uniformity of certain sequences of phenomena from our observation of that uniformity."

"Assuredly."

"And as all mankind obviously act upon that same principle in most cases, and we believe that it is part of the very uniformity in question that human nature is radically the same in all ages and in all countries, I think we *ought* to conclude, that it is not you and I only, but the *vast majority* of mankind at all events, who have maintained the impossibility of miracles."

"We *ought* to be able to conclude so," said Fellowes, "but it is very far from being the case. So far from it, that nothing can be plainer than that miraculous legends have been most greedily taken up by the vast majority of mankind, and have made a very common part of almost every form of religion."

"Men do not, then, it appears, in this instance, at all regard the uniform tenor of their experience; so that it is a part of *our* uniform experience, that mankind disregard and disbelieve the lessons of *their* uniform experience. This is almost a miracle of itself,—at all events a curious paradox,—but one which we must not stay to examine: though I confess it leads to one other humiliating conclusion—a little corollary, which I think it is not unimportant to mark; and that is, that we can never expect these enlightened views of ours to spread amongst the mass of mankind."

"Nay, I cannot agree with you. I hope far otherwise, and far better for the human race."

"But will the result not contradict your uniform experience, if your hopes be realised? Is not your experience sufficiently long and sufficiently varied to show, that the belief of miracles and all sorts of prodigies is the *normal* condition of mankind, and that it is only a *comparatively* few who can discern that uniform experience justifies man in believing that no miracle is *possible?* While it teaches us that a miracle is impossible, does it not also teach us that, though none is possible, it is nevertheless impossible that they should not be *generally* believed? Is not this taught us as plainly by our uniform experience as any thing else? See how fairly Hume admits this at the commencement of his Essay on Miracles. He says, 'I flatter myself that I have discovered an argument which, if just, will, with the *wise and learned*, be an everlasting check to all kinds of superstitious delusion, and consequently will be useful as long as the world endures. *For so long, I presume, will the accounts of miracles and prodigies be found in all history, sacred and profane.*' Thus are we led to the conclusion that though miracles never can be real, they will nevertheless be always believed; and that though the truth is with us, it never can be established in the minds of men in general. And, my dear friend, let us be thankful that it never can; for if it could, that fact would have proved the possibility of miracles by contradicting one of those very deductions from uniform experience on the validity of which their impossibility is demonstrated.

"These are some of the perplexities," continued Harrington, "which, as Theætetus says, sometimes make 'my head dizzy,' when I revolve the subject. Meantime, surely a nobler spectacle can hardly present itself than our fairly abiding by our *principle*, amidst so many plausible difficulties as assail it. I know no one principle in theology or philosophy which has been so battered as that of Hume. Not only Campbell, Paley, and so many more, confidently affirm errors in it,—such as his assuming individual or general experience to be universal; his quietly attributing to individual experience a belief of facts which are believed by the vast mass of mankind on *testimony*, and nothing else; his representing the experience of a man who says he has seen a certain event as 'contrary' to the experience of him who says he has *not* seen a *similar* one ; his implying that *no* amount of testimony can establish a miracle, which might compel us to believe *moral* miracles to get rid of physical miracles ; I say not only so, but the most recent investigators of the theory of evidence cruelly abandon him. The argument of Hume and Paley, says De Morgan, in his treatise on Probabilities*, 'is (so far as its mathematical bearing is concerned) a fallacy answered by fallacies'—meaning by this last that Paley had conceded to his opponent more than he *ought* to have done. With similar vexatious opposition, Mr. J. S. Mill says, that to make any alleged fact contradictory to a law of causation, ' the allegation must be that this happened in the absence of *any adequate counteracting* cause. Now in the case of an alleged miracle, the assertion is the exact opposite of this.' He says, ' that all which Hume has made out is that no evidence can prove a miracle to any one who did not previously believe the existence of a being or beings with supernatural power ; or who believed himself to have *full proof* that the character'† of such being or beings is inconsistent with such an interference ; that is, the argument could have no force unless either a man believed there was no God at all, or the objector happened to be something like a God himself! And now, lastly, I have shown that the predicament of Hume and Voltaire, and Strauss, and you and myself (if consistent), is just the reverse of that in which the argument from Transubstantiation represents it. But never mind ; so much more glory is due to us for abiding by our principle. I begin almost to think that I am arriving at that transcendental ' faith' which you admire so much, and which is totally independent of logic and argument, and all ' intellectual processes whatever.'"

---

* Encyclopædia Metropolitana : Theory of Probabilities, § 182.
† System of Logic, vol. ii. pp. 186, 187.

July 23. I this day read to Mr. Fellowes the paper I had promised a week or two before, and which I had entitled—

AN EXTERNAL REVELATION EVEN OF ELEMENTARY "SPIRITUAL AND MORAL TRUTH," VERY POSSIBLE, AND VERY USEFUL; AND IN ANALOGY WITH THE CONDITIONS OF HUMAN DEVELOPMENT, WHETHER IN THE INDIVIDUAL OR THE SPECIES.

It is necessary to observe in the outset that even if I were to grant your proposition, " that a revelation of moral and spiritual truth is impossible "—understanding by such " truth " what you seem to mean—the truth which " Natural Religion," as it is called, has recognised in *some shape or other*, (for it has varied not a little,)— it would leave the *chief* reasons for imparting an external revelation just where they were. I, at least, should never contend that the *sole* or even *chief* object of an external revelation is to impart elementary moral or spiritual truth, however *possible* I may deem it. On the contrary, I am fully persuaded that the great purpose for which such a revelation has been given, is to communicate facts and truths, many of which were quite transcendental to the human faculties; which man would never have discovered, and most of which he would never have surmised. All this your favourite Mr. Newman perceived in his earlier days clearly enough, and has recorded his sentiments held at that period in his " Phases." * If I were to grant you, therefore, your proposition, it would leave the question of an external revelation untouched; your hasty inference from it that *every* book-revelation is to be rejected is perfectly gratuitous.

But I am thoroughly persuaded that the notion of the impossibility of an external revelation of moral and spiritual truth, even of the elementary form already referred to, is a fallacy.

Whether the religious faculty in men be a simple faculty or (as Sir James Mackintosh seemed to think

---

* P. 42.

might possibly be the case with conscience), a complex one, constituted by means of several different powers and principles of our nature, is a question not essential to the argument; for I frankly admit at once, with Mr. Newman and Mr. Parker, that there *is* such a susceptibility (simple or complex), and not a mere abortive tendency, as Harrington seems to suppose possible. Otherwise I cannot, I confess, account for the fact (so largely insisted upon by Mr. Parker) of the very general, the all but universal adoption by man of *some* religion, and the *power*, the prodigious power, which, even when false, hideously false, it exerts over him. But, then, I must as frankly confess that I can as little account for all the (not only terrible but) uniform aberrations of this susceptibility, on which Harrington has insisted, and which, I do think, prove, (if ever truth was proved by induction,) one of two things; either that, as he says, this susceptibility in man was originally defective and rudimentary, or that man is no longer in his normal state; in other words, that he is, as the Scriptures declare, depraved. I acknowledge I accept this last solution; and firmly believe, with Pascal, that *without* it, moral and religious philosophy must toil over the problem of humanity in vain.

If this be so, we have, of course, no difficulty in believing that there may be, in spite of the existence of the religious faculty in man, ample scope for an external revelation, to correct its aberrations and remedy its maladies.

But you will say that this fact is not to be taken for granted. I admit it; and, therefore, lay no further stress upon it. I go one step further; and shall endeavour at least, to prove, that supposing man is just as he was created, yet *also* supposing, what neither Mr. Parker nor Mr. Newman will deny, (and if they did, the whole history of the world would confute them,) that man's religious faculty is not uniform or determinate in its action, but is dependent on *external* development and culture for assuming the form it does, ample scope is still left for an *external* revelation. I contend that the entire condition of this susceptibility (as shown by experience) proves that if in truth an external revelation be impossible, it is not because it has superseded the necessity for one; and that the declaration of the elder Deists and modern "spiritualists" on this subject, in the face of what all history proves man to be, is the most preposterous in the world.

Further; I contend that all the analogies derived from the fundamental laws of the development of man's nature — from a consideration of the relations in which that nature stands to the external world — from the absolute dependence of the individual on *external* culture, and that of the whole species on its *historic* development — are all in favour of the notion both of the possibility and utility of an external revelation, and even in favour of that particular *form* of it which Mr. Newman and you so contemptuously call a "*book*" revelation.

I. I argue from all the analogies of the fundamental laws of the development of the human mind. Nor do I fear to apply the reasoning even to the cases in which it has been so confidently asserted that there *can* be no revelation, on the fallacious ground that a revelation "of spiritual and moral truth" presupposes in man certain principles to which it appeals. To possess certain faculties for the appreciation of spiritual and moral truth, is one thing; to acquire the conscious possession of that truth, is another; the former fact would not make an external revelation superfluous, or an empty name. Every thing in the process of the mind's development, goes to show that, whatever its capacities, tendencies, faculties, 'potentialities," (call them what you will,) a certain external influence is necessary to awaken its dormant life; to turn a "potentiality" into an "energy;" to transform a dim *inkling* of a truth into an intelligent, vital, conscious recognition of it. — Nor is this law confined to mind alone; all nature attests its presence. All effects are the result of properties or susceptibilities in one thing, solicited by external contact with those of others. The fire no doubt may smoulder in the dull and languid embers; it is when the external breeze sweeps over them, that they begin to sparkle and glow, and vindicate the vital element they contain. The diamond in the mine has the same internal properties in the darkness as in the light; it is not till the sun shines upon it, that it flashes on the eye its splendour. Look at a flower of any particular species; we see that as it is developed in connection with a variety of external influences—as it comes successively under the action of the sun, rain, dew, soil, it expands in a particular manner, and in that only. It exhibits a certain configuration of parts, a certain form of leaf, a certain colour, fragrance, and no other. We do not doubt, on the one hand, that without the "skiey influences" these things could never have been; or, on the other, that the flower assumes this form of development, and this alone, in virtue of its internal structure and organisation. But both sets of conditions must conspire in the result.

It is much the same with the mind. That it possesses certain tendencies and faculties, which, as it develops itself, will terminate in certain ideas and sentiments, is admitted; but apart from certain external conditions of development, those sentiments and ideas will, in effect, never be formed—the mind will be in perpetual slumber. Thus, in point of fact, this controversy is connected ultimately with that ancient dispute as to the origin, sources, and genesis of human knowledge and sentiments. I shall simply take for granted that you are (as most philosophers are) an advocate of innate capacities, but not of "innate ideas," of "innate susceptibilities," but not of "innate sentiments;" that is, I presume, you do not contend that the mind possesses more than the faculties — the *laws* of thought and feeling — which, under conditions of external development, actually give birth to *thoughts* and *feelings*. These faculties and susceptibilities are, no doubt, congenital with the mind—or rather, are the mind itself. But its actually manifested phenomena wait the touch of the *external;* and they will be modified accordingly. It is absolutely dependent on experience in this sense, that it is only as it is operated upon by the outward world that the dormant faculties, whatever they are, and whatever their nature, be they few or many,—intellectual, moral, or spiritual,—are first awakened. If a mind were created (it is, at least, a conceivable case) with all the avenues to the external world closed,—in fact, we sometimes see approximations to such a condition in certain unhappy individuals,—we do not doubt that such a mind, by the present laws of the human constitution, could not possess *any* thoughts, feelings, emotions; in fact, could exhibit none of the phenomena, spiritual, intellectual, moral, or sensational, which now diversify it. In proportion as we see human beings approach this condition, —in fact, we sometimes see them approach it very nearly—we see the "potentialities" of the soul (I do not like the word, but it expresses my meaning better than any other I know) held in abeyance, and such an imperfectly awakened *man* does not, in some cases, manifest the degree of sensibility or intelligence manifested in many animals. If the seclusion from sense and experience be quite complete, the life of such a soul would be wrapped up in the germ, and possess no more consciousness than a vegetable.

It appears, then, universally, that however true it may be, and doubtless is, that the laws of thought and feeling enable us to derive from external influence what it alone would never give, yet that this external influence *is* an indispensable condition, as we are at present constituted, of the development of any and of all our faculties.

As this seems the law of development universally, it is so of the spiritual and religious part of our nature as well as the rest; and in this very fact, we have abundant scope for the possibility and utility of a revelation,—if God be pleased to give one,—even of elementary moral and spiritual truth; since, though conceding the perfect congruity between that truth and the structure of the soul, it is only as it is in some way actually presented to us from without, that the soul arrives at the conscious possession of it. And what, after all, but such an *external* source of revelation is that Volume of Nature, which, operating in perfect analogy with the aforesaid conditions of the soul's development, awakens, though imperfectly, the dormant elements of religious and spiritual life? So far from its being true in any intelligible sense that an external revelation of moral and spiritual truth is impossible, it is absolutely necessary, in *some* form, as a condition of the evolution of that truth in the human soul; so far from its being true that such revelation is an absurdity, it is in strict analogy with the fundamental laws of our being. Whether, if this be so, the *express* external presentation of such truth in a book constructed by divine wisdom and expressed in human language—this last being the most universal and most appropriate instrument by which man's dormant powers are actually awakened,—may not be a more effective method of attaining the end than any of man's devising, whether instinctive or artificial; or than the casual influences of external nature, well or ill deciphered; all this is another question. But *some* such external apparatus—applied to the faculties of men—is essential, whether it be in the Volume of Nature, or in the "Bible," or in a *book* of Mr. Newman or Mr. Parker. All that makes the difference between you and a Hottentot (to recur to that illustration which Harrington, I really think, fairly employed) depends on external influences, and the consequent development of the spiritual and religious faculties.

And this very fact — the unspeakable differences between man and man, nation and nation, as regards the recognition, the conscious possession of even elementary "moral and spiritual truth" (varying, as it perpetually does, as those external influences vary, and more or less perfect, according as that external "revelation" which in some degree, and of some species, is indispensable, is more or less perfect), affords another indication of the ample utility of an external *divine* revelation, as well as of its possibility; and a proof that if there be one, it is in harmony, again, with the conditions of human nature. And here I may employ, in further illustration, one of the analogies I adverted to a little time ago. Not only is the flower *never* independent of external influences for its actual development,—not only would it remain in the germ without them,—but we see that within certain limits, often very wide, the *kind* of external influence operates powerfully on the species, and on the individual itself;—according as it is in one climate or another—in this soil or that—submitted to culture or suffered to grow wild. It is needless to apply the analogy. While we see that the moral and spiritual faculties of man, no more than his other faculties, can attain their development except in co-operation with *some* external influences, we also see that they exhibit every degree and variety of development according to the *quality* of those external influences. Is there then not even a possibility left for an external revelation? If the *actual* exhibition of any spiritual and religious phenomena in man not only depends on *some* external influences and culture, but perpetually varies with them, what would such a revelation be but a provision in analogy with these facts? But it is sufficient to rebut this gratuitous dictum,—of an external revelation of "spiritual and moral truth being impossible,"—that some external influence is necessary for any development of the religious faculty at all. If the last be *necessary*, I cannot conceive how the other should be *impossible*.

Nor is it any reply to say,—as I think has been abundantly shown in your debates with Harrington,—that any such external influences only make articulate that which already existed inarticulately in the heart; that they only chafe and stimulate into life "the ivory of Pygmalion's statue," to use his expression,—the dormant principles and sentiments which somehow existed, but were in deep slumber. That which makes them vital, active, the objects of consciousness, and the sources of power, may well be called a "revelation." Nay, since it seems that, in some way, this outward voice *must* be heard first, I think it is more properly so called than the internal response of the heart. *That* is rather the echo.

It may be admitted that the elementary truths of religion, once propounded, are promptly admitted, but still in *some* external shape they require to be propounded. There is such a thing in the human mind as unrealised truth, both intellectual and spiritual: the inarticulate muttering of an obscurely felt sentiment; a vague appetency for something we are not distinctly conscious of. The clear utterance of it—its distinct proposition to us, is the *very thing* that is often wanted to convert this dim feeling into distinct vision. This is the electric spark which transforms two invisible gases into a visible and transparent fluid; this is the influence which evolves the latent caloric, and makes it a powerful and active element.

I cannot help thinking that the great source of your fallacy on this subject arises from confounding the idea of certain characteristic tendencies and potentialities of our nature with the supposition — contradicted by the whole religious history of man in all ages — that they must be everywhere efficaciously active, and spontaneously exhibit a normal manifestation; than which there cannot, I conceive, be a greater error.

I must entreat you to recollect Harrington's dilemma. Either the supposed truths of your spiritual theory or that of Mr. Newman or Mr. Parker are known to all mankind or not; if they are, surely their books, and every such book is the most impertinent in the world; if not, these authors did well to write, supposing them to have truth on their side; but then that vindicates the possibility and utility of a "book-revelation."

II. But I go a step further, and not only contend that from the very law of the soul's development, there is ample scope for a revelation, even of elementary "moral and spiritual truth," but that even if we supposed all men in *actual* possession of that truth, in some shape or other, there would still be abundant scope for a divinely constructed external instrument for giving it efficacy; and that this, again, is in perfect analogy with the fundamental condition of the soul's action. The principles of spiritual and religious life are capable, in an infinite variety of ways, of being modified, intensified, vivified by the external influences brought to bear upon them from time to time. Not only must that external influence be exerted for the first awakening of the soul, but it must be continued all our life long, in order to maintain the principles, thus elicited in a state of activity. Sometimes they seem for awhile to have been half-obliterated—to fade away from the consciousness; they are re-illumined, made to blaze out again in brilliant light on the "walls of the chambers of imagery," by some outward stimulus; by a "word spoken in season"—by the recollection of some weighty apothegm which embodies truth—some ennobling image which illustrates it; by the utterance of certain "charmed words," hallowed by association as they fall on the external sense, or are recalled by memory. How familiar to us all is this dependence on the external! How dull, how sluggish, has often been the soul! A single word, the sight of an object surrounded with vivid associations, the sudden suggestion of a half-forgotten strain of poetry or song, what power have these to stir its stagnant depths, and awaken "spiritual" and every other species of emotion as well as intellectual activity! The lightning does not more suddenly cleave the cloud in which it slumbered, the sleeping ocean is not more suddenly ruffled by the descending tempest, than the soul of man is thus capable of being vivified and animated by the presentation of appropriate objects,—nay often, by even the most casual external impulses. If this be so, is it not *possible* that an external instrument for thus stimulating and vivifying spiritual life might be given us by God? which if not, in literal strictness, a "revelation," would virtually have all the effect of one, as rekindling the dying light, re-illumining the fading characters, of spiritual truth?

Nor, surely, is there much presumption in supposing that the appropriate influences of such an instrumentality might be brought to bear upon us with infinite advantage by Him who alone possesses perfect access to all the avenues of our spirits; a perfect mastery of our whole nature; of intellect, imagination, and conscience; of those laws of association and emotion which he himself has framed. If Shakspeare and Milton can daily exercise over myriads of minds an ascendancy which makes their admirers speak of them almost with the "Bibliolatry" with which Mr. Newman makes the Christian speak of the Bible, I apprehend God could construct a "book," even though it told man *nothing* which was strictly a revelation, which might be of infinite value to him; simply from the fact that the *modes* in which truths operate upon us, and by which our faculties are educated to their perfection, are scarcely less important than either the truths or the faculties themselves.

But I need say the less upon this point, inasmuch as Mr. Newman has spoken of the New Testament, and its influence over his mental history, in terms which conclusively show that if it be not a "revelation," ample space is left for such a divinely constructed book, if God were pleased to give one.

"There is no book in all the world," says he, "which I love and esteem so much as the New Testament, with the devotional parts of the Old. There is none which I know so intimately, the very *words* of which dwell close to me *in my most sacred thoughts*, none for which I so thank God, none on which *my soul and heart have been to so great an extent moulded*. In my *early boyhood*, it was my private delight and daily companion; and to it I owe the best part of whatever wisdom there is in my manhood."*

I only doubt whether even this testimony, strong as it is, *fully* represents the power which the Book has had in modifying his interior life, though he would now fain renounce its *proper* authority; whether it has not had more to do than he thinks in *originating* his conception of such "moral and spiritual" truth as he still recognises. Its very language comes so spontaneously to his lips, that his dialect of "spiritualism" is one continued plagiarism from David and Isaiah, Paul and Christ. Nay, it may well be doubted whether the entire substance of his spiritual theory be any thing else than a distorted and mutilated Christianity.

* Soul, pp. 241, 242.

Some of the previous observations also apply to the possibility and utility of a divinely originated statement of "*ethical* truth;" nor will they be neutralised by an objection which Mr. Newman is fond of urging,—namely, that a *book* cannot express (as it is freely acknowledged no book can) the limitations with which maxims of ethical truth are to be received and applied; that all it can do is to give general principles, and leave them to be applied by the individual reason and conscience. The reasoning is refuted by *fact*. The same thing precisely is done, and necessarily done in every department in which men attempt to convey instruction in any particular art or method. It is thus with the general principles of mechanics, of law, of medicine. Yet men never entertain a notion that the collection and inculcation of such maxims are of no use, or of little, merely because they must be intelligently modified and not blindly applied in action. If indeed there were any force in the objection, it would put an end to all instruction — that of Mr. Newman's "spiritual faculty" amongst the rest, for *that* too can only prompt us by general impulses, and leaves us in the same ignorance and perplexity how far we are to obey them. That is still a point to be otherwise determined. The genuine result of such reasoning, if it were acted upon, would be that we need never, in any science or art whatever, trouble ourselves to enunciate any general principle or maxim, because perfectly useless! Similarly, we need never inculcate on children the duty of obeying their parents, honouring their superiors, of being frugal or diligent, humble or aspiring, the particular circumstances and limitations in which they are to be applied being indeterminate! But is not the experience of every day and of all the world against it? Is not the early and sedulous inculcation of just maxims of duty *felt* to be a great auxiliary to its performance in the circumstances in which it is necessary to apply them? Is not the possession of a general rule, with the advantages of a clear and concise expression — in the form of familiar proverbs, or embodied in powerful imagery — a potent *suggestive* to the mind? not only whispering of duty, but, by perpetual recurrence, aiding the *habit* of attending to it? Is not the early and earnest iteration of such sententious wisdom in the ears of the young — the honour which has been paid to sages who have elicited it, or felicitously expressed it — the care with which these treasures of moral wisdom have been garnered up — the perpetual efforts to conjoin elementary moral truth with the fancy and association — is not all this a standing testimony to a consciousness of the value of such auxiliaries of virtue and duty? Is it not felt, that, however general such truths may be, the very forms of expression — the *portable* shape in which the truth is presented — have an immense value in relation to practice? Admitting, therefore, as before — but, as before, only conceding it for argument's sake (for the limits of variation, even as regards the elementary truths of *morals*, are, as experience shows, very wide) — that each man in some shape could anticipate for himself the more important ethical truth, there would be yet ample scope left for the utility of a divinely constructed instrument for its exhibition and enforcement, in perfect harmony with the *modes* in which it is actually exhibited and enforced by man, and in close analogy with the form in which he attempts the same task, whenever he teaches any practical art or method whatever.

Only may it not be again presumed here, that he who knows perfectly "what is in man" would be able to perform the work with correspondent perfection? Whether he has performed it in the Bible or not, that book does, at all events, contain not merely a larger portion of pure ethical truth than any other in the world — but ethical truth expressed and exhibited (as Mr. Newman himself, and most other persons, would admit) in modes incomparably better adapted than in any other book to lay hold of the memory, the imagination, the conscience, and the heart.

Even, then, if we conceded that elementary "spiritual and moral truth" is not only *congruous* to man's faculties, but in some shape universally recognised and possessed, it might yet be contended, from the *manner* in which such truth is dependent for its power and vitality on the forms in which it comes in contact with the human spirit and stimulates it, that ample space is left for such a divine instrument as the Bible; and that it would be in perfect conformity with the laws of our nature — in analogy with the known modes in which external aids give efficacy to such truth. At the same time, be pleased once more to remember, that I concede so much only for argument's sake; I contend that in the stricter sense, without some external aid — and the Bible may be at least as effectual — the religious faculty will not expand at all; and that even where there are these indispensable external influences, the recognition of the truth is obscure or bright, as those influences vary in their degrees of appropriateness. Where they are rude and imperfect (as amongst barbarous nations) we have the spectacle of a soul which struggles towards the light, like a plant to which but a small portion of the sun's rays is admitted; it depends on the free admission of that light whether or not it shall arrive at its full development — its beauty, its fragrance, and its colour. The most that merely human culture can promise, even under the most favourable circumstances (witness ancient Greece!), is that men, in some few favoured instances, may possibly attain those truths which it may be admitted are congenial to the soul, and easily recognised when once propounded, but which, in fact, few men, by nature's sole teaching, ever do clearly attain. It is infinitely important that the path, dimly explored by sages alone, should be thrown open to mankind. Is it not even *possible* then that this task should be performed by a book like the Bible? and if such a book were given, would it not be, I once more ask, in analogy with the fundamental laws of the soul's development? its uniform dependence on external influences for *any* result, and the variable nature of that result, as the influence itself is more or less appropriate? To affirm that each man at once, by internal illumination alone, attains a clear recognition of even elementary "moral and spiritual truth," is to ignore the laws according to which the soul's activity is developed, and to contradict universal experience, which tells us that the great majority of mankind are but in partial possession of this "spiritual and moral truth," and hold it for the most part in connection with the most prodigious and pernicious errors.

You will perceive that I have here chosen to argue the question of the possibility and utility of a "revelation" on your own grounds; but, recollect what I have said, that, in fact, the *principal* reasons for a revelation would still remain in force even if all you demand were conceded. It is a point which I do not find that Mr. Newman's dictum affects.

There may obviously be other facts and other truths as intimately connected with man's destinies and happiness as the elementary truths of religious and moral science; facts and truths which may be necessary to give efficacy to mere elementary principles, and to supply motives to the performance of moral precepts. And how ample in this respect are man's necessities, and how large the field for a "divine revelation," if we content ourselves with such a meagre theology as that of Mr. Parker and Mr. Newman, you see plainly enough in the questions asked by Harrington! How many of Mr. Newman's and Mr. Parker's assumptions, — the moment they step beyond such "spiritual and moral truth" as is "elementary" indeed, — does Harrington declare that he finds unverified by his own consciousness, and needing, if true, an authority to confirm them far more weighty than theirs! As to the terms of access to the Supreme Being — his aspects towards man — man's duties towards him — the future destinies, even the future *existence*, of the soul (a point on which these writers are themselves divided) — the boasted "progress" of the race, which they "prophesy" indeed, but without any credentials of their mission, you see how on all these points Harrington maintains — and oh! how many, if the Bible be untrue, must maintain with him — that he is in total darkness!

III. But I must proceed to show yet further, if you will have patience with me, that, supposing a divine *external* revelation to be given, it is in striking analogy not only with the primary laws of development of our whole intellectual and spiritual being, but with the *fact* — undeniable, however unaccountable, — that our subjection to *external influences* does, in truth, not only mould and modify, but usually determine our intellectual and religious position. We see not only that some external influence is necessary to awaken any activity at all, but that it is actually so powerful and so inevitable from the manner in which man enters the world, and is brought up in it, — his long years of dependence, absolute dependence on the education which is given him (and what an education it has ever been for the mass of the race!), — that it makes all the difference, intellectually and morally, between a New Zealand savage and an Englishman — between the grossest idolater and the most enlightened Christian. This fact affects alike our intellectual and spiritual condition. The savage can use his senses better than the civilised; but the interval is trifling compared with that between the intellectual condition of a man who can appreciate Milton and Newton, and that of our Teutonic ancestors. In the sentiments of a spiritual nature there is the same wide gulf — or rather wider — between a Hottentot and a Paul. Yet the same "susceptibilities" and "potentialities" are in each human mind. The same remark applies to the sense of the beautiful and sublime; the characteristic faculties are in all mankind; it is education which elicits them. Nay, would you not stare at a man who should affirm that education was not itself a species of "revelation," simply because the truths thus communicated were all "potentially" in the mind before? The fact is, that education is of co-ordinate importance with the very faculties without which it cannot be imparted.

Now we cannot break away from that law of development with which our individual existence is involved, and which necessarily (as far as any will of ours is concerned) is a most important, nay, *the* most important, element in that *tertium quid* which man becomes in virtue of the threefold elements which constitute him: — 1°, a given internal constitution of mind; 2°, the modifying effects of the actual exercise of his faculties and their interaction with one another, resulting in *habits* ; and, 3°, that external world of influences which supplies the *matériel* from which this strange plant extracts its aliment, and ultimately derives its fair fruits or its poisonous berries. All this is inevitable, upon the supposition that man was to be a social, not a solitary being — linked by an indissoluble chain to those who came before and to those who come after him — dependent, absolutely dependent upon others for his being, his training, his whole condition, civil, social, intellectual, moral, and religious. If, then, an external instrument of moral and religious culture were given by God to man, would it not be in strict analogy with this tremendous and mysterious law of human development?

IV. I must be permitted to proceed yet one step further, and affirm that the very *form* in which this presumed revelation has (as we say) been given — that of a *Book* — is also in strict analogy with the law by which God himself has made this an indispensable instrument of *all* human progress. We have just seen that man is what he is, as much (to say the least) by the influence of external causes as by the influence of the internal principles of his constitution; it must be added that to make that external influence of much efficiency at all, still more to render it either universally or progressively beneficial, the world waits for a — BOOK. Among the varied external influences amidst which the human race is developed, this is incomparably the most important, and the only one that is absolutely *essential*. Upon it the collective education of the race depends. It is the sole instrument of registering, perpetuating, transmitting thought.

Yes — whatever trivial and vulgar associations may impair our due conceptions of the grandeur of this material and artificial organon of man's development, as compared with the intellectual and moral energies, which have recourse to it, but which are almost impotent without it — God has made man's whole career of triumphs dependent upon this same art of writing! The whole progress of the world he has created he has made dependent upon the Alphabet! Without this the progress of the individual is inconceivably slow, and with him, for the most part, progress terminates. By this alone can we garner the fruits of experience — become wise by the wisdom of others, and strong by their strength. Without this, man everywhere remains, age after age, immovably a savage; and if he were to lose it when he has once gained it, would, after a little ineffectual flutter by the aid of tradition, sink into barbarism again. Till this cardinal want is supplied, all considerable "progress" is impossible. It may look odd to say that the whole world is dependent on any thing so purely artificial; but, in point of fact, it is only another way of stating the truth, that God has constituted the race a *series* of mutually dependent beings; and as each term of this series is perishable and evanescent, the development and improvement of the race must depend on an instrument by which an interconnection can be maintained between its parts; till then, progress must not only be most precarious, but virtually impossible. To the truth of this all history testifies. I say, then, not only that if God has given man a revelation at all, he has but acted in analogy with that law by which he has made him so absolutely dependent upon external culture, but that if he has given it in the very *shape of a book*, he has acted also in strict analogy with the very *form* in which he has imposed that law on the world. He has simply made use of that instrument, which, by the very constitution of our nature and of the world, he has made absolutely essential to the progress and advancement of humanity. May we not conclude from analogy that if God has indeed thus constituted the world, and if he busies himself at all in the fortunes of miserable humanity, he has not disdained to take part in its education, by condescendingly using that very instrument which himself has made the condition of all human progress? I think, even if you hesitate to admit that God *has* given us a "book-revelation," you must admit it would be at least in manifest coincidence with the laws of human development and the "constitution and course of nature."

To conclude: I must say that Mr. Newman, in his account of the *genesis* of religion, does himself in effect admit (as Harrington has remarked) an "external revelation," though not in a book. For what else is that apparatus of external influences by which the several preparatory or auxiliary emotions are awakened and the development of your "spiritual faculty" effected?—contact with the outward world—with visible and material nature—the instruction of the living voice! If you acknowledge all this without derogation, as you imagine, to the sublime and divine functions of the indwelling "spiritual" power, why this rabid, this, I might almost say, puerile (if I ought not rather to say fanatical) hatred of the very notion of a "book-revelation?"

Let us confess that if a revelation be *possible* at all, it cannot be more worthy of God to give one even from "*within*," than in such a shape as a "book;" since without a "BOOK" man remains an idolater, in spite of his fine "spiritual faculties," and a barbarian, in spite of his sublime intellect; in fact, not much better than the beasts, in spite of all those noble capacities which, although they are *in* him, are as it were hopelessly locked up till he has obtained this key to their treasures.

Nor do I think that the invectives of the modern spiritualists on this point are particularly becoming, when we reflect not only that they freely give mankind what Harrington declares to be to him, and I must say are equally to me, *their* "book-revelations," but in very deed, as he truly affirms, have given us nothing else. It has been much the same with all who have rejected historical Christianity, from Lord Herbert's time downwards.

I paused, and Fellowes mused. At last he said, "I cannot feel convinced that the 'absolute religion' is not (as Mr. Parker says) essentially the same in all men, and internally revealed. The *want* exists in all, and there must, according to the arrangements of universal nature, be the *supply;* just as the eye is for the light, and the light is for the eye. As he says, 'we feel instinctively it *must* be so.'"

"Unhappily," said Harrington, "Mr. Parker says that many things *must* be which we find *are* not, and this among the number. At least, I for one, shall not grant that the sort of spiritual 'supply' which is given to the Calmuck, or the savage 'besmeared with the blood of human sacrifices,' at all resembles that uniform light which is made for all people's eyes."

Fellowes seemed still perplexed with his old difficulty.

"I cannot help thinking," he began again, "that the 'spiritual faculty' acts by immediate 'insight,' and has nothing to do with 'logical processes' or 'intellectual propositions,' or the sensational or the imaginative parts of our nature; that it 'gazes immediately upon spiritual truth.' Now in the argument you have constructed you have expressly implied the contrary. You have said, you know, that even if you granted men to be in possession of 'spiritual and moral truth,' there might still be large space for a divinely constructed book from the reflex operation of the intellect, the imagination, and so forth, upon the products of the spiritual faculty; both directly, and also indirectly, inasmuch as external influences modify or stimulate them."

"But," said I, "does not Mr. Newman himself, in the first part of his Treatise on the Soul, admit the reciprocal action of all these on the too plastic spiritual products; and as to 'logical and intellectual processes,' does he not continually employ them—*for* his system of opinions, though he will not allow them to be employed *against* it? And by what other means than through the intervention of your *senses*, by which you read his pages—your *imagination*, by which you seize his illustrations—your *intellect*, by which you comprehend his arguments, did he reclaim you, as you say he has done, from many of your ancient errors? How else, in the name of common sense, did he get access to your soul at all?"

"I cannot pretend to defend Mr. Newman's consistency," said he, "in his various statements on this subject. I acknowledge I am even puzzled to find out how he *did convince* me, upon his hypothesis."

"Are you sure," said I, laughing, "that he ever convinced you at all? However, all your perplexity seems to me to arise from supposing the spiritual powers of man to act in greater isolation from his other powers than is conceivable or even possible. Not apart from these, but in intimate conjunction with them, are the functions of the soul performed. The divorce between the 'spiritual faculties' and the intellect, which your favourite, Mr. Newman, has attemped to effect, is impossible. It is an attempt to sever phenomena which co-exist in the unity of our own consciousness. I am bound in justice to admit that there are others of our 'modern spiritualists' who condemn this preposterous attempt to separate what God hath joined so inseparably. Even Mr. Newman does practically contradict his own assertions; and outraged reason and intellect have avenged his wrongs upon them by deserting him when he has invoked them, and left him to express his paradoxes in endless perplexity and confusion. But this conversation is no bad preface to some observations on this important fallacy, (as I conceive,) which I have appended to the paper I have read, and, with your leave, I will finish with them." They assented, and I proceeded.

It is very common for philosophers, spiritual and otherwise, to be guilty of two opposite errors, both exposed in the first book of the Novum Organum. One is, that of supposing the phenomena which they have to analyse, more simple, more capable of being reduced to some one principle than is really the case; the other, that of introducing a cumbrous complexity of operations unknown to nature. It is unnecessary here to adduce examples of the last; quite as frequently, at least, is man apt to be guilty of the first. He imagines that the complex and generally deeply convoluted phenomena he is called to investigate are capable of being more summarily analysed than they can be. The ends to be answered in nature by the same *set* of instruments are in many cases so various, and in some respects so limit and traverse one another, that, though the same multiplicity of ends is attained more completely, and in higher aggregate perfection, than by any device which man's ingenuity could substitute for them, yet those instruments are necessarily very complex at the best. Look, for example, at the system of organs by which, variously employed, we utter the infinite variety of articulate sounds, perform the most necessary of all vital functions (that of respiration), masticate solid food, and swallow fluids. The miracle is, that any *one set* of organs in any conceivable juxtaposition should suffice to discharge with such amazing facility and rapidity these different and rapidly alternated functions; yet, I suppose, few who have studied anatomy will deny that, though relatively to the variety of purposes it has to perform, the apparatus is very simple, it is *absolutely* very complex; and that its parts play into one another with great facility indeed, but with endless intricacy.

To apply these observations to my special object. To one who attentively studies man's *immaterial* anatomy, much the same complexity is, I think, apparent; the philosopher is too apt to assume it to be much more simple than it is. It is the very error, as I conceive, into which some of you modern "spiritualists" fall when considering the phenomena of our religious nature. You do not sufficiently regard man as a complicated unity; — you represent, if you do not suppose, the several capacities of his nature—the different parts of it, sensational, emotional, intellectual, moral, spiritual, — as set off from one another by a sharper boundary line than nature acknowledges. They all work for immediate ends, indeed; but they all also work for, with, and upon each other, for other ends than their own. Yet as they all exist in one indivisible mind, or rather constitute it, they form one most intricate machine : and it can rarely happen that the particular phenomena of our interior nature we happen to be investigating do not involve many others. Throughout his book on the " Soul," we find Mr. Newman employing expressions (though I admit there are others which contradict them) which imply that the phenomena of religion — of what he calls "spiritual insight," may be viewed in clearer distinction from those of the intellect, than, as I conceive, they ever can be; and that a much clearer separation can be effected between them than nature has made possible. To hear him sometimes speak, one would imagine that the logical, the moral, and the spiritual are held together by no vital bond of connection; nay, from some expressions, one would think that the "logical" faculty had nothing to do with religion, if it is not to be supposed rather to stand in the way of it; that the "intellect" and the "spiritual faculty" may each retire to its "vacant interlunar cave," and never trouble its head about what the other is doing. Thus he says in one place, "All the grounds of belief proposed to the mere understanding have *nothing to do* with Faith *at all.*"* In another, "The processes of *thought* have *nothing* to quicken the conscience or *affect* the soul."† "How then can the state of the soul be tested by the conclusion to which the intellect is led?"‡ And accordingly you see he everywhere affirms that we ought not to have any better or worse opinion of any man for his "intellectual creed;" and that "religious progress" cannot be "anticipated" till intellectual "creeds are destroyed."§

Here one would imagine that the intellectual, moral, and spiritual had even less to do with the production of each other's results than matter and mind reciprocally have with theirs. These last, we see, in a thousand cases act and react upon one another; and modify each other's peculiar products and operations in a most important manner. How much more reasonably may we infer that the elementary faculties of the same indivisible mind will not discharge their functions without important reciprocal action; that in no case can we have the process pure and simple as the result of the operation of a single faculty!

* Soul, p. 223. † Ibid. p. 245.
‡ Ibid. p. 245. § Phases, p. 222.

If it were not so, I see not how we are to perform any of the functions of a spiritual nature, even as defined by you and your favourite writers; unless, indeed, you would equip the soul with an entire Sunday suit of separate capacities of reasoning, remembering, imagining, hoping, rejoicing, and so on, to be expressly used by the "soul" alone when engaged in her spiritual functions; quite different from that old, threadbare, much-worn suit of faculties, having similar functions indeed, but exercised on other objects.

What can be more obvious (and it must be admitted that the most fanatical "spiritualist" employs expressions, and, what is more, uses methods which imply it), than that whether we have a distinct religious faculty, or whether it be the result of the action of many faculties, the functions of our "spiritual" nature are performed by the instrumentality, and involve the intervention of the very same much-abused faculties which enable us to perform any other function. It is one and the same indivisible mind which is the subject of *religious* thought and emotion, and of any *other* thought and emotion. Religious *truth*, like any other truth, is embraced by the understanding — as indeed it would be a queer kind of truth that is not; is stated in propositions, yields inferences, is adorned by eloquence, is illustrated by the imagination, and is thus, as well as from its intrinsic claims, rendered powerful over the emotions, the affections, and the will. In brief, when the soul apprehends, reasons, remembers, rejoices, hopes, fears, *spiritually*, it surely does not perform these functions by totally different faculties from those by which *similar* things are done on other occasions. All experience and consciousness are against the supposition. In religion, men's minds are employed on more sublime and elevated themes indeed, but the operations themselves are essentially of the same nature as in other cases. Hence we see the dependence of the true development of religion on the just and harmonious action of all our faculties. They march together, and it is the glorious prerogative of true religion that it makes them do so; that all the elements of our nature being indissolubly connected, and perpetually acting and reacting on one another, should aid one another, and attain a more just conjoint action. If there be acceptable *faith*, it presupposes belief of the *truth*, as well as love of it in the heart; if there be holy habit, it implies just *knowledge* of duty; if there be spiritual emotion awakened, it will still be in accordance with the laws which ordinarily produce it; that is, because that which *should* produce it is perceived by the senses or the intellect, is recalled by the memory, is vivified by the imagination. If faith, and hope, and love often kindle into activity and hallow these instruments by which and through which they act, it is not the less true, that apart from these — as constituting the same indivisible mind — faith, and hope, and love cannot exist; and not only so; but when faith is languid, and hope faint, and love expiring, these faculties themselves shall often in their turn initiate the process which shall revive them all; some outward object, some incident of life, some "magic word," some glorious image, some stalwart truth, suddenly and energetically stated, shall, through the medium of the senses, the imagination or the intellect, set the soul once more in a blaze, and revive the emotions which it is at other times only their office to express. A sanctified intellect, a hallowed imagination, devout affections, have a reciprocal tendency to stimulate each other. In whatever faculty of our nature the stimulus may be felt — in the intellect or the imagination — it is thence propagated through the mysterious network of the soul to the emotions, the affections, the conscience, the will: or, conversely, these last may commence the movement and propagate it in reverse order. Each may become in turn a centre of influence; but so indivisible is the soul and mind of man, so indissolubly bound together the elements which constitute them, that the influence once commenced never stops where it began, but acts upon them all. The ripple, as that of a stone dropped into still water, no matter where, may be fainter and fainter the further from the spot where the commotion began, but it will stop only with the bank.

Ordinarily, many functions of the mind are involved in each, and sometimes all in one.

July 24. Yesterday, a somewhat interesting conversation took place between Harrington and Edward Robinson, a youth at College, a friend of George Fellowes's family. He is a devout admirer of Strauss, and thinks that writer has completely destroyed the historical character of the Gospels. I was, as usual, struck with the candour and logical consistency with which our Sceptic was disposed to regard the subject.

"You have Lingard and Macaulay here, I see," said young Robinson. "I need hardly ask, I think, which you find the more pleasant reading?"

"You need not, indeed," cried Harrington. "Mr. Macaulay is so superior to the Roman Catholic historian (though his merits are great too) in genius, in eloquence, in variety and amplitude of knowledge, in imagination, in style, that there is no comparison between them."

"And do you think Mr. Macaulay as *accurate* as he is full of genius and eloquence?"

"If he be *not*," said Harrington, laughing, "I am afraid there are very few of us deeply versed enough in history to detect his delinquencies, or even to say whether they have been committed. There may be, for aught I know, some cases (of infinite importance of course) in which he has represented an event as having taken place on the 20th Dec. 1693, whereas it took place on the 3rd Jan. 1694; or he may have said that Sir Thomas Nobody was the son of another Sir Thomas Nobody, whereas two or three antiquaries can incontestibly prove that he was the son of Sir *John* Nobody, and nephew of the above. To me, I confess, he appears distinguished scarcely more by the splendour of his imagination than by the opulence of his knowledge, and the imperial command which he possesses over it. But, in truth, the accuracy or otherwise of history when it is at all remote, is a matter in which I feel less interest than I once did. I read, indeed, Mr. Macaulay with perpetual renewal of wonder and delight. But though I believe that his vivid pictures are the result of a faithful use of his materials, yet, if I must confess the full extent of my scepticism, *his* work, and every other work which involves a reference to events which transpired only a century or two ago, is poisoned as *history* by the suspicion that to ascertain the truth is impossible. I know it must be so, if the principles of your favourite Strauss are to be received; and yet it seems so absurd, that I am sometimes inclined, on that account alone, to laugh at Strauss's criticisms, just as David Hume did at his own speculative doubts when he got into society and sat down to backgammon with a friend. At other times, as I say, the whole field of historic investigation seems more or less the territory of scepticism."

"I know not," said the other, "how you can justify any such general scepticism from anything that Strauss has written."

"Do you not? and yet I think it is a perfectly legitimate inference. Does not Strauss argue that certain discrepancies are to be observed, — certain apparent contradictions and inconsistencies detected in the New Testament narratives; and that therefore we are to reckon, if not the whole, yet by far the larger part, as utterly fabulous or doubtful, mythic or legendary? Now, I cannot but feel, on the other hand, that these narratives are *as* strikingly marked by all the usual indications of historic truthfulness as any historic writings in the world. The artlessness, simplicity, and speciality of the narrative, — a certain inimitable tone and air of reality, earnestness, and candour, — the *general* harmony of these so-called sacred writers with themselves, and with profane authors (quite as general, to say the least, as usually distinguishes other narratives by different hands); above all, the long-concealed, and yet most numerous, 'coincidences' which lie deep beneath the surface, and which only a very industrious *mining* brings to light; coincidences which, if ingenuity had been subtle enough to fabricate, that same ingenuity would have been too sagacious to conceal so deep, and which are too numerous and striking (one would imagine) to be the effect of accident; — all these things, I say, would seem to argue (if any thing can) the integrity of the narrative. Yet all these things must necessarily, of course, go for nothing, on Strauss's hypothesis. There are, you say, certain discrepancies, and from them you proceed to conclude that the narrative is uncertain, and unworthy of credit; that if there be a residuum of truth at all, no man can know with any certainty what or how much it is. We must therefore leave the whole problematical. Now the question comes, whether we must not in consistency apply the same principle further; and, if so, whether we can find in any history whatever stronger marks of credibility; whether any was ever submitted to an examination more severe, or so severe; whether any can boast of a larger number of minds, of the first order, giving their assent to it."

"Let me stop you there," said the other; "you must consider that those minds were prejudiced in favour of the conclusion. They were *inclined* to believe the supernatural wonders which these pretended historians retail."

"How differently men may argue with the same premises! I was about to mention the suspicion attaching to miraculous narratives, as *attesting* (I still think so, notwithstanding your observation) that stress and pressure of supposed historic credibility under which so many powerful minds — minds, many of them of the first order — have felt themselves compelled to receive these histories as true in spite of such obstacles. Surely, you do not think that a miracle is in our age, or has been for many ages, an antecedent ground of credibility; or that if a history does but contain *enough* of them, as this assuredly does, it is certain to be believed. No; do not you with Strauss contend that a miracle is not to be believed at all, because it contradicts uniform experience? And yet thousands of powerful minds have believed the truth of these historic records against all this uniform experience! Their prejudices against it must surely have been stronger than those for it. — But to resume the statement of my difficulties. I say the question returns whether there is any history in the world which either presents in *itself* greater marks of historic credibility, or in which as numerous and equally inexplicable discrepancies cannot be discovered. If there be none, then how far shall we adopt and carry out the principles of Strauss? for if we carry them out with rigid equity, the whole field of history is abandoned to scepticism: it is henceforth the domain of doubt and contention; as in truth, a very large part of it in Germany has already become, in virtue of these very principles. Much of profane history is abandoned as well as the sacred; and Homer becomes as much a shadow as Christ."

"You seem," said Robinson, "to be almost in the condition to entertain Dr. Whately's ingenious 'Historic Doubts,' touching the existence of Napoleon Buonaparte!"*

"I believe that it is simply our proximity to the events which renders it difficult to entertain them. If the injuries of time and the caprice of fortune should in the remote future leave as large gaps in the evidence, and as large scope for ingenious plausibilities as in relation to the remote past, I believe multitudes would find no *difficulty* in entertaining those 'doubts.' They seem to me perfectly well argued, and absolutely conclusive on the historic canons on which Strauss's work is constructed — namely, that if you find what seem discrepancies and improbabilities in a reputed history, the mass of that historic texture in which they are found may be regarded as mythical or fabulous, doubtful or false. If you say the principles of Strauss are false, that is another matter. I shall not think it worth while to contest their truth or their falsehood with you. But if you adhere to them, I will take the liberty of showing you that you do not hold them consistently, if you think any remote history is to be regarded as absolutely placed beyond doubt."

* Are the ingenious "Historic Certainties," by "Aristarchus Newlight," from the same admirable mint?— Probably suggested by the "Historic Doubts," like Harrington's paper on the "Papal Aggression."— ED.

"Well, if you will be grave," said Robinson, "though, upon my word, I thought you in jest,—is it possible that you do not see that there is a vast difference between rejecting, *on the same ground of discrepancies*, the credibility of the narratives of the Gospel, and that of any common history?"

"I must honestly confess, then, that I do not,—if the *discrepancies*, as Strauss alleges, and not something else, is to be assigned as the cause of their rejection. If indeed, like some criminals, under despotic governments, they are apprehended and convicted on a certain charge, but really hanged for an entirely different reason, I can understand that there may be *policy* in the proceeding; but I do not comprehend its argumentative honesty. Be pleased therefore (that I may form some conclusion) to tell me what are those circumstances which so wonderfully discriminate the *discrepancies* in the New Testament histories from those in other histories, as that the inevitable consequence of finding a certain amount of said discrepancies in the former leads to the rejection of the entire, or nearly entire, documents in which they are found; while their presence in other histories, even to a far greater extent, shall not authorise their rejection at all, or the rejection only of the *parts* in which the discrepancies are found. And yet I think I can guess."

"Well, what do you guess?"

"That you think that the *miraculous* nature of the events which form a portion of the New Testament history makes a great difference in the case."

"And do not you?"

"I cannot say I do; for though it is doubtless Strauss's principal object to get rid of these *miracles*, it is not as *miracles*, but as history, that his canons of historic criticism are applied to them. It is as history that he attacks the books in which they are contained. His weapons are directed against the miracles, indeed; but it is only by piercing the history, with which alone the supposed discrepancies had any thing to do."

"But I cannot conceive that the historic discrepancies occurring in *connection* with such topics must not have more weight attached to them than if they occurred in any other history."

"This is because you have already resolved that miracles are impossible on *totally different grounds*. But you may see the fallacy in a moment. Talk with a man who does *not* believe miracles *à priori* impossible, and that though, of course, *improbable* (otherwise they would be none, I suppose), the authentication of a divine revelation is a sufficient reason for their being wrought; and he evades your argument. You are then compelled, you see, to throw yourself exclusively upon the alleged *historic discrepancies;* they become your sole weapon; and if it pierces the New Testament history, I want to know whether it does not equally pierce all other remote history too? In truth, if as you and Mr. Fellowes agree — I only doubt — a miracle is *impossible*, nothing can (as I think) be more strange, than that, instead of reposing in that simple fact which you say is demonstrable, you should fly to *historic* proofs."

"And do *you* not think that miracles are impossible and absurd?"

"I think nothing; because, as I told Fellowes the other day, I am half inclined to *doubt* whether I *doubt* whether a miracle is possible or not, like a genuine sceptic, as I am. And this doubt, you see, even of a doubt, makes me cautious. — But to resume. If that principle be sound, it seems much more natural to adhere to it than to attack the Gospels as *history*. Strauss, however, has thought otherwise; and while he has left this main dictum unproved — nay, has not even attempted a proof of it, he has endeavoured to shake the historic character of these records, treating them like any other records. I say, therefore, that to adduce the circumstance that the narrative is miraculous, is nothing to the purpose, until the *impossibility* of miracles is proved; and then, when this is proved, it is unnecessary to adduce the discrepancies. If, on the other hand, a man has *no* difficulty (as the Christian, for example) in believing miracles to be possible, and that they have really occurred, Strauss's argument, as I have said, is evaded, and the seeming discrepancies can do no more against the credibility of the New Testament history than equal discrepancies can prove against any other document. I will, if possible, make my meaning plain by yet another example. Let us suppose some Walter Scott had compiled some purely fictitious history, professedly laid in the Middle Ages (and surely even miraculous occurrences cannot be more *unreal* than these products of sheer imagination); and suppose some critic had engaged to prove it fiction from internal evidence supplied by contradictions and discrepancies, and so on; would you not think it strange if he were to enforce that argument by saying, 'And besides all this, what is more *suspicious*, is that they occur in a work of imagination?' Would you not say, 'Learned sir, we humbly thought this was the point you were engaged in making out? Is it not to assume the very point in debate? And if it be true, would it not be better to stop there at once, instead of taking us so circuitous a road to the same result, which we perceive you had already reached beforehand? Are you not a little like that worthy Mayor who told Henri Quatre that he had nineteen good reasons for omitting to fire a salute on his Majesty's arrival; the *first* of which was, that he had no artillery; whereupon his Majesty graciously told him that he might spare the remaining eighteen?' So I should say in the supposed case.—To return, then: you must, if you would consider the validity of Strauss's argument, lay aside the *miraculous* objection, which must be decided on quite different grounds, and which, in fact, if valid, settles the controversy without his critical aid. All who read Strauss's book either believe that miracles are impossible, or not: the former need not his criticisms: they have already arrived at the result by a shorter road; the latter can only reject the history, by supposing the discrepancies in it, *as* history, justify them. I ask you, then, supposing you one who, like the Christian, believes miracles possible, whether these historic discrepancies would justify you in saying that the New Testament records, considered simply as history, no longer deserve credit, and that you are left in absolute ignorance how much of them, or whether any part, is to be received—aye or no?"

"Well, then, I should say that Strauss has shown that the history, *as history*, is to be rejected."

"Very well; only then do not be surprised that, in virtue of such conclusions, I doubt whether you ought not to push the principle a little further, and contend that, as there are no writings in the world which seem to bear more marks of historic sincerity and trustworthiness, and certainly none of any magnitude or variety, in which far greater discrepancies are not to be found, it is doubtful whether we can receive any thing as absolutely veritable history; and that the Book of Genesis, and Gospel of Luke, and History of Lingard, and History of Hume, are alike covered with a mist of sceptical obscurity."

"But, really, Mr. Harrington, this is absurd and preposterous!"

"It *may* be so; but you must *prove* it, and not simply content yourself with affirming it. I am, at all events, more consistent than you, who tell the man who does not see your *à priori* objection to the belief of miracles, that a history which certainly contains as many marks of historic veracity as any history in the world, and discrepancies neither greater nor more numerous, must be reduced (ninety-nine hundredths of it) to *myth* on account of those discrepancies, while the others may still legitimate their claims to be considered as genuine history! Your only escape, as I conceive, from this dilemma, is, by saying that the marks of historic truth in the New Testament, looked at as mere *history*, are not so great as those of other histories, or that the discrepancies are greater; and I think even you will not venture to assert *that*. But if you do, and choose to put it on that issue, I shall be most happy to try the criterion by examining Luke and Paul, Matthew and Mark on the one side; and Clarendon and May, or Hume, Lingard, and Macaulay on the other; or, if you prefer them, Livy and Polybius, or Tacitus and Josephus."

"But I have bethought me of another answer," said Robinson. "Suppose the sacred writers affirm that every syllable they utter is infallibly true, being inspired?"

"Why then," said Harrington, "first, you must find such a passage, which many say you cannot; secondly, you must find one which says that every syllable *would* remain always infallibly true in spite of all errors of transcription and corruptions of time, otherwise your discrepancies will not touch the writers; and lastly, it does not affect my argument, whether you find any such absurdities or not, since you and I would know what to say, though the Christian would not like to say it— namely, that these writers were mistaken in the notion of their plenary inspiration. It would still leave the mass of their history to be dealt with like any *other* history. Now I want to know why, if I reject the *mass* of the one on the ground of certain discrepancies, I must not reject the mass of the other on the score of equal or greater."

After a few minutes, Harrington turned to Fellowes, and said—"That in relation to the bulk of mankind there can be no authentic history of remote events, plainly appears from a statement of Mr. Newman. He says, you know, after having relinquished the investigation of the evidences of Christianity, that he might have spared much weary thought and useless labour, if at an earlier time, this *simple truth* had been pressed upon him, that since the 'poor and half-educated cannot investigate historical and literary questions, *therefore* these questions cannot constitute an essential part of religion.' You, if you recollect, mentioned it to my uncle the other night; and, in spite of what he replied, it does appear a weighty objection: on the other hand, if I admit it to be conclusive, I seem to be driven to the most paradoxical conclusions, at direct variance with the experience of all mankind,—at least, so they say.— For why cannot an historical fact constitute any part of religion?"

"Because, as Mr. Newman says, it is impossible that

the bulk of people can have any certainty in relation to such remote facts of history," said Fellowes.

"And, therefore, in relation to any other remote history; for if the bulk of men cannot obtain certainty on *such* historical questions, neither can they obtain certainty on other historical questions."

"Perhaps not; but then what does it *matter*, in that case, whether they can obtain certainty or not?"

"I am not talking—I am not thinking—as to whether it would *matter* or not. I merely remark that in relation to the generality of people, at all events, they cannot obtain certainty on any remote historical questions. Of course, with regard to ordinary history, it is neither a man's duty, strictly speaking, to believe or disbelieve; and, therefore, I said nothing about *duty*. But in neither the one case nor the other is it possible for the bulk of mankind to obtain satisfaction, from a personal investigation, as to the facts of remote history, or indeed any history at all, except of a man's own life, and that perhaps of his own family, *up* to his father and *down* to his son! What do you say to this—yes or no?"

"I do not know that I should object to say that the great bulk of mankind never can obtain a sufficiently certain knowledge of any fact of history to warrant their belief of it?"

"Very consistent, I think; for you doubtless perceive that if we say they *can* obtain a reasonable ground of assurance of the facts of remote history—so that, if any thing *did* or *does* depend on their believing it, they are truly in possession of a warrant for acting on that belief —I say you then see whither our argument, Mr. Newman's and yours and mine, is going; it vanishes—$o\"i\chi\epsilon\tau a\iota$, as Socrates would say. If, for example, men can attain reasonable certainty in relation to Alfred and Cromwell, alas! they may do the like in reference to Christ; and many persons will say, much more easily.—Now, with my too habitual scepticism, I confess to a feeling of difficulty here. You know there are thousands and tens of thousands amongst us who, if asked respecting the history of Alfred the Great or Oliver Cromwell, would glibly repeat to you all the principal facts of the story — as they suppose; and if you ask them whether they have ever investigated critically the sources whence they had obtained their knowledge, they will say, No; but that they have read the things in Hume's history; or, perhaps (save the mark!), in Goldsmith's Abridgment! But they are profoundly ignorant of even the names of the principal authorities, and have never investigated one of the many doubtful points which have perplexed historians; nay, as to most of them, are not even aware that such points exist. Yet nothing can be more certain than that their supposed knowledge would embrace by far the most important conclusions at which the most accurate historians have arrived. It would be principally in a supposed juster comprehension of minor points — of details — that the latter would have an advantage over them; compensated, however, by a 'plentiful assortment' of doubts on *other* points from which these simple souls are free; doubts which are the direct result of more extensive investigation, but which can scarcely be thought additions to our *knowledge;* — they are rather additions to our ignorance. The impressions of the mass of readers on all the main facts of the two memorable periods respectively would be the same as those of more accurate critics. Now, what I want to know is, whether you would admit that these superficial inquirers — the bulk of your decent countrymen, recollect — can be said to have an *intelligent belief* in any such history; whether you think them justified in saying that they are *certain* of the substantial accuracy of their impressions, and that they may laugh in your face (which they assuredly would do) if you told them that it is possible that Alfred may have existed, and been a wise and patriotic prince; and that probably Oliver Cromwell was Protector of England, and died in 1658; but that really they *know* nothing about the matter."

"Of course they would affirm that they are as assured of the substantial accuracy of their impressions as of their own existence," replied Fellowes.

"But what answer do *you* think they ought to give, my friend? Do you think that they can affirm a reasonable ground of belief in these things?"

"I confess I think they can."

"Ah! then I fear you are grossly inconsistent with Mr. Newman's principles, and must so far distrust his argument against historic religion. If you think that this ready assent to remote historic events may pass for a reasonable conviction, and an intelligent belief, I cannot see why it should be more difficult to attain a similar confidence in the general results of a *religious* history; and in that case it may also become men's *duty* to act upon that belief. On the other hand, if it be not possible to obtain this degree of satisfaction in the latter case, neither for similar reasons will it be in the former. If you hold Mr. Newman's principle consistently, seeing that neither in the one case nor the other can the bulk of mankind attain that sort of critical knowledge which *he* supposes necessary to certainty, you ought to deny that any common man has any business to say that he believes that he is *certain* of the main facts in the history either of Alfred or Cromwell."

"You do not surely mean to compare the importance of a belief in the one case with the importance of a belief in the other?" rejoined Fellowes.

"I do not; and can as little disguise from myself that such a question has nothing to do with the matter. The *duty* in the one case depends entirely on the question whether such a conviction of the accuracy of the main facts and more memorable events, as may pass for moral certainty, and justify its language and acts, be possible or not. If, from a want of capacity, and opportunity for a thorough investigation of all the conditions of the problem, it be not in the one case, where duty is involved, neither will it be in the other, though no duty is involved. If this be a fallacy, be pleased to prove it such —I shall not be sorry to have it so proved. But at present you seem to me grossly inconsistent in this matter.—I have also my *doubts* (to speak frankly) whether we must not apply Mr. Newman's principle (to the great relief of mankind) in other most momentous questions, in which the notion of *duty* cannot be excluded, but enters as an essential element. I cannot help fancying that, if his principle be true, mankind ought to be much obliged to him; for he has exempted them from the necessity of acting in all the most important affairs of life. For example, you are, I know, a great political philanthropist; you plead for the duty of enlightening the masses of the people on political questions — of making them intelligently acquainted with the main points of political and economical science. You do not despair of all this?"

"I certainly do not," said Fellowes.

"A most hopeless task," said Harrington, "on Mr. Newman's principle. The questions on which you seek to enlighten them are, many of them, of the most intricate and difficult character, — are, all of them, dependent on principles, and involve controversies, with which the great bulk of mankind are no more competent to deal than with Newton's 'Principia.' An easy, and often erroneous, assent on ill-comprehended data is all that you can expect of the mass; and how can it be their *duty*, when it may often be their *ruin*, to act upon this? A superficial knowledge is all that you can give them; thorough investigation is out of the question. Most men, I fear, will continue to believe it at least as possible for the common people to form a judgment on the validity of Paley's 'Evidences' as on the reasonings of Smith's 'Political Economy.' They will say, if the common people can be sufficiently sure of their conclusions in the latter case to take action upon them, — that is to render action a *duty*, — the like is possible in the former. Ought you not to hold by your principle, and say, that as from the difficulty of the investigation it is not possible for the bulk of mankind to attain such a degree of certainty as to make belief in an 'historical religion' a duty, so neither for the like reason can it be their duty to come to any definite conclusion, or to take any definite action in relation to the equally difficult questions of politics, legislation, political economy, and a variety of other sciences?

—I will take another case. I believe you will not deny that you are profoundly ignorant of medicine, nor that, though the most necessary, it is at the same time the most difficult and uncertain of all the sciences. You know that the great bulk of mankind are as ignorant as yourself; nay, some affirm that physicians themselves are about as ignorant as their patients; it is certain, that in reference to many classes of disease, doctors take the most opposite views of the appropriate treatment, and even treat disease in general on principles diametrically opposed! A more miserable condition for an unhappy patient can hardly be imagined. Though our own life, or that of our dearest friend in the world, hangs in the balance, it is impossible for us to tell whether the art of the doctor will save or kill. I doubt, therefore, whether you ought not to conclude from the principle on which we have already said so much, that God cannot have made it a poor wretch's duty to take any step whatever; nay, since even the medical man himself often confesses that he does not know whether the remedies he uses will do harm or good, it may be a question whether he himself ought not to relinquish his profession; at least if it be a *duty* in man to act only in cases in which he can form something better than conjectures."

"Well," said Fellowes, laughing; "and some even in the profession itself say, that perhaps it might not be amiss if the patient never called in such equivocal aid; if he allowed himself to die, not *secundum artem*, but *secundum naturam*."

"And yet I fancy, that in the sudden illness of a wife or child, you would send to the first medical man in your street, or the next, though you might be ignorant of his name, and *he* might be almost as ignorant of his profession; at least, that is what the generality of mankind would do."

"They certainly would."

"But yet, upon your principles, how can it be their duty to act on such slender probabilities, or, rather, mere conjectures, in cases so infinitely important?"

"I know not how that may be, but it is assuredly *necessary*."

"Well, then, shall we say it is only *necessary*, but not a duty? But then if in a case of such importance God has made it thus *necessary* for man to act in such ignorance, people will say he may possibly have left them in something less than absolute *certainty* in the matter of an 'historical religion.'—Ah! it is impossible to unravel these difficulties. I only know, that if the principle be true, then as men in general cannot form any reasonable judgment, not only on the principles of medical science, but even on the knowledge and skill of any particular professor of it (by their ludicrous mis-estimate of which they are daily duped both of money and life to an enormous extent), it cannot be their duty to take any steps in this matter at all. The fair application, therefore, of the principle in question would, as I say, save mankind a great deal of trouble;—but, alas! it involves us *philosophers* in a great deal."

"I cannot help thinking," said Fellowes, "that you have caricatured the principle." And he appealed to me.

"However ludicrous the results," said I, "of Harrington's argument, I do not think that his representation, if the principle is to be fairly carried out, is any caricature at all. The absurdity, if anywhere, is in the principle affirmed; viz., that God cannot have constituted it man's duty to *act*, in cases of very imperfect knowledge; and yet we see that he has perpetually compelled him to do so; nay, often in a condition next-door to stark ignorance. To vindicate the wisdom of such a constitution may be impossible; but the fact cannot be denied. The Christian admits the difficulty alike in relation to religion, and to the affairs of this world. He believes, with Butler, that 'probability is the guide of life;' that man may have sufficient evidence, in a thousand cases,—varying, however, in different individuals,— to warrant his action, and a reasonable confidence in the results, though that evidence is very far removed from certitude;—that similarly the mass of men are justified in saying that they *know* a thousand facts of history to be true, though they never had the opportunity or capacity of thoroughly investigating them, and that the great facts of science are true, though they may know no more of science than of the geology of the moon;—that the statesman, the lawyer, and the physician are justified in acting, where they yet are compelled to acknowledge that they act only on most unsatisfactory calculations of probabilities, and amidst a thousand doubts and difficulties; that *you*, Mr. Fellowes, are justified in endeavouring to enlighten the common people on many important subjects connected with political and social science, in which it is yet quite certain that not one in a hundred thousand can ever go to the bottom of them; of which very few can do more than attain a rough and crude notion, and in which the bulk must *act*, solely because they are *persuaded* that other men know more about the matters in question than themselves; all which, say we Christians, is true in relation to the Christian religion, the evidence for which is plainer, after all, than that on which man in ten thousand cases is necessitated to hazard his fortune or his life. If you follow out Mr. Newman's principle, I think you must, with Harrington, liberate mankind from the necessity of acting altogether in all the most important relations of human life. If it be thought not only hard that men should be called perpetually to act on defective, grossly defective evidence, but still harder that they should possess varying degrees even of that evidence, it may be said that the difference is perhaps rather apparent than real. Those whom we call *profoundly* versed in the more difficult matters which depend on moral evidence, are virtually in the same condition as their humbler neighbours; they are *profound* only by comparison with the superficiality of these last. Where men must act, the decisive facts, as was said in relation to history, may be pretty equally grasped by all; and as for the rest, the enlargement of the circle of a man's knowlege is, in a still greater proportion, the enlargement of the circle of his ignorance; for the circumscribing periphery lies in darkness. Doubts, in proportion to the advance of knowledge, spring up where they were before unknown; and though the previous *ignorance* of these was not knowledge, the knowledge of them (as Harrington has said) is little better than an increase of our ignorance.

"If, as you suppose, it cannot be our duty to act in reference to any 'historical religion' because a satisfactory investigation is impossible to the mass of mankind, the argument may be retorted on your own theory. You assert, indeed, that in relation to *religion*, we have an internal 'spiritual faculty' which evades this difficulty; yet men persist in saying, in spite of you, that it is doubtful, 1st, whether they have any such; 2nd, whether, if there be one, it be not so debauched and sophisticated by other faculties, that they can no longer trust it implicitly; 3rd, what is the amount of its genuine utterances; 4th, what that of its aberrations; 5th, whether it is not so dependent on development, education, and association, as to leave room enough for an auxiliary external revelation: — on all which questions the generality of mankind are just as incapable of deciding as about any historical question whatever."

Here Fellowes was called out of the room. Harrington, who had been glancing at the newspaper, exclaimed, —" Talk about the conditions on which man is left to act, indeed! Only think of his gross ignorance and folly being left a prey to such quack advertisements as half fill this column. Here empirics every day almost invite men to be immortal for the small charge of half-a-crown. Here is a panacea for nearly every disease under heaven in the shape of some divine elixir, and, what is more, we know that thousands are gulled by it. How satisfactory is that condition of the human intellect in which quack promises can be proffered with any plausible chance of success!"

I told him I thought the science of medicine would yield an argument against religious sceptics which they would find it very difficult to reply to.

"How so?"

"Ah! it is well masked; but I know you too well to allow me to doubt that you suspect what I am referring to."

"Upon my word — I am all in the dark."

"Is there not," said I, "a close analogy between the condition of men in reference to the health of their bodies and the science by which they hope to conserve or restore it, and the health of their souls and the science by which they hope to conserve or restore *that?* Has not God placed them in precisely the same difficulty and perplexity in *both* cases — nay, as I think, in greater in relation to medicine? and yet, is not man most willing and eager to apply to its most problematic aid, imparted even by the most ignorant practitioners, rather than be without it altogether? The possession which man holds most valuable in this world, and most men, alas! more valuable than aught in any other world — LIFE itself — is at stake; it is subjected to a science, or rather an art, proverbially difficult in theory and uncertain in practice, about which there have been ten thousand varieties of opinion — whimsically corresponding to the diversity of sect, creed, and priesthood, on which sceptics like you lay so much stress; nay, even the wisest and most cautious practitioners confess that their art is at best only a species of guessing; while the patient can no more judge of the remedies he consents, with so much *faith*, to swallow, or the knowledge of him who prescribes them, than he can of the perturbations of Jupiter's satellites. Yet the moment he is sick, away he goes to this dubious oracle, and trusts it with a most instinctive faith and docility as if it were infallible. All his doubts are mastered in an instant. I strongly suspect yours would be. Ought you not in consistency to refuse to act at all in such deplorable deficiency of evidence?"

"Well," said he, "consistent or inconsistent, it must be admitted that the parallel is very complete — and amusing." And he then went on, as he was apt to do, when an analogy struck his fancy. "Let me see, — yes, our unlucky race is condemned to put its most valued possession on the hazard of a wise choice, without any of the essential qualifications for wisely making it; a man cannot at all tell whether his particular *priest* in medicine understands and can skilfully apply even his own theory. Yes," he went on, "and I think (as you say) we might find, not only in the partisans of different systems of physic, the representatives of the various priesthoods, but in their too credulous — or shall we say, too *faithful* patients? — the representatives of all sects. There is, for example, the superstitious vulgar in medicine — the gross worshipper of the Fetish, who believes in the efficacy of charm, and spell, and incantation, of mere ceremonial and *opus operatum;* then there is the polytheist, who will adore any thing in the shape of a *drug*, and who is continually quacking himself with some nostrum or other from morning till night; who not only takes his regular physician's prescriptions, but has his household gods of empirical remedies, to which he applies with equal devotion. Then there is the Romanist in medicine, who swears by the infallibility of some papal Abernethy, and the unfailing efficacy of some *viaticum* of a blue pill."

"And who," said I, "would represent our friend who has just left the room, and who has tried every thing?"

"Why," he replied, "I think he is in the condition of a little boy of whom I heard a little while ago, whose mother was a homœopathist, and kept a little chest, from which she dispensed to her family and friends, perhaps as skilfully as the doctor himself could have done. The little fellow going into her dressing room, opened this box, and thinking that he had fallen on a store of 'millions' (as children call them) swallowed up his mother's whole doctor's shop before he could be stopped. It was happy, said the doctor, when called in, that the little patient had swallowed so *many*, or he would have been infallibly killed. Or perhaps we may liken our friend to that humorous traveller Mr. Stephens, who tells us, that having been provided at Cairo, by a skilful physician there, with a number of remedies for some serious complaint to which he was subject, he found, to his dismay, when suffering under a severe paroxysm in the fortress of Akaba, that he had lost the directions which told him in what *order* the medicines were to be taken. Whether pill, powder, or draught was to come first, he knew not, 'on which,' says he, 'in a fit of desperation, I placed them all in a row before me, and resolved to swallow them all *seriatim* till I obtained relief.' George has equal faith."

"You have omitted," said I, "one character, — that of the sceptic, who believes in no medicine at all; who sturdily dies with his doubts unresolved, and unattended by any physician. But it must be confessed that he is a still *rarer* character than the sceptic in religion. Nature, my dear Harrington, every where decides against you."

"I acknowledge," he said, "that we are but a scanty flock in any department of life; but, upon my word, the parallel you have suggested is so striking, that I think I must, in consistency, *extend* my scepticism to physic at least, and, if I am ill, refrain from availing myself of so uncertain an art, practised by such uncertain hands, and which are to be selected by one who cannot even guess whether they are ignorant or skilful —doctors, who may, perhaps, as Voltaire said, put drugs of which they know *nothing*, into bodies of which they know still *less*."

"*Act* upon that resolution, Harrington," said I, "and you will at least be consistent; but, depend upon it, nature will confute you."

"Why," said he, jestingly, "perhaps in the case of medicine, at all events, I might face the consequences of scepticism. I remember reading, in some account of Madagascar, that the natives are absolutely without the healing art; 'and yet,' says the author, with grave surprise, 'it is not observed that the number of deaths is increased.' Perhaps, thought I, that is the cause of it."

"The statistics," I replied, "of more civilised countries amply refute you, and show you that dubious as is the evidence on which God has destined and compelled men to act in this the most important affair of the present life, and absolute as is the faith they are summoned to exercise, neither is the study of the art (uncertain as it is in itself), nor the dependence of patients upon it (still more precarious as *that* is), unjustified on the whole by the result; and as to the abuses of downright quackery, a little prudence and common sense are no doubt required, and, if exercised, are sufficient to preserve men from them."

He mused, and, I thought, seemed struck by this analogy between man's temporal and spiritual condition. I said no more, hoping that he would ponder it.

July 25. I had been so much interested in the discussion between Harrington and young Robinson on the fair application of the principles of Strauss to history in general, that I could not resist the temptation to tell the youth in secret that I thought the matter would admit of further discussion, and that he would do well to challenge Harrington plausibly to show that some undoubted modern event might, when it became remote history, be rendered dubious to posterity. He willingly acted on the hint the next morning. To some remark of his Harrington replied thus:—

"Assuming with you, that Strauss has really cast suspicion on the historic character of the bulk of the transactions recorded in the New Testament, I must suspect that there is not an event in history, if at all remote, which, arguing exactly on the same principles, may not be made doubtful; and that is——"

"Why now," replied the other, "do you think it possible, that the events of the present year" (referring to the Papal Aggression), "which are making such a prodigious noise in England, will ever stand a chance of being similarly treated some centuries hence?"

"If they are ever treated at all," said Harrington; "but you must have observed that it is the tendency of man to make ridiculous mis-estimates of the importance of the transactions of his own age, and to imagine that posterity will have nothing to do but to recount them. He is much mistaken; they forget or care not a doit for nine-tenths of what he does; and misrepresent the tenth," continued he, laughing.

"Well, then, upon the supposition that Pio Nono and Cardinal Wiseman are of sufficient importance to be remembered at all eighteen hundred and fifty years hence, that is in the year 3700 of the Christian era,—though in all probability some new and more rational epoch will have jostled out both the Christian era and the Mahometan hegira by that time,——."

"Pray be sure," interrupted I, "before you predict a new epoch, that it will be wanted; that Christianity is really dead before you bury her. You will please to remember that the experiment was tried in France with much formality, but somehow came to a speedy and ignominious conclusion; the new era did not survive its infancy. As Paulus thinks that Christ was only in a trance when he seemed to be dead, so it certainly often is (figuratively speaking) with his religion; it seems to be dead when it is only in a trance. It is apt to rise again, and be more active than ever; and never more so than when, as in the middle of the last century, our infidel undertakers were providing for its funeral. But I beg your pardon for interrupting your conversation; you were saying——"

"I was saying," said Robinson, "that I doubt whether Cardinal Wiseman and his doings, eighteen hundred and fifty years hence, could be as much the subject of doubt and controversy (if remembered at all) as the events which Strauss has shown to be unhistorical. I think the press alone, with its diffusion and multiplication of the *sources* of knowledge, will prevent, in the future, the doubts which gather over the past. There will never again be the same dearth of historic materials."

"In spite of all that," replied Harrington, "I suspect it will be very possible for men to entertain the same doubts about many events of our time eighteen hundred and fifty years hence, as they entertain of many which happened eighteen hundred and fifty years ago."

"I can hardly imagine this to be possible."

"Because, I apprehend, first, that you are labouring

under the delusion already mentioned, by which men ever magnify the importance of the events of their own age, and forget how readily future generations will let them slip from their memory, and let documents which contain the record of them slip out of existence; and, secondly, because you do not give yourself time to realise all that is implied in supposing eighteen hundred years to have elapsed, nor to transport yourself fairly into that distant age. As to the first; let us recollect that the importance of historic events is by no means in proportion to the excitement they produce at the time of their occurrence. We have many exemplifications of this even in our own time; see the rapidity with which every trace of a political storm, which for a moment may have lashed the whole nation into fury, is appeased again: the surface is as smooth after a few short years as if it had never been ruffled at all! In all such cases, the constant tendency is, to let the events which have been thus transient in their effects sink into oblivion. But even of those which have been far more significant (since each future age will teem with fresh events *equally* significant, all claiming a part in the page of general history), the importance will be perpetually diminishing in estimate, and still more in interest, from the intenser feeling with which each age will in turn regard the events which stand in immediate proximity to its own. As time rolls on, all of the past that can be spared will be gradually jostled out. Details will be lost; and then, when remote ages turn to re-investigate the half-forgotten past, the want of those details will issue in the customary problems and 'historic doubts.' In the page of *general* history, events of a remote age, except those of a surpassing interest, will be reduced to more and more meagre outlines, till abridgments are abridged, and even these compendiums thought tedious. The interval between decad and decad now will be as much as that between century and century then. History will have to employ a sort of Bramah press in her compositions, and its application will compress into mere films the loose and pulpy textures submitted to it by each age. Let human vanity think what it will, many events and many names which seem imperishable will speedily die out of remembrance; many lights in the firmament destined (as we deem) to shine 'like the stars for ever and ever,' will hereafter be missing from the catalogue of the historic astronomer."

"But, at all events," said the other, "though there are thousands of facts which will be virtually forgotten, it will be at all times *easy* to ascertain (if a sufficiently strong motive exists) the real character of past events by a reference to the documents preserved by the press. The press—the *press* it is, which will preserve us from the doubts of the past."

"I *doubt* that. Has there been any lack of historic controversy respecting a thousand facts which have transpired since the press was in full activity? You forget that, in the first place, neither the press, nor any thing else, can preserve any *original* documents. Time will not be inactive in the future more than in the past; it will have no more respect for printed books than for manuscripts. An immense mass of print is every year silently perishing by mere decay. The original documents to which you refer, will, eighteen hundred years hence, have almost all perished; few will be preserved except in copies, and how many disputes *that alone* will cause, it is hard to say; but we may form some guess from the experience of the past. Of thousands of these documents again, no importance having been attached to them, and no one having imagined that any importance *would* ever be attached to them, no copies will have been taken, and there will be here again the usual field for conjectures. This is a common trick of Time;—silently destroying what a present age thinks may as well be left to his maw. It is not even discovered that valuable documents are lost till something turns up to make mankind wish they may be found. But neither is this the sole nor the chief source of future historic doubts. Do not flatter yourself too much on the wonders which the press can work, amongst which one unquestionably is, that it will bury at least as much as it will preserve.

Several considerations will suffice to show that here too we labour under a delusion. Oblivion will practically cover many events, owing to the mere accumulations of the press itself. You talk of the case of consulting 'original documents;' but when they lie buried in the depths of national museums, amidst mountain loads of forgotten and decaying literature, it will not be so *easy*, even supposing the present activity of the press only *maintained* for eighteen hundred and fifty years (although, in all probability, it will proceed at a rapidly increased ratio), I say it will not be so *easy* to lay your hands on what you want. The materials, again, will often exist by that time in dead or half-obsolete languages, or at least in languages full of archaic forms. It will be almost as difficult to unearth and collate the documents which bear upon any events less than the most momentous, as to recover the memorials of Egypt from the pyramids, or of ancient Assyria from the mounds of Nineveh. The historian of a remote period must be a sort of Belzoni or Layard. If we can suppose any thing so extravagant as that the British Museum will be in existence then, having preserved during these centuries (as it does now) all new books, and accumulated ancient and foreign literature only at the rate it has during these few years past, the library alone will extend over hundreds of acres at least. This, unless our posterity are fools, can hardly be the case; and therefore much will be rejected and left to the mercy of the great destroyer. But the very existence of any such repository is itself a very doubtful supposition. Comprehensive, indeed, may be the destruction of many large portions of our archives, essentially necessary to minute accuracy at so distant a date; nay, England herself may have ceased to exist. If her subterranean fuel be not exhausted, a cheaper and equally abundant supply of it may have been found elsewhere, and transfer for ever the chief elements of her manufacturing or commercial prosperity; or entirely new and more transcendent resources of science may have done the same thing, and our country may be left like a stranded vessel to rot upon the beach! Her furnaces extinguished, her manufactories deserted, her cities decayed, the hum of her busy population silenced, she may present a spectacle of desolation like that of so many other famous nations which have risen, culminated, and set for ever."

"Or," interrupted I, "(and may God avert the omen!) the same ruin may be accomplished still earlier, and by more potent causes. Her nobles enervated by luxury, her lower classes sunk in vice and ignorance, and both the one and the other decaying in piety and religion (a sure result of neglecting that Bible which has directly and indirectly formed her strength), she may have fallen a victim to the consequences of her own degeneracy, or to an irresistible combination of the enemies who envy and hate her. That picture of the splendid imagination of the great historian of our day may be realised, ' when some traveller from New Zealand shall, in the midst of a vast solitude, take his stand on a broken arch of London Bridge to sketch the ruins of St. Paul's.'"

"In short," resumed Harrington, "in several ways that appalling catastrophe may have taken place; and, should this be the case, how many questions will be asked of history, but asked in vain! As for Rome,— that other great name in the present strife pitted against England,—for aught we can tell she may by that time be in desolation far more remediless than when the grim Attilas and Alarics stormed her walls. For aught we know, the agency of those terrible elements which more or less mine the soil of Italy may have made her 'like unto' Herculaneum or Pompeii; or that silent desolator, the malaria, which Dr. Arnold thinks will be perpetual and will increase, may long before that period have reduced, not only the Campagna of Rome, but the whole region of the 'seven hills,' to a pestilential solitude."

"But all this is mere vision?" said Robinson.

"Certainly; but it is the vision of the *possible*. Similarly wonderful and equally unexpected revolutions have taken place in the history of nations and empires in a less space of time; and some enormous changes, we know, must happen during the next eighteen hundred and fifty years; and they will tend both to jostle out thousands of events of meaner moment, and to effect a comparative destruction of the memorials of the past. You do not suppose, I presume, that London and Rome are absolutely privileged from the fate which has overtaken Babylon and Memphis. I, for one, therefore, do not expect that the time will arrive when, in the historic investigations of the past, our Strausses will not find abundant scope for ingenious theories; nay, many real sources of perplexity even in reference to events which, at the time of their occurrence, seemed written as 'with a pen of iron on the rock for ever.' But even supposing no other difficulty, I cannot lay small stress upon the mere accumulation of materials on which the historian, two thousand years hence, will have to operate, if he would recover an exact account of the events of our time. It is much the same whether you have to dig into the pyramids of Egypt or into the catacombs of the buried literature of two thousand years for the memorials which are to enable you to arrive at the exact truth, at least as to any events of transient interest, however important at the time of their occurrence. It will be like 'hunting for a needle in a bundle of hay,' as the proverb says."

"Still, I cannot imagine that facts like those with which our ears have been ringing during the last eight months, can ever be contested."

"Can you not?" said Harrington. "I cannot imagine anything more likely than that, eighteen hundred and fifty years hence, such an event, on Strauss's principles, may be shown to be very problematical."

"Will you endeavour to show how it may probably be?" rejoined Robinson.

"Well, I have no objection, if you will give me till this evening to prepare so important a document."

In the evening, after supper, he amused us by reading us a brief paper entitled—

THE PAPAL AGGRESSION SHOWN TO BE IMPOSSIBLE.

"I shall proceed on the supposition that some Dr. Dickkopf or Dr. Scharfsinn, for either name will do, has to deal (as my uncle here believes our modern critics have to deal in the Gospels) with an account literally true. This learned man I shall imagine as existing in some nation at the antipodes 1850 years hence, and intellectually, if not literally, descended from some erudite critics of our age. Let me further suppose that the principal memorials of the current events are found in the page of some *continuator* of Macaulay (may the Fates have pity on him! I am afraid he will be far worse than even Smollett after Hume), who publishes his work only sixty years hence. Let us suppose him (as surely we well may) proceeding thus: ' During the year 1850-51 our countrymen are represented to us by the accounts of those who lived at the time (some few still survive), as having been in a condition of political and religious excitement almost unprecedented in their history. It was occasioned by the attempt of the Pope to re-establish the Roman Catholic hierarchy, which had been extinct since the Reformation. As these events, though all-absorbing to the actors in them (as are so many others of very secondary importance), have now shrunk to their true dimensions, and are, in fact, infinitely less momentous than others which were silently transpiring at the time almost without notice, I shall content myself with simply condensing a brief contemporaneous document which gives the chief points, without passion or prejudice, in a narrative so simple that it vouches for its own veracity:—

' Without permission of the Crown, or any negotiations with the Government whatever, Pope Pius the Ninth divided the whole of England into twelve sees, and assigned these to as many Roman Catholic bishops with local titles and territorial jurisdiction. The chief of them was one Nicholas Wiseman (by birth, it is said, a Spaniard), who was created Archbishop of Westminster and Cardinal.

' The said Wiseman issued a pastoral letter, which was read on the 27th day of October, 1850, in all the churches and chapels of the Romanists, congratulating Catholic England on the re-establishment of the Roman hierarchy. In it, he used the startling expression, "our beloved country has been restored to its orbit in the ecclesiastical firmament, from which its light had long vanished."

'The nation was the more surprised at all this, inasmuch as the position of Pio Nono was not such as to warrant any expectation of a step so audacious. Little more than a year had elapsed since his own subjects in Rome itself rebelled against him, murdered his Prime Minister, and compelled him, in the disguise of a menial, to fly from Rome; nor was he restored except by the arms of the French, who besieged and took Rome in 1849.

'That the Pope, while holding his own little dominions on so precarious a tenure, should venture to assume such an exercise of supremacy over the most powerful nation in the world,—a nation so jealous of its independence, which had so long been, and which still was, most averse to his claims, seemed almost incredible to the people of England; and they were proportionably indignant.

'Some affirmed that the aforesaid Cardinal Wiseman was the chief cause of it all,—the spectacle of many conversions from the Church of England to that of Rome having deceived him into a notion that the national mind was far more generally disposed to receive Romanism, and to make up the long-standing breach with the Papacy, than was really the case. The principal cause of the conversions above mentioned was what was called the "Oxford movement." In the university of Oxford had sprung up a body of men who had consecrated their lives to the diffusion of doctrines indefinitely near those of Rome. They spoke of the Reformation contemptuously; advocated very many obsolete rites and usages; and magnified the power of the Church and the prerogatives of the priesthood. Many of them, at length, finding that they could not, with any shadow of consistency, remain in the English Church, abandoned it; but many others remained, and propagated the same opinions with impunity. They were regarded as traitors by their brethren, though no steps were taken to prevent them from teaching their notions, nor to deprive them of their benefices and emoluments. Among those who gave up their livings, of their own accord, from the feeling that they could not hold them with a safe conscience, the principal was one afterwards called Father Newman.

'Now this Newman must by no means be confounded with another of the same name, Professor Newman — in fact his own brother — who was also educated at Oxford, but whose history was in most singular contrast with his. While the one brother went over to Rome, exceeded in zeal and credulity even the Romanists themselves, and sighed for a restoration of mediæval puerilities, the other lapsed into downright infidelity, and denied even the *possibility* of an external revelation.

'Very many thought, that if the Oxford party had been wise enough to proceed more gently in the propagation of their notions, they would have accomplished much greater things, and perhaps eventually brought the popular mind to embrace the Romish Church. But their later publications (and especially No. 90.) opened the eyes of many, and the frequent defections from the English Church, which were almost daily announced in the papers, opened the eyes of many more.

'But, whether or not Wiseman and other principal persons were misled by erroneous representations of the state of the English mind, certain it is that he advised the Pope to take this perilous step. The Pope was persuaded; he assured the people of England that he should not cease to supplicate the Virgin Mary and all the saints whose virtues had made this country illustrious, that they would deign to obtain, by their intercessions with God, a happy issue to his enterprise.

'The excitement produced by the publication of the Pope's proceedings throughout England was prodigious, and can hardly be conceived by us at this day. Every county, city, and almost every town, held meetings in the utmost alarm and indignation; and resolved on petitioning the Queen and Parliament to do something or other to prevent the Pope's measures from taking effect, and especially to annul all claims to local and territorial jurisdiction in this country. The universities;

the clergy in their dioceses; the Bishops collectively—even Philpotts of Exeter, though intoxicated with zeal for those Oxford notions which had done all the mischief; the municipalities; almost all organised bodies, whether of Churchmen or Dissenters, remonstrated and petitioned. Amongst these meetings one was held at the Guildhall of London, which was crowded with the merchant princes of that great city, and all that could represent its wealth, intelligence, and energy. One Masterman opened the proceedings, made a vehement speech against the Bishop of Rome and his pretensions, and proposed a stringent resolution, which was carried by acclamation.

'At a dinner given by the Lord Mayor, at which were present many of the Ministers of the Crown, the Lord Chancellor Wilde spoke very boldly, and, as some thought, unadvisedly, on his possible *future* relations to the Cardinal.

'Cardinal Wiseman published a subtle defence of himself and the Popish measure, which he addressed to the people of England; and whether consistently or inconsistently, pleaded in the most strenuous manner for the inviolable observance of the principles of "religious liberty."

'A single and indeed inexplicable circumstance occurred in the course of this controversy. In a lecture, delivered at the Hanover-Square Rooms, a certain Presbyterian Clergyman had asserted that the oath prescribed in the Pontificale Romanum, which the Cardinal Wiseman must have taken to the Pope when he received the Pallium as Archbishop of Westminster, notoriously contained a clause enjoining the *duty* of persecution. This clause a facetious Englishman said, ought to be translated, "I will persecute and *pitch into* all heretics to the utmost of my power;" and every one knew that the Pope of Rome looked upon the English as the greatest heretics in the world.

'When Wiseman heard of the representations thus made, he caused his secretary to write to the Protestant Lecturer, to say that the clause in the oath to which he had referred, was not insisted upon, in his (the Cardinal's) case, by the Pope, and that if his calumniator chose to go to the Cardinal's library, he would see that it was cancelled in his copy of the Pontifical. The Protestant accepted his challenge, and went to the said library. He was then shown the oath, and found the clause in question, *totidem verbis;* not cancelled, however, but marked off by a line in black ink drawn over it, and (as it seemed) very recently.

'Pamphlets were published on this curious circumstance on both sides; the Roman Catholics contended that the mere fact of Wiseman's challenge was a sufficient proof of his consciousness of rectitude.

'On the whole, after half a year of perpetual agitation, both in and out of Parliament, a measure was passed which was notoriously inadequate to suppress the offence, and which was broken with impunity.

'It is gratifying to add, that notwithstanding the dangerous and vehement excitement which so long inflamed the minds of the people, no life was lost except on one occasion. The sufferer—contrary to what might have been expected—was of the dominant party; a policeman, who was endeavouring to repress the party violence of some Irish Catholics in the north of England.'

"Now it need not be said," proceeded Harrington, "that these sentences contain what is perfectly well known by you — for myself I say nothing — to be the merest matter of fact, narrated in the simplest language, without any art or embellishment. Would you like to hear how Dr. Dickkopf, of New Zealand, or Kamschatka, or Caffre-land, might treat such a document eighteen hundred and fifty years hence, amidst that imperfect light which we well know rests upon so many portions of the past, and which may, very possibly, be felt in the future? I think it would not be difficult for him to show that the 'Papal Aggression' *was impossible.*"

"We will, at least, listen to you," said Robinson.

"Let us suppose, then, some learned Theban stumbling upon this brief record of an obscure event, and, as usual, making (if only because he had discovered what nobody in the world either knew or cared about) a huge commentary upon it; concluding from the internal evidence, the simplicity of the style, the absence of all imaginable motives for misrepresentation, and some external corroborative fragments painfully gleaned from the history of the period, that these sentences formed a genuine, literal, historic account, of certain events which transpired in England in the year 1850. This, of course, would of itself, be sufficient to make ten Dr. Dickkopfs turn to, and prove the contrary; and any one of them, I imagine, might, and probably would, thus reply. Excuse his clumsy style. He would say:

'That there may have been, and very probably was, some *nucleus* of fact which may have served as a groundwork for these pseudo-historical memorials, is not denied: but to regard that document, of which they are professedly a *condensation*, as a genuine record of events which transpired at the period in question, can only, we conceive, be the infelicity of an essentially uncritical mind. Most evidently, whether we regard the known events and relations of that age (as far as they have come down to us) or the internal characteristics of the document itself, we discover unequivocal traces of an unhistoric origin. Let us look at both these sources of evidence in order. If we mistake not, the document, even as it now stands, bears on its very front, that the *original* document, so far from being a literal description of the events of the time to which it professedly related, was allegorical, or at most, historico-allegorical, and most likely designed broadly to caricature and satirise some perceived tendencies or conditions of the English religious *development* in certain parties of that age. But whether it be, or be not, reducible to the class of allegorico-ecclesiastico-political satire, certainly no person of critical discernment can for a moment allow it to be a literal statement of historic events. And first to look at the internal evidence.

'Is it possible to overlook the *singular* character of the names which every where meet us? They, in fact, tell their own tale, and almost, as it were, proclaim of themselves, that they are allegorical. *Wiseman, Newman* (two of them, be it observed), *Masterman, Philpotts, Wilde.* Who, that has been gifted with even a moderate share of critical acumen, can fail to see that these are all fictitious names invented by the allegorist either to set forth certain qualities or attributes of certain persons whose true names are concealed, or, as I rather think, to embody certain tendencies of the times, or represent certain party characteristics? Thus the name "Wiseman" is evidently chosen to represent the proverbial craft which was attributed to the Church of Rome; and Nicholas has also been chosen (as I apprehend) for the purpose of indicating the sources whence that craft was derived. In all probability the name was selected just in the same manner as Bunyan in his immortal Pilgrim's Progress (which still delights the world) has chosen "Worldly Wiseman" for one of his characters. It is said that he was a Spaniard: but who so fit as a Spaniard to be represented as the agent of the Holy See? while, as there never was a Spaniard of that name, every one can see that historic probability has not been regarded. The word Newman again (and observe the significant fact that there were two of them) was, in all probability, I may say, certainly, designed to embody two opposite *tendencies,* both of which, perhaps, claimed, in impatience of the effete humanity of that age (a dead and stereotyped Protestantism), to introduce a new order of things. These parties (if I may form a conjecture from the document itself) were essaying to extricate the mind of the age from the difficulties of its intellectual position: an age, asserting inconsistently, on the one hand, the freedom of spiritual life, and, on the other, claiming for the Bible an authorised supremacy over all the phenomena of that spiritual life. One of these parties sought to solve this difficulty by endeavouring to resuscitate the spirit of the *past:* the other, by attempting to set human intellect and consciousness free from the yoke of *all* external authority. In all probability the names were suggested to the somewhat profane allegoricosatirical writer by that text in the English version, "put on the Newman," the new man of the *spirit*. We are almost driven to this interpretation, indeed, by the extreme and ludicrous improbability of two men — brothers — brought up at the same university, gradually receding, *pari passu*, from the same point in opposite directions, to the uttermost extreme; one till he had embraced the most puerile legends of the middle ages, the other till he had proceeded to open infidelity. Probably such a curious coincidence of events was never heard of since the world began: and this must, at all events, be rejected.

'Similar observations apply to the name *Masterman*, which, in ancient English, was applied to him who was not a "servant," or "journeyman," and is not unfitly used to indicate *collectively* the assemblage of wealthy merchants who, like those of Tyre, were "princes;" as well as to imply that the powerful class to which they belonged were the "Mastermen" in the country, and, in fact, spoke in a *potential* voice in all such crises as that supposed. It might also, perhaps, be designed obliquely to intimate that whatever the clergy and the theologians of different parties might wish to realise, it was, after all, the powerful and independent class of the laity who were the "mastermen," and would not succumb to any spiritual guides whatever, even though called by the specious names of Wisemen and Newmen. The mere singularity of the names alone ought to decide the point. And what further confirms our view is that it is impossible to point out any Englishman of any distinction who ever had any of these names. Here we do not argue from conjecture, after merely looking into the most recent biographical repertories, (as, for example, the "Bibliotheca Clarissimorum Virorum," in three hundred and fifty volumes folio;) for it is no argument that this meagre collection makes no mention of any such names; since, in the successive compilations of such works (as the world grows older), it has been found necessary to extrude from time to time thousands of lesser names, which had twinkled in preceding ages.

But, deeply anxious to establish truth, we have at infinite pains caused to be fished up from the depths of the archives of our national museums, very rare reprints of some of the works of the age nearest that in which these events are said to have occurred, and in none of these works is there an individual mentioned of the name of Newman or Masterman, and only one comparatively obscure person of the name of Wiseman—a presumptive proof that they were fictitious names. Is it possible that these curious and varied coincidences can be the mere effect of chance?'

"I shall spare you," said Harrington, "Dr. Dickkopf's learned etymological disquisitions on the names Wilde and Philpotts, which, aided by the imputed 'rashness' of the one, and the 'intoxicated zeal' of the other, he clearly demonstrated to be fictitious.

"After which, I will suppose him to proceed thus:—

'We presume we have said enough to convince any acute and candid mind of the extreme improbability of the document being designed to convey to posterity a literal statement of facts; not that we for a moment think it necessary to suppose that any evil design actuated the writer, whoever he might be. It was most likely intended, as we have already said, to be an allegorico-political caricature of certain events which did undeniably occur, and which formed a slender basis of historic fact on which to found it.

'Nor is the particularity of some of the dates and alleged circumstances of much weight in our judgment. He must be a miserable inventor of fiction indeed, who cannot clothe a narrative in some verisimilitude of this kind. It is said, that the historian makes a seeming reference to those who were living at the very time. "Some," he says, "still survive." But who does not see that the word "survive" may refer to the *accounts* (which he, it appears, knew little how to interpret), not the *persons;* though, be it observed, that on such a supposition he does not vouch for having *seen* them, and may have spoken merely from report. This very clause, too, has undeniably much the appearance of an interpolation. There are many other little circumstances which, to those who have been accustomed to detect unhistoric characteristics in ancient documents, and to draw a sharp line between the mythic or allegoric, and the historic, sufficiently proclaim the origin of this supposed narrative of facts.

'But the internal evidence, conclusive as it is, is as nothing to the external. If we examine the document by the light of the facts which contemporary history supplies, nay, even by the probability or otherwise of its own contents, we shall see the extreme absurdity of supposing that the account from which it was borrowed was ever meant to be a record of facts. We hesitate not to say, that the political events of which it makes mention are many of them in the highest degree incredible. That there may have been a rebellion at Rome is very possible; but assuredly the very nation in Europe (if we except England), that was *least* likely to take the Pope's part against a popular movement, or reseat him on his throne, was the French. To suppose *them* thus acting is contrary to all that we know of the history of that nation, and of human nature. The traces of the terrible revolutions which in that century and at the close of the preceding one, shook France again and again to her centre, and the outlines of which still live in authentic history, all show the extent to which infidelity and democratic violence prevailed in France; nay, we know that during the dominion of the Emperor Napoleon (if we are to regard his history as literally true, and not a collection of fables and legends*, as some even of that age maintained), that great conqueror arrested and imprisoned the Pope. That France should have undertaken the task of subduing a republican movement, just when she had come out of a similar revolution, or rather, many such — and of reseating the Pope on his throne, when she had been more impatient of the re-

---

* Dr. Dickkopf may here be supposed to refer to the "Historic Doubts" of Archbishop Whately, which may well deceive even more astute critics. — ED.

straints of all religion than any other nation in Europe, is perfectly incredible! But, further; supposing (as may, perhaps, be true) that there was a basis of fact in the asserted rebellion of the Romans, and Pio Nono's restoration to his dominions, (though not by France, *that* the intelligent reader will on politico-logical grounds pronounce impossible, but more probably by the Spaniards,) —yet can we suppose that a power which was always celebrated for its astuteness and subtlety, would choose that very moment of humiliation and ignominy to rush into an act so audacious as that of re-establishing the Romish hierarchy in England; in a nation by far the most powerful in the world at that time, a nation which, if it had pleased, could have blown Rome into the air in three months? It must needs have strengthened a thousand-fold the strong antipathies of the English to the See of Rome. It would, indeed, have justified that storm of indignation with which it is *said* to have been met.

'There is much that is palpably improbable in many other parts of the statement (simple as it seems to be) when submitted to the searching spirit of modern criticism. How ridiculous is the story of Cardinal Wiseman's pretending that the oath in receiving the Pallium had been modified for his convenience; little less so, indeed, than his challenge to his Presbyterian antagonist to examine it, and that, too, in the very book in which the contested clause was *not* cancelled! All this is such a maze of absurdity that it is impossible to believe it. In the first place, do we not know that throughout the whole history of the Papal power, the inflexible character, not only of its doctrines, but of its official forms and solemnities, was always maintained, and that this pertinacity was continually placing it at a disadvantage in the contest with the more flexible spirit of Protestantism? It would not renounce in terms or words, the very things which it *did* renounce in deeds, and never could prevail upon itself to get over this unaccommodating spirit! Yet here we are to believe that at the Cardinal's request a certain part of a most solemn ceremonial—that of receiving the Pallium—was remitted by the Pope! If it were so, the Cardinal would certainly have desired to conceal it. If he could not have done that, he would, at least, never have given so easy a triumph to his adversary as to challenge him to inspect the very copy of the Pontifical, in which, after all, the oath was *not* cancelled, in order that he might be satisfied that it was! Who can believe that a Cardinal of the Romish Church, Wiseman or fool, would have been simple enough for such a step as this? It is plain that the historian himself was not unaware that such an objection would immediately suggest itself, and endeavours to guard against it—a suspicious circumstance *in itself*—which may serve to warn us how little we can depend on the historic character of the document.

'Again; what can be more improbable than that, when a great nation was convulsed from one end to the other, as the English are said to have been, there should have been *no* violence, not even accidentally, attending those huge and excited assemblages; a thing so natural, nay, so certain! Who can believe that only *one* man was sacrificed, and *he* on the predominant side! I have discovered in my laborious researches on this important subject, that only seventy years before, when a cry of the same nature, but much less potent, was raised, London was filled with conflagration and bloodshed. Who ever heard, indeed, of commotion such as this is pretended to have been, and its ending in *vox et præterea nihil?*

'It is superfluous to point out the absurdity of supposing a Cardinal of the Romish Church lecturing the people of England on "the claims of religious liberty;" or so great a nation, in such a paroxysm, spending many months in the concoction of a measure confessed to be a feeble one, and suffered to be broken with impunity!

'But lastly, my laborious researches have led to the important discovery that in this very year of pretended hot commotion, England—in peace with all the world—profound peace within and profound peace without—celebrated a sort of jubilee of the nations, in a vast building of glass (wonderful for those times) called the

Great Exhibition, to which every country had contributed specimens of the comparatively rude manufactures of that rude age! London was filled with foreigners from all parts of the earth; the whole kingdom was in a commotion indeed, but a commotion of hospitable festivity in which it shook hands with all the world! This is a piece of positive evidence which ought to settle the whole matter. In short, the external and internal evidence alike warrants us in rejecting this absurd story as utterly incredible.'

"Upon my word," said young Robinson, "you have said more than I thought you could have said on such a theme. I really almost doubt whether Dr. Dickkopf has not the best of it, and whether we ought not to agree that the 'Papal Aggression' is a sheer delusion."

"Oh!" said Harrington, "I have not given you half the arguments by which an historian, eighteen hundred years hence, might prove that what has actually occurred never could have occurred, and that what has not occurred must, in the very nature of things, have occurred, by a necessity alike political, historical, ethical, logical, and psychological. And no doubt Dr. Dickkopf is right on the principles on which acute critics may argue; that is, the assumption that certain *probabilities* will justify conclusions on such subjects. One might naturally have supposed the Pope to have been more politic than to take this step — the French more consistent than to suppress the Republican movement of Italy — the English less *moderate* in expressing their indignation — and certainly that there would never have been such an array of odd names to garnish one brief document. And now, I bethink me, it is far from impossible that some Dr. Dickkopf may even apply to Strauss's Leben Jesu, and Dr. Whately's 'Historic Doubts,' similar reasoning to prove that the first was elaborate irony; and the second, a sincere expression of scepticism."

"How can that be?"

"Thus: he will prove that the age was remarkably fond of such species of ironical literature. As Strauss, in his preface, has expressly admitted (though we all know what he means) that Christianity is true, and has suggested an unimaginably absurd hypothesis as to its true import, founded on the principles of the Hegelian philosophy, the learned Dr. Dickkopf will say that no one who so spoke of Christianity could have intended seriously to discredit it, and yet certainly could not possibly believe the absurd theory of it concocted out of German philosophy; *ergo*, that we must regard the whole book as a piece of prolonged irony,—a little too characteristic of German pedantry, it is true, but sincerely designed to expose that extravagance of historic criticism and biblical exegesis which had so distinguished the author's countrymen; by which Homer had been annihilated, a great part of ancient history rendered doubtful, and the Bible turned into a riddle-book;— that this hypothesis is confirmed by the space which Strauss gives to the exposure of the absurdities of the Rationalists, which, in fact, occupies at least half his work. Dr. D. will even very likely prove that Strauss himself is a fictitious name; Strauss, in the German, meaning an ostrich, which, according to the proverb, can digest anything. On the other hand, as he will be able to show that Strauss's work is a piece of prolonged irony, he will very likely show that Whately's 'Historic Doubts' may be a sincere expression of opinion (which, in fact, many have even in our day wisely believed it to be), and he will argue it with a gravity worthy of one of the commentators who interpret the irony of Socrates literally; he will prove it from the air of sobriety and sincerity which pervades the pamphlet. Nay, for aught I know, he may show that there was an 'historic place' for such a piece, in the undoubted *myths* to which the wondrous achievements of Napoleon had given rise; he will say that these had produced a natural feeling of scepticism as to the greater part of the facts, though he will think Dr. Whately has gone a *little* too far in doubting his very existence; there being sufficient evidence that such a man as Napoleon existed, although the world really knows little more about him than about Semiramis or Genghis Khan."

"Well," said I, "having proved that Dr. Strauss's work is irony, and Whately's *brochure* a sincere expression of opinion, it would be hard for even Dr. Dickkopf to go further. But, seriously, it is no laughing matter. This is a strange power the future historian has over us."

"Oh, be assured," said Harrington, "he can make of us just what he pleases. Never was a question more unreasonable than that of the Irishman who, being conjured, on some occasion, to think of *posterity*, said, 'What, I should like to know, has posterity done for us?' It will do something for us, depend upon it. A future historian will not only make us confess, with the Prayer-Book, 'that we have done the things we ought not to have done, and have left undone the things we ought to have done,' but, 'that we have done the things that we have *not* done, and have left undone the things that we *have* done!'"

"I wonder," said I, "that some of Dr. Strauss's countrymen have not proved him to be an imaginary being — a myth. It were very easy to do it on such principles."

"It has been done long since," said Harrington, "by Wolfang Menzel."

"Thank you," said I, in conclusion, "you have clearly proved that a *true* history may plausibly be shown to be *false*."

"And therefore, my dear uncle, you will, I hope, justify my scepticism on all such matters," said he, archly. I acknowledge, as Socrates says, that I felt for a moment as if I had received a sudden blow, and hardly knew what to say. "No," said I, at last, "unless you can justify Dr. Strauss's theory of historical criticism, of which you yourself acknowledge you have *doubts*. With *that*, any thing may be proved false; meantime it appears that the *facts* to which it is applied may be undoubtedly *true*."

On retiring to my chamber, I mused for some time on the facility with which man's ingenuity or inclinations can pervert any facts which he resolves shall be otherwise than they are. "Dubious as is the EVIDENCE," Harrington was fond of saying, "I distrust the JUDGE still more;" an admission, I told him, of which I should one day remind him. Tired at last of this unpleasant theme, I took up a volume of Leibnitz's Theodicée, which happened to lie on the table, and read those striking passages towards the conclusion in which he represents Theodore (reluctant to accept the iron theory of necessity) as privileged with a peep into a number of the infinite *possible* worlds; from which he has the satisfaction of seeing that, bad as is the lot of Sextus in the best of all possible worlds, that lot, Sextus being what he is, could not possibly be any better: a queer consolation, by the way, till we know why Sextus *must* be what he is, or why Sextus *must* be at all.

I sank off to slumber in my chair, no doubt under the soporific effects of this metaphysical morphine. While I slept, the previous discussions of the day and the dose of Theodicée operating together suggested a very strange dream, which I shall here record. It shall be entitled—

THE PARADISE OF FOOLS.

Methought I saw a grave and very venerable old man with a long white beard enter my chamber, and quietly seat himself opposite to me. Instead of asking who he was, and how he came there, nothing seemed more natural and proper. We all know how easily in dreams the mind dispenses with all ceremony; little or no introduction is required; every one is at once on a most delightful footing of familiarity with all the world; and the greatest possible incongruities appear just *comme il faut*.

He told me that he had come from a very curious part of the "best of all possible worlds"—the "Paradise of Fools;" and on my looking surprised, said,

"Are you ignorant, then, that there is a spot in the universe where a vicegerent of the Deity has at his disposal unlimited power and wisdom to enable him to comply with the somewhat whimsical conditions of the theories of those wonderful philosophers who have taken upon them to say how the universe might have been constructed without any supreme or presiding intelligence at all; or have modestly suggested, that had they been consulted, certain notable improvements might have been effected in its fabrication or government; or lastly, who have complained of the revelation which God has vouchsafed to man, or contended, that, if true, it might have been more unexceptionably framed, and more skilfully promulgated?"

"And what is the result?" I asked.

"The result is a part of the 'everlasting shame and contempt' which are the heritage of impiety."

"There must have been enough for the said vicegerent to do," I remarked.

"Not so much as you imagine," said he, smiling. "The conditions of these wise men's theories, so far as even omniscience can comprehend or omnipotence realise them, are indeed exactly complied with; but nevertheless, they often baffle both. Sometimes the reproof, thus implied, obliquely strikes more than its immediate objects; it alights even on some of the profoundest philosophers who never had it in their thoughts to call in question the infinite superiority of divine Power and Wisdom, but who have delivered themselves a little too positively about 'monads' and 'atoms,' and ultimate constituents of the universe. They have sometimes been not a little scandalised, as well as laughed at, when some half-witted, muddle-headed followers, glad to escape their trial, pretended to have founded systems of Pantheism or—what is just the same thing—Atheism, on some of their too obscure definitions. One man declared that he could do nothing without the Monads of Leibnitz, each of which, says that philosopher, 'is a mirror representing the universe, though obscurely, and knows everything but confusedly;' which last clause is unexceptionable enough. Another rogue asked for the archetypes of Plato — he had had a notion, he said, that a good deal might be made out of them without Plato's Demiurgus;— another, for the constituents of the vital automata of Descartes; he had been misled to believe that if animals could be mechanically produced, the whole universe might have been so produced also. The Archangel assured them and others, with much politeness, that, if the philosophers in question could in any way make their meaning intelligible, heaven would do its poor best to realise their conceptions, but that it was impossible for even omnipotence to execute commands which even omniscience could not comprehend.

" Similarly, one man requested that he might be provided with a little of Aristotle's ' Eternal Matter;' but he was told that there was no such thing *in rerum naturâ*, and that it was unfortunately *too late* to *make* it. He seemed to think himself very unjustly treated. Another demanded some of the Atoms of Epicurus, to make a slight experiment with; unexceptionably spherical, indivisible, and so forth. These, he was told, he might be accommodated with; and that all he had to do was to shake them *long enough*, and doubtless the fortuitous jumble would come out at last a miniature world.

" Above all, there were several German philosophers, who, having founded various physical theories, more or less extensive, on the perspicuous metaphysics of their countrymen,' were confident that if they had not hit on *the* modes which Supreme Wisdom had adopted, their modes were yet very excellent modes; and they were absolutely clamorous that their experiments should begin. But, alas! many of them stood but little chance of being ever tried, for the very same reason which prevented the disciple of Leibnitz from obtaining his ' Monads;' their authors could not make their meaning intelligible to the delegated omniscience. As to some of the metaphysicians of the same country, since their theories embraced nothing less than the evolution of the ' totality ' of the universe, the ' infinite ' and the ' absolute ' included — it was of course impossible that they could be tried. But it was thought an appropriate punishment for their authors to be condemned to write on till they had made their meaning intelligible. Some have laboured with incredible industry to comply with this very reasonable request, but their notions seem to grow darker and darker at every step; and one in particular has written a .huge folio, in which, by universal consent of men and angels, there is not the smallest glimmer of meaning from one end to the other. Another even complains in private of the want of *philosophical genius* in the court of celestial criticism, and declares that in Germany they could have constructed ten theories of the universe, and given twenty solutions of the ' infinite ' and the ' absolute,' in the time he has been vainly endeavouring to explain his meaning to personages so deplorably deficient in metaphysical acumen."

He was going on with some other details of the hapless philosophers.

" I would much rather hear from you," said I, " for it is a subject in which I take a far deeper interest, — how those have sped who have objected to the Revelation with which God has favoured man, on the ground that it cannot be true, else it would have been more unexceptionably framed or more wisely promulgated. I take it for granted that these have not been destitute of opportunities of trying their experiment."

" Surely not," replied my new acquaintance. " ' The Paradise of Fools ' is well stocked with creatures of this description. Many of the experiments which required time to test them were commenced hundreds of years ago, and are completed. Others are still unfinished, while there have been many which required only to be commenced and they were completed instantly, to the confusion of their authors."

" I should much like," said I, " to hear an account of some of these experiments."

" Willingly," answered he; "only you must bear in mind that they were all to be performed under certain limitations, without which no revelation which God can give to man would be of the slightest value."

He then informed me, that the evidence afforded must not be such as to annihilate the conditions on which man is to be made virtuous and happy, if he is to be made so at all. It must not be inconsistent with the exercises of either his reason or his faith; nor prevent the play of his moral dispositions, nor triumph by mere violence over his prejudices; it must not operate purely upon the passions or the senses, nor overbear all possibility of offering resistance; — as would be the case, for example, if a man were placed on the edge of a precipice, and told that he would immediately be thrown over it if he transgressed the rules of temperance or chastity. The happiness, he said, which God originally designed for his intelligent and moral creatures was a *voluntary* happiness, springing out of the well-balanced and well-directed activity of all the principles of their nature. Any revelation, therefore, must proceed on the same basis, both as regards itself and the *mode* in which it is given. Arguments and motives morally sufficient, but not more than sufficient, must be addressed to the intellect and the conscience. All this is necessary to render the felicity and perfection of man stable and permanent; for without such a trial, triumphantly sustained, he would have no security that in the presence of objects which tend to exert an overpowering influence on his senses or his feelings, he might not at some period of the unknown future be impelled to take a wrong path, and err and be miserable. This ordeal, originally designed for man, and not superseded by revelation, must be continued long enough to render the principles, on which he *ought* to act, practical habits; after which he may go forth (sublime and glorious privilege!) to any part of this world, or of *any* world to which God may call him, master of himself and his destiny; not afraid lest temptations should warp him from a steadfastness that is founded on the decision of an inflexible will itself directed by enlightened intelligence and moral rectitude; in a word, in possession of the appropriate, and alone appropriate, happiness of an intellectual and moral agent; an image of the felicity of the great Creator himself.—This condition, he said, of giving a revelation, so far from being a hardship, is not only in harmony with the nature of things, but is itself an expression of the Divine Beneficence; which designed for man no casual, precarious safety, as the result of transient external violence to the principles of his nature, but a permanent and inviolable equilibrium of the powers *within* him. "Heaven itself," he concluded, "can *be* heaven only to those who are *internally* prepared for it."

"Were there many," I cried, "who were willing to make the experiment of giving a revelation more unexceptionably than it has been given, on the proposed conditions?"

"Not very many, as you may well suppose," said he; "but if objectors had been unwilling, they would have been compelled to make it."

"But upon whom were the experiments to be made?" said I; "for unless they were beings of the same intellectual and moral condition as themselves, I see not how aught could come of it."

"Oh, be satisfied," he replied; "the beings who are provided for these projectors are as like the inhabitants of your world as one egg is like another. They are men themselves; communities made up of those who have lived in your world, and who have gone out of it with the same thoughts, passions, and emotions as they had on earth; many of them having rejected or disregarded the *true* revelation, and others never having had that revelation to reject. Of course they are ignorant, in this intermediate state, of the tricks which these experimenters play with them, till they are concluded; but in rejecting the new revelations, many of them reject the very conditions of belief which when on earth they said would have been sufficient, while the result in those who make the experiment, and in those on whom the experiment is made, is, to 'vindicate the ways of God to man.'"

There is a wonderful power in getting over trifling difficulties in our dreams, or I should certainly have demurred to some parts of this statement. Instead of that, I let my mind, as usual in such cases, dwell on a point which was no difficulty at all. "If," said I, "they are dead, they are probably very different beings from what they were when alive."

"And do you think," said he, with an unpleasant half-sneer, "that mere change of place makes any difference in man; or that the merely physical effects of death operate a magical change on his intellect, affections, emotions, and volitions, or can render him a more reasonable creature than he was before?"

"I did not mean exactly that," said I; "but surely it is not possible that the soul without the body can be exactly like the soul with it."

"Have not your philosophers," said he, "often founded, or *pretended* to found scepticism on the argument, that it is difficult to tell whether life itself may not be a series of illusions like those in dreams? Have they not even declared, that as in dreams all seems to be real, so in their waking moments all *may* be no more than a dream? Nay, have not some said, that it is impossible to tell which is the real and which the dreaming part of their existence?"

"There have been such," said I, "but I never knew any one convinced by their reasoning."

"Perhaps not," he answered; "but it may be of use to show you that in that intermediate state men may, as in dreams, be capable of a series of thoughts and emotions exactly similar to what they experienced in this world; quite as vivid," and he added, with a quiet smile, "perhaps as rational."

"But they must be more coherent than those which now visit our slumbers," said I.

"It is hardly worth while to contend about the difference," he replied, with a sarcastic expression which I did not much like. "It is sufficient to say, however, that these projectors have no reason to complain; for with whatever show of reason men think or act here, so, under exactly the same laws of thought and emotion, do those shadows act there."

"But I, who am now awake and perfectly sensible—"

He laughed outright. "Are you so sure," said he, "that you are awake? How do you know it?"

"Because I am conscious of it," said I.

"And this, too, I suppose, is a philosopher," he muttered to himself. "Well," he continued aloud, "we must not discuss these matters just now; you must believe me when I say that the communities to which our experimenters go to work, on their own hypothesis, are just as capable of ingenious reasoning and impartial and candid deliberation as you are now in your present waking moments. You wish to hear a few of these experiments?"

I nodded.

"Well, then; first, there was one worthy philosopher, who, having seen the advantages which infidelity has gained from the discrepancies and other difficulties occasioned by the *varied* testimonies which the evangelical historians have left behind them, resolved, after having wrought a number of splendid miracles (uniformly affirmed and never denied by the parties in whose presence they were performed), that they should all be consigned to one single history so admirably constructed that there was not a single discrepancy from beginning to end."

"And what was the effect?"

"Why, in the first place, you must recollect that, according to that or any other mode of authenticating a divine communication by miracles, there were a great many more of those who never saw the miracles than of those who did; for if miracles had been common, they would have ceased to be miracles. There were vast numbers, therefore, who even in the age in which they were performed never believed them; but what is more, in four generations there was not a soul that did not treat them as old wives' fables."

"Surely they were very unreasonable," I said.

"Not at all; it was inevitable; for it was asked (and every one assented to it), whether it was reasonable that a story so marvellous, and so contrary to experience, should be believed on any single testimony, however unexceptionable? There were also keen critics who said that as there was proof that in the very age in which the miracles were wrought there were many who did not believe the message which they professedly confirmed, it was a strong indication that the whole was a fiction; while some others of still greater acumen discovered that the very *freedom* from all discrepancies and contradictions in the account itself smelt very strongly of art and design; that this perfection of consistency was not the characteristic of any history ever written by an honest man; and that no doubt it had been elaborately contrived by a single highly inventive mind."

"The idiots!" I exclaimed. "Why, this very circumstance ought surely to have led them to argue the other way."

"They thought otherwise; and I must say I think they argued very plausibly, and that very much is to be said for them. They thought that perfect self-consistency might possibly be attained by a single mind of highly inventive power, and they preferred believing *that*, to receiving such wonderful things supported by any single testimony."

"But did none attempt to remedy this defect of the unhappy speculator?"

"O yes; another attempted to establish in a second community of our reasonable *shadows* a revelation on the same basis of miracles; but instead of trusting to one witness, he recorded the results by ten; and with such perfection of art that all the ingenuity of all the critics of succeeding ages could not detect a single variation other than in language; the records themselves and their contents were precisely the same."

"And what was the result?"

"Much the same as before; for this identity of substance and almost of manner showed most evidently, said the critics, that there had been *collusion* between the several parties who had framed the revelation:— and in the course of three or four generations it was universally rejected as totally unworthy of belief."

"I see not, then, how a revelation by any such means could be authenticated at all!"

"Why, our *reasonable* creatures require a great deal of management — that is the truth. There are always ways in which you may prove to your own satisfaction, that no one of any divine communications (given under the conditions aforesaid) is to be believed; but, perhaps, after all, the method would have been more sure, had these sages consigned these communications to different testimonies, in which the general harmony and undesigned coincidences should be manifest, but which should contain slight discrepancies, and even some apparent contradictions, which the parties, if there had been collusion, would certainly have obviated. This would, perhaps, have been the *best* guarantee that there could not be any fraud in the case."

"But this," I remarked, "was just the mode in which the Gospels of Christ *were* consigned to mankind."

"And you see with what mixed result. It was sufficient indeed to justify the method, if it was attended with *less* disastrous effects than any other mode. For it is a problem of limits even at the very best."

Prompted, I suppose, by some recollection of Woolston's opinion, that the miracles of Jesus Christ would have been better worthy of attention, and more likely to be credited by posterity, if they had been performed on royal or notable public characters, or in their presence, I felt curious to know if any one had been determined to guard against a similar error. I was told that there had been; and for a time every thing went on well. This sage's doctrine and pretensions were rapidly propagated within certain limits of space and time. But alas! while even in his lifetime the *zeal* of some of the royal or noble converts caused the doctrine to be regarded with considerable suspicion among the rival great, to whom the fame of the miracles was known only by hearsay, its early success proved an insurmountable objection in a few generations; for several learned infidels showed to the satisfaction of the entire community, that the pretended revelation could have been nothing else than a conspiracy of crafty statesmen for *political* purposes. It was sagely remarked, that it was not wonderful that a doctrine had been believed, and had rapidly diffused itself, which had all the *prestige* of rank, and power, and statesmanship in its favour: that if, indeed, it had appeared amongst the *poor* and *ignorant* portion of mankind, and the miracles had been witnessed by such as from their situation were rather likely to be persecuted by the great and powerful than to be favoured by them; and lastly, if the pretended revelation had *vanquished* such resistance instead of being suspiciously *allied* with it, something more might be said in its behalf; but as it was, the whole thing was evidently — a lie.

"Really," said I, "it seems a more difficult thing for God to make known his will to mankind than I had supposed."

"It is," said he, "on those conditions to which his wisdom for man's own sake has restricted him, and apart from which condition, I have already stated, that a revelation would be worthless. It is a far more difficult matter than those who have not reflected upon the subject would suppose; and you would have more reason to say so still, if you knew, as I do, how ludicrously as well as how utterly many other attempts have failed."

He then amused me with an account of a sage who seeing the ill consequences which had followed from the very local or limited character of Miracles (when a few generations had passed by), resolved to remedy this by a series of wonders so stupendous and magnificent, that the very echo of them, as it were, should reverberate through the hollow of future ages, and so impress all tradition as to render them independent of the voice of individual historians. He accordingly passed to the very extreme limit (if he did not go beyond it) by which a miracle is necessarily restricted, — that of not disturbing *general* laws. He succeeded perfectly in the place in which these phenomena were witnessed; though as there were multitudes who knew nothing of the operator, but were only conscious that nature was playing some strange pranks, no connection was established in their minds between the doctrine and the miracles. But the consequences in the *future* were the direct contrary of what the sanguine philosopher had contemplated! If the impression of those who saw these splendid wonders could have been prolonged, all had been well; but so far from the *report* of them conciliating the regard of posterity, their very grandeur and vastness were the principal arguments against them, and condemned them to universal rejection. Who could believe, men said, that phenomena so strange and so portentous — not only so different from, and so contrary to, the uniform course of nature, but so much beyond the *limited purpose* which must have been contemplated by a *truly* miraculous interposition, had ever happened? If they had been *single* events, very transient and local disturbances of the laws of nature for a high object, the case, they candidly avowed, would have been wholly different; but such wholesale infractions of the fixed laws of the universe were at once to be summarily rejected! They were unquestionably the offspring of an age of fable and superstition.

It did not fare much better with another miracle-monger of the same species. In one community, which he had engaged to instruct in the mysteries of his revelation, the wonders he wrought extended to such large classes of phenomena, and for a time were so constant, that they ceased to be miracles at all. As he could not add ubiquity to his other attributes, few attached any importance to his declaration that *he* was the author of such vast and distant operations, and fewer absolutely believed him. Moreover, men became accustomed to phenomena which they daily witnessed; for such, it seems, is the constitution of human nature in any world, that things cease to be wonderful when they cease to be novel. Were it otherwise, men would be always wondering; for no miracles are more wonderful than the phenomena of every day in every part of the universe. Not a few wise men, therefore, in this community, succeeded in giving a perfectly plausible account of these wholesale infractions of the uniformity of nature. Nature, it was said, was unquestionably uniform, but only in the several larger *portions* of her operations; that within certain cycles, she varied her operations, as was clearly seen in the introduction of new races, and so forth; that the generation which had just witnessed such departures from what seemed the *established* order of things were doubtless living at an epoch in which the huge evolution of the universe was about to exhibit one of these new phases, and that the series of sequences to which they were just becoming accustomed would afterwards continue uniform for a number of ages; that such things were no miracles, but merely indicated that nature was, within certain limits, only *variably uniform*, though she was also, within certain limits, *uniformly invariable.* After this very clear deliverance of philosophy, few people troubled themselves about the claims of this seer, and were so fast getting accustomed to the new uniformity, that it seemed highly probable that the very next generation, or at most the second, would begin to prate in the old style about the *invariable uniformity* of nature, and to treat all the ancient order of things which their progenitors had seen changed as a lying fable of those remote ages. Enraged at such an unexpected result of his operations, the projector changed his plan, and broke in upon nature with such a startling explosion of single miracles that there could be no longer any doubt that nature was neither " variably uniform " nor " uniformly invariable : " the only question was, whether nature was not " uniformly variable." He set the sun spinning through the heavens at such a rate, or rather at such a jaunty pace, that no one knew when to expect either light or darkness; men now froze with cold, and now melted with heat; the seasons seemed playing one grand masquerade : the longest day and the shortest day, and no day at all, succeeded one another in rapid succession; and the whole universe seemed threatened with ruin and desolation. Now, he thought, was the time to put an end to all this strange disorder, and avow himself the great agent in all these marvels! But he found, to his chagrin, that so far from having convinced men of the being and attributes of God, and of the truth of the revelation which he had brought them, they were never less disposed to listen to any such story; and, in fact, that the very few whose terror had left them at all in possession of their senses, had become perfectly convinced that the universe was under the dominion of Chance, and that the only orthodox belief in such a world was stark Atheism. As there will always be men who will speculate upon chance itself, there were not wanting philosophers who concocted admirable theories of all this disorder, but not one of them dreamed of the true. They all agreed, however, that the state of things admitted of no remedy from any gods, celestial or infernal; for if a divine artificer had existed, they said, it could not have occurred. And thus the miracles which were designed by this great man to convince the world of a God, served for a demonstration that there was and could be none! They equally served also to stifle the sage's claims to be considered God's messenger, for unhappily exhorting a large crowd to believe that he was the cause of all the misery and terror which they had suffered, they were so exasperated that they took summary vengeance on him: upon which the sun resumed his wonted quiet pace again through the heavens, and everything fell into the old harmonious jogtrot of uniformity. Philosophers who lived at a distance from the scene of the prophet's exit, quietly adjusted their old theory to the new phenomena, and showed most conclusively that the whole train of things had been just what must necessarily have been, and could not but have happened, without the most serious consequences; while those who lived near to the scene aforesaid, and were privy to the circumstances, speculated upon the curious *coincidence* between the impostor's death and the return of nature to her order. It was well, they said, that such things did not happen often, or they could not fail to give rise to some superstitious notions as to some law of causation between ignorant fanaticism and the sublimest phenomena of the universe.

I asked my visitor how it fared with the many who have objected to the clearness and force of prophecy, and who have not scrupled to assert that if prophecies had been given, they would have been given in such a shape as would have made their claims more plain, and their fulfilment more incontrovertible. "Were there none who relied on this mode of demonstrating the reality of a divine revelation, and manifesting their claims to be regarded as an embassy from heaven?"

"Many," he replied; "so many that it were tedious to detail them. But you are quite mistaken if you suppose it possible that even God can employ any moral methods which man cannot evade; how much less the fools who think they can improve upon his! The wisdom of God," said he, with a melancholy smile, "is no match for the ingenuity of man. As to your present question, you know there have been persons who have continually complained in your world that prophecy is so obscure that the event cannot be certainly known to have been referred to by it, or else so *plain* that, *ipso facto*, it proves that the prediction must have been composed *after* the event. Now it was precisely in attempting the *juste milieu* between these extremes that our prophetical speculators wrecked themselves. Men always had it to say that their prophecies had been either too plain or too obscure; or, if very plain, and yet as plainly written *before* the event, that their very plainness had ensured their own accomplishment by prompting to the very actions and conduct they so clearly indicated!"

"I can easily conceive that," I answered. "But now for another problem. Not a few of our older infidels complained of the revelation in the Bible on the score that the maxims of conduct which it delivers are too general to be of any use, because the application of them is still left to be adjusted by a reference to particular circumstances; and that if a revelation were framed it ought to take in all the limitations of actions, and furnish, in fact, a complete system of casuistry; otherwise it would be of no avail. Were there none who attempted this task?"

"Five-and-twenty men," he answered, "who were destined to be a torment to one another, were instructed to compile such a system of rules, and publish them for the benefit of a certain community as an infallible rule of life."

"And have they completed it?"

"Completed it! They have been sitting now for two hundred years, and have not yet exhausted the infinitude of cases to be digested under their very first capitulary." He said that being all of them ingenious men, all anxious to show their ingenuity, and knowing that their credit was staked upon the completeness of their system, it was incredible what strange and ridiculous contingencies and combinations of circumstance they had suggested as modifying the application of their general rules. The books of law, voluminous as they are in most civilised countries, were conciseness itself compared with this new code of morals. It was thought by many that the labours of the commissioners would not come to an end till long after the race for whose benefit it was designed had ceased to exist. Afraid, apparently, of such a direful contingency, they had published, about three years before, the first part in seventy-five folio volumes, containing limitations, illustrative cases, exceptions, and modifications, in relation to that very obscure general maxim, "Do unto others as ye would that others should do unto you." All questions appertaining to this point were from that time to be decided by the precise statements contained in these statutes at large. But their mere publication sufficed to make an incredible number of infidels in the authority of the commission. Such a voluminous rule, they truly said, could be no rule at all, and could be fruitful of nothing but everlasting litigation. If (they admitted) general maxims had been as briefly as possible laid down, and men's common sense had been left to interpret and apply them with the requisite restrictions, there would be much more to be said for their divine origin. But on such a system, no man, if he lived for a thousand years, could tell what his duty was. Many complained that before they found the rule for which they were in search, the time for its application had passed away. Many excused themselves from complying with the dictates of justice and charity because they could not discover the cases that related to their special circumstances; some even denied that the rules could have been devised by heavenly wisdom, because, having carefully studied the whole of the seventy-five volumes, they did not hesitate to say that there were many cases which had *not* been provided for at all!

I was so amused with this last disastrous attempt to construct a revelation, that I laughed outright, and in so doing awoke. I found that my lamp was fast going out; so, dismissing the innocent volume of Leibnitz which had suggested all these incongruities, I went to bed; firmly convinced that the shadows of men in the "Paradise of Fools" are about as wise and ingenious as are men themselves.

July 28. I had this morning some curious, and if it had not been for the grave importance of the subject, amusing conversation with Mr. Fellowes on his views, or rather his *no* views, respecting a "future life." He said he wished he could make up his mind whether the doctrine was true; also whether, as some of his favourite writers supposed, it was of no "spiritual" importance to decide it. I said it certainly *did* seem of some importance. I reminded him of Pascal's saying, that he could excuse men's contented ignorance with any thing rather than *that.* "They are not obliged," says he, "to examine the Copernican system; but it is vital to the whole of existence to ascertain whether the soul is mortal or not."

"Mr. Newman," said Fellowes, "thinks very differently: but then his whole mind is differently constituted from Pascal's."

I admitted it, of course.

"Mr. Newman's views," he continued, "on this subject certainly do not quite satisfy me; and yet they are very sublime. If he has any hope in this matter (of which he appears not absolutely destitute) it is from the sheer strength of a '*faith*,' which triumphs over all obstacles, or rather hangs upon nothing. He ridicules all intellectual proofs, and at the same time declares, that his 'spiritual insight' deserts him. It is a faith pure from all reason, and from all 'insight' too.—As to insight in this matter, I must agree with him, that to ascertain the fact of a future life by '*direct vision*,' is ' to me hitherto impossible.'"

Harrington, who was sitting by, smiled: "You speak of your 'insight' and 'direct vision' much as a Highlander might talk of his 'second sight.' As to your present difficulty, do you remember the advice of Ranald of the Mist to Allan M'Aulay, when the 'vision' obstinately averted its face from him? 'Have you reversed your own plaid,' said Ranald, 'according to the rule of the experienced Seers in such cases?' You do not wear a *plaid*, George, but suppose you try the experiment of *turning your coat* inside out."

"Really Harrington," said Fellowes, with becoming solemnity, "'insight' is far too serious a subject to joke upon."

"Why, my dear fellow," said the other, "you do not think I am going to treat your 'insight' with more respect than we treat the Bible."

"*Odi profanum*," said Fellowes, almost angrily.

"No man hateth his *own* flesh," said Harrington, with provoking quiet; "and that, I am sure, is from no *profane* writer. As to the '*odi profanum*,' why, I shall simply say, that

'You can quote it,
With as much truth as he who wrote it.'"

So saying, he left the room. I was not sorry that he was gone, as I thought perhaps Fellowes might be more communicative. I asked him why he felt Mr. Newman's arguments on this subject unsatisfactory? Why he could not acquiesce in them?

"In the first place, then," said he, "I was struck with the fact, that while admitting that he had no 'spiritual insight' on the subject of a future life, he yet admits that *others* may have enjoyed what is impossible to him: that there may be souls favoured with this 'vision,' though clouds obscure his own. It is true he has admitted, (and, indeed, who can deny it?) that the spiritual faculty is not equally *developed* in all men; — though as it is *not*, I feel some difficulty in rejecting the arguments hence arising for the *possibility* and *utility* of an external revelation; — yet at the best, if the faculty may be *so* uncertain in reference to *so* important a question, when consulted by *so* diligent and deep a student of its oracles as Mr. Newman, — if even *his* soul may be dubious on such a point, — why, upon *my* soul, I sometimes hardly know what to think. Again, Mr. Newman says, that some may have, as by special privilege from God, what is denied to *him*. Now really this looks a little too much like favouring the vulgar view of inspiration, nay, a sort of Calvinistic 'election' in this matter; it seems to me to cast doubts both on the competency and the uniformity of the sublime 'spiritual faculty,' even when most sedulously consulted."

"It does look a little like it," said I; "and what next?"

"In the next place, I am free to confess, that if I *may* be allowed to argue against such an authority——"

"Oh! remember, I pray, that you are of the school of *free* thought: do not *Bibliolatrize*."

"To state my views freely, then: I must say, that if this suspected doctrine be *not* one of the unsophisticated utterances of the spiritual nature of man, I am almost led to doubt whether the clearness with which the spiritualist 'gazes' on the rest, may not possibly be an illusion. For if any truth would seem to be a dictate of nature, it is a sort of dim conviction or impression of a future state. We see it, in some shape or other, extensively believed by all nations, and forming a feature of all systems of religion, however degraded they may be. Mr. W. J. Fox mentions it as one of those things which are certainly characteristic of the absolute religion; so does Mr. Parker. Mr. Fox expressly affirms that the approximate universality of the belief justifies the application of his criterion for detecting the eternally 'true' under the Protean shapes of the 'false' in religions; it is one of the points, he says, in which they are all *agreed*."

"Which," said I, "if true, is perhaps the *only* point in which all religions are agreed, unless we affirm that they have all recognised *a* Deity, because most of them have recognised *thousands*. Yet as men's Gods have varied between the infinite Creator and a monkey, so, in relation to this article of a 'future life,' it must be confessed that there is a *little* difference between the Heaven of a Christian, the Paradise of a Mahometan, and the Valhalla of an ancient Goth. Still, as you say, it is true that, *in some shape or other*, nations have more generally recognised the idea of an after existence, than any other assignable religious tenet."

"You know," resumed Fellowes, "that in the draught of 'natural religion' given us by Lord Herbert, that writer particularly insists on this as one of the articles which nature itself teaches us, as amongst the 'common notions,' a sentiment innate to the human mind. Now if such masters as Mr. Newman may be in doubt about our *innate* sentiments, truly I scarcely know what to think."

"You can easily decide," said I gravely, "and decide infallibly."

"How so?"

"Consult that spiritual faculty of which Mr. Newman says you have as well as he or Lord Herbert. If your theory be true, how can there be any doubt as to your '*innate*' sentiments? If you say they are written in very small characters, and require to be magnified by somebody's microscope, that, recollect, is tantamount to acknowledging the possible utility of an external revelation. But what next?"

"Well, then, if I must confess all the truth, I thought Mr. Newman hardly fair in his exhibition of Paul's reasoning on this matter. He, if you recollect, says, that Paul seems to have rested the belief of Christ's resurrection very little upon *evidence*, which he received very credulously upon very insufficient proof, and in a manner which would have moved the laughter of Paley;

that, in short, he cared very little *about* the evidence, and arrived mainly at his convictions in virtue of his 'spiritual aspirations;' that it was rather his strong aspirations after immortality which made Paul believe the supposed fact, than the supposed fact which gave strength to his aspirations after immortality. Now it is very clear (from texts which, for whatsoever reasons, are not quoted by Mr. Newman), that the Apostle Paul made his whole argument depend on the alleged fact of Christ's resurrection, whether carelessly received or not: 'If Christ be not risen, then is your faith vain, and our preaching is also vain. . . . Then are we of all men most miserable.'"

"But you recollect that Mr. Newman alleges that Paul deals very superficially with the evidence—with that of the 'five hundred,' for example. He observes that Paley would have made a widely different matter of it."

"See how variously men may argue," replied Fellowes, candidly. "I was talking on that very point with one of the orthodox the other day, and *he* reasoned in some such way as this:—

"On the supposition, he said, that the possession of miraculous powers was notorious in the Church — that many of those whom Paul addressed had actually witnessed them — that the Gospel when preached by him and by the other Apostles, was confirmed 'by signs and wonders'—nothing could be more *natural* than the very tone which the Apostles employed: that so far from its being suspicious, it was one of the truest touches of nature and verisimilitude in their compositions; so much so, that, supposing there were *no* miracles, that very tone required itself to be accounted for as unnatural; he said that it is, in fact, just the way in which men talk and write of any other extraordinary events which *notoriously* happened in their time. They never think of posterity, and what *it* may think; of anticipating either future doubts or charges of fraud. It is natural that men should speak in this, as we should call it, *loose* way, of what is transpiring under their very noses. On the other hand, unless there had been miracles to appeal to, so as to render this style as natural as, on the contrary supposition, it was the reverse, he could not, he declared, imagine, that in that or any other age, any men, especially men *opposed* to such pretensions, would so easily have been satisfied, even had the Apostles confined themselves to rumours of alleged distant miracles; but much less where similar wonders were said to have been brought under the eyes of the very parties to whom the appeal was made! He said he would even go a step further, and affirm that, under the circumstances of the professed notoriety of the miraculous occurrences to which Paul and the other Apostles appealed, any declaration that they had instituted that careful scrutiny of evidence, that minute circumstantial cross-examination of the witnesses, which would be a course all very well in the days of Paley 1800 years after, but absolutely preposterous then,—would have appeared to *our* age a much more suspicious thing than the tone actually adopted; that the scrupulous deposition of technical proof would have been *finessing* too much, and would have been to us the strongest proof of collusion. The very tone objected to, he said, supposing there were no miracles, is one of the most striking proofs of the astonishing sagacity of these men; for it is just the tone which, and which alone, they would have used if there had been miracles. So differently may men reason from the same data! Whether, (my friend concluded) Mr. Newman's view of the facts or his was founded on a deeper and more comprehensive knowledge of human nature, he must leave to my judgment."

"I protest," said I, "I think the *orthodox* had the best of it.—But what struck you next as unaccountable in Mr. Newman's view of this subject of a future life?"

"I confess, then, that the reasoning by which he endeavours to show that even admitting the *fact* of Christ's resurrection, there could be nothing in it to warrant the expectation of the resurrection of any *other* human beings, simply because he must have differed so stupendously from all the rest of mankind, appears to me very damaging to us. Of what use is it to argue upon such an *hypothesis?*"

" Of none in the world, certainly," said I, laughing.

" Surely not," he replied; " for if Christ's resurrection be admitted, we know very well it will carry with it in the estimation of the bulk of mankind all the other great facts implicated with the Christian system. They will concede, at once, the supernatural character, the divine origin of the New Testament. I suppose there scarcely ever was a man who admitted these premises who would trouble himself to contest the conclusion."

"But seriously," continued this half-repentant admirer, almost frightened at the extent of his own freedom of thought, " though I cannot say I am satisfied with Mr. Newman's notions on this subject—and, in fact, cannot make up my mind upon it—can there be anything morally more sublime than the view, that the doctrine of immortality which has been superficially supposed, if not necessary, yet so conducive to sincere and elevated piety, may be readily dispensed with, as no way necessary, (as Mr. Newman feels,) for the spiritual nourishment of the soul? ' *Confidence,*' he says, 'there is none; and hopeful aspiration is the soul's highest state. But, then, there is herein nothing whatever to distress her: no cloud of grief crosses the area of her vision, as she gazes upwards.' He even intimates that from the stress laid upon immortality by ' modern divines,' they might seem to be ' incarnations of selfishness.' He says it tends to ' degrade religion into a *prudential* regard for our interests after death;' that ' conscience, the love of virtue for its own sake, and much more the love of God, are ignored.'—Many of the ' spiritual' school agree with him in this; and some even affirm that the hope of immortal felicity is but a bribe to selfishness! Can any thing be more elevated or original than *this* view?"

" As to the elevation," said I, "I confess I prefer the spectacle of Socrates, relying even on feeble arguments, rather than sink to this tame acquiescence in a notion so degrading to the Deity as that man was created for a dog's life, with a tormenting aspiration for something better. The spectacle of the heathen sage, who, amidst the thick gloom, the 'palpable obscure,' which involved this subject, gazed intently into the darkness, and 'longed for the day;' who strained every nerve of an insufficient logic, and was willing to take even the whispers of hope for the oracles of truth, rather than part with the prospect of immortality, is, to my mind, much more attractive. As to the *originality* of the view you just now expressed, why, it is merely a resurrection of one of the theories of some of our very 'spiritual deists' a century ago. Collins and Shaftesbury were, in like manner, apprehensive lest an elevated 'virtue' should suffer at all from this bribery of a hope of a 'blessed immortality;' as you may see in the Characteristics. For my own part, I certainly have my doubts whether virtue will be the less virtuous, or spirituality the less spiritual, for such a doctrine; and I must believe it even on the hypothesis of you spiritual folks; for you generally affirm that the Belief of a Future Life does not really exercise any thing more than an insignificant influence on human nature; the hopes and the fears of that so distant a morrow are too vague to be operative. Now if it be so, immortality can be no more a bribe than a menace."

"Yet," said Fellowes, "in justice to Mr. Newman, it must not be forgotten, that he thinks that 'a firm belief of immortality must have very energetic force,' provided it '*rises out of insight;*' it is as 'an *external dogma*' that he thinks it of little efficacy. He says, you know, that, supposing Paul to have had this insight, '*his* light can do *us* no good, while it is a light *outside of us.* If he in any way confused the conclusions of his logic (*which is often extremely inconsequent and mistaken*) with the perceptions of his divinely illuminated soul, our belief might prove baseless.'* These are his very words."

"Very well, then; say that Mr. Newman thinks the otion of a future hell of little efficacy; and of a future

---

* Soul, pp. 226, 227.

heaven of as little, except when it rises from 'insight;' — he confessing that he has not that 'insight,' and, from the necessity of the case, not knowing whether any body else has, it being a 'light outside him.' If so, I think he is much like the rest of you, and cannot in fact suppose the thought of a future life to operate strongly either as a bribe or a menace."

"But surely, whatever his views, or those of any other individual, you must admit that a piety, which is sustained without any hopes of immortality, is less *selfish* than that which is."

"Why," replied I, laughing; "*I* cannot conceive how the hope of a virtuous immortality can produce a vicious self-love. But if the hope and the consciousness of happiness *now* exercise any influence at all, your argument proves too much; and there is a simple impossibility of being unselfishly religious at all."

"How so?"

"Do you think that, admitting not only the uncertainty of any future life, but the certainty that there is none, and that nevertheless (as you affirm), man, under that conviction, is just as capable of manifesting a true devotion and piety towards God, any felicity flows from his so doing?"

"The highest, of course," said he.

"Do you think that the happiness so derived and expected from day to day has any *sinister* influence on the spiritual life of him who feels it?"

"Of course, none."

"The contrary, perhaps?"

"I think so."

"Then neither need the expectation of an *eternity* of such blessedness be any impediment. — Again; let us come to *facts;* are not the declarations of those whom Mr. Newman, however oddly, is willing to admit have been the best specimens yet afforded of his true 'spiritual' man — the Doddridges, the Fletchers, the Baxters, and Paul especially, full of this sentiment? 'I desire to *depart*,' says Paul, 'and to be with Christ, which is far better;' and similar selfish hopes inspired those excellent men whose names still rise spontaneously to Mr. Newman's memory when he would remind us of examples of his 'spiritual' religion! Tell me, do you not think Paul a 'spiritual' man?"

"Yes; with *all* his *blunders*," said Fellowes, "I do; and Mr. Newman's writings are full of that admission."

"Very true. But then Paul is so *selfish*, you know, as to say, not merely that the immortality of man is true, and that the 'light afflictions which are but for a moment' are to be despised, *because* unworthy 'to be compared with the glory to be revealed;' but that if immortality be *not* true, Christians, as deluded in such hopes, are of all men most miserable. All this shows how powerfully the 'spiritual' Paul thought that the doctrine of a future state operated and ought to operate on the mind of a Christian; he never supposed that it could possibly have a negative, still less a sinister influence."

"But then, surely, what Mr. Newman says is true, that many of the saints of the Old Testament exemplified all the heroism of a true faith, and kindled with the ardours of a true devotion in an ignorance of any such state, and in the absence of all such expectations."

"I answer, that Mr. Newman too often speaks as if his individual *impressions* were to be taken for demonstration. That the Old Testament is unpervaded by any distinct traces of expectations of a future life is, at all events, *not* the opinion of the majority of men, many of them at least as capable of judging as Mr. Newman. It is not the opinion of the writers of the New Testament that the Old Testament worthies were in this deplorable darkness; nor of the majority of the Jewish interpreters of their ancestors' writings; nor is it the impression of the great majority of those who now read them. How it can be the opinion of any one who has not some hypothesis to serve, is to me a mystery. Meanwhile Mr. Newman himself at least gives some notable passages to the *contrary*, though he chooses to call them only personal aspirations. Think of the absurdity, my good friend, of supposing that Job, David, Isaiah, failed to realise a doctrine (imperfectly it may be) which, as you truly affirm, has, in some shape or other, animated all forms of religion! that these brightest specimens of 'spiritual religion' in the ancient world somehow missed what many of the lowest savages have managed to stumble upon!"*

"Well," he replied, "but after all, he who loves God without any thought of heaven, must surely be more unselfish than he who hopes for it."

I laughed — for I could not help it.

---

* One of the most philosophical and comprehensive estimates of the degree in which the doctrine of a future state may be fairly said to be disclosed in the Old Testament — proving that, though not fully or dogmatically taught there, it was sufficiently implied to secure its being actually apprehended by the chief lights of the nation, and to awaken the aspirations of every devout student of the sacred records in every age, — may be found in an admirable discourse by the Rev. Thomas Binney, entitled "Life and Immortality brought to *Light* in the Gospel;" — brought to light, he contends, not at once out of *absolute* darkness, but (in harmony with the whole preparatory dispensation) after many gradations from the first faint twilight through an ever brightening dawn. It were to be wished, that the eloquent author, who writes in a vein of singularly clear, nervous, and idiomatic English, would expand his thoughts on this *vexata quæstio*, and publish them in a little volume, detached from all matter of a temporary or incidental interest. — For the omission of the doctrine in question, from all the statutory matter of the Mosaic law, Michaelis, in his great work, gives a cogent reason. He says that it were as unreasonable for a legislator to enforce by the sanctions of a future world a code designed to take effect in this, as it would be for "an act of Parliament to threaten criminals with the penalties of hell-fire." Nay, perhaps, we might say it were more unreasonable in Moses than in any other, since the Mosaic dispensation was professedly founded on a precise present distribution of punishment and reward. See *Laws of Moses*, Vol. I. Book i. Art. 14.

On this whole subject, the reader will also do well to consult Dr. Whately's elaborate Essay on the "Revelation of a Future State." (*Peculiarities of the Christian Religion.*) The first part — showing how little the heathen had achieved in relation to the great subject — is most triumphant. Many, probably, will be disposed to think he has underrated the intimations of a future life in the *historical* portions of the Pentateuch; but he expressly admits, and has well illustrated the fact, that, taking the whole of the Old Testament together, — though the doctrine is not dogmatically taught or adequately revealed, — it does appear there as a continually dawning light, sufficient to guide the diligent reader to the truth. — It in fact led, long before the advent of Christ, to very general, though not universal, convictions on the subject. The Sadducees, says Josephus. were not a numerous sect. — Ed.

"Unhappy Paul!" interjected Harrington, who had again entered the library; "unhappy Paul! burdened with the *hopes* of immortality; what an impediment he must have found it in his Christian course! I wonder he did not throw aside 'this weight, which so easily beset him.' Pity that when he became a Christian, and ceased to be a Pharisee, he did not, like so many 'spiritual' Christians of our day, know that when he became a Christian, he might still remain in one of the Jewish sects, and turn Sadducee."

"Be it so," said Fellowes; "a Christian Sadducee, *cæteris paribus*, might perhaps be a more virtuous man, having no hopes of heaven by which he can possibly be bribed."

"Religious love and hope," said I, "will, with difficulty, exist in such an atmosphere as you create. It is at a sublime altitude, doubtless, but no ordinary 'spiritual' beings can breathe that rarefied air. It is for the honour of Shaftesbury and some few other deists, that they aspired to this transcendental virtue! You are imitating them. I fear you will not be more successful. Once leave a man to conclude, or even to suspect, that he and his cat end together, and if a bad man, he will gladly accept a release from every claim but that of his passions and appetites (the effects being more or less philosophically calculated according to his intellectual power); while the best man would be liable to contemplate God and religion with a depressed and faltering heart. He would be apt to lose all energy; he would feel it impossible to repress doubts of the infinite wisdom and benignity of Him (whatever he might think of his power) who had given him the soul of a man and the life of a butterfly; conceptions and aspirations so totally disproportioned to the evanescence of his being! If, however, you really think that the hopes of an immortality of virtuous happiness will stand in the way of a sublime disinterestedness of spirituality, you ought to recollect that *any* expectation of happiness, even for a day, will, in its measure, have the same effect. So that the only way in which you can accommodate so 'spiritual' a piety, and absolutely insure yourself against 'spiritual bribery,' is to deprive yourself of all possibility of being so misled. If your piety would be absolutely sure that it loves God on these sublime terms, it should take care to neutralize the happiness which that love brings with it; so that if God has not made you miserable, you should never fail, like the ascetics, to make yourself so. I fear you never can be perfectly 'spiritual' till you have made yourself supremely wretched.— But to quit this point," I continued; "if immortality be a delusion, I fear we must say that it covers the divine administration with an impenetrable cloud— one which we cannot hope will be removed. The inequalities of that administration cannot be redressed."

"But do you not recollect," replied Fellowes, "the reason Mr. Newman gives for despising any such mitigation? Does he not say that it is a strange argument for a day of recompense that man has unsatisfied claims upon God? He says, 'Christians have added an argument of their own for a future state, but, unfortunately, one that cannot bring personal comfort or assurance. A future state (it seems) is requisite *to redress the inequalities of this life.* And can I go to the Supreme Judge, and tell Him that I deserve more happiness than he has granted me in this life?' Do you not recollect this?— or has this sarcasm escaped you?"

"It has not escaped me— I remember it well; but it seems to have escaped *you*, that it is a very transparent sophism. For what is it but a pretence that the Christian in general is confident enough of his virtue to think that he has not been sufficiently well treated, and that his Creator and Judge cannot do less than make amends for his injustice by giving him compensation in another world?"

"And is not that the true statement of the case?"

"I imagine not; whether men be Christians or otherwise. The generality, when they reason upon this subject (you and I, for example, at this very moment), are not at all considering the aspect of such a day upon themselves; how much they will *lose* if there be none; perhaps the bulk would wish that it could be proved that it would never come! It has been from a wish to escape great speculative perplexities, connected with the divine administration, and not in relation to man's deserts, that the question has been argued. When dictated by other feelings, the conviction of a future state has been quite as generally the utterance of remorse and fear, the response of an accusing conscience, as of hope and aspiration; and derives, perhaps, a terrible significance from that circumstance. But it has certainly not been, in the Christian, the result of any absurd expectation of virtues to be rewarded, or rights to be redressed. As to the Christian, though he feels that he would not, and dare not, go to the divine tribunal with any such absurd plea as Mr. Newman is pleased to put into his mouth,— though he cannot impeach the divine goodness, — he none the less feels that that goodness, if this scene be all, is open to very grievous impeachment in relation to millions who have suffered much, and done *no* wrong, and to multitudes more who have inflicted infinite wrong, and suffered next to nothing; and they would fain, if they could, get over difficulties which Mr. Newman chooses, from the mere exigencies of his theology, to represent as no difficulties at all. To escape them or to solve them is the thing principally in the minds of those who contend for a day of recompense: not the imaginary compensation of individual wrongs. I do contend that, if this world be all, the divine administration in many points is more hopelessly opposed to our moral instincts, and to all our notions of equity and benevolence, than any thing on which you spiritualists are accustomed to justify your censure of Scripture. You ought, as Harrington says, to go further."

July 30. I was much interested yesterday morning by a conversation between Harrington and two pleasant youths, acquaintances of Mr. Fellowes, both younger by three or four years than either he or Harrington. They are now at college, and have imbibed in different degrees that curious theory which professedly recognising Christianity (as consigned to the New Testament) as a truly *divine* revelation, yet asserts that it is intermingled with a large amount of error and absurdity, and tells each man to eliminate the divine 'element' for himself. According to this theory, the problem of eliciting revealed truth may be said to be indeterminate; the value of the unknown x varies through all degrees of magnitude; it is equal to anything, equal to everything, equal to nothing, equal to infinity.

The whole party thought, with the exception of Harrington, who knew not what to think, that the "religious faculty or faculties" (one or many — no man seems to know exactly) are quite sufficient to decide all doubts and difficulties in religious matters.

Harrington knew not whether to say there was any truth in Christianity or not; Fellowes knew that there was *none*, except in that "religious element," which is found alike essentially in all religions; that its miracles, its inspiration, its peculiar doctrines, are totally false.

The young gentlemen just referred to believed "that it might be admitted that an external revelation was *possible*," and, "that the condition of man, considering the aspects of his history, has not been altogether so felicitous as to show that he never needed, and might not be benefited by such light." I could cordially agree with them so far; superabundance of religious illumination not being amongst the things of which humanity can legitimately complain.

But then, as they both believed that each man was to distil the "elixir vitæ" for himself from the crude mass of truth and falsehood, which the New Testament presents, Harrington, with his interrogations, soon compelled them to see how inconsistent they were both with themselves and with one another. One of them believed, he said, that the Apostles might have been favoured by a true revelation; but not in such a sense "as to prevent their often falling into serious errors," wherever the distinctly "*religious element*" was not concerned; this was the only truly "divine" thing about it; but he saw no particular objection to receiving the miracles; at least some of them — the best authenticated and most reasonable; perhaps they were of value as part of the complex evidence needful to establish doctrines which, if not absolutely transcendental to the human faculties — as the doctrine of a future life, for example — yet, apart from revelation, are but matter of conjecture.

The other was also not unwilling to admit the miraculous and inspired character of the revelation, but contended, further, that the "religious element" was to be submitted to human judgment as well as the rest; and that if *apparently* absurd, contradictory, or pernicious, as judged by that infallible and ultimate standard, it was to be rejected.

It was amusing to think that in this little company of three devout believers in the "internal oracle," no two thought alike! After the two youths had frankly stated their opinions, Harrington quietly said, "I should much like to ask each of you a few questions. There are certain difficulties connected with each hypothesis just stated, on which I should be glad to receive some light. I frankly confess beforehand, however, that I fear that that curiously-constructed book, which gives us all so much trouble, — which will not allow me to say *positively* either that it is true or false,—will still less permit you to reject a part or parts at your pleasure. It is, I must admit, a most independent book in that respect, and treats your *spiritual illumination* most cavalierly. It says to you, ' receive me altogether or reject me altogether, just as you please;' and when men *have* rejected it altogether, it leaves them certain literary and historical, and moral problems, in all fairness demanding solution, which I *doubt* whether it is in our power to solve, or to give any decent account of."

"What do you mean," said the younger of the two youths, "by affirming that we are compelled to receive the whole book, or to reject it all?"

"Let us see," said Harrington, "whether there is any consistent stopping-place between. It appears to me, that whether by the most singular series of 'coincidences,' or by immense subtlety of design, this book evidently composed by different hands, has yet its materials so interwoven, and its parts so reciprocally dependent, that it is impossible to separate them, — to set some aside, and say 'we will accept these and reject those:' just as in certain textures, no sooner do we begin to take out a particular thread, than we find it is inextricably entangled with others, and those again with others; so that there immediately takes place a prodigious 'gathering' at that point, and if we persevere, a *rent;* but the obstinate part at which we tug will not come away alone. Whether it is so or not, we shall soon see, by examining the results of the application of your theories. I will begin with you" (addressing the younger), "because you believe least; you say, I think, that you admit the records of the New Testament contain a *real* revelation,—a religious element — and that it has been authenticated to you by miracles and other evidence; but that the human mind is still the judge as to how much of that revelation is to be received, 'and sits in judgment' on the 'religious element' as well as the rest."

The other assented.

"You admit, probably, the doctrine of the soul's immortality as a part of that revelation — perhaps even the doctrine of a *resurrection?*"

"I do — both these doctrines."

"But perhaps you reject the idea of an 'atonement,' though you admit it to be in the book?"

"Yes. At the same time it is contended by many (as you are aware) that such a doctrine is *not* there."

"I am aware of it, of course; but with *them* we have no controversy here. They are consistent, so far as the present argument goes; as consistent as the orthodox themselves. They do not allege a liberty of rejecting what they admit the book *does* contain, but only deny that it does contain some things which they reject. They would admit that *if* those doctrines be there, then either they must concede them, because authenticated by the miracles and other evidence, which proves what *else* they concede, or they must reject the said evidence altogether, because it authenticated what they found it impossible to concede. The controversy between them and the orthodox is one of *interpretation*, and is quite different from that in which we are now engaged."

"I must admit it."

"They may go, then?" said Harrington.

"They may."

"You admit, then, the miraculous authentication of such an event as the resurrection of man, but deny the doctrine of the atonement, though *equally* found in the said records."

"I do."

"May I ask why?"

"Because the one doctrine does *not* seem to me to contradict my 'spiritual consciousness,' and the other does."

"You receive the one, I suppose you will say, on account of the miracles, and so on; since, while not contradicting your impressions of spiritual truth, it could not be authenticated without external evidence?"

"Exactly so."

"But is not the *other* doctrine as much authenticated by the miracles and so forth? or have you any thing to show that while all those passages which relate to the former are *true* assertions, as well as *truly* the assertions of those who published the revelation, those which relate to the latter are not?"

"I acknowledge I have not," replied the youth.

"Or supposing they are *not* their sayings at all, have you any evidence by which you can show that they are not, so as to separate them from those that are?"

"I must admit that I have no criterion of this kind."

"For aught you know, then, since you know nothing of Christianity except from those documents in which the miracles and the doctrines are alike consigned to you, the said miracles, together with the other evidence, do equally establish the truths which you say are a part of divine revelation, and the errors which you say your 'spiritual faculty,' 'moral intuitions,' or what you will, tells you that you are to reject. You believe, then, in the force of evidence, which equally establishes truth and falsehood?"

"You can hardly expect me to admit that."

"But I expect you to answer a plain question."

"Why," said the youth, with a little flippancy, but with a good-humoured laugh too, "the proverb says 'even a fool may ask questions which a wise man cannot answer.'"

"I acknowledge myself to be a fool," said Harrington, with a half serious, half comic, air; "and you shall be the wise man who does not—for I will not say *cannot*—answer the fool's question."

"I beg your pardon," said the other. "I acknowledge that it was an uncourteous expression."

"Enough said," replied Harrington; "and now, since you are not pleased to answer my question, I will answer it myself; and I say, it is plain that the evidence to which you refer *does* affirm equally the truths you declare thus revealed to you, and the errors you declare you must reject. Now, either the evidence is not sufficient to prove the *one*, or it is sufficient to prove *both*. So far then, I think we may say, and say justly, that the supposed revelation is so constructed that you cannot accept a part, and reject a part, on *such* a theory. But to make the case a little plainer still if possible. There have been men, you know, who have taken precisely opposite views of the two doctrines you have mentioned; who have declared that the doctrine, not of man's immortality, but of the resurrection, so far from being conceivable, is, in *their* judgment, a physical contradiction; but who have also declared that the doctrine of *atonement*, in some shape, is instinctively taught by human nature, and has *consequently* formed a part of almost every religion; that it is in analogy with many singular facts of this world's constitution, and is not absolutely contradicted by any principle of our nature, intellectual or moral. Such a man, therefore, might take the very opposite of the course you have taken. He would proceed upon your common basis of a miraculously confirmed revelation, grossly infested with errors and falsehoods; he might say that he believed the authentication of the doctrine of 'atonement' in virtue of the evidence, because, though transcendental to his reason, it was not repugnant to it; but that he rejected the doctrine of the 'resurrection,' though equally established by the evidence, because contrary to the plainest conclusions of his reason."

"I cannot in candour deny," said the other, "the possibility of such a case."

"And in such a case, we might say, he does the very opposite of what *you* do."

"Neither can I help admitting that."

"The miracles, then, and other evidence, not only play the part of equally supporting truth and falsehood; but what is still more wonderful, convert the same things in *different* men, into truth and falsehood alternately. Miracles they must verily be if they can do *that!* A wonderful revelation it certainly is, which thus accommodates itself to the varying conditions of the human intellect and conscience, and demonstrates just so much as each of you is pleased to accept, and no more. No doubt the whole 'corpus dogmatum,' so supported, will by the entire body of such believers be eaten up: just as was the Mahometan hog, so humorously referred to by Cowper; but even that had not all its 'forbidden parts' miraculously shown to be 'unforbidden' to different minds! I do not wonder that such a revelation should *need* miracles; that any should be *sufficient*, is the greatest wonder of all; if indeed we except two;— the first, that Supreme *Wisdom* should have constructed such a curious revelation, in which it has revealed alternately, to different people, truth and falsehood, and has established each on the very same evidence; and the second (almost as great), that any rational creature should be got to receive a revelation on such evidence as equally applies to points which he says it does *not* prove, and to points which he says it *does*; these points, however, being, it appears, totally different in different men! But I will now go to your friend, who has got a point further in his belief, and graciously accepts *all* the 'religious elements' in this revelation."

"Excuse me," said the last; "before you go to him,

permit me to mention a difficulty which occurred to me while we were speaking."

"By all means; but I do not promise to solve it. Perhaps *I* on this occasion shall prove the 'wise man,' though I am sure you will not be the fool."

"You recollect," said the other, blushing, "our dismissing those who, while contending, like myself, that such and such doctrines are to be *rejected*, differ from me in this, that they contend that the said doctrines are *not* contained in the records of the supposed revelation at all; while others contend that they are. Now, if, while the two parties admit the general evidence which is to substantiate all that *is* in the records, they arrive by different interpretation at such very different results as to the supposed truth which it supports, are they in any better condition than I? There is the *same* difference, though arrived at in different ways; and the revelation still remains indeterminate."

"Your objection is ingenious," replied Harrington. "First, however, it is rather hard to ask *me* to solve a difficulty with which I am in no way concerned, who profess to be altogether sceptical on the subject. Secondly, it certainly does not at all mend your case to prove that there are other men who possibly are as inconsistent as yourself. It makes your theory neither better nor worse. But, thirdly, if I were a *Christian*, I should not hesitate to contend that there was an obvious and vital difference in the two cases."

"Indeed! If you can show *that*."

"I should attempt it at all events. I should say that in the latter case the evidence to which the appeal was made did not equally serve to establish truth and falsehood, or, what is still worse, alternately to make falsehood truth and truth falsehood, to different minds; that it was designed to establish *all* that was really in the records, though what that *all* was might give rise to different views, from the prejudices and the ignorance, the different degrees of intelligence and candour, of those who interpreted the records; that *they* made the falsehoods, and not the records or the evidence. I should, therefore, have no difficulty in relation to what, on your theory, is so incomprehensible; namely, that *God* should have given man so peculiarly constructed a revelation. That men shall differ or err in its interpretation, is not, I presume, very wonderful, because man, they *say*, is a creature of prejudice and passion as well as reason."

"But God would still have given the revelation, and yet it is capable, it appears, of being variously interpreted!" said the other.

"Very true; and it is very plain to me that, supposing him to have given *any*, he could have given no other than would have been liable to this, unless his omnipotence had been immediately exerted separately upon each individual of the human race, and then in such a way as to supersede all the moral discipline which Christians affirm is involved in the reception of any such revelation. Supposing this discipline (as those who believe in a revelation contend) to be an essential condition, I cannot conceive God himself to give a document which man's ingenuity cannot easily misinterpret. You see man plays the same trick equally well with that faculty of 'spiritual insight,' which some say is the *sole source* of religious truth, and which *you* say is the sole *arbiter* of an external revelation! We cannot find two of you who think alike, or who will give us the same transcript of religious truth. Similarly, we see the same ingenuity manifested by a man whenever it is his *interest* to find in a document a different meaning from that which it apparently carries on its face. Does not the endless controversy, the perpetual litigation of men respecting the meaning of seemingly the plainest documents, assure us that if a revelation were really given, the like would be possible with that? It is *doubtful* with me, therefore, whether God himself could give a revelation, such that men could not misrepresent and pervert it; that is, as long as they were *rational* creatures," he continued, bitterly. "But the mischief of *your* theory is, that it charges the inevitable result of man's perverseness or ignorance on God and the revelation he has been supposed to construct, and that is to me an absurdity."

"I do not see that these answers are satisfactory," said the other.

"I must leave *you* to judge of that," said Harrington, "or to contest it with my uncle here. I am keeping my next friend waiting, who, I can see, is impatient to run a course in favour of *his* view of revelation. He tells us, too, that a divine revelation, as conveyed in the New Testament, is to be admitted, but he cannot away with the notion that its certainty extends to any thing more than to what he calls the 'religious element?' Is not that your notion?"

"It is."

"You think, for example, that it is possible that the Apostles, and writers of the New Testament (in fact, whoever had the charge of recording, and transmitting to posterity, the doctrines of this revelation), were left liable, just as any other men, to all sorts of errors, geographical, chronological, logical, historical, political, moral ——"

"No, no, not moral," said the other; "I did not say *moral:* their morality is implied in their theology."

"Oh! very well, we shall better see that presently; only I have to remind you, for the glory of your Rationalism, that *other* Rationalists make the errors extend even to the '*moral* element;' but it is all one to me. You say, that, as far as regards every thing else, it is very possible that these 'inspired' men might err to any amount."

"Yes; I believe it."

"You have, doubtless, some reason for saying that they were made infallible in religion and morality, but liable to all sorts of errors on other subjects?"

"Nothing but this; that if, to give us 'spiritual truth' (as is *supposed*) was their proper function, (and we cannot but *suppose* that it was,) they must have been invested (we must *suppose*) with all the necessary qualities for this end, since I am *supposing* that even miracles were thought worth working in order to confirm their doctrine."

"You use the word *suppose* rather frequently, my

friend; however, I will not quarrel with you for that: only you ought not to be surprised if, adopting your last *supposition*, — that when miracles and inspiration have been *supposed* to be vouchsafed to authenticate a particular revelation, all such endowments, at least, will be granted as shall secure that object from defeat, — other Christians further *suppose* that the documents in which the revelation was to be consigned to all future ages would not be disfigured (and in many respects obscured) by the liability of their authors to all sorts of errors on an infinity of points, hopelessly entangled, as we shall soon see, with this one! that when heaven was at the trouble to embark its cargo of diamonds and pearls for this world, it would not send them in a vessel with a great hole in the bottom! If the Apostles were plenarily inspired with regard to this one subject, men *will* think it strange, perhaps, that divine aid should not have gone a little further, and since the destined revelation was to be recorded, or rather imbedded, in *history*, illustrated by *imagination*, enforced by *argument*, and expressed in *human language*, — its authors should have been left liable to destroy the substance by egregious and perpetual blunders as to the form; to run the chance of knocking out the brains of the unfortunate revelation by upsetting the *vehicle* in which it was to be conveyed!"

"But, then, these presumed endowments are purely a *supposition* on the part of Christians in general."

"Just as yours, we may say, of an indefectible wisdom on *one* point is a supposition on your part. I think in that respect that you are both well matched. But I freely confess that I think their *supposition* more plausible than yours; and if I were an advocate for Christianity, I should certainly rather *suppose* with them than *suppose* with you; that is, I should think it more credible, if God interposed with such stupendous instruments as miracles, inspiration, and prophecy at all, he would endow the men thus favoured (not with all knowledge, indeed, but) with whatever was necessary to prevent their encountering a certainty of vitiating their testimony."

"But how would their testimony be liable to be vitiated? I am supposing them to be absolutely free from error as regards the religious element — which they deliver pure."

"We shall see in a minute whether their testimony was liable to be vitiated or not, and whether the separation for which you contend be conceivable or even possible. I fear that you have no winnowing-fan which will separate the chaff from the wheat."

"To me, nothing seems more easy than the supposition I have made."

"Few things *are* more easy than to make suppositions; but let us see. I am sure you will answer as fairly as I shall ask questions. To do otherwise would be to separate the 'moral element' from the 'logical,' whatever the New Testament writers may have done. You believe, you say, in the resurrection of Christ?"

"I do."

"As a *fact* or *doctrine*?"

"Both as a fact and doctrine."

"For it is both, if true," said Harrington; "and so, I apprehend, it will be found with the other doctrines of Christianity. Whether, in *your* particular latitude of Rationalism, you believe many or few of them, still, if true at all (which we at present take for granted), they are both *facts* and *doctrines*, from the Incarnation to the Resurrection. But to confine ourselves to *one* — that of the resurrection — for one will answer my purpose as well as a thousand; — that, you say, is a fact — a *fact* of history?"

"It is."

"It is, then, conveyed to us as such."

"Certainly."

"Were the recorders of that fact liable to error in conveying it to us? In other words, might they so blunder in conveying that fact (as we know the unaided historian may, and often does), as to leave us in just doubt whether it ever took place or not?"

"Well," said the youth, "and you know they *have*

exhibited it in such a way as to suggest many apparent discrepancies, and those very difficult to be reconciled."

"I am aware of it, and for that very reason selected this particular fact. In my judgment there are no passages which more exercise the ingenuity of the harmonists than those which record the transactions connected with the resurrection. But still, in spite of them all, I presume that you do not think that those discrepancies *really* call the fact in question, else you would not continue to believe it. I should then suddenly find myself arguing with a very different person."

"Certainly, you are quite right. I agree that the substantial facts are as the writers have delivered them; although they may, from their liability to error, have delivered some of the details erroneously."

"But might this *liability* to error have led them a little further in their discrepancies, so as to involve the fact itself in just doubt, and so of other great facts which constitute the *doctrines* as well as the *facts* of Scripture?"

"Of course, I think it *might*, since I suppose them unaided by any supernatural wisdom in this respect."

"The answer is honest. I thought, perhaps, you would have answered differently, in which case you would have given me the trouble of pursuing the argument one step further. It appears, then, that, though inspired to give mankind a true statement of *doctrines*, yet that, when these *doctrines* assume the form of *facts* (which, unhappily, they do perpetually), this hazardous liability to error, as historians, may counteract their inspiration, and they may give them in such a form as to throw upon them all manner of doubts and suspicion; and possibly they have done so, for aught you can tell.— But, again, you also affirm that these so-called inspired men were liable to make all sorts of logical blunders just as the uninspired?"

"Certainly; and I must confess I think the logic of the Apostle Paul, in particular, often exceedingly absurd."

"Very fair and candid. For example, I dare say that

you do not think much of his arguments or inferences from certain doctrines; or his proofs of those doctrines from the Old Testament or——"

"They are not, indeed, worth much in my estimation."

"Candid again; but then it is plain, first, that you will have to distinguish between the *pure doctrines* which Paul derived from a celestial source, and his erroneous proofs or inferences, which are delivered in precisely the same manner and with the same assumption of authority. And this, I think, would be an insuperable task; at least, it seems so, for you Rationalists decide this matter very differently. When any of you favour me with your sketches of the true heaven-descended Pauline theology, I find them widely different from each other. Your 'religious element' is of the most variable volume. Some of you include nearly the whole creed of ordinary orthodoxy; others, fifty or even eighty per cent. less, both in bulk and weight."

"Perhaps so."

"Perhaps so! But then, what becomes of your principle, that you may separate the pure 'religious element,' as conveyed to the minds of the sacred writers by direct illumination, from the errors of vicious logic which have been permitted to mingle with it? To me, it appears any thing but easy to separate the functions of a revealer of *truly* inspired truth, from the vitiating influences of a fallacious logic. The 'heavenly vision,' however 'obedient' a Paul may be to it, will be but obscurely represented, and suffer egregiously from that distorted image which the ill-constructed mirror will convey to us.—But once more, I think you do not hold Paul's rhetoric to be always of the first excellence?"

"Certainly not; I think his representations are often as faulty as his logic is vicious; especially when, under the influence of his Jewish education, he throws old Gamaliel's mantle over his shoulders, and dotes about 'allegories' founded on the Old Testament."

"Fair and candid once more; but then, I suppose, you will admit that the Divine truths which he was, nevertheless, commissioned to teach mankind, will, like any other truths, be much affected by the mode in which they are represented to the imagination; will become brighter or more obscure, more animated or more feeble, and even more just or distorted, as this task is wisely and judiciously, or preposterously performed?"

"No doubt."

"Then it appears, I think, that if there were nothing to control the Apostle Paul's *manner* of exhibiting Divine verities, even in relation only to the imagination, there might be all the difference between sober truth and fanatical perversions of it. I might, in the same manner, proceed to show that the *feelings*, uncontrolled by a superior influence, would be also likely to give distortion or exaggeration to the doctrines. But it is enough. It appears very plain that, according to *your* hypothesis, even though the Apostles were commissioned to teach by supernatural illumination certain truths, yet that, being liable to be infected with all the faults of false history, bad logic, vicious rhetoric, fanatical feeling, these divine truths might, possibly, be most falsely presented to us. We have, really, no guarantee but your gratuitous 'supposition' that they have been taught at all. We have no criterion for separating what is thus divine from what is merely human. I fear, therefore, your distinction will not hold. The stream, whatever the crystal purity of its fountain, could not fail to be horribly impure by the time it had flowed through such foul conduits."

"In short," continued Harrington, with a bitter smile at the same time, "there are but three consistent characters in the world; the Bible Christian, and the genuine Atheist,—or the absolute Sceptic."

"No—no—no," exclaimed the whole trio at once; "and you yourself must be true to your principles, and, therefore, sceptical as to this."

"It is," he replied, "one of the very few things which I am *not* sceptical about. At all events, right or wrong, I am, as usual, willing to give you my reasons for my belief."

"Rather say your *doubts*," said Fellowes.

"Well, for my *doubts*, then. You see, my friends, the matter is as follows. The Christian speaks on this wise:—

"'I find in reference to Christianity, as in reference to Theism, what appears to me an immense preponderance of evidence of various kinds in favour of its truth; but both alike, I find, involved in many difficulties which I acknowledge to be insurmountable, and in many mysteries which I cannot fathom. I believe the conclusions *in spite* of them. As to the revelation, I see some of its discrepancies are the effect of transcription and corruption; others are the result of omissions of one or more of the writers which, if supplied, would show that they are apparent only; of others I can suggest no explanations at all; and, over and above these, I see difficulties of *doctrine* which I can no more profess to solve than I can the *parallel* perplexities in Nature and Providence, and especially those involved in the permitted phenomenon of an infinity of physical and moral evil. As to these difficulties, I simply submit to them, because I think the rejection of the evidence for the truths which they embarrass would involve me in a much greater difficulty. With regard to many of the difficulties, in *both* cases, I see that the progress of knowledge and science is continually tending to dissipate some, and to diminish, if not remove, the weight of others: I see that a dawning light now glimmers on many portions of the void where continuous darkness once reigned; though that very light has also a tendency to disclose other difficulties; for, as the sphere of knowledge increases, the outline of darkness beyond also increases, and increases even in a greater ratio. But I also find, I frankly admit, that on many of my difficulties, and especially that connected with the origin of evil, and other precisely analogous difficulties of Scripture, *no* light whatever is cast; to the solution of them man has not made the slightest conceivable approximation. These things I submit to, as an exercise of my faith and a test of my docility, and that is all I have to say about them; you will not alter my views by dwelling on them, for *your* sense of them cannot be stronger than *mine*.' Thus speaks the Christian; and the Atheist and the Sceptic occupy ground as consistent. They say, 'We agree with you Christians, that the Bible contains no greater difficulties than those involved in the inscrutable ' constitution and course of nature;' but on the very principles on which the Rationalist, or Spiritualist, or Deist, or whatever he pleases to call himself, rejects the Divine origin of the former, we are compelled to go a few steps further, and *deny*—or *doubt*—the Divine origin of the latter. It is true that the Bible presents no greater difficulties than the external universe and its administration (it cannot involve greater); but if those difficulties are sufficient to justify the denial or doubt of the Divine authorship of the one, they are sufficient to justify denial or *doubt* about the Divine origin of the other.'—Such is *his* position; but as to *you*, what consistent position can you take so long as you affirm and deny so capriciously? who 'strain at the gnats' of the Bible, and 'swallow the camels' of your Natural Religion? You ought, on the principle on which you reject so much of the Bible— namely, that it does not harmonise with the deductions of your intellect, the instincts of conscience, the intuitions of the 'spiritual faculty,' and heaven knows what—to become Manichæans at the least."

"But these very arguments," said one of the youths, "are just the old-fashioned arguments of BUTLER, which it is surely droll of all things to find a *sceptic* making use of."

"I admit they are his, my friend; but not that there is any inconsistency in *my* employing them. I affirm that Butler is quite right in his premises, though I may reject the conclusion to which he would bring me. He leaves two alternatives, and only two, in my judgment, open; leaves two parties untouched; one is the Christian, and the other is the Atheist or the Sceptic, whichever you please; but I am profoundly convinced he does not leave a consistent footing for any thing between. His fire does not injure the Christian, for it comes out of his own camp; nor me, for it falls short of my lines; but for *you*, who have pitched your tents between, take heed to yourselves. He proves clearly enough that the very difficulties for which you reject Christianity exist equally, sometimes to a still greater amount, in the domain of nature."

"Oh!" said the youngest, "we do not think that Butler's argument is *sound*."

"Then," said Harrington, "the sooner you *refute* it the better. All you have to do is, just to show that this world does *not* exhibit the inequalities — the miseries — the apparent caprice in its administration — the involuntary ignorance — the enormous wrongs — the wide-spread sorrows and death it does. You will do greater service to the Deist than the whole of his tribe have ever done them yet. I am convinced that Butler is not to be refuted."

"But do you not recollect what no less a man than Pitt said, — 'Analogy is an argument so easily retorted?'" replied the same youth.

"Then you will have the *less* difficulty in retorting it," said Harrington, coolly. "Pitt's observation only shows that he had forgotten the true object of the work, or never understood it. For the purposes of *refutation*, it does not follow that an analogy may be easily retorted; it may be, and often is, irresistible. It is when employed to establish a supposed truth, not to expose an error, that it is often feeble. If Butler had attempted to prove that the inhabitants of Jupiter *must* be miserable, nothing could have been more ridiculous than to adduce the *analogy* of our planet. But if he merely wished to show that it did not follow that that beautiful orb, being created by infinite power, wisdom, and goodness, *must* be an abode of happiness (just the Rationalist style of reasoning), it would be quite sufficient to introduce the speculator to this ill-starred planet of ours."

There are few who will not acquiesce in this remark of Harrington's, however they may lament the alternative he seemed disposed to take. Assuredly, for the specific object in view, no book written by man was ever more conclusive than that of Butler. For if you can show to an unbeliever in Christianity, who is yet (as most are) a theist, that any objection derived from its apparent repugnance to wisdom or goodness applies equally to the "constitution and course of nature," you do fairly compel him (as long as he remains a theist) to admit that that objection *ought* not to have weight with him. He has indeed an alternative; that of Atheism or Scepticism; but it is clear he must give up either his argument or his — theism. It may be called, indeed, an argument *ad hominem;* but as almost every unbeliever in Christianity is a man of the above stamp, it is of wide application. This is the fair issue to which Butler brings the argument; and the conclusiveness of his logic has been shown in this, that, however easily "analogies" may be "retorted," the parties affected by it have never answered it. I was amused with the criticism with which Harrington wound up. "Butler," said he, "wrote but little; but when reading him, I have often thought of Walter Scott's old wolf-dog Maida, who seldom was tempted to join in the bark of his lesser canine associates. 'He seldom opens his mouth,' said his master; 'but when he does, he shakes the Eildon hills. Maida is like the great gun at Constantinople — it takes a long time to load it; but when it *does* go off, it goes off for something!'"

Aug. 1. I this day put into Mr. Fellowes's hands the brief notes on the three questions on which he had solicited my opinion. They were as follows: —

I. Mr. Newman says that it is an idle boast that the elevation of woman is in any high degree attributable to the Gospel. "In point of fact," says he, "Christian doctrine, as propounded by Paul, is not at all so honourable to woman as that which German soundness of heart has established. With Paul the *sole* reason for marriage is that a man may without sin vent his sensual desires."

If indeed there were no other passage in the New

Testament than that to which Mr. Newman refers, there might be something to be said for him. But it is only one of many, and the question really at issue is consequently blinked; namely, what is the aspect of the entire New Testament Institute upon the relations of woman? It is true, indeed, that the reason for marriage which Mr. Newman contends is the only thing Paul thought about, is very properly urged; for from the constitution of human nature (as every comprehensive philosopher and legislator would admit), as well as from the horrible condition of things where marriage is neglected, prominence is very justly given to the preservation of chastity as one of the primary objects of the institution. But the question as between Mr. Newman and Christianity is this: Is this the only aspect under which the relations of man and woman are represented to us? That every thing is not said in one passage is true enough. From the desultory manner in which the ethics as well as doctrines of the New Testament are expounded to us, and especially from the casual form which they assume in the Apostolic Epistles, where the particular circumstances of the parties addressed naturally suggested the degree of prominence given to each topic, we must fairly examine the whole volume in order to comprehend the spirit of the whole, and not take up a solitary passage as though it were the only one. Now, if we examine other passages, we cannot fail to see that the New Testament consecrates married life by enjoining the utmost purity, devotion, and tenderness of affection. Look at only one or two of the passages in which the New Testament enjoins the reciprocal duties of husbands and wives; what sort of model it proposes for their love. "Husbands, love your wives, even as Christ also loved the Church, and gave himself for it. . . . . . Let every one in particular so love his wife even as himself; and the wife see that she reverence her husband. So ought men to love their wives as their own bodies . . . . . giving honour unto the wife as unto the weaker vessel, and as being heirs together of the grace of life."

Is this like condemning women to be "elegant toys and voluptuous appendages?"

Admitting, for the sake of argument, that the whole of Christianity is a delusion; that Christ never lived, and therefore never died; that he is a more palpable myth than even Dr. Strauss contends for; still it is impossible not to see that the writers of the New Testament represent his love for man as the ideal of pure, disinterested, self-sacrificing affection; this appears whether we listen to the words which the Evangelists have put into his mouth, or those in which they have spoken of him. "Greater love hath no man than this, that a man lay down his life for his friends." Now, let there be as much or as little historic truth in such statements, in the doings and sufferings of Christ on behalf of humanity, as you will, the conclusion is irresistible, that his conduct (real or imaginary) is set forth as the exhibition of unequalled patience, gentleness, meekness, and forbearance; of a love anxious to purchase, at the dearest cost, the purest and highest happiness of its objects. Now such is the pattern of affection which the Apostles commend to the imitation of "husbands and wives" in their conduct towards one another. Such is to be the lofty standard which *their* love is to emulate, Is it possible to go further? Does not the fantastical observance, or rather the absolute idolatry of women cherished by chivalry—itself, however rooted in the influences of a corrupt Christianity—look like a caricature beside the picture? And who are the "poets of Germanic culture" who have risen to an equal ideal of the reciprocal duties and sentiments of wedded life? I must contend that so beautiful a picture of a real equality between man and woman—founded on the love of the common Lord of both—such a picture of woman's *true* elevation was never realised in the ancient world, nor would have been to this day had not Christianity been promulgated; nor is *now*, except where Christianity is known, though alas! not always where it is. But if you think otherwise, beg Mr. Newman to give you a catena of passages from the "poets of Germanic culture" (he has not adduced a syllable in proof); and recollect it *ought* to be from Germanic poets who lived before the Germans were Christians! Or perhaps you would wish to seek the Germanic "sentiment" towards woman *pure* in its source, as given in the certainly not unfavourable estimate of Tacitus. In their respect for woman, and the stress they laid on chastity, the ancient Germans transcended without doubt many savages. Still, few readers will suppose there was much reason to boast of the elevation of women, or the presence of much refined "sentiment" between the sexes. As long as women do all the drudgery of house and *field* work, while their lazy husbands drink and gamble; as long as they are liable (and their children too) to be sold or put on the hazard of a cast of the dice; as long as they are themselves ferocious enough to go out to battle with their husbands; I presume you will think the "Germanic culture" very far short of the "culture" likely to be produced by the New Testament! Well says Gibbon, "Heroines of such a cast may claim admiration; but they were most assuredly neither lovely nor very susceptible of love."

II. Mr. Newman says that undue credit has been claimed for Christianity as the foe and extirpator of slavery. He says, that at this day, the "New Testament is the argumentative stronghold of those who are trying to keep up the accursed system." Would it not have been candid to add, that the New Testament has ever been also the stronghold of those who oppose it, as well in this country as in America? It is on the express ground of its supposed inconsistency with the *maxims* and *spirit* of Christianity that the great mass of abolitionists hate and loathe it. A public clamour against it was never raised in the days of ancient slavery, nor is now in any country where Christianity is unknown. The opposition to it in *our own* country was a religious one; that we know full well; and so is the opposition of the American abolitionists at the present day. If selfish cupidity, on the one hand, appeals to the New Testament for its continuance, so does philanthropy, on the other, for its abolition; and though in my judgment the inferences of the latter are far more reasonable, the mere fact that *both* parties appeal to the book shows that the New Testament neither sanctions it — rather the contrary by *implication* — nor expressly denounces it; — Mr. Newman doubtless can do it safely. This very moderation of language, however, has, to many minds, and those of no mean capacity (the late Dr. Chalmers, for example), been regarded as an indication of the wisdom which has presided over the construction of the New Testament; it was not only a tone peremptorily demanded by the necessary conditions of publishing Christianity at all, but was best adapted — nay alone adapted — in the actual condition of the world in relation to slavery to make any salutary impression.

Admitting that the great, the primary end of the Gospel was spiritual; that it was the object of the Apostles to obtain for it a dispassionate hearing among all nations; and that, however they might hope indirectly to affect the temporal prosperity and political welfare of mankind, all good of this kind was in their view subordinate to that spiritual amelioration, which, if effected, would necessarily involve all inferior social and political improvements; — I say, admitting this, it is really difficult to imagine any other course open to a wise choice than that which was actually adopted. I contend, that in not passionately denouncing slavery, and in contenting themselves with quietly depositing those principles and sentiments which, while achieving objects infinitely more important, would infallibly abolish it, the Apostles took the wisest course, even with relation to this latter object — though it was doubtless not the course into which a blind fanaticism would have plunged. To enter upon an open crusade against slavery in *that* age would have been to render the preaching of the Gospel a simple impossibility, and to convert a professedly moral and spiritual institute into an engine of political agitation; it would have afforded the indignant governments of the world — quite prompt enough to charge it with seditious tendencies — a plausible pretext for its suppression. Both the primary and the secondary objects would have been sacrificed; and the chains of slavery riveted, not relaxed. Slavery, in that age, we must recollect, was interwoven with the entire fabric of society in almost all nations. To denounce it would have been a provocation, nay, a challenge to a servile war in every country to which the zeal of the Christian emissaries might carry the Gospel. Contenting themselves, therefore, with the enunciation of those principles which, where they are truly embraced, are inconsistent with the permanent existence of slavery, and if triumphant, insure its downfall, the Apostles pursued that which was their great object; and for those of an inferior order, patiently waited for the time when the seed they had sown broad cast in the earth should yield its harvest.

And surely the event has justified their sagacity. For to what after all have just notions on this most important subject been owing except to this said Christianity? Though it is true that, owing to the imperfect exemplification of its principles by men who profess it, it has not yet done its work, it is doing it; though some Christian nations — more shame for them! — have slaves, none but Christian nations are without them. Not only is the sincere admission of the maxims and principles of the New Testament inconsistent with the permanent existence of slavery, but the history of Christianity affords perpetual illustrations of its tendency to destroy it. Even during the dark ages — even in its most corrupted form — Christianity wrought for the practical extinction of serfdom. Mr. Newman says that it was *Christians*, not *men*, that the Church sought to enfranchise: it little matters; she sought to abolish all villenage. He says, that even Mahometans do not like to enslave Mahometans; I ask, can he find *immense bodies of Mahometans* who contend that it is contrary to the spirit, tendencies, and maxims, if not precise letter, of their religion to enslave *any body?* For it was such a principle which expressly called forth the abhorrence and condemnation of slavery in our own age and nation. It cannot be denied that the movement by which this accursed system was, after so long a struggle, exterminated amongst us, was an eminently religious one, as regards its main supporters, the grounds they took, and the sacrifices they made.

"But Christian nations have defended and practised slavery!" you will say.

They have; and Christian nations have often practised the vices which the "Book" expressly condemns — just as all nations have practised many things which their codes of morals or laws condemn. The question is, whether, in the one case, the *Book*, or in the other case the *codes*, approve them; not, I presume, whether man is a very inconsistent animal. But no system is made answerable for the violations of its spirit — *except* Christianity.

Mr. Newman says, that slaveholders make the "New Testament the stronghold of the accursed system." It had been more to the purpose if he had pointed out a passage or two which *recommend* it. He knows that it is simply because it does not (for reasons already stated) *denounce* it, that they say it approves it. Are you satisfied with this reasoning? Then try it on another case — for despotism is exactly parallel. The New Testament does not expressly denounce *that*, and for the same reasons; and the arguments for passive obedience have been with equal plausibility drawn from its pages. Will the Transatlantic republicans approve despotism on the same authority? — Despotism has wrought at least as much misery to mankind as slavery, and probably much more. Was it a duty of the Apostles, instead of laying down principles, which, though having another object, would infallibly undermine it, to denounce despotism everywhere, and invite all people to an insurrection against their rulers? If they had, the spiritual objects of the Gospel would have been easily understood and very properly treated. Let me apply the "argumentum ad hominem." Mr. Newman has favoured the world with his views of religious truth, and the "spiritual" weapons by which its "champion" is to make it victorious over mankind; he has also recorded his hatred of slavery and despotism, where such magnanimity is perfectly safe, and perfectly superfluous. Let me now suppose you not only partly, but wholly of his mind, and animated (if "spiritualism" will ever prompt men to do anything, except, as Harrington says, to write books against book-revelations) — let me suppose you animated to go as missionary to the East to preach this spiritual system; would you, in addition to all the rest, publicly denounce the social and political evils under which the nations groan? If so, your spiritual projects would soon be perfectly understood, and summarily dealt with.*

It is in vain to say that if commissioned by Heaven, and endowed with power of working miracles, you would do so; for you cannot tell under what limitations your commission would be given: it is pretty certain that it would leave you to work a moral and spiritual system by moral and spiritual means, and not allow you to turn the world upside down, nor mendaciously tell it that you came only to "preach peace," while every syllable you uttered would be an incentive to sedition.

III. The last point on which you ask a few remarks is in relation to the early spread of Christianity. Mr. Newman makes easy work of this great problem. He says, "Before Constantine, Christians were but a *small*

---

* A *similar* reply to *another* objection of infidelity (founded on Paul's recognition of the authority which the *actually prevailing laws and customs* of the age gave to parents in the disposal of their daughters in marriage) is urged in the admirable work on the "Life and Epistles of Paul," by Messrs. Conybeare and Howson. Mr. Conybeare says, "We must suppose this writer" (evidently Mr. Newman) "would on the same grounds" (on which he condemns Paul) "require a modern missionary to Persia to preach the absolute incompatibility of despotic government with sound morality." The whole work was not completed till after the publication of the "Eclipse of Faith," though the *Number* containing these words must have been published a few months before, and when this last work was preparing for the press. Had the Author seen the passage in time, he would have been glad to refer to it; for such coincidences, when, as in the present case, perfectly independent, add much to the weight of an argument. But he would have been still better pleased to make the reference for the purpose of doing what he now does — expressing his sense of the value and beauty of the elaborate work on Paul, and earnestly recommending it to the attention of the reader.

fraction of the empire. . . . . . *In fact it was the Christian soldiers in Constantine's army who conquered the empire for Christianity.*"*

In the first place, supposing the facts just as stated, — namely, that it was the Christian soldiers of Constantine who conquered the empire for Christianity; who was it that conquered the army for Christianity? When I find Mahometanism the *prevalent* religion through the English regiments, I shall shrewdly suspect that the conquest of England for Mahometanism will have been made an easy task by its having already made equal progress amongst the people generally!

I suppose it will not be denied that the soldiers, by whose aid Constantine achieved this great victory, were themselves *professedly* converts to Christianity; and Christianity, as it had existed in the times of the recent persecutions, was not likely to *allure* men to the profession of arms. I think, therefore, we may fairly assume, that if the imperial armies were to any considerable extent — and it must have been *ex hypothesi* to a prevailing extent — composed of Christians, Christianity had made at least equal progress in the ranks of civil life. The one may be taken as the measure of the other; though we *might* fairly suppose, both from the principles and habits of the Christians, that they would be found in civil life in a larger ratio. The camp was not precisely the place for them; the Gospel might find them there, it rarely sent them. So that the question returns, how came it to pass that the bulk of the armies which "conquered the empire for Christianity" came to be Christians — at least in name and profession?

"Ah!" you will say, "in *name* — but they were strange Christians who became soldiers." Very true; and it makes my argument the stronger. *Mere* professors of a religious system only follow in the wake of its triumphs. When those who do not care much for a system, profess and embrace it, depend upon it, it has largely triumphed.

* Phases, p. 162

To suppose, therefore, that Constantine conquered the empire for Christianity, while we admit that the army was already Christian, is very like getting rid of the objection in the way the Irishman proposed to get rid of some superfluous cart-loads of earth. "Let us dig a hole," said he, "and put it in." It is much the same here.

Constantine became a convert, *perhaps* from conviction, but certainly rather late. Supposing him a *political* convert, as many have done, it could only be because he saw that Christianity had done its work to such an extent as to render it more probable that it would assist *him* than that he could assist *it*. This induced him to take it under the wing of his patronage. And on such a theory, what but such a conviction could have justified him in the attempt for a moment? How could he be fool enough to add to the difficulties of his position — a candidate for empire — the stupendous difficulty of forcing upon his unwilling or indifferent subjects a religion which by supposition they were any thing but prepared to receive? If the prospects of Christianity had not already decided the question for him, so far from receiving credit for political sagacity, as he ever has done, he would deserve rather to be considered an absolute idiot!

Again; is it not plain from history in general, and must we not infer it from the nature of the case *à priori*, that Christianity must in some fashion have conquered its millions before Constantine or any other man was likely to attempt to conquer the empire *for* Christianity, or to succeed in so doing if he had? Is there an instance on record of a people suddenly, at a moment's notice, changing its religion, or rather — for this is the true representation — of *many* different nations changing their *many* different religions, at the simple command of their sovereign, and he too an upstart? In two cases, and in only two, it may be done; first, by an unsparing use of the sword, the brief, simple alternative of Mahomet, Death or the Koran; the other, when the new form of belief has converted the bulk or a large portion of the nation; of which, in this case, the conversion of the army is a tolerably significant indication.

But again; if it be said that the people, or rather the many different nations, abandoned their religions out of complaisance to their sovereign; I answer, why do we not see the same thing repeated when Julian wished to reverse the experiment? They were not so pliant then; then was it seen very clearly that the people were, as in every other case, unwilling, as regards their religion, to be mere puppets in the hands of their governors. Julian was animated by at least as strong a hatred of Christianity as Constantine by a love of it. Yet we see all the way through that there was not a chance of success for him.

"But there were *some* persecutions," you will say, "by Constantine." True, but they were so trifling compared with what would have been required had the conversion of an unbelieving and refractory *empire* depended on such means, that few who read the history of religious revolutions will believe that they were the *cause* of the change. Every thing shows that a vast preceding moral revolution in the empire is the only sufficient explanation of so sudden an event. Gibbon himself admits Constantine's tolerant disposition.

"But," it may be said, "the old heathenism was worn out and effete; no one thought it worth his while to stand up in its defence."

I answer, first, it seems to have been sufficiently loved, or at least Christianity was sufficiently hated, to insure frequent and sanguinary persecutions of the latter, almost up to the eve of Constantine's accession. Secondly, you are to consider, that though in the schools of philosophers, in the Epicurean or Sceptical atmosphere of the luxurious capital and other great cities, there was unquestionably a numerous party to ·whom the old superstition was a laughing-stock, there were vast multitudes to whom it was still, in its various forms, a thing of power. You are to recollect that the Roman empire was made up of many nations, each with a different mode of religion, and to suppose that these different religions had ceased to exercise the usual influence on vast multitudes of the people would be mere delusion. If they were surrendered at last so easily, it could only be because a great party—antagonistic to each—had been silently forming in each nation, and undermining the power of the popular superstitions. But, thirdly, if the representation were true, to what can so singular a phenomenon—this simultaneous decay of different religions—this epidemic pestilence amongst the gods of the Pantheon—be ascribed, but to the previous influence of Christianity, and its extensive conquests? And, fourthly, supposing this not the case, and yet that the indifference in question existed, this indifference to the *old* systems of religion would not presuppose equal indifference to *new*, or induce the people to embrace them at the mere bidding of their new master. If this were so, we ought to see the same phenomenon repeated in the case of Julian. If in their presumed indifference to the old and the new, they listened to Constantine when he commanded them to become Christians, why did not they manifest an equally compliant temper when the Apostate enjoined them to become heathens, and, like Constantine, gave them both precept and example?

But look at the historic evidence on the subject long before the establishment of Christianity. Is it possible for any candid person to read the Epistle of Pliny to Trajan, and not see in that alone, after making every deduction for any supposed bias under which the letter may have been written (though, in fact, it is difficult to suppose *any* bias that would not rather lead the writer to diminish the number of the Christians than to exaggerate it),—is it possible, I say, to read that singular state paper and not feel that the new religion had made prodigious progress in that remote province? and that, *à fortiori*, if in Bithynia it had conquered its thousands of proselytes, in other and more favoured provinces it must have gained its tens of thousands? To me the letter of Pliny speaks volumes; and if so much could be said at so early a period as A. D. 107, what was the state of things two centuries later?

Precisely the same conclusion must be arrived at if we consult the uniform tone of the Christian apologists, from Justin Martyr to Minucius Felix. Making here, again, what deductions you please for the fervid eloquence and rhetorical exaggerations of such a man as Tertullian, it is too much to suppose even his "African" impetuosity would have ventured, not merely on the virulent invective, the bold taunts with which he every where assails the popular superstitions, but on such strong assertions of the triumphant progress of the upstart religion, unless there had been obvious approximation to truth in his statements. "We were but of yesterday," says he, "and we have filled your cities, islands, towns, and assemblies; the camp, the senate, the palace, and the forum, swarm with converts to Christianity." Apologist for Christianity! Unless these words had been enforced by very much of truth, he would have made Christianity simply ridiculous; and Christians would have been necessitated to apologise for their mad apologist.

The same conclusion equally follows from the consideration of those very corruptions of Christianity, which no candid student of ecclesiastical history will be slow to admit had already infected it, many years before Constantine ventured to aid it by his equivocal patronage. It was obviously its triumphant progress — its attraction to itself of much wealth — the accession, to a considerable extent, of fashion, rank, and power — that chiefly caused those corruptions. So long as the Christian Church was poor and despised, such scenes as often attended the election of bishops in the great cities of the empire would be quite impossible.

Under such circumstances the argument of Mr. Newman — judiciously compressed into a few sentences — appears to me even ludicrous. How different the course which Gibbon pursues! What a pity that the great historian did not perceive that this statement would have led him equally well to his desired end; that so brief a demonstration would suffice to account for that unmanageable phenomenon, the rapid progress and ultimate triumph of Christianity! He, on the contrary, seems to have read history with very different eyes; and yet I suppose no man will question either his learning or his sagacity. He finds himself obliged to admit the conspicuous advance which the Gospel had made before Constantine's accession, and employs every nerve to invent sufficient *natural* causes to account for it. What a facile task would he have had of it if he had but bethought him that Christianity, instead of having been to an enormous extent successful, was, in fact, waiting, in comparative failure, the triumphant aid of a military conqueror. He might then have dispensed with the *celebrated chapter*, and substituted for it the two pregnant sentences by which Mr. Newman has, in effect, declared it superfluous.

August 7. Three days ago (the evening before my return home) I managed to prevail upon myself to have a close and formal discussion with Harrington on the subject of his scepticism. We had a regular fight, which lasted till midnight and beyond. A good deal of it was (in a double sense, perhaps) a νυκτομαχια. As I had no one to jot down shorthand notes of our controversy — perhaps it is as well for me and for truth that there was none — it is impossible that I should do more than give you a succinct summary of its course. But its principal topics are too indelibly impressed on my memory to leave me in doubt about general accuracy.

I hardly know what led to it; I believe, however, it was an observation he made on the different fates of metaphysical and physical science,—the last all progress, and the first perpetual uncertainty. He had been reading a remark of some philosopher who attributed this difference to the more substantial incentives offered to the cultivation of the physical sciences. "So that," said he, "they are, it seems, what our German friends would call 'Brodwissenschaften!' Not the *brain*, as some idly suppose, but the *stomach*, is the true organon of discovery, and if the metaphysician could but be punctually assured of his dinner (which has not always been the case), or at all events of a fortune, we should soon have the *true* theories of the Sublime and Beautiful—of Ethics—of the Infinite—of the Absolute—of Mind and Matter—of Liberty and Necessity; whereas *I* think we should only have a multiplication of *doubtful* theories."

He remarked that he doubted the truth of the hypothesis in both its parts: that not the want of adequate motives, but the intrinsic difficulty of the subjects, had kept metaphysics back (on what subjects had men expended more gigantic toil?); nor, on the other hand, was it *necessity* that chiefly impelled man to cultivate physical science; it was the desire of knowledge—or rather, he added, the love of truth; for what else was man's admitted *curiosity*, in the last resort, unless he is equally curious about falsehood and truth; "that is," said he, laughing, "as curious after *ignorance* as after *knowledge!* No," he continued, "the sciences are made *arts* for utilitarian purposes; but the sciences themselves have a very different origin. For my own part, I would as soon believe that Sir Isaac Newton excogitated his system of the universe in hopes of being made one day Master of the Mint." I assented, and, smiling, told him I was glad to find him admit that there was in man a love of knowledge, identical with the love of truth. He said he admitted the *appetite*, but denied that there was always an adequate supply of food. He admitted that in physical science man seemed capable of unlimited progress; but it seemed doubtful whether this was the case in other directions. "What was there inconsistent with scepticism in that?" he asked.

I answered that it was not for me to say at what point of the scale a man might become an orthodox doubter; but I was, at all events, glad that he had not gone all the lengths which some had gone, or professed to have gone; who, if they had not reached that climax of Pyrrhonism—to doubt even if they doubt, yet had declared the attainment of all truth impossible. I then bantered him a little on the *advantages* of "absolute scepticism;" told him I wondered that he should throw them away; and reminded him of the success with which the sceptic might train on his adversary into the "bosky depths" of German metaphysics — the theories of Schelling, Fichte, Hegel. "If truth be in any of those dusky labyrinths," said I, "you are not compelled to find her; the more unintelligible the discussion becomes, the better for the sceptic; you may not only doubt, but doubt whether you even understand your doubts. You may play 'hide and seek' there for ten thousand years." "For all eternity," was his reply. But he said he had no wish to seek any such covert, nor to *play* the sceptic.

I told him I was glad to find that his scepticism did not — to use Burke's expression on another subject — "go down to the foundations." He answered that he was afraid it did on all subjects *really* of any significance to man. "As to the present life," he continued, "I am quite willing to accept Bayle's dictum: 'Les Sceptiques ne nioient pas qu'il ne se fallût conformer aux coûtumes de son pays, et pratiquer des devoirs de la morale, et prendre parti en ces choses là *sur des probabilités*, sans attendre la certitude.'"

I was not sorry that he took Bayle's limits of scepticism rather than Hume's: I told him so.

Hume, he said, was evidently playing with scepticism; for himself, he had no heart to jest upon the subject. The Scotch sceptic acknowledged that the metaphysical riddles of his "absolute scepticism" exercised, and ought to exercise, no practical influence on himself or any man; that the moment he quitted them and entered into society, "they appeared to him so frigid and unnatural," that he could not get himself to interest himself about them any further; that a dinner with a friend, or a game at backgammon, put them all to flight, and restored him to the undoubting belief of all the maxims which his meditative hours had stripped him of. It was *natural*, Harrington said; for such scepticism was impossible. He added, however, that had Hume been honest, he would never have employed his subtlety in the one-sided way he did; "for," said he, "if his principles be true, they tell just as much against those who *deny* any religious dogmas as against those who *maintain* them. Yet every where in relation to religion—take the question of miracles for example—he argues not as a sceptic at all, but as a dogmatist,—only on the *negative* side. If his doctrine of 'Ideas' and of 'Causation' be true, he ought to have maintained that, for any thing we know, miracles may have occurred a thousand times, and may as often occur again. Hume," he said, "was amusing himself; but I am not: nor can any one really feel—many pretend to do so, without feeling at all—the pressure of such doubts as envelope me, and be content to *amuse* themselves with them."

I found it very difficult to attack him in the entrenchments he had thrown up. I thought I would just try for a moment to act on the Spiritualist's advice, and, throwing aside all "intellectual and logical processes," all appeals to the "critical faculties," advance "lightly equipped as Priestley himself," making my appeal to the "spiritual faculty." I cannot say that the result was at all what "spiritualism" promises. On the contrary, Harrington parried all such appeals in a twinkling. He said he did not admit that he had any "spiritual faculty" which acted in isolation from the intellect; that religious faith must be founded on religious truth, and even *quasi*-religious faith on *quasi*-religious truth. That the intellect and the moral and spiritual faculties (if he had any) acted together, since he felt that he was indivisible, and that the former must be satisfied as well as the latter; that it was so with all his faculties, none of which acted in isolation; that however hunger might prompt to food, he never took what his senses of sight and touch told him was sand or gravel; that if he indulged love, or pity, or anger, it was only as his senses, and the imagination, and the understanding were busied with objects adequate to elicit them; that if beautiful poetry excited emotion, it was only as he *understood* the meaning and connection of the words. "And what else are you doing *now*, while urging me to realise by direct 'insight,' by 'gazing' on 'spiritual truth,' and so forth, the things you wish me to realise,—I say what are you doing but appealing to me, through these same media of the senses and the imagination, by rhetoric and logic? How else can you gain any access to my supposed 'spiritual faculties?'" I replied, that even the spiritualist did that—he endeavoured to *convince* men, I supposed. "Yes," he replied, laughing, "because he is privileged doubly to abuse logic at one and the same time; to abuse it in one sense as a *fallacious* instrument of religious conviction in the hands of others, and to abuse it in another sense, as an instrument of *fallacious* conviction in his own. But you are not so privileged."

Harrington insisted on the fact that the whole thing was a delusion: I might appeal, he said, if I thought proper, to any faculties, or rudiments of faculties, he possessed, spiritual or otherwise; but he really could not pretend even to comprehend one syllable I said, if I denied him the use of his understanding. I might as well, and for the same reasons, appeal to him without the intervention of his *senses*—for his "soul" could not be more different from his "intellect" than from them. "Besides," he continued, "I know you do not imagine that any spiritual faculty acts thus independently of the intellect; and, therefore, you are only mocking me."

I thought it best to cut my cable, and leave this unsafe anchorage.

I told him that, as he doubted whether man had any distinctly marked religious and spiritual faculties, while I affirmed that he had, — although he was quite right in supposing that I did not believe that they acted except in close conjunction with the intellect, — it made it difficult to hold any discourse with him. Doubting the Bible, he had also learned to doubt that doctrine of human depravity, which he once thought harmonised, and I still thought did alone harmonise — the great facts of man's essentially religious *constitution* and his eternally varied and most egregiously corrupt religious *development*.

However, I told him that even in the concession of the *probable* as a sufficient rule of conduct in this life, he had granted enough to condemn utterly his sceptical position.

He now looked sincerely interested. "Let me," said I, "ask you a few questions." He glanced towards me an arch look. "What," he said, "you wish to get the Socratic weather-gage of me, do you? You forget, my dear uncle, that you introduced me to the Platonic dialectics."

"Heaven forgive you," said I, "for the thought. You know I make little pretension to your favourite erotetic method: and if I did — oh! do you not know, Harrington, my son, that if I could but convince you on this one subject, I would consent to be confuted by you, on every other, every day in the year? — nay, to be trampled under your feet?" I added, with a faltering voice. "And, besides that, do you not know that there can be no rivalry between father and son; that it is the only human affection which forbids it; that pride, and not envy, swells a father's heart, when he finds himself outdone?"

He was not unmoved; told me he knew that I loved him well, and desired me to ask any questions I pleased.

He saw how gratified his affection made me feel. I said, gaily, "Well then, let me ask (as our old friend with the queer face might have said), Do you not grant there is such a thing as prudence?"

"I do," he said.

"But to be *prudent* is, I think, to do that which is most likely to promote our happiness."

"That which *seems* most likely, for I do not admit that we *know* what will."

"That which *seems*, then; for it is of no consequence."

"Of no consequence! surely there is a little difference between *being* and *seeming to be*."

"All the difference in the world," I replied, "but not in relation to our choice of conduct. We choose, if prudent, that conduct which, on the whole, deliberately *seems* most likely to promote our happiness, and as far as that goes, what seems, is."

"I grant it; and that probabilities are the measure of it," said Harrington.

"You are of Bayle's opinion, that there is in relation to the present life, a probable prudent, and that it would be gross folly to neglect it?"

"Certainly."

"And in proportion as the interest was greater, and extended over a longer time, you would be content with less and less *probabilities* to justify action."

"I freely grant I should."

"If now a servant came into the room to say that he feared your farm-house at King's O—— was on fire, though you might think it but faintly probable, you would not think it prudent to neglect the information?"

"I certainly should not."

"And if you were immortal here on earth, and the neglect of some probably, or (we will say) only possibly true information in relation to some vital interest, might affect it through that whole immortality, you would consider it prudent to act on almost *no* probability at all, on the very faintest presumption of the truth?"

"I must in honesty agree with you so far."

"What does your scepticism promise you, if it be well-founded? Much happiness?"

"To me none; rather the contrary; and to none, I think, can it promise much."

"And if Christianity be true—for I speak only of that, I know there is not in your estimate any other religion that comes into competition with it,—immortal felicity, immortal misery depends on it?"

"Yes: it cannot be denied."

"You admit that scepticism may be false, even though it has a thousand to one in its favour; for by its very principles you know nothing, and can know nothing, on the subjects to which its doubts extend."

"I acknowledge it."

"And Christianity may be true by the very same reasoning, though the chances be only as one to a thousand?"

"It is so."

"Then by your own confession you are not prudent, for you do not act in relation to Christianity on the principles on which you say you act in the affairs of the present life; where you acknowledge that the *least* presumption will move you when the interests are sufficiently permanent and great."

He told me, with a smile, I might have arrived at the same conclusion without any argument; for he was willing to acknowledge *in general* that he was not prudent, and in relation to this very subject should always admit with Byron, "that the sincere Christian had an undeniable advantage over both the infidel and the sceptic, since," he added, putting the admission into a very concise form, " their *best* is his *worst*."

"Very well," said I, "Harrington; only remember that your imprudence is none the less for your admission of it."

"None in the world," he admitted; but he contended there was a flaw in the argument; for that it was impossible to accept any religion on merely *prudential* grounds. And he then went on, in his curious way, to lament that an unreasonable *candour* prevented him from here taking advantage of an ingenious argument adopted by some of the modern "spiritualists" in reasoning on the probabilities of a "future life." They contend that it is necessary to insulate the soul (if it would discover "spiritual truth") from all bias of self-interest—from all oblique glances at prospective advantage; in fact, that only *he* is fully equipped for discovering "spiritual truth" who is disinterestedly indifferent as to whether it be discovered or not. Harrington said he could not pretend that even the sceptic was so favourably circumstanced as that. "For my part," he said, "I cannot honestly adopt this view, and always think it *prudent* to accept as large an armful of happiness as I can grasp, when truth and duty do not come in the way."

"And in the name of common sense," I said, "what truth and duty are to stand in *your* way? Is not your truth, that there is none?"

"Yes," he replied, smiling; " but is not the truth the

truth, as Falstaff said? though to be sure it was when he was manufacturing his eleven men in buckram out of two. However, as Mr. Newman, when some one foretold that he would be some day a Socinian or an infidel, replied, 'Well, if Socinianism *or any thing else* be the truth, Socinians *or any thing else* let us be;' so I must say, if *no truth* be the truth, *no-truth-men* let us be."

"Very well," I replied. "Then, it seems, truth stands in the way of acting *prudently;* and instead of remedying our first paradox, we have started on another, that truth and prudence are here opposed: for in no other cases (I think) in which you apply your own rule of the probable to the present life will a mind of your comprehensiveness say they *are* opposed; I am sure you will admit the general maxims, that to lie is inexpedient, and that honesty is the best policy, and so on." He granted it.

"But further," said I, "what sort of truth is this, which involves duty, and yet is opposed to prudence? It is, that there is *no truth* it seems, and this completes the paradox. This strange truth — the Alpha and Omega of the sceptic, his first and his last, — is to involve *duty;* he is to be a confessor and martyr for it! Nothing less than happiness and prudence are to be sacrificed to *conscience* in the matter. Truly, if the truth that there is *no truth* involves any duty, it ought to be the duty of believing that there is *no duty* to be performed; and you might as well call yourself a *no-duty-man* as a *no-truth-man.*"

He smiled, but replied, that, seriously, it was impossible to adopt any religious opinions, or to change them at the bidding of the will.

I admitted, of course, that the will had no *direct* power in the matter; but reminded him, that if he meant it had no influence, or even a little, on the formation or retention of opinions, no one could be a more strenuous asserter of the contrary than he had often been. I reminded him it was so notorious, that man usually managed to believe as he *wished,* that there was no maxim more frequently on the lips of the greatest philosophers, orators, and poets. But I added, that there is also a legitimate way of influencing the will, and that is through the understanding; and that it was with the hope of inducing him to reconsider the paradoxes of scepticism, and not with any expectation of instant or violent change, that I was anxious to enumerate them on the present occasion.

It is impossible for me to recollect exactly the course of the long conversation that ensued; suffice it to say, that he willingly granted many other paradoxes, some of them so readily, as to confirm the suspicion I had sometimes felt, that he must often have *doubted* the validity of his *doubts*. He admitted, for example, that since men *in general* (whether from the possession of a distinct religious faculty, though it might be corrupt and depraved, or a mere rudimentary tendency to religion) had adopted *some* religion, religious scepticism, in an intelligible sense, was opposed to *nature*;—that it was equally opposed to *nature*, inasmuch as the general constitution of man sought and loved *certainty*, or supposed *certainty*, and found a state of perpetual doubt intolerable; and that if this be attributed to a tendency to *dogmatism*, that is the very tendency of *nature* which is affirmed;— that it is opposed to *nature* again in this way, that whereas restlessness and agitation of mind are, usually at all events, warnings to seek relief, scepticism produces these as its pure and proper result;—that, since by the confession of every mind worthy of respect, the great doctrines of religion, if *not* true, are such that we cannot but *wish* they were: since, by his *own* confession, scepticism has nothing to allure in it, and rather causes misery than happiness; and since by his confession, and that of every one else, men *in general* easily believe as they *wish*,—it is an unaccountable paradox that any one should remain a sceptic for a day, except, indeed, from a guilty fear of the truth;—that since scepticism tends to misery, it is better *not* to know its truth, and that therefore ignorance is better than knowledge;—that if Christianity be an illusion, it at all events tends to make men happier than the *truth* of scepticism, and that therefore error is better than truth;—that religious scepticism is open to the same objection as scepticism absolute; for whereas the last is taunted with trusting to reason to prove that reason can in nothing be trusted, religious scepticism is chargeable with declaring the certainty of all uncertainty, and, while proclaiming that there is nothing true, avowing that that *is* the truth; and lastly, that if, in consistency, it leaves even that uncertainty uncertain, it arrives at a conclusion which everlastingly remits us to renewed investigation!

"But," said he, "the sceptic *does* affirm the certainty of all uncertainty. That is precisely my state of mind, even in relation to Christianity. Both its truth and falsehood are — uncertain."

"Then," said I, "I must not say you reject Christianity, but only that you do not receive it."

"Precisely so," said he, with a smile and a blush at the same time. I was much amused with this logical ceremoniousness, by which a man is not to say that he *rejects* any thing so conditioned, but only that he does not receive it. I told him I imagined they came to much the same thing.

"It is impossible," said he, after a pause, "to affirm any thing on these subjects."

"It is equally impossible," said I, "to affirm nothing; on the contrary, you sceptics have two conclusions, though in a negative form, for every body else's one — together with the pleasant addition that they are contraries to one another; and as Pascal said that the man who attempted to be neuter between the sceptic and dogmatist was a sceptic *par excellence*, so the genuine sceptic may be called a dogmatist *par excellence*."

"For my part," said he, smiling sadly, "I hardly think it is very difficult either to believe nothing or everything. Fellowes, you see, has believed everything, and now he is in a fair way to believe nothing. However, all I mean is, that the evidence on these subjects reduces one to a state of complete mental suspense, in which it is equally unreasonable to say that we believe, as to say that we believe not. However, I grant you most of the paradoxes you mention; but a sceptic is not to be startled by paradoxes, I trow: and alas! they *prove* nothing."

"Prove nothing! nay, I think you do your system injustice; I think it is entitled to the distinction of making great discoveries. You confess that the only truth on these subjects is, that there is no truth; that to act on this truth necessitates a conduct opposed to nature, to prudence, to happiness; that it is a knowledge worse than ignorance; that it is a truth that is worse than error; that it never was, will be, or can be embraced by many, and that it makes the few who embrace it, miserable; you admit further, with me, that men generally believe as they *wish*. Why, then, do you not fly from so hideous a monster, on the very ground (only in this case it is stronger) on which you doubt all religious systems— that is, on account of the supposed paradoxes they involve? It may be but a little argument with you who seem to demand demonstration of religious truth; but for myself, I feel that whatever be the truth, such a chimera as scepticism, bristling all over with paradoxes, must be—a lie."

"Well," he replied, "but then *which* religion is the true?"

"Nay," I said, "that is an after consideration; if you can but be brought to believe that *any* is true, I know you will believe but *one*."

"You touched just now," he replied, "on the very difficulty. I shall believe as soon as any one gives me what you truly say I ask,—demonstration of the truth of some one of the thousand and one religious systems which men have believed."

"And that demonstration," said I, "you cannot have; for God has not granted demonstration to man on that or any other subject in which *duty* is involved."

"But why might I not have had it? and should I *not* have had it, if it had been *incumbent* on me to believe it?"

We had now come to the very knot of the whole argument.

"Incumbent on you to believe! I suppose you mean if there had been any system which you could not *but* believe; which you *must* believe whether you would or not. No doubt, in that case, the requisite evidence would have been such that scepticism would have been impossible; that word 'incumbent' implies *duty;* and that word *duty* is the key to the whole mystery, for it implies the possibility of resisting its claims. We do not speak of its being *incumbent* on a man to run out of a burning house, or to swim, if he can, when thrown into deep water. He cannot help it. If there be a Supreme Ruler of the universe, and if the posture of his intelligent creatures be that of submissive obedience to him, it is inconceivable that a man can ever have *experience* of his being willing to perform that duty with the sort of demonstration which you demand; and for aught we know, it may be impossible, constituted as we are, that we should ever be actually trained to that duty except in the midst of very much less than certainty. Now, if this be so—and I defy you or any man to prove that it may not be so—then we are asking a simple impossibility when we ask that we may be freed from these conditions; for it is asking that we may perform our *duty* under circumstances which shall render *all* duty impossible."—I pursued this subject at some length, and reminded him that the supposed law of our religious condition was throughout in analogy with that of the entire condition of our present life, and in conformity with his own rule of the *probable;* that it is *probable* evidence only that is given to man in either case, and "probable evidence," as Bishop Butler says, "often of even wretchedly insufficient character." Nature, or rather God himself, everywhere cries aloud to us, "Oh! mortals—certainty, demonstration, infallibility, are not for you, and shall not be given to you; for there must be a sphere for faith, hope, sincerity, diligence, patience." And as if to prove to us not only that this evidence is what we must trust to, but that we safely may—He impels us by strong necessities of our lower nature operating on the higher (which would otherwise, perhaps, plead for the sceptic's inaction in relation to this as well as to another world), to play our part; if we stand shivering on the brink of action, necessity plunges us headlong in; if we fear to hoist the sail, the strength of the current of life snaps our moorings, and compels us to drive. I reminded him that the general result also shows that, as man *must* thus act, so, in thus acting, he *may, can, will, shall* (and so through all the moods and tenses of contingency) do well; that faith in that same sort of evidence which the sceptic rejects when urged in behalf of religion, prompts the farmer to cast in his seed, though he can command no blink of sunshine, nor a drop of rain; the merchant to commit his treasures to the deep, though they may all go to the bottom, and sometimes do; the physician to essay the cure of his patient, though often half in doubt whether his remedy will kill or save. "It is," said I, "in that same faith that we build and plant, and lay our little plans each day; sometimes coming to nothing, but generally, and according to the fidelity and manliness with which we have conducted ourselves, securing more than a return for the moral capital embarked; and even where this is not the case, issuing, when there have been the qualities which would naturally secure success, in a vigour and robustness of character which, like the rude health glowing in the weather-beaten mariner, who has buffeted with wind and wave, are a more precious recompense than success itself. In these examples, God says to us in effect, 'On such evidence you *must* and *shall* act,' and shows us that we safely may. Without promising us absolute success in all our plans, or absolute truth in the investigation of evidence, he says, in either case, 'Do your best; be faithful to the light you have, diligent and conscientious in your investigations of available evidence, great or little—act fearlessly on what appears the truth, and leave the rest to me.'"

Harrington here asked the question I expected: "But suppose different men coming (as they do) on religious subjects to different conclusions, after the diligence and fidelity of which you speak: what then?"

"Then, if the fidelity and diligence have been *absolute*—if all has been done which, under the circumstances, could be done—I doubt not they are blameless. But I fear there are very few who can absolutely say this; and for those who cannot say it at all, their guilt is proportionate to the demands which the momentous nature of the subject made on diligence and fidelity."

"I suppose," said he, with some hesitation, "you will not allow that *I* have exercised this impartial search; and yet, supposing that I have, will you not hold me blameless on the very principles now laid down?"

It was a painful question; but I was resolved I would have nothing to reproach myself with; and therefore answered steadily, that it was not for me to judge the degree of blame which attached to his present state of mind, which I trusted was only transient; that the argument, from sincerity, was itself only one of the *probable* things of which we had been speaking; that so subtle are the operations of the human mind, so mysterious the play of the passions and affections, the reason and conscience, so intimate the connection amongst all our powers and faculties, that it is one of the most difficult things to be able to say, with truth, that we *are* perfectly sincere; that I did not see any difficulty in believing that there is many a man who, without hesitation and without any conscious hypocrisy, would avow his sincerity, who, upon being suffered to look into his own mind through a moral solar microscope, would see there all sorts of misshapen monsters, and turn away from the spectacle with disgust and horror; that such a microscope (to speak in figure) might one day be applied by that Power to whom only the human heart is fully known. I added, however, that if I knew more of his mental history for some years past (into which my affection should never induce me impertinently to pry), I might, perhaps, in some measure, account for his scepticism; that I could even conceive cases of minds so "encompassed with infirmity," or so dependent on states of health, as to render such a condition involuntary, and therefore to take them out of the sphere of our argument. But apart from some such causes, I plainly told him I could not permit myself to believe that religious scepticism could be free from heavy blame, if only on the ground that such as feel it do not act consistently with its maxims in *other cases,* where the evidence is of the same dubious nature, or rather is much more dubious. The parallel case would be (if we could find it), of a man whose interests urgently required him to act one way or the other, and who, instead of acting accordingly, sat down in absolute inaction, on the score that he did not know what course to pursue. That indecision would be always blameable. "Ah!" said I, "those cool heads and skilful hands which pilot the little bark of their worldly fortunes amidst such dangerous rocks and breakers, under such dark and stormy skies, what *can* they say if asked why they gave up all thought of religion on the score of doubt, when its hopes are at least as high as those of the schemes of earthly success, and its claims at least as strong as those of present duty? What *will* they be able to say?"

"Oh! Harrington," I continued, in some such words as these, "supposing the draught of our present condition not to be such as I have sketched; that the sceptical view of the gloom in which we are placed is the true one, and that the Christian's is false; which, nevertheless, is likely to be not merely the happier, but the nobler being,—he who sits down in querulous repining or slothful inactivity, as the result of doubt; or he who, buoyant with faith and hope, encounters the gloom, and, while longing for the dawn, is confident that it will come? But if that sketch be a true one — if the trial of which I have spoken be necessary for you and for all — to develop and discipline those qualities which alone will elicit and mature an Immortal Virtue, and secure to us at last the privilege of indefectible 'children of God,' then with what feelings will you hear the Great Master say, 'In every other case but this, you acted on the principles and maxims by which I taught you (not obscurely), that I summoned you to act in this case also: doubts and difficulties were necessary to you as to all, and I exacted of you no more than were necessary ultimately to secure for you an eternal exemption from them! But because you could not have *that* certainty which the very necessity of the case excluded, you declined the trial, and have 'accounted yourself unworthy of eternal life!' Ah! how different if you could hear him say, 'It was indeed a temptation; amidst numberless blessings denied to others, I yet gave you, too, your trial;—the questionable talent of an inquisitive intellect, and leisure to use or abuse it. Tempted to absolute doubt, you would not succumb to it; you would not be so inconsistent here as to relinquish those maxims on which I compelled you to act in every other case in life, nor deny to ME the confidence which you granted to every common friend! Warned by the very misery which was sent to caution you that in that direction lay death, you struggled against the incursions of your subtle foes, and you overcame. Welcome, child of clay! welcome to that world in which there is no more NIGHT.'"

We had been talking on till long past midnight; and the lamp suddenly warned us that its light was just expiring. Harrington took off the shade, and was about to light a candle by the dying flame, when it went out. "It matters not," he said, "I have the means of kindling a light close at hand." "Let it alone," said I, rising, and gently laying my hand on his arm, and speaking in a low voice, but with much earnestness; "this darkness is an emblem of our present life. You cannot see me, but you hear my voice and feel the touch of my hand. For any thing you know, I may be seized with a sudden fit of insanity. I may be about to stab you in this darkness; such things have been. You have lost, with the light, more than half the indications of affection which that would disclose. But you trust to the *probable;* your pulse does not beat any the quicker, nor do your nerves tremble. You may have similar, nay, how much stronger proofs (if you will) of the confidence with which you may trust God, and Him, the compassionate One, 'whom he hath sent,' in spite of all the gloom in which this life is involved. That certainty for which you have just now asked will only be granted when the darkness is passed away; and then you will 'rejoice in the light of his countenance.' And further," I continued "there is yet one thing which I wish to say to you; and I feel as if I could say it better in this darkness; for I will not venture to say that I should not manifest more feeling than is consistent in a hard-hearted metaphysician. Yes! it is on the side of feeling that I would also address you. You will say, feeling is not argument? No; but is man *all* reason? I firmly believe, indeed, that man is not called upon to do anything for which his reason does not tell him that he has sufficient evidence; but a part of that very evidence is often the dictate of feeling; and *genuine* reason will listen to the heart, as not *always*, nor perhaps more frequently than otherwise, a suspicious pleader. If, as Pascal says so truly, it sometimes has its reasons, which the reason cannot comprehend, it has also its reasons which the reason thoroughly understands.

"You were early an orphan; you do not remember your mother; but I do; ah! how well. I saw her the last time she ever saw you. You were brought to her bedside when she was in the full possession of all her faculties, and deeply conscious that she had not many hours to live. She looked at you as you were held in your nurse's arms, smiling upon her with to me an agonising unconsciousness of your approaching orphanage. She gazed upon you with that intense look of inexpressible affection which only maternal love, sharpened by death, can give; she looked long and earnestly, but spoke not one syllable. As you were at length taken from the room, she followed you with her eyes till the door closed, and then it seemed as if the light of this world had been quenched in them for ever. 'I charge you,' she said at length, 'let me see him again.' I made a motion as if to recall the attendant. 'Not *here*,' she added, laying her hand gently on my arm; and I understood her but too well. *You* know whether I have in any degree fulfilled my trust. But is it possible that I can think of an utter failure, and not be more than troubled? And if Christianity be true, and if *I* am so happy as to obtain admission to that 'blessed country into which an enemy never entered, and from which a friend never went away,' and she whom I loved so well should ask me why you come not,— that she had tarried for you long, — must I say that you will never come? that her child had wandered from the fold of the Good Shepherd, and had gone I knew not whither; that I sought him in the lonely glens and mountains, but found him not? I hardly know, but I almost think,— such was the love she had for you — that such reply would shade that radiant face even amidst the glories of paradise. And now — let all this be a dream;— suppose that not simply by your own fault you will never see that mother more, but that from the sad truth of your *no* truth — you never *can;* that the '*vale, vale, in æternum, vale,*' is all that you can say to her: yet I say this,— that to live only in the hope of the possibility of fulfilling the better wishes of such a friend, and rejoining her for ever in (if you will) the fabulous 'islands of the blest,' would not only make you a happier, but even a nobler being than your present mood can ever make you. My FABULOUS, as you deem it, is better than your TRUE."

I felt that he was not unmoved. I was myself moved too much to allow me to stay any longer, and saying that I could find my way very well to my chamber in the dark, where I had the means of kindling a light, I softly closed the door and left him.

* * * * *

As I was to leave very early in the morning, I had told Harrington that I should depart for the neighbouring town (whither his servant was to drive me), without disturbing him. But I could not tear myself away, after the singular close of our interview on the last evening, without a more express farewell. I tapped at his chamber door, but receiving no reply, gently entered. He was resting in unquiet slumber. A table, lamp, and books, by his bedside, bore witness to his perseverance in that pernicious habit which he had early formed! I gently drew back one of the curtains and let in the light of the summer morning on his pallid, but most speaking features, and gazed on them with a sad and foreboding feeling. I recalled those days when I used nightly to visit the slumbers of the little orphan, and trace in his features the image of his mother. He was not aroused by my entrance; most likely he had sunk to slumber at a late hour. Presently he began to talk in his sleep, which was almost a constant habit in his younger days, and which I used to consider one of the symptoms of that intense cerebral activity by which he was distinguished. On the present occasion I thought I could interpret the fitful and fleeting images which were chasing each other by the laws of association through his mind. "But how shall I know that these things, which I call real, are different from the phenomena of sleep which I call real?" Alas! thought I, the ruling passion is strong in sleep as in waking moments! How I dread lest it should be strong "in death" itself, of which this sleep is the image! After a pause, an expression of deepest sadness crept over the features, and he murmured, with a slight alteration, two lines from Coleridge's translation of that glorious scene in which Wallenstein looks forth into the windy night in search of his "star," and thinks of that brighter light of his life which had been just extinguished. Harrington used to say that he preferred the translation of that scene even to the magnificent original itself. These lines (now a little varied) I had often heard him quote with delight.

> ...... "Methinks
> If I but saw her, 'twould be well with me;
> She was the star of my nativity."

Was he, by the magic of dream-land, transported back to childhood? Was he, as an orphan child, thinking of his mother, the image of whose dying hours I had so lately called up before him? Or was it the recollection of a still brighter, and more recently extinguished "star," which thus troubled his wandering fancy?—There was another pause, and again the fitful breeze of association awakened the sad and plaintive melody of the Æolian lyre: but I could not distinguish the words.

Presently the scene again changed; and he suddenly

said, "Beautiful shadow! if thou *art* a shadow,—thou hast said, Come to me all ye that are weary,—and surely, if ever man was weary—To whom can I go——." It was with intense feeling that I watched for something more; but to my disappointment (I may almost call it anguish), he continued silent. I could not find it in my heart to rouse him, and softly leaving the chamber, departed for home.

* * * * *

Oct. 31. The young Sceptic has since gone where doubts are solved for ever; but I am not without hope that in his last hours he was able to finish the sentence which his dream left incomplete. "To whom can I go, but unto Thee? THOU ONLY HAST THE WORDS OF ETERNAL LIFE." For me—I have nothing more to live for here. In a few weeks I gladly go to join my brother in his distant exile; and for Thee, my Country, "peace be within thy dwellings, and prosperity within thy palaces!" And that it may be so,—may that Christianity, which, all imperfectly as it has been exemplified, has yet been thy Palladium and thy Glory, be ever and increasingly dear to thee!

* * * * *

Dec. 27. I have resolved that the fragments, which originally constituted this journal, shall not be destroyed. I have employed the interval since the last date in adapting and disguising them for publication. How far an embroidery of fiction has been necessary in attaining this object is a matter of no consequence to any one; since the book aspires to none of the appropriate attractions of either a novel or a history. No doubt, a much stronger interest, of a certain kind, might have been secured by a free employment of fictitious embellishment, or even by a more liberal indulgence in biographical details. But I have been content, for a special object, to do what some tell us is to be done with the Bible—to separate, from the mass of incident which might have varied or adorned the narrative, the exclusively "Religious Element." If the discussions in the preceding pages shall in any instance convince the youthful reader of the precarious nature of those modern book-revelations which are somewhat inconsistently given us in books which tell us that all book-revelations of religious truth are superfluous or even impossible; if they shall convince him how easily an *impartial* doubter can retort with interest the deistical arguments against Christianity, or how little merely insoluble objections can avail against anything; if they shall convince him that the differences with which the assailants of the Bible taunt its advocates are neither so numerous nor half so appalling as those which divide its enemies; or, lastly, if they shall, *par avance*, in any degree protect those who like Harrington D——, are being made, or are in danger of being made *sceptical* as to all religious truth, by the religious distractions of the present day, I shall be well content to bear the charge of having spoiled a Fiction, or even of having mutilated a Biography.

F. B.

THE END.

LONDON
PRINTED BY SPOTTISWOODE AND CO.
NEW-STREET SQUARE

By the same Author,

I

A DEFENCE OF THE ECLIPSE OF FAITH:
Being a Rejoinder to Professor Newman's "Reply." *Third Edition*, revised. Fcp. 8vo. price 3s. 6d.

OF the *Defence of the Eclipse of Faith*, first published in 1854, the present is a new and cheaper edition; and it may therefore be proper to briefly explain its scope. Although it is in substance a rejoinder to Mr. Newman's *Reply* to the *Eclipse*, it would be a mistake to suppose that it is exclusively occupied with the personal controversy. It is an expansion as well as defence of many of the arguments of the *Eclipse*, while many fresh topics of great theological importance in these times are also discussed in it. The following extract from the Author's Preface explains the chief modifications introduced into the Third Edition. "In preparing the present edition of the *Defence of the Eclipse of Faith* for the press, I have omitted a few passages— more especially in the Introductory chapter—which seemed unnecessarily to prolong the personal part of the controversy, and to detain the reader from the great points in dispute between my opponent and myself. I should have been very well pleased if, at this distance of time, when all trace of polemical animosity, I should hope, has died out of the minds both of Mr. Newman and myself, I could have proceeded much further in this direction, and confined myself almost entirely to the general topics, which though involved with the personal argument, are, it must be confessed, of the last importance and of enduring interest. But I found that this course was utterly impracticable without writing an entirely new work. Nor perhaps would the exclusion of the personal vindication be quite just to myself; for Mr. Newman's diatribe is not only circulated in the *Phases* (which was natural enough), but has been separately published in the shape of a cheap tract. It is true, indeed, that the attack has not impeded the sale of the *Eclipse*; but it is a reason for not letting the reader remain ignorant of the *Defence*. I have therefore acceded to the request of the publishers, and the often expressed wishes of readers of the *Eclipse*, that I would reissue the present work in a shape uniform with the cheap editions of the *Eclipse* and at a proportionably diminished price. In the two previous editions of this *Defence*, large citations — occupying twelve pages of the Appendix, "pp. 205-217—were given from Mr. Newman's chapter on the *Moral Perfection of Christ*. This was done that I might not be again charged 'with not quoting enough,' and lest it should be supposed that in the remarks I made on that chapter in Section 11, I had taken any advantage by insulating sentences from their context.... As the sentiments of Mr. Newman expressed in the obnoxious chapter are notorious to the world, I have not thought it worth while to print them a third time, and they are therefore omitted in the present edition."

"THE Author's main design is to apply Butler's great argument to some recent modifications of Deism. He has thrown his reasoning, for the most part, into the form of dialogue; and we think that the Socratic weapons have never, since the time of Plato, been wielded with more grace and spirit. Various talkers are brought upon the stage, who state fairly the opinions of the different Deistic schools, and are successively foiled by a sceptical friend, who overthrows them in succession by the very objections they have urged against Christianity. This task is accomplished not only with very great power of logic, but also with unusual liveliness of illustration, seasoned with a plentiful mixture of sarcastic humour; the latter being never intruded needlessly into the argument, but springing naturally out of it. The principal representative of Deism in the dialogue is a disciple of Mr. Francis Newman, whose writings are made to supply a large contribution to this species of entertainment.... Let us thank Mr. Rogers for the addition he has made to the philosophical literature of England, and to the defensive armoury of Christendom, and still more for his promise to deal with Pantheism as he has already dealt with Deism. We trust that he may be spared to redeem this pledge in the amplest manner, and also to recast his present work by omitting those ephemeral topics which might hinder its permanent appreciation. If he lives to accomplish our expectations, we feel little doubt that his name will share with those of Butler and of Pascal in the gratitude and veneration of posterity." QUARTERLY REVIEW.

London: LONGMAN, GREEN, and CO. Paternoster Row.

II

SELECTIONS from the CORRESPONDENCE of R. E. GREYSON, Esq. Edited by the Author of *The Eclipse of Faith*. New Edition, complete in One Volume. Crown 8vo. price 7s. 6d.

"THESE are the letters of a very able and accomplished man, deeply impressed with the necessity of meeting distinctly and firmly, on intellectual grounds, the infidelity of educated society...There is a neatness, an aptitude, a truthfulness of statement in speaking of commonplace things, which are often very striking in these letters." GUARDIAN.

III

ESSAYS selected from Contributions to the EDINBURGH REVIEW. By HENRY ROGERS. *Second Edition*, revised; with Additions. 3 vols. fcp. 8vo. price 21s.

Contents:—

I. *Biographical and Critical.*

1. LIFE AND WRITINGS OF THOS. FULLER.
2. ANDREW MARVELL.
3. LUTHER'S CORRESPONDENCE AND CHARACTER.
4. LIFE AND GENIUS OF LEIBNITZ.
5. GENIUS AND WRITINGS OF PASCAL.
6. LITERARY GENIUS OF PLATO—CHARACTER OF SOCRATES.
7. GENIUS AND WRITINGS OF DESCARTES.

II. *Literary and Critical.*

8. JOHN LOCKE.
9. SYDNEY SMITH'S LECTURES.
10. STRUCTURE OF THE ENGLISH LANGUAGE.
11. HISTORY OF THE ENGLISH LANGUAGE.
12. SACRED ELOQUENCE—THE BRITISH PULPIT.
13. THE VANITY AND GLORY OF LITERATURE.
14. ULTRAMONTANE DOUBTS.
15. RIGHT OF PRIVATE JUDGMENT.

III. *Theological and Controversial.*

16. ANGLICANISM; or, THE OXFORD TRACTARIAN SCHOOLS.
17. RECENT DEVELOPMENTS OF TRACTARIANISM.
18. REASON AND FAITH—THEIR CLAIMS AND CONFLICTS.
19. REVOLUTION AND REFORM.
20. TREATMENT OF CRIMINALS.
21. PREVENTION OF CRIME.

IV

REASON and FAITH; their Claims and Conflicts. Reprinted from the EDINBURGH REVIEW. By HENRY ROGERS. The *Fourth Edition*, revised; with Additions and an Appendix. Fcp. 8vo. price Eighteenpence.

"HIS treatment of the Christian Evidences gives a most happy and popular turn to the graver learning and weightier logic which their discussion has at various times drawn forth from the leaders of religious controversy; while in grappling with Strauss he ventures into less trodden ground, where he displays unquestionable originality and vigour of a very telling kind. Re-assurance will come to many a doubt-tossed reader from his eloquent and closely-reasoned pages." EXAMINER.

www.ingramcontent.com/pod-product-compliance
Lightning Source LLC
Chambersburg PA
CBHW030425300426
44112CB00009B/851